RNAC

"An Oklahoma I Had Never Seen Before"

"An Oklahoma I Had Never Seen Before"

Alternative Views of Oklahoma History

Edited by Davis D. Joyce

UNIVERSITY OF OKLAHOMA PRESS : NORMAN AND LONDON

For my stepchildren,
Elizabeth, Bret, and Barry

Also by Davis D. Joyce

Edward Channing and the Great Work (The Hague, 1974)
History and Historians: Some Essays (Washington, D.C., 1983)
(with Michael Kraus) *The Writing of American History,* rev. ed. (Norman, 1985); paperback ed. (Norman, 1990)
(ed. and abr.) *A History of the United States* by Edward Channing (Lanham, Md., 1993)

This book is published with the generous assistance of
Edith Gaylord Harper.

Library of Congress Cataloging-in-Publication Data

An Oklahoma I had never seen before : alternative views of Oklahoma
history / edited by Davis D. Joyce.
 p. cm.
 Includes index.
 ISBN 0-8061-2599-3
 1. Oklahoma—History. 2. Oklahoma—Social conditions. I. Joyce,
Davis D., 1940– .
 F700.O34 1994
 976.6—dc20   93-27247
                                   CIP

Book designed by Bill Cason

The paper in this book meets the guidelines for permanence and durability
of the Committee on Production Guidelines for Book Longevity of the
Council on Library Resources, Inc. ∞

1 2 3 4 5 6 7 8 9 10

CONTENTS

EDITOR'S PREFACE

In the fall semester of 1988, the first time I taught Oklahoma history at East Central University, in the "further comments (if you wish)" section of the evaluation form I designed for the course, one student said: "I saw an Oklahoma I had never seen before." What I had done in the course that led to that comment was to begin to try to introduce the kind of material found in this volume.

I love Oklahoma. I love its land, its people. I love its history. But, just as I always thought the bumper sticker slogan "America: Love It or Leave It" was silly, narrow-minded, and inappropriate—I always liked "America: Change It or Lose It" better—I react negatively to those who react predictably negatively to every criticism of Oklahoma. Love it or leave it? No. Some of us love it enough to stay and try to change it—America *and* Oklahoma.

My love affair with Oklahoma began in 1958 when I began to drive its long, diverse, beautiful east-west reach from Moffett, just across the Arkansas River from Fort Smith, Arkansas, to Texola, adjacent to the Texas Panhandle. (I had just graduated from high school at Greenwood, Arkansas, and started college at Eastern New Mexico University in Portales.) The love affair intensified when I moved to Norman in 1963 to begin work on my Ph.D. at the University of Oklahoma. I have been an "Okie" ever since; the four years that I spent out of the state, in Illinois and Washington from 1983 to 1987, just had the effect, it seems now, of making me realize how attached to Oklahoma I have become. I hope to live out my life here.

But I've been known to criticize Oklahoma (and America) and its history. Indeed, one of the things I love is that I am free to criticize. I criticize, in part, because I love. I want to help make Oklahoma (and America) live up to its potential. Oklahoma, like America, is too good not to be better.

Not that all the material included in this volume is necessarily critical of Oklahoma. But it does, much of it, present an Oklahoma many have "never seen before." Its focus is on women, ethnic minorities, gay people, working people, radicals. Or, in some cases, if the topic is familiar, its treatment is not, for it might be dealt with from a new, different, "revisionist" perspective.

But why the comparison of Oklahoma to America here? Because this book was inspired in part by Howard Zinn's 1980 book, *A People's History of the United States*. Zinn was one of the leading "New Left" or "radical" scholars of the 1960s. In his textbook he gives us a view of American history which involves "a reversal of perspective, a reshuffling of heroes and villains. The book bears the same relation to traditional texts as a photographic negative does to a print: the areas of darkness and light have been reversed."[1] Or, as one reviewer put it, Zinn wrote "from the point of view of those who have been exploited politically and economically and whose plight has been largely omitted from most histories."[2]

Zinn said in the last chapter of *A People's History of the United States:* "As for the title of this book, it is not quite accurate; a 'people's history' promises more than any one person can fulfill, and it is the most difficult kind of history to recapture. I call it that anyway because, with all its limitations, it is a history disrespectful of governments and respectful of people's movements of resistance." As Zinn readily acknowledged, "That makes it a biased account, one that leans in a certain direction." To this he added, "I am not troubled by that, because the mountain of history books under which we all stand leans so heavily in the other direction—so tremblingly respectful of states and statesmen and so disrespectful, by inattention, to people's movements—that we need some counterforce to avoid being crushed into submission."[3]

Clearly, one goal that Zinn hoped to accomplish by his approach was to encourage the people to make their own history. "All the histories of this country centered on the Founding Fathers and the Presidents," Zinn wrote, "weigh oppressively on the capacity of the ordinary citizen to act. They suggest that in times of crisis we must look to someone to save us: in the Revolutionary crisis, the

Founding Fathers; in the slavery crisis, Lincoln; in the Depression, Roosevelt; in the Vietnam-Watergate crisis, Carter. And that between occasional crises everything is all right, and it is sufficient for us to be restored to that normal state." Traditional American history books, he continued, also teach us that "the supreme act of citizenship is to choose among saviors, by going into a voting booth every four years to choose between two white and well-off Anglo-Saxon males of inoffensive personality and orthodox opinions."[4]

The people should be allowed to a great extent to *tell* their own history as well. As James Levin said of A *People's History,* "Seldom have quotations been so effectively used; the stories of blacks, women, Indians, and poor laborers of all nationalities are told in their own words."[5] As Zinn explains further:

in that inevitable taking of sides which comes from selection and emphasis in history, I prefer to try to tell the story of the discovery of America from the viewpoint of the Arawaks, of the Constitution from the standpoint of the slaves, of Andrew Jackson as seen by the Cherokees, of the Civil War as seen by the New York Irish, of the Mexican war as seen by the deserting soldiers of Scott's army, of the rise of industrialism as seen by the young women in the Lowell textile mills, of the Spanish-American war as seen by the Cubans, the conquest of the Philippines as seen by black soldiers on Luzon, the Gilded Age as seen by southern farmers, the First World War as seen by socialists, the Second World War as seen by pacifists, the New Deal as seen by blacks in Harlem, the postwar American empire as seen by peons in Latin America. And so on, to the limited extent that any one person, however he or she strains, can "see" history from the standpoint of others.[6]

Finally, Zinn makes clear a major part of what he wants to accomplish with this kind of history:

I don't want to invent victories for people's movements. But to think that history-writing must aim simply to recapitulate the failures that dominate the past is to make historians collaborators in an endless cycle of defeat. If history is to be creative, to anticipate a possible future without denying the past, it should, I believe, emphasize new possibilities by disclosing those hidden episodes of the past when, even if in brief flashes, people showed their ability to resist, to join together, occasionally to win. I am supposing, or perhaps only hoping, that our future may be found in the past's fugitive moments of compassion rather than in its solid centuries of warfare.[7]

So what does all this have to do with Oklahoma? A great deal, I would suggest. Couldn't our view of Oklahoma history use a little reshuffling of heroes and villains? Why, for example, isn't Woody Guthrie in the Oklahoma Hall of Fame? Could it be that he was too "radical" for the state's image of itself? But as humorist John Henry Faulk once said, Guthrie was "one of Oklahoma's most famous sons, if you consider the number of people throughout the U.S. who still sing his songs and repeat his stories. . . . Who else from Oklahoma has millions of Americans chorusing his song, 'This Land is Your Land'?"[8] We know that Governor William H. ("Alfalfa Bill") Murray was a colorful character, but do we know as well the arguably more important fact that he cared only for people of his own color? Our questions could go on.

In that inevitable taking of sides which comes from selection and emphasis in Oklahoma history, I prefer to try to tell the story of Oklahoma's prehistory from the point of view of the Spiro Mound people; of Indian removal from the viewpoint of the Cherokees; of the Civil War from the standpoint of the Seminole slaves; of the Run of '89 as seen by the Indians already here; of the coming of statehood as seen by the Sequoyah Convention; the First World War as seen by those who participated in the Green Corn Rebellion; the state's petroleum industry as seen by the workers in the fields; the coal mining industry as seen by the radical Italian labor organizer; the Ku Klux Klan as seen by the victims of the Tulsa Race Riot in 1921; the 1930s exodus as seen by the "Okies"; the state's "macho" image as seen by the victim of domestic violence or the gay individual; the state's failure to ratify the Equal Rights Amendment as seen by women; the University of Oklahoma's much-vaunted football success as seen by the bright students who feel compelled to leave the state for high-quality education and jobs, or as seen by the athlete who never gets a degree; and so on, to the limited extent that any one person, however he or she strains, can "see" history from the standpoint of others.

Like Zinn, I must also make something of a disclaimer. A "people's history," he said, "promises more than any one person can fulfill." Just so, a "people's history of Oklahoma" promises more than any one person can fulfill, at least at this time. Certainly this volume is not comprehensive. (It does not, for example, address all

the topics suggested in the preceding paragraph.) Textbooks, presumably, are that; the problem, of course, is that they are not. This
volume, then, is a collection of pieces, most of them seeing print
here for the first time, which should be thought of as supplementary
to Oklahoma history textbooks. It addresses aspects of Oklahoma's
history which do not usually get attention in the standard works or
presents alternative interpretations of standard topics. Perhaps it can
stimulate further work toward a true and complete "people's history
of Oklahoma"—which is to say a true and complete history of
Oklahoma. Perhaps it can also serve as a model for other states of
what can be done with this approach to history at the state level.

The topics here are diverse, ranging from an Indian view of the
land run centennial to a history of gay rights in Oklahoma and
from a reinterpretation of the Progressive era in Oklahoma to a first-
hand account of the early sit-in demonstrations for integration in
Oklahoma City. The style is diverse as well, from the traditional
scholarly essay to what I like to call the personal/historical essay—
historical in the sense of involving change over time, personal in the
sense that the author was a participant in the events described.

But what ties this diversity together is that it is the beginning of
an effort to show an Oklahoma that many have never seen before—
the underside of Oklahoma history, a people's history of Oklahoma,
Oklahoma history from the bottom up, alternative views of Oklahoma history. Though not traditionally included in the standard
treatments of the state's history, such material is clearly interesting,
important, relevant: our unknown history does not fail to have consequences just because we ignore it.

Danney Goble's book *Progressive Oklahoma* was lying on my
desk recently.[9] A colleague outside of history saw it and remarked,
"That's kind of an oxymoron, isn't it?" I appreciated the humor,
but I also thought, "How sad." Parts of Oklahoma's past, including
its progressive, even radical past, go largely ignored, forgotten. Yet
many of us find those the most exciting parts of our past, in part
because of their potential relevance for the present and the future.

Part of the agenda of a book such as this one is, broadly speaking,
a political one. New Left historian Staughton Lynd wrote in the
preface of his 1968 book, *Intellectual Origins of American Radicalism,* ". . . let me put the baldest face on my intention. In one sense

the concern of the following chapters is ahistorical. I am less interested in eighteenth-century radicalism than in twentieth-century radicalism. . . . The characteristic concepts of the . . . radicalism of today have a long and honorable history. Acquaintance with that history may help in sharpening intellectual tools for the work of tomorrow."[10]

Not all of the pieces included in this volume are in line with that kind of thinking, obviously. But many are. We do our students of Oklahoma history a grave disservice by not telling them the story of socialism, communism, gay rights, domestic violence, pro-choice (on abortion), radical protest, women's activism, "radical" Indians, radicalism in general, and so on, as part of the total story of our state's history. Is it not possible that Oklahoma's past radicals can serve to remind us of changes that still need to be made, maybe even provide models of how (and how not) to go about making them, and, perhaps most important of all, provide inspiration for the job? Finally, even those at different points on the political spectrum would surely agree that the stories of Freda Hogan Ameringer, Clara Luper, Kate Barnard, Nicholas Comfort, and Woody Guthrie are a vital part of our still young state's vital history and need to be told in addition to the better-known stories of Will Rogers and Alfalfa Bill Murray.

NOTES

1. Eric Foner, review in *New York Times Book Review,* Mar. 2, 1980, p. 10.

2. James Levin, review in *Library Journal,* Jan. 1, 1980, p. 101.

3. Howard Zinn, *A People's History of the United States* (New York: Harper and Row, 1980), 570.

4. Ibid.

5. Levin, review in *Library Journal,* p. 101.

6. Zinn, *People's History,* 10.

7. Ibid., 10–11.

8. Letter from John Henry Faulk to Davis D. Joyce, Aug. 3, 1989.

9. Danney Goble, *Progressive Oklahoma: The Making of a New Kind of State* (Norman, University of Oklahoma Press, 1980).

10. Staughton Lynd, *Intellectual Origins of American Radicalism* (New York: Pantheon Books, 1968), vii.

ACKNOWLEDGMENTS

As with any book, there are many people to thank. Indeed, with such a work as this, that need seems even more intense, for the thank-yous must begin with all the contributors; obviously, without them the volume simply would not exist.

At East Central University, the Research Committee, chaired by Shirley A. Mixon, assisted me by reducing my teaching load in the fall 1989 semester; John Walker and Linda Powers of the Linscheid Library kindly allowed me to set up shop in the Special Collections Room so that I would have a nice, quiet place to work; my departmental chairman, Marvin E. Kroeker, was very cooperative in providing a schedule that maximized blocks of time for research and writing; my colleague Palmer H. Boeger, though he had just retired, graciously agreed to take up the slack created by my reduced load by teaching Oklahoma history; Brenda Bean, Lois Collins, Lisa Griffits, and Teresa Leon all helped with the typing; and Monica Jackson helped with the final editing.

At the University of Oklahoma Press, John N. Drayton, editor-in-chief, earned my thanks, as he did on my previous book published by them, by his early encouragement and consistent interest and direction.

Finally, at home, my wife, Carole, not only contributed an essay for the volume but also took an early interest in it, helped me shape it, and along with Muckle (our basset hound) helped create an environment that encourages all sorts of wonderful things, including the writing of books.

''An Oklahoma I Had Never Seen Before''

OKLAHOMA

George Milburn

Oklahoma's great historian Angie Debo wrote of George Milburn in Oklahoma: Foot-loose and Fancy-free *in 1949: "Nearly all his settings are of
rural and small-town Oklahoma—to him very unpleasant places filled with
disagreeable people. Naturally he is not loved in his home state."[1] Naturally. And these days he is not very well known, either. Milburn was from
Coweta but spent most of his professional life in New York. His books were*
Oklahoma Town, Catalog, No More Trumpets, *and* Flannigan's Folly.
Much of his writing appeared in H. L. Mencken's American Mercury.
The following essay from the Yale Review *in March 1946—with its
blend of solid information, sound insights, humor, and sometimes biting
criticism—seems an appropriate way to begin a collection of alternative
views of Oklahoma history.*

It may seem needless to explain
that Oklahoma is one of the forty-eight United States of America.
But as a proud native of Oklahoma, born in the Indian Territory
before statehood, I have found this less a matter of common knowledge than might be supposed. When I visit such distant Babylons as
New York, or London, I have learned to go braced for people, well-
informed otherwise, who have only the vaguest notions of what

---

"Oklahoma," by George Milburn, first appeared in *Yale Review* (March 1946): 515–26.
Reprinted with permission.

Oklahoma (without the exclamation point) is, much less any idea of where it is.

The faint air of disbelief with which my earnest definitions of Oklahoma often have been met places me under some constraint even now. There was a time when confusion of Oklahoma with a new nervous disorder, or a patent breakfast food, or a Japanese seaport, could be shrugged off as gross ignorance. Lately, however, it has been difficult to cope with a growing tendency to identify the State as the fictitious setting of a current comic opera.

Many people seem to have got the idea that Oklahoma is like one of those Balkan kingdoms where musical comedies used to be set in the good old care-free days. This is a sorry misconception. Oklahoma is a real place. Here I am setting down a few facts about Oklahoma, and I cross-my-heart-and-hope-to-die if I say anything untrue about the place where I was born and raised.

Oklahoma, in spite of skeptics, is easy to find on up-to-date maps of America. The official state guidebook says that its outline is that of ''a butcher's cleaver: the Panhandle of the west representing the handle, the north line its straight-back edge, the east line its square-cut end, the Red River on the south its irregular cutting edge.'' A more prosaic description of Oklahoma's outline would be hard to think up. The same stretch of fancy might have discerned the shape of a sawed-off shotgun, or a chewed-up tomahawk. Either of these blunt instruments is more symbolic of Oklahoma than a dull meat ax.

As a matter of fact, an outline map of Oklahoma looks like an index fist (☞), that arbitrary sign printers use to mark items worthy of special note. The finger of Oklahoma points in the other direction. That, too, is worthy of special note.

Oklahoma always has been wayward. Nestled close to the geographic centre of the United States, it has little in common with its neighbors. Kansas on its north is a typical Middle-Western farm State, a Republican stronghold. Arkansas on its east is a typical Southern State—where any white man who has paid his poll tax is free to vote as he likes, just so he votes the straight Democratic ticket. Colorado, New Mexico, and Missouri merely touch its corners. Texas, the largest State in the Union, borders the other two sides of Oklahoma. Texas strives to be another country, and suc-

ceeds only in being typically Southwestern. But the regional tag to
fit Oklahoma has not been made.

Oklahoma is to sociology as Australia is to zoölogy. It is a place
where the trials and errors of men, instead of nature, have been
made only yesterday, and the results are as egregious as a duckbill,
or a kangaroo. Oklahoma is filled with man-made contradictions,
perversities and monstrosities.

Oklahoma has scarcely any history beyond the memory of living
man, and yet it has a vein of well-documented history which dates
back farther than that of the original thirteen colonies. Sevillian
archives prove that Spanish prospectors were working Oklahoma
mines while the Plymouth Rock was still a pebble. Coronado left his
trail across Oklahoma before the Pilgrim Fathers were so much as
conceived.

A hundred years ago Oklahoma was turned into a vast concentration camp for Red Indians, because it was such worthless land. Fifty
years ago, white people from every State in the Union swarmed in
to dispossess the banished Indians, because Oklahoma was such
valuable land. Land was free for the taking in Oklahoma a generation ago. So today Oklahoma has a greater percentage of white
farm-tenancy than any other State in the Union.

Politically Oklahoma is fickle—just when Democratic candidates
are counting on it most strongly, it goes Republican. Once it polled
more socialist votes than any other State except Wisconsin. Nowadays it is almost as reactionary as Mississippi. It is a criminal
offense, for example, in Oklahoma, to have a copy of Karl Marx's
"Das Kapital" in one's library, and anyone suspected of possessing
seditious literature is liable to search, seizure, and arrest. Indeed,
certain scholarly citizens have been prosecuted criminally and faced
with penitentiary sentences, because sober political treatises,
regarded as classics elsewhere, in Oklahoma are even more illicit
than a bottle of bootleg booze. But the whole subject of Oklahoma
politics is so complex and bizarre that it would require a separate
study.

Many white people who settled in Oklahoma were decent home-
seekers. Most white people who came to Oklahoma were, perforce,
either scoundrels or transient paupers. Oklahoma was the Dust
Bowl. And yet no spot on earth has more verdant scenic beauty than

Oklahoma. The western plains of Oklahoma are so high above sea level that they make its rugged eastern hills seem like holes in the ground.

Oklahomans are an irascible humorless breed, set wild by the mildest criticism. Contradictory to this, Oklahomans have a peculiar wit, and the late Will Rogers is a popular prototype.

The first settlers of Oklahoma did not come there through any choice of their own. Although by legal technicality they were Indians, many had more Scotch-Irish and English than they had aboriginal ancestry. It was an apt historian who said that first the colonists fell on their knees, then they fell on the aborigines. Members of the Five Civilized Tribes (distinct from the nomadic predatory Plains Indians) often bore such stout patronymics as McIntosh, Porter, McCurtain, LeFlore, Childers, Rogers, Ross, Colbert, Logan, and McGillivray. Some had been educated in New England colleges. They were as deeply attached to their ancestral homes as any Boston Brahmin was to his. They owned Negro slaves, and prosperous plantations. They were torn from their villages and farms to be transported a thousand miles overland to the wilderness of Oklahoma. This forcible resettlement of a minority people was as ruthless as anything in modern times. Hundreds died on the road of disease and starvation. The routes taken by the "emigrating companies" still may be traced by graves. Many were brought in irons. The forlorn "Indians" sowed flower seeds to mark the way, and they called it "The Trail of Tears."

The name Oklahoma is a combination of two Choctaw words— *okla,* people; *humma,* red. It should be understood that *red* has the same connotations to a Choctaw that *white* has to an Anglo-Saxon. "Oklahoma" was a title of honor the Choctaws had conferred on their chieftains for hundreds of years. "Oklahoma" figuratively means honorable, square-dealing, or distinguished. The irony of its being applied to stolen territory just being parcelled out to the offscourings of white civilization, must have been deliberate.

By way of contrast, the white settlers of Oklahoma proudly adopted the nickname of "Sooner." Oklahoma became "the Sooner State." The current edition of Webster's Dictionary defines a *sooner* as "one who settles on government land before it is legally open to settlement; hence, one who does a thing prematurely or anticipates another in acting, in order to get an unfair advantage.'' In other words, a kind of sneaking crook. Then Oklahomans anticipated a basic American advertising principle. This is to pick out the weakest part of your product, and make a virtue of it. Oklahoma's official state guidebook points out that "for a long time the term *Sooner* was one of reproach, but with the passing of years the word began to lose its original connotations. As its origin was gradually forgotten, it eventually came to mean merely one who is alert, ambitious, and enterprising, or one who gets up earlier than others, always takes the lead, and strives to excel.''

Thus it might appear that Oklahoma is populated with people who scarcely go to bed at all, so eager is everyone to get up earlier than the other fellow. This is hardly true. Although Oklahoma is one of the wealthiest States in the Union, at the same time it is one of the most poverty-stricken. Although education is a fetish in Oklahoma, its illiteracy rating is twice that of the national average.

Each of these statements shows, like an index finger pointed the wrong way, that Oklahoma can be a controversial subject even to people who know the place well. It is difficult to set down the solemn facts about Oklahoma without their reading like something copied out of an insane encyclopaedia—Baedeker gone berserker. (Standard reference works get around such inconsistencies by leaving much to be said.) Bearing in mind that Oklahomans are a proud and touchy people—and the more disreputable their past, the more opulent their present, the more proud and touchy they are apt to be—the reader should appreciate that writing a brief, informative piece about Oklahoma is a delicate task, to be approached with trepidation, even by a native son.

Once while I was a perennial sophomore at the University of Oklahoma, I wrote a magazine article about Oklahoma that almost got me lynched. The campus auxiliary of the Ku Klux Klan, doing business under the mystic initials D.D.M.C., regularly kidnapped and flogged students who incurred its displeasure. Its secret councils decided that nothing short of mayhem would do for my offense. I had characterized my Alma Mater as a " 'college comic' college in a comic-opera State.'' (A college comic is, of course, a student periodical which burlesques school life with cartoons, jokes, doggerel, and such.) Even my professors took a dim view of my youthful perspicacity.

That was over fifteen years ago. Two years later, having eluded mob violence, to say nothing of formal education, at Oklahoma's outstanding seat of higher learning, I was emboldened to write another magazine piece about my native State. Published in "Vanity Fair," this began: "Miss Edna Ferber, the lady novelist, wrote by way of preface to her novel *Cimarron:* 'Anything can happen in Oklahoma. Practically everything has.' Miss Ferber's statement, obviously, is extravagant, but it is true that some unusual things do happen in Oklahoma. However, any reasonably accurate narrative based on the State's history would not resemble Miss Ferber's super-spectacle scenario so much as it would the plot for a hilarious comic opera. . . ." Whereupon the daily newspapers of Oklahoma burst into a frenzy of denunciation.

My early recommendation was, nevertheless, sound. One of the most popular shows in New York is a musical play called "Oklahoma!" As everyone knows, this has been crowding theatres there and elsewhere for years. Some optimists says that it will go on forever. Not to be compared with "Tobacco Road," another regional play which enjoyed a long run without being set to music, "Oklahoma!" is an authentic portrayal of rural manners and speech lingering in Oklahoma to this day, even though the time is tactfully set as just before statehood, some forty years ago.

But are Oklahomans outraged by such a happy realization of my modest proposal, made a few years before? Not at all. No one is more highly pleased by the success of "Oklahoma!" than the people who cried for my scalp when I said that Oklahoma was an ideal subject for a comic opera. Believe it or not, there was a movement to have the legislature adopt the finale of "Oklahoma!" as the official state anthem. The Governor of Oklahoma, the Honorable Robert S. Kerr—a large man who holds the distinction of being the first native-born Oklahoman ever elected to that high office, not to mention his having escaped impeachment proceedings which have routed several predecessors—boasts that he has "gone to see 'Oklahoma!' about umpteen times, both in New York and Chicago." Furthermore, Governor Kerr has published with impunity a popular magazine commentary, illustrated by colored scenes from "Oklahoma!" which makes some of the same observations that aroused such furious editorial resentment against me a few years ago.

This is given as proof of how quickly attitudes may change in Oklahoma. Attitudes in Oklahoma are almost as unpredictable as the weather. And Oklahoma is a place where a man comes home in the evening with a fringe of icicles on his straw hat.

Miss Edna Ferber has written an enlightening passage in her autobiography. She owns to a clairvoyant power which lets her project herself "into any age, environment, condition, situation, character, or emotion." She says she doesn't expect anyone to believe this, but that it's nevertheless true. She adduces proof by reporting that she wrote *Cimarron,* her widely read novel about the State, "after spending exactly ten days in Oklahoma." As soon as *Cimarron* was published, Miss Ferber goes on to say, "Oklahoma read the book, stood up on its hind legs, and howled."

Miss Ferber's faith in her oracle was not shaken for an instant. "By now I had realized that an American regional novel always is resented by the people of its locale, unless, of course, all descriptions and background are sweetness and light. Oklahoma had all the self-consciousness and inferiority feeling of the new and unsure. A flood of letters poured in upon me. They ranged from remonstrance to vilification."

In Oklahoma, oddly enough for a place populated with failures, nothing succeeds like success. When Miss Ferber's novel had sold a quarter of a million copies and had been made into a highly successful motion picture, she was startled to find that she had suddenly become Oklahoma's darling.

At least Miss Ferber was conscientious enough to spend ten days in Oklahoma. John Steinbeck, who wrote "The Grapes of Wrath" a few years later, was content, it would seem, to get his information from a road map, with ludicrous results. It is evident that Mr. Steinbeck wrote his book without ever having set foot in the State. The eastern part of Oklahoma, which Mr. Steinbeck, using real place names, describes as a vast Dust Bowl created by mechanized farming, is actually a region of wooded hills, broad lakes and beautiful streams flowing through high bluffs. There is no more beautiful scenery in all America than that of eastern Oklahoma. Nor do people anywhere dwell more serene in the ways of their ancestors. The so-called Dust Bowl was in the more up-and-coming western part of the State. Really the Dust Bowl lay, for the most part, in Texas and Kansas, and was touched only by the extreme western finger of Oklahoma.

The pathetic Okies about whom John Steinbeck wrote in "The Grapes of Wrath," were seldom, if ever, natives of Oklahoma. Although the name Okies is a contraction of the word Oklahoman, and is contemptuously applied to any transient laborer, most Okies, in saying that they are from Oklahoma, are merely giving their most recent place of residence.

I must add as a first-hand witness that the exodus of Okies from Oklahoma to California began long before there was a Dust Bowl. A contemporary observer noted that the land lotteries which opened the region to settlement between 1889 and 1903 attracted "a large class of farmers who had met with failure in other parts of the country. . . . It was one of this class who had as his motto painted on the canvas side of his prairie schooner: 'Chinch-bugged in Illinois, Bald-nobbed in Mizzouri, Prohibited in Kansas, Oklihommy or Bust.'" So, many people who came to Oklahoma in covered wagons took to the roads again a few years later in battered flivvers. These failures, called "Okies," at least had the courage to move on when they knew they were licked. The tenant farmers who stayed in Oklahoma are another story.

Even the Indians, who are the real aristocrats of Oklahoma, regard the State as alien soil. There are some thirty tribes of them there, comprising thirty-six per cent of the entire Indian population of the United States, and they range in culture from the Five Civilized Tribes, who were much less migratory than the white people who uprooted them, to the once wild, now tamed but unregenerate, Comanches and Apaches of the plains.

It is difficult to make clear, even to Americans in adjoining States, the peculiar social status Indians enjoy in Oklahoma today. Often the most refined white girl there feels that she has made a lucky catch if she can win a man with Indian blood, and there are Oklahomans of pure "Aryan" ancestry who like to boast that they have "a sixteenth Cherokee." This is all the more confusing when it is observed that Oklahoma draws a strict color line against the

Negro, who forms only a small percentage of the population, in spite of the fact that the slave-owning tribes usually regarded an admixture of Negro blood with somewhat less disfavor than they did white miscegenation. Oklahoma, nevertheless, harshly enforces its Jim Crow law (full-blood Indians often carry credentials to prove their right to ride in the train coaches forbidden to Negroes), and its history has been smirched by numerous sanguinary race riots "to keep the nigger in his place." On the other hand, several all-Negro communities in Oklahoma assert their right to prohibit any white man from staying over night in their towns.

It should not be assumed that wealth is all that makes Indians matrimonially attractive to white people. The riches of the Oklahoma Indians have been greatly exaggerated by inspired news stories, which seek to show how generous the white invader has been towards the Indians, and how foolishly the Indians make use of their money. (No Oklahoman, for example, has ever seen a wealthy Indian sitting in a rocking chair, riding in a plate-glass motor hearse he has just bought for his pleasure. This is a familiar newspaper myth, and my investigations have prepared me to challenge that it has any basis in fact.) Actually, many of the Indians in Oklahoma, perhaps the majority, are desperately poor. Their congenital opposition to manual labor and to engaging in trade for profit is not being erased by time. It is true that the Osage tribe, numbering about 3,000 head, enjoyed an income of $22 million as recently as 1926, which they divided under a communal system, but even the income of this tribe, once said to be the wealthiest people per capita in the world, has been reduced almost to the vanishing point by the outrageous exploitation and waste of the mineral wealth beneath their land.

Oklahoma is a combination of two Choctaw words, meaning red people. *Oka-homa* is a combination of two Choctaw words, meaning whisky (red water). One word is about as applicable to the State as the other—even though Oklahoma is one of the few States in the Union now enjoying statewide prohibition of the sale and manufacture of intoxicating liquors. There is, nevertheless, a considerable traffic in potables. Some of these are revenue-paid brands smuggled in from Arkansas, Texas, and Missouri. (Bootlegging—indeed, both the word and the profession—was invented in Oklahoma.)

Also there are local products, a distillation of about 150 proof, pure white, euphemistically called "panther sweat," and a brew known as Choctaw beer, made of water and corn meal, sometimes spiced with a native berry, once used by the Indians to poison fish, which provides a narcotic ingredient in lieu of alcohol.

Oklahoma exceeds New England in size by about 4,000 square miles, ranking seventeenth among the forty-eight States in area. It ranks twenty-second in population among the States with 2,336,434 people, white, red, and black. Even today the majority of Oklahomans are natives of other States, although few of them are foreign-born. In 1940 it had 43 towns and cities of more than 5,000 population, the largest of which are Oklahoma City, the capital (204,424), Tulsa (142,157), Muskogee (32,332) and Enid (28,118). But recently it is said to have lost population.

Visitors are often impressed by the cleanliness of cities in Oklahoma, because natural gas is used as fuel, and there is no soot. Both Oklahoma City and Tulsa, which calls itself the "oil capital of the world," are model cities, little replicas of New York, boasting skyscrapers and smart shops. Muskogee, a fine old Territory town, is more sedate. It may seem odd to a stranger approaching these cities when he sees a cluster of twenty-story buildings rising suddenly out of the wide open spaces—for no reason at all.

Oklahoma has been kept as an agricultural State, partly through vicious, discriminatory freight rates that were imposed by the very railroads which were such a powerful force in opening the Territory to white ownership. Its main crops are cotton in the southern part of the State, wheat in the north, and cattle-raising in the west. In normal times, the only manufacturing industries worth mentioning are petroleum refineries (oil is the main source of wealth), lead and zinc smelters, flour mills, and broom factories.

It is no longer possible to write of Oklahoma's industry in the manner of a decade ago. The State's eastern terrain, which differs from that of its west as much as Scotland does from England, always had been conducive to brigandage, and once enjoyed the reputation of being the most lawless part of the United States. But bank-robbing, which for many years was a profitable occupation there, now has become obsolete. Times have changed since 1933, when I noted for publication:

"Oklahoma has, in addition to its prohibition statute, a law against bank-robberies, but it is all to no avail. Every other bank cashier in Oklahoma has his coat sleeves pulled out at the arm-pits from reaching up. The outlaws conduct their interviews with all the gallantry and swagger of frontier days.

"Lately one 'Pretty Boy' Floyd and his band have been getting the blame for nearly everything. 'Pretty Boy's' whereabouts are usually known, and the officers have been talking about attending to him, but he has such a dreadful reputation, they hesitate. The bankers and bonding companies, of course, are pretty indignant, and they pass resolutions and things when they have their conventions. But the citizens are not much aroused, since there is a feeling current among them that when thieves and robbers fall out, then honest men will get their due."

"Pretty Boy" Floyd made the choice that many another Okie had made before him. He wandered elsewhere—and unsympathetic G-men mowed him down. His home town of Sallisaw put on for him one of the grandest funerals that any community ever gave a homecoming hero. Other Oklahoma outlaws, broadening their scope, met the same fate. Since then the State has become almost as law-abiding as Iowa or Kansas.

Indeed, Oklahoma has changed so much within the last few years it seems too bad that those choleric editors who so roundly denounced me a few years ago cannot see the place now. It is a matter of sincere regret to me that so few of these men have survived apoplexy since I first called attention to Oklahoma as a comic-opera State.

Nowadays, when music on the radio inevitably goes into a medley from the musical comedy "Oklahoma!" I'm sorry I ever said that Oklahoma was the ideal comic-opera State. The oddities and complexities of my native heath, as years have gone by, do not seem as funny to me as they did in my youth. It would be well if one of the endowed foundations with which America is blessed could send a party of disinterested sociologists to look at Oklahoma. Sober explorations might have discovered how such a commonwealth, starting new with every natural advantage, could run the gamut of "free enterprise" within the first four decades of the twentieth century.

Of course, Oklahoma is still on the map. And even if its history is not a subject for schoolboys, it is still a good one for political scientists because, in my opinion, no other place in the world offers a more gruesome study of democracy in the raw—nor of how thoroughly it can be cooked.

NOTES

1. Angie Debo, *Oklahoma, Foot-loose and Fancy-free* (Norman: University of Oklahoma Press, 1949), 241.

2

THE DIFFICULTY OF CELEBRATING AN INVASION

Jerald C. Walker

In the spring of 1989, a friend in Ohio who had been watching news coverage of the "celebration" of the centennial of the Oklahoma Land Run of 1889 gave me a really hard time over the phone. I was able to respond rather meekly that at least some alternatives to the celebration were taking place. At the annual meeting of the Oklahoma Historical Society that year, appropriately held in Guthrie, the alternative was provided in an insightful personal/historical address by Dr. Jerald C. Walker, president of Oklahoma City University. A revised version of that address follows.

PERSONAL HISTORY: BETWEEN TWO WORLDS

The tensions and conflicts in the Walker family over the last eighty years mirror the complex history of what came to be known as Oklahoma. My father's family, joined by several related families, moved to Indian Territory from the mountains of East Tennessee to buy "surplus land" in the Creek Nation. It was, of course, surplus land only in the minds of federal officials and non-Creek land seekers.

This grandfather, coming from a Union-supporting family, was firmly Republican. My father insisted that grandfather was "one-fifth of the Republican party" in Fry Township, Tulsa County. It was clear Joseph Dulaney Walker regarded the Democratic party as the party of secession, Jim Crow laws, and fiscal irresponsibility.

Educated as a lawyer at Cumberland University in Tennessee, J. D. Walker had been a schoolteacher, merchant, and lawyer "back home." He was, for a time, a partner in a general store in Broken Arrow and managed the local cotton gin. He gave up these pursuits to devote full time to farming and the importing of mules from Missouri for resale to the area's farmers.

J. D. Walker did not fit white rural eastern Oklahoma stereotypes in any form or fashion. Although he was adamantly opposed to Franklin D. Roosevelt, he was a man of great compassion and an uncanny sense of fairness. Even though he would not have understood the term, he was the community's "liberal." He was so in the sense that he had no use for the Jim Crow laws enacted after statehood. He gave legal counsel free of cost or consideration to the area's whites, blacks, and Indians of modest financial means.

J. D. Walker, as an Oklahoman, moved from the Cumberland Presbyterian community of faith to that of the Methodist Episcopal Church. He would never have joined the Methodist Episcopal Church, South.

Grandfather, finally, all but abandoned his town home for the farm and the Haikey Chapel community's farming people. He made especially close friendships with a number of Creek families. My father and one uncle identified with their father in these matters. The other four children did not so identify and remained "town bound" with their mother.

The mixed-blood Jackson-England side of the family did not welcome the Anglo and black newcomers to Indian Territory. This Cherokee, Scotch-Irish, and English family grouping opposed a willful federal government that all but destroyed the five Indian republics of Indian Territory and forced the "allotment" property system on the citizens of the five nations. As more white settlers forced their way into Indian Territory with the aid and support of the federal government, the political and social influence of the Jacksons and Englands waned, as was the case with many mixed-blood and full-blood families in the five republics.

The "surplus" land eagerly sought by the Walker family and their relatives was seen as land stolen from its rightful owners by my mother's clan. To them Elias C. Boudinot was a traitor of the first order. They, like many of my mixed-blood relatives, worked toward acceptance of their neighbors no matter what they thought of statehood and the demise of the five Indian republics. But one thing was clear then and now: these folk never forgot or forgave the loss of the Cherokee republic. Many of their descendants hold exactly the same unreconstructed view in the present.

As Cherokee Baptists, fervent Democrats, Southern sympathizers, and opponents to the allotment property system, my mother's family found areas of profound disagreement and tension between themselves and my father's kin. Religion, Oklahoma history, and political issues were seldom discussed at gatherings which included both sides of the family.

As the years proceeded, my paternal grandfather developed more and more sympathy for and understanding of his daughter-in-law's interpretation of Oklahoma history, as did my father and my favorite uncle. This was, however, not necessarily the case for the remaining members of the family. J. D. Walker's views on FDR, the New Deal, religion, and the Jim Crow laws remained intact.[1]

If I were to write an autobiography, it would be entitled, *Between Two Worlds*. I have, effectively, lived my life between the two often conflicting worlds of values, opinions, and historical interpretations into which I was born on Walker's Hill, Fry Township, Tulsa County, Oklahoma, in 1938. Upon reading such a projected volume, one would understand why I find it easier to identify with Sam Houston than many other prominent figures in American history. Unlike Mr. Houston, however, I have no plans to leave Oklahoma.

AN ALTERNATIVE VIEW OF HISTORY

It has been said that those who win the wars write the histories. It could also be said that those who win the wars organize the celebrations.

Because I was fortunate enough to have access to an alternative perspective on Oklahoma history and events such as the Oklahoma Land Run of April 22, 1889, I will present a basic but not popular image of the Land Rush of '89 and the eventual destruction of Oklahoma as exclusively Indian country in a legal, political, and social sense.[2]

The Land Rush of '89 has been celebrated in song and story, in novel and film, and now by a centennial celebration of significant proportions. Despite the attention lavished on this event over the years, as Rennard Strickland has correctly pointed out, how the Oklahoma Indians came to April 22, 1889, and what has happened to them subsequently has been largely ignored in public school textbooks and civic celebrations of this colorful dash for land.[3]

Rennard Strickland is on the mark when he says "the Run of '89 was an epic if condensed enactment of the entire frontier settlement process."[4] Danney Goble also puts it well when he suggests the run squeezed into one "supreme moment" the national experience of three centuries in terms of white dealings with this country's native peoples and nations.[5] It was, from the perspective of the great majority of the Indian population of what was to have been a uniquely Indian area, another invasion of Indian land by non-Indians. It was a perfectly legal invasion from the non-Indian perspective, but nothing more than another land grab by property hungry non-Indians from the Native American perspective.

Strickland provides a concise and helpful paragraph outlining key developments leading to April 22, 1889: "The story of the dissolution of the Oklahoma Indian nations is primarily one of white policy and white power. By 1865, Indian tribes had begun to lose whatever hint of equality they may have once possessed. Indians were left primarily to react to the initiatives of white policy. By 1871 the treaty era had formally ended, and even the pretense of negotiated equality had been replaced by the terrorizing potential of executive order and congressional governance."[6]

As a consequence of these unhappy developments, by 1890 the majority of the people in what is now Oklahoma were white. The combination of the relentless waves of these new immigrants— invaders, if you will—and the federally mandated destruction of Indian forms of governance and common life overwhelmed the invaded Native American peoples socially, economically, and politically.

When I entered public school I was warned by my mother, her family, and our Creek neighbors to beware of the white bias that colored the schoolroom presentation of American history in general and Oklahoma history in particular. Mother read Grant Foreman's work on the five tribes with special care. He was her intellectual hero.

Our family's long-time Creek friends, Geronimo and Alsophene Alexander, read Angie Debo with interest and concern equal to my mother's reading of Foreman. Mother, her family, and the Alexanders and their relatives provided me an alternative to the indifferent instruction in Oklahoma history I received in public school.

The dominant image of the white immigrants to the "new world" was not that of brave, hardy pioneer heroes but, rather, of never-ending waves of greedy and overbearing invaders. It should be pointed out that my mother's family and the Alexanders and their Creek kinsmen adapted to Oklahoma's "new order" in remarkably successful ways, but they did not forget what had been cherished and lost to the invaders.[7]

One oft-repeated bitter joke in the full-blood and mixed-blood circles of my childhood stated that "the Scotch-Irish kept the sabbath on the American frontier and everything else they could get their hands on." Will Rogers ironically joked, "We spoiled the best territory in the world to make a state." A white state like Oklahoma was inevitable, Rogers said, because "Indians were so cruel that they were all killed by civilized white men for encroaching on white domain."[8]

The dominant view of Oklahoma history in my public school classroom was the standard assimilationist view that saw the allotment system, the radical emasculation of Indian political and social self-determination, and statehood for Oklahoma as desirable and proper.

I will now offer a brief outline of the standard objections to the invader image applied to the Run of '89 and the subsequent events leading to statehood for Oklahoma and, in the process, answer the objections.

1. *Those persons making the Run of '89 were, in the main, well-meaning people seeking freedom and the means to better their economic and social circumstances.* Those folk making the run were, knowingly or unknowingly, busily re-creating the national experience of westward expansion.[9] The great irony of the non-Indian

westward expansion in the United States is that the freedom of the newcomers to develop economically and socially was purchased by the progressive denial of freedom and self-determination for the nation's Native American peoples. The invasion carried out on April 22, 1889, was clearly in the mainstream of this dubious American tradition.

2. *The invaders had a mandate, yes, and an overriding moral responsibility to foster private ownership of the land controlled by Indian peoples and, in the process, to fully develop the agricultural and commercial potential of what would become Oklahoma.* This was the theme of David Payne's company of invaders, the railroad promoters, and many other groups pressuring the federal government for the opening of Indian lands. The constant agitation of groups espousing this theme eventually prompted the federal government to repudiate its entire Indian policy.[10]

"We can better develop and manage the resources now controlled by the soon-to-be invaded" has been a consistent rationalization of invaders over the centuries to justify their invasions. The National Socialists used this reasoning, for example, to support Germany's invasion of the Ukraine during World War II. Their Italian counterparts used much the same rationale for their adventures in Africa during the same period. There are examples ad nauseam of this theme employed to support invasion.

Thomas Jefferson Morgan, U.S. Senator Henry Dawes, and other alleged "reformers" were intent on following the dogmatic position that private landownership would enhance the prosperity of Indian land in what is now Oklahoma. Although the deep-rooted tradition of communal land tenure was contrary to the ways of the individualistic white man, the Indian people of the five nations operated their affairs with this convention in a manner that produced contentment.[11]

Senator Dawes, visiting the Cherokee Nation in preparation for the writing of what became the Dawes Act, said of the Cherokee Nation, "There was not a family in that whole nation that had not a home of its own. There was not a pauper in that Nation, and the Nation did not owe a dollar. It built its own capitol . . . and it built its own schools and its hospitals. Yet the defect of the system was apparent. They have got as far as they can go, because they own their land in common. . . . there is no enterprise to make your home any better than that of your neighbors. There is no selfishness which is at the bottom of civilization.'' The most partisan Indian, as Angie Debo pointed out, would hardly have painted such an idealized picture of his people's happiness, prosperity, and culture, but, illogically, the senator from Massachusetts advocated a change in this prosperous society because it held to the wrong principles of property ownership.[12]

The new system of private landownership has not, in fact, promoted the prosperity for the Indian people in eastern Oklahoma that its advocates in theory claimed would inevitably be the case. The twenty million acres of land that made up the five nations were marked by general prosperity on the part of their Indian citizens. That area is now marked by significant contrasts of prosperity and poverty.

Just as socialist ideology can blind one to the realities discoverable through empirical observation, rightist ideology can produce the same myopia. The five Indian republics had developed an ingenious halfway position which produced prosperity for the Indian people of eastern Oklahoma, but, given the economic dogmatism of Dawes, Morgan, and others, it was an ideologically impure form of land use policy and ownership.

It is important to note that well-defined non-Indian groups took stands against abolishing tribal governments, the allotment system, and selling ''surplus'' Indian land and opening it to non-Indian settlement. Many churchmen, especially the missionaries who worked among the Indian tribes, were opponents of white settlement. White public pressure informed by the opposite opinion bowled over such opposition.

3. *White immigration to the Indian lands upgraded the population of this section of the United States.* The noncitizens in the Indian republics proclaimed they were subject to taxation without representation. Statehood was needed, they said, in order for these noncitizens in the Indian nations to have their full rights as American citizens. The year 1889 was the time when white farmers came with their families in great numbers to what had been Indian land. Until that fateful year, although subject to many federal regulations, Indians owned all the lands that were to become Oklahoma. By 1890

there were three times as many non-Indians living on Indian land as there were Native Americans. The Land Rush of '89 brought non-Indians in larger numbers to previously Indian-controlled territory.[13] The immigration of noncitizen, nonintermarried, non-Indian immigrants that, as Angie Debo correctly stated, "began as a trickle" into Indian lands soon after the Civil War "became a deluge that engulfed the Indian settlements by the end of the century."[14]

Because the noncitizens in the republics wanted title to the land they cultivated and paid taxes to support governments in which they had no voice and school systems that did not serve them, these "guests" on Indian lands clamored for the abolition of the Indian governments and the establishment of a governmental system representative of the whole population. The federal government ultimately bowed to such pressure, and there are still those among us who believe such capitulation was proper.[15]

The living arrangements of the "guests" of the republics rested on the most solemn commitments made by the federal government. The non-Indians, noncitizens had *voluntarily subjected themselves to such arrangements*. The noncitizens living on Indian lands, in fact, had no more right to press for the right to vote, determine land-ownership policies, and participate in governance and school administration in the "dependent, domestic Indian nations" than I have to press for such rights in the crown colonies of the United Kingdom. The long-standing commitments of the federal government in this vital matter were swept away under non-Indian pressure. It is as simple and as sad as that. The national experience of dealing with the nation's native peoples simply repeated itself, and such repetition was of no credit to those inside and outside the Indian lands who pressured for such change.[16]

Each republic operated its school system without federal participation or interference. As a result of their educational endeavors, there was a larger proportion of educated people among the Cherokees, Choctaws, Creeks, and Chickasaws than among the white people of the neighboring states. There is good reason to believe that illiteracy in the five nations increased as the non-Indian population grew.[17]

The political leaders of the five nations, often better educated than the governors and legislators of the neighboring states of Texas and

Arkansas, promoted better education among their peoples for many reasons, including that of attempting to fend off the ever-encroaching world of white America.[18]

Large numbers of the non-Indian immigrants to Indian lands were simply illegal and often lawless intruders. It is difficult to overestimate the disruption to the Indian republics caused by the unwelcome and unprincipled white rabble that took up unlawful residence in the five nations.

4. *Corruption in tribal government made statehood necessary.* This is the most curious of all major rationalizations for the legal invasions of Indian lands and statehood for Oklahoma. As a variety of historians have pointed out, there is no reason to believe governmental corruption in the five nations exceeded that which has marked the politics of governance in the new legal entity known as the State of Oklahoma from 1907 to the present. There was, of course, much corruption among the government agents who dealt with the tribes and pieces of tribes living outside the boundaries of the five republics in what is now Oklahoma. If the degree of political corruption were the test for states' regressing or not regressing to territorial status, Oklahoma and a great many of her sister states would have returned to territorial status decades ago.

This essay has dealt primarily with the fate of the five "civilized" tribes in relation to the advent of statehood for Oklahoma. There are strong parallels between the experiences of the Native American peoples living in the five republics and their ethnic kinsmen elsewhere in what is now the State of Oklahoma.

The allotment system, with support from some Indian leaders and the active opposition of the Indian Rights Association and other reform groups, was, for example, forced on the Comanches, Kiowas, and Kiowa-Apaches by a coalition of the Rock Island Railroad, cattle ranchers long involved in ranching activity on Indian land, homesteaders envisioning new homes, and Democrats viewing such a move as a step for Oklahoma statehood, along with an increase in party strength in Congress.[19]

I am hopeful the points made in this brief essay will help many understand why the Run of '89 is not seen as the dawn of a bright new day by many Oklahomans in both the eastern and western sections of the state. These "noncelebrating" folk, more often than not, have roots in this part of the United States older than the events and actions that allowed more and more non-Indians to settle Indian lands in what is now known as the State of Oklahoma.

Despite often tough opposition, Oklahoma shows a marked tendency to come to terms with its past as an Indian land. The Indian nations are undergoing a revival of vigor and strength. We must be very firm toward reactionary attitudes among some of our fellow Oklahomans who would see Indian nations as simply another set of American ethnic organizations. Governor Henry Bellmon and State Senator Enoch Kelly Haney deserve much credit among those in state government and legislative circles for these hopeful and positive developments.

The efforts in Oklahoma to come to terms with its past as an Indian land can be divided, as Senator Haney suggests, into the categories of the "symbolic" and the "concrete":[20] "To the native people of this country, symbolism is very important. Symbolism is probably the core of philosophy and theology for Indian beliefs. Subsequently, the Oklahoma State Legislature, with the help of Governor Bellmon, have taken certain steps which symbolize to the Indian nations the willingness of the State of Oklahoma to work with tribes on a government-to-government basis. Let me list some of the key symbolic acts." Senator Haney's list includes: (1) The bill which made the Indian Blanket the official state wild flower. (2) The use of the Osage shield as the logo on the state automobile tag. (3) The use of the Osage shield as the logo to be used on the State Flag Plaza in front of the Oklahoma State Capitol. Legislation has been passed whereby we will fly the flags of the thirty-seven tribal governments functioning in Oklahoma on the plaza. (4) The State of Oklahoma's giving significant funds to develop the impressive Red Earth Celebrations in Oklahoma City.

The Indian Burial Desecration Bill, making it a felony in the state of Oklahoma to desecrate the graves of native peoples; the passing of the Oklahoma Indian Child Welfare Act; and the passing of Senate Bill 210 are important concrete steps taken by Oklahoma to come to terms with its past and to normalize the relationships of the tribal governments and the State of Oklahoma. Senate Bill 210 provided the State of Oklahoma the opportunity, for the first time in its history, to recognize the existence of the federally recognized Indian tribal governments operating within its borders. In its amended form, Senate Bill 210 provided the authority for the political subdivisions of the State of Oklahoma, such as cities, towns, and counties, to enter into agreements with the Native American national governments. This change in the legislation provides safeguards that protect both the tribes' and state's interests. Significant economic development projects, benefiting Indian peoples and Oklahomans in general, have resulted from the provisions of Senate Bill 210. The Oklahoma Department of Commerce now has an Indian Business Desk.

While Oklahoma is increasingly seen as a pacesetter in normalizing relations between tribal governments and its state government, significant problems remain unsettled. These problems relate to the fact that the Oklahoma State Tax Commission sees its responsibility in the collection of taxes in a different way than do the Native American national governments. The issues at stake in the disputes between the Indian nations and the tax commission revolve around the matters of tribal sovereignty and governmental jurisdiction. It is likely some of the outstanding issues between the nations and the tax commission will be resolved by negotiation and others in the courts.

There is very good reason to believe the posture of the tax commission oftentimes works against Oklahoma in the vital area of economic development. There is also good reason to believe that, as Senator Haney points out, the tax commission wastes valuable tax dollars by taking the Indian national governments to court over and over again in cases generally won by the tribes.

The installing of the impressive statues *As Long as the Waters Flow,* by the world-renowned Apache sculptor Alan House, in front of the Oklahoma state capitol is almost, as Senator Haney suggests, an "offering of peace" from the State of Oklahoma to its Native American peoples.[21] This monumental statue, it is to be hoped, bodes well for the relationship of the State of Oklahoma to its citizens holding dual citizenship.

NOTES

1. Material in this section is covered in Jerald C. Walker and Daisy Decazes, *The State of Sequoyah* (Kansas City: Lowell Press, 1985), 1–2.

2. Rennard Strickland, *The Indians of Oklahoma* (Norman: University of Oklahoma Press,1980), 34.

3. Ibid.

4. Ibid.

5. Danney Goble, *Progressive Oklahoma: The Making of a New Kind of State* (Norman: University of Oklahoma Press, 1980), 3.

6. Strickland, *Indians,* 34.

7. Geronimo and Alsophene Alexander adopted my sister and me in the ''Indian Way'' upon the death of my parents in the late 1970s. Because it was a wholly voluntary act devoid of political or financial considerations, I consider it the highest honor one can receive.

8. Strickland, *Indians,* 53.

9. Goble, *Progressive Oklahoma,* 13.

10. Ibid., 7.

11. Angie Debo, *And Still the Waters Run* (Princeton, N.J.: Princeton University Press, 1940), 14.

12. Ibid., 21–22.

13. Strickland, *Indians,* 34.

14. Debo, *And Still the Waters Run,* 12.

15. Ibid., 20.

16. Ibid.

17. Ibid., 7.

18. Donald E. Green, *The Creek People* (Phoenix: Indian Tribal Series, 1973), 56.

19. H. Glenn Jordan and Peter MacDonald, Jr., ''Quanah Parker: Patriot or Opportunist,'' in *Indian Leaders: Oklahoma's First Statesmen,* ed. H. Glenn Jordan and Thomas M. Holm (Oklahoma City: Oklahoma Historical Society, 1979), 158–75.

20. From comments made to Christopher Mauldin, Oklahoma City University administrative staff member, by Senator Enoch Kelly Haney, Sept. 19, 1989.

21. Ibid.

3

PROGRESSIVISM IN OKLAHOMA POLITICS, 1900–1913:

A Reinterpretation

Kenny L. Brown

Kenny L. Brown teaches at the University of Central Oklahoma in Edmond. He wrote the volume The Italians in Oklahoma *in the "Newcomers to a New Land" series. Some of the rethinking of progressivism in Oklahoma which he does in the following essay began, he says, in a National Endowment for the Humanities seminar he and I participated in together at Vanderbilt University in 1988 under Paul K. Conkin ("The American Regulatory and Welfare State, 1887 to the Present"). After surveying the historiography of progressivism at the national and state level, Brown presents his own interpretation and seems almost to conclude that "progressivism" is meaningless in looking at Oklahoma's history, or at least not a label which describes any well-defined movement.*

"I regard Haskell as a criminal and an organizer of criminals," Senator Robert L. Owen wrote to presidential hopeful Woodrow Wilson early in October 1912. Two months earlier, Owen had defeated former Oklahoma Governor Charles N. Haskell in the Democratic preferential primary for U.S. senator. The incumbent Owen wanted to make sure that Haskell and his campaign manager would have no influence in the future Wilson administration. To Owen the issue was clear: only honest, "progressive" politicians should prevail. He wrote, "Honest government can only be established in Oklahoma, as in New Jersey, by overthrowing the corrupt machine elements in this state, which fought me to a man and which I have overthrown by an overwhelming majority."[1]

Within a month after Wilson's inauguration in March 1913, the defeated Haskell retaliated against Owen. In a lengthy letter to Wilson, Haskell accused Owen of dishonest manipulations and outright graft in acquiring Indian lands in Oklahoma. Haskell cautioned Wilson not to follow Owen's advice in hiring governmental officials to oversee Indian affairs in the state. And finally, he warned Wilson that Owen's self-professed progressivism was a fraud. "I also submit . . . that when the Senator lays claim of being the founder of progressive ideas, that he is not a founder but a follower of the ideas that have been developed in the constitution and laws of our state."[2]

These letters from Owen and Haskell illustrate the difficulty in defining "progressivism" and in identifying the "real progressives." By 1912 most politicians laid claim to the label of progressive, and like most political labels it offered the utility of vagueness and flexibility. It meant that you were one of the righteous, honest, and modern leaders fighting the evil forces of the "monopolies," the "special interests," and the "trusts." But these corporate villains were vague and poorly defined, meaning different things to different interest groups.

Initially, this anticorporatism had no name. It was simply a widely held fear of the potential power of new giant corporations which had arisen at the turn of the century. But beginning about 1909 and 1910, politicians throughout the country began calling it "progressivism," and, like most contrivances of politicians, it created an illusion of cohesion among disparate groups. In reality, the supporters and goals of this nebulous progressivism varied according to the local economic and demographic mix. As elsewhere, in Oklahoma there was no unified group of people with common goals who called themselves progressives. There were several separate interest groups that arose and used the prevailing anticorporate sentiment to achieve their ends. In particular, Oklahoma farmers and labor union members convinced politicians to draft provisions in the constitution and legislation favorable to agriculture and labor. Legislators also approved laws designed to restrict the actions of various types of corporations. But the language, goals, and results of this political activity were contradictory, inconsistent, and vague.

Despite similar previous observations from other historians, most scholars have persisted in embracing the concept of progressivism as some sort of coherent, unified philosophy that adequately described reality. After reviewing some of the previous efforts to describe Oklahoma politics from 1900 to 1914, this essay will offer an alternative interpretation. It will demonstrate how several different local interest groups formed and used anticorporate sentiment to achieve their goals. But it will also show how the interests of each group often conflicted with those of their supposed allies and how politicians often fell victim to the inconsistencies inherent in the vague concept of progressivism.

In order to understand interpretations of Oklahoma progressivism, a brief survey of the views of historians of national progressivism is necessary.[3] The first scholar to write extensively about the topic, Benjamin Parke De Witt, accepted the politicians and various reform advocates at face value. De Witt explained that progressives opposed the "trusts" and "monopolies." They desired to regulate and curtail corporate activities using the government as an intervener, and they wanted the people as a whole to have more influence in government through various new electoral devices.[4]

Following De Witt's effort in 1915, most historians over the next several decades repeated the same basic formula. With few exceptions, historians explicitly or implicitly considered their "progressives" to be good guys fighting the villains of big business. Some of these claimed the ideas of the progressive "movement" had originated under the Populists of the 1890s. Other writers argued that the movement developed later, led by politicians from the Midwest. And by the 1950s several historians concluded that the best conceptualization was to consider the progressives as "middle class professionals."[5]

In the 1950s Richard Hofstadter rose to be the chief advocate of the middle-class theory of progressivism. However, he added a new negatively critical assessment. These middle-class professionals suffered status anxiety. They disliked the new power and prestige of the emerging industrialists, and they feared the rumblings from the working-class segment of society. These fearful professionals wanted to return to the old social system in which they had been the elites. Thus, progressives were nostalgic, a bit neurotic, and often intolerant of those outside their class. But even Hofstadter viewed the progressives as basically good fellows who wanted a better world and who were fighting against harmful corporate forces.[6]

In the 1960s historians Samuel P. Hays and Robert H. Wiebe challenged the basic premises of the previous interpretations of progressivism. Hays wisely used the word "progressive" sparingly in his books, *Conservation and the Gospel of Efficiency: The Progressive Conservation Movement, 1890–1920,* and *The Response to Industrialism, 1885–1914.* Hays said that the late nineteenth and early twentieth centuries were a time of adjustment to the emerging American industrial system. Scientists, businessmen, and other professionals sought to make the new system efficient and rational. Political passions and the overwhelming revulsion to monopolies and trusts, according to Hays, did not result in any major changes. Political posturing and rhetoric simply diverted attention from the real issues from time to time and interfered with the larger problem of imposing efficiency on the American economic system.[7] In his various similar works, historian Wiebe used the word *progressive* much more frequently than did Hays, but he also concluded that businessmen and professional managers molded the legislation and reforms of the era. According to Wiebe, the businessmen were the "real" progressives, and they were seeking to impose some sort of order on the new economic system.[8]

Although the Hays-Wiebe "organizational" synthesis soon became the leading interpretation, several other new variations emerged as well. Gabriel Kolko and James Weinstein endorsed the basic pattern outlined by Hays and Wiebe, yet Weinstein and Kolko saw the businessmen as deceitful and conspiratorial when they convinced the public that the changes were in the "people's" interest.[9] The businessmen themselves represented the very interests they claimed to have been opposing. Other historians, such as J. Joseph Huthmacher and John D. Buenker, said reform was often promoted and supported by urban workers, immigrants, and political bosses.

Irwin Yellowitz argued that the labor unions should be included in any discussion of progressivism. And David P. Thelen concluded that progressivism was a taxpayers' and consumers' revolt, while Richard L. McCormick insisted that antibusiness sentiment acted as a catalyst to bring about ironical and unexpected legislative results.[10]

Such widely variant interpretations as these led Peter G. Filene to conclude that a reconceptualization was in order. In his essay entitled "An Obituary to the Progressive Movement" (1970), Filene reviewed existing scholarship and found no unity in goals, values, membership, or supporters of so-called progressivism. He also chastised the principal historians of progressivism for their imprecise, contradictory, and muddled definitions of the "progressive movement."[11]

Filene was right. American historians have interpreted "progressivism" as a unified movement, a diverse movement, a collection of varied yet still similar movements, an impulse, an impulse with many "strains," a spirit of the age, a reform ethos, a reform wave, or some other type of elusive and ill-defined entity. According to various interpretations, "progressives" were liberal, conservative, working-class, middle-class, upper-class, rural, urban, forward-looking, backward-looking, Christian, scientific, Middle Western, found in every part of the country yet different in each section, pro-consumer, probusiness, or proefficiency.

Like the histories of national politics from 1900 to 1914, most works on Oklahoma suffer from weak definitions and convoluted descriptions of progressivism. These histories are quite good in the presentation of factual information; they simply suffer from the mistaken belief that politicians' generalizations can be accepted at face value. The first historian to deal extensively with the topic in Oklahoma was Keith L. Bryant, Jr. In his excellent biography of William H. ("Alfalfa Bill") Murray, Bryant described the popular issues in Oklahoma during the time of the constitutional convention, over which Murray presided in 1906 and 1907. Bryant wrote, "The constitution represented an amalgamation of the Populist and Progressive ideologies. Indeed, the two philosophies became so intermeshed in the document that it is impossible to determine which was the more important influence."[12] According to Bryant, the regulation of railroads, the control of corporations, and the initiative and referendum were reforms from both the populist and the progressive traditions. Uniquely progressive were the child labor provisions, prolabor sections, and the prohibition amendment. Bryant further explained that many of these populist and progressive elements were "fused" in the person of Alfalfa Bill Murray.[13]

Yet much of Bryant's analysis was contradictory. Although many of the populist and progressive elements may have been fused into Murray, he had outright rejected the Populist party and distrusted labor unions. In fact, Murray later became a target of labor union animosity because of his failure to support several of their legislative efforts. Finally, Bryant's major premise was that Murray was fundamentally an "agrarian." He sought the equal and fair distribution of land to make farming available to all Americans. Thus, any "fusing" of progressive elements into the person of Murray was in truth only partial and did not eradicate his strong agrarian inclinations.[14]

Within two years Bryant followed up his biography of Murray with two articles on progressivism ("Kate Barnard, Organized Labor, and Social Justice in Oklahoma during the Progressive Era," in the *Journal of Southern History,* and "Labor in Politics: The Oklahoma State Federation of Labor in the Age of Reform," in *Labor History*). These articles proved that social justice advocate Kate Barnard and labor union activists led the fight for many of the provisions included in the Oklahoma Constitution. Bryant said that their involvement in the passage of "progressive" reforms contradicted the prevailing opinion among historians that only middle-class professionals were progressives. To Bryant, Barnard and her union allies made up the core of progressivism in Oklahoma. But he also acknowledged that their success came because of an alliance with the powerful Oklahoma Farmers Union, and farmers have usually been excluded from most definitions of progressivism. The coalition of Barnard, union leaders, and farmers caused the constitution to be loaded with popular reforms designed to protect their own interests and control the "selfish corporate interests."[15]

In the early 1970s following Bryant's efforts, George O. Carney produced an analysis of Oklahoma "progressives." In his dissertation and two related articles, Carney traced the voting records of thirteen Oklahomans who served in the U.S. House of Representatives from 1901 to 1917.[16] Carney conceded there was no "large group of men who were in agreement on all of the goals" that can be called progressive. Progressivism was a "trend" in politics in the early twentieth century. Nonetheless, a working definition of a progressive program could easily be identified, according to Carney. His list of progressive reforms included tariff, banking, and tax reforms; railroad and trust regulations; prolabor laws; agricultural legislation; child labor restrictions; and electoral changes, such as the initiative and referendum, direct election of senators, and direct primary. Carney seemed to convey that these reforms were good and that a congressman who supported a majority of the reforms was worthy of being designated progressive.[17]

Carney surveyed the books of eight prominent historians of the progressive era to compile a list of several dozen characteristically progressive bills and resolutions. He concluded that ten out of the thirteen Oklahoma representatives supported this agenda. Dennis Flynn, who had actually been a territorial delegate, had not voted or spoken out on the reforms because he had served only one term during the time frame of Carney's study. Nevertheless, Flynn had been friendly to "stand pat," antiprogressive Republican leaders and thus could be convicted of being nonprogressive through guilt by association. Bird McGuire, who served several terms, likewise associated with stand patters. He did support a few of Carney's progressive reforms, but not enough to escape the "conservative" label. Charles E. Creager, who served one term, came close but did not support a majority of the reforms. The progressive label could be applied to the rest: Elmer L. Fulton, Dick T. Morgan, James S. Davenport, Charles D. Carter, Scott Ferris, William W. Hastings, William H. Murray, Joseph B. Thompson, James V. McClintic, and Claude Weaver.[18]

Carney's study favored Democrats over Republicans. Nine of the ten progressives were Democrats, while all three nonprogressives were Republicans. Perhaps part of this slant was a result of the tariff issue. Several of the roll call votes in Carney's list were on tariff rates. The Republicans tended to stick with their party's old protectionist tendencies, while the Democrats usually voted to lower rates. Leaving out the tariff issue, even the Republicans look more "progressive'' than Carney's original assessment. Bird McGuire in particular was posturing himself as a supporter of progressive reform by 1910; therefore, he supported the popular changes in word if not totally in deed. Thus, those congressmen whom Carney said do not deserve the label at least disguised themselves as progressives, and an overwhelming majority of the delegation approved Carney's agenda.[19]

The list of legislation that Carney offered as a working definition includes much that is contradictory and is so broad that most politicians of the day supported some of the agenda. This problem of defining progressivism is endemic in most histories of progressivism. A banker could have supported banking reform and railroad regulation, but he could also have adamantly opposed child labor restrictions and electoral reforms. In other words, the wide spectrum of legislation is too broad and too unrelated to say any unity of thought existed.

About the same time that Carney was evaluating the House delegation from Oklahoma, Rennard J. Strickland and James C. Thomas analyzed the intent of the framers at the Oklahoma Constitutional Convention. These two law professors wrote an article in 1973 for *Tulsa Law Journal* entitled, ''Most Sensibly Conservative and Safely Radical: Oklahoma's Constitutional Regulation of Economic Power, Land Ownership, and Corporate Monopoly.'' Relying heavily on the official proceedings of the constitutional convention, Strickland and Thomas concluded that some provisions of the Oklahoma Constitution were several years ahead of similar changes at the national level, but for the most part, the Oklahoma Constitution sought to maintain the status quo. It represented a strong consensus based upon conventional beliefs that the small landholder and farmer were preferable to large corporate owners of land. The authors contended that the delegates to the constitutional convention were ''more strongly *pro farmer than anti corporation*'' but had some concerns about monopolies as well. Strickland and Thomas wrote, ''Their concern with antitrust and monopoly was mostly focused on those points at which corporate power might endanger the survival of the rural neighbors, small town shopkeeper, and the family farm as a social unit.''[20] The principal objections were to any monopolies, to railroads that expanded into other fields, and to large real estate corporations. Otherwise, corporations properly organized and properly operated were both necessary and good.

Strickland and Thomas argued that the regulatory system established under the constitution was not "radical." But they also recognized the ambiguity of the term *radical*. In one sense *radical* means simply any extreme departure from the status quo. In another sense it is used to identify a measure specifically socialistic or communistic. Under neither definition of the word was Oklahoma's constitution radical. However, in several ways Oklahoma's regulations were more stringent than the federal government's similar laws governing corporations. Oklahoma required corporations to make their books available at any time, allowed governmental officials broad investigatory powers, and exempted labor unions from antitrust provisions. But the federal government adopted similar measures seven years later (1914) in the Clayton Anti-Trust Act and with the creation of the Federal Trade Commission. Therefore, according to Strickland and Thomas, Oklahoma's approach was balanced and only a few years ahead of federal changes. It was "sensibly conservative and safely radical." Although lengthy, their article offers fairly clear terms and wisely avoids the concept of progressivism.[21]

The most thorough attempt to define and explain progressivism in Oklahoma came from Danney Goble in his *Progressive Oklahoma: The Making of a New Kind of State* (1980). Goble argued that the Oklahoma Constitution exemplified the progressive movement in its most advanced form. According to Goble, most of Oklahoma's new settlers, who came primarily between 1889 and 1907, had one thing in common: they shared the "boomer spirit." They had a vision of a new life with bountiful rewards for their toils and the chance for wealth and comfort. However, after a few years in the Twin Territories (Oklahoma Territory and Indian Territory), most settlers found their dreams unfulfilled. Some were ruined by bad weather and drought, and others found the business opportunities had been exaggerated, yet most concluded that distant market forces and capricious bankers and big businesses were robbing them of their wealth.

Following the earlier trend of national "muckraking," local newspapers published articles uncovering fraud and corruption perpetrated by businessmen against the public. Many Oklahomans reacted with a new consumer consciousness that was combined with a vigorous growth in interest-group politics. Drawing heavily upon the previous work of Keith L. Bryant, Jr., Goble described the actions of the Oklahoma Farmers Union, the Twin Territories Federation of Labor, and Kate Barnard in forcing certain provisions in the constitution. Thus, consumerism, interest-group activism from farmers and workers, and the actions of Barnard formed the essence of "progressivism" and brought about the "progressive" constitution.[22]

Goble's book is generally straightforward, factual, and very well written; however, its principal difficulty is the absence of a clear-cut definition of progressivism. Goble observed that historians hold widely varying views on the meaning of progressivism, but he argued that most scholars of progressivism have concluded that "the Oklahoma Constitution of 1907 was a particularly lucid example of Progressive reform."[23] Therefore, the principal provisions of the constitution that outlaw monopolies, regulate railroads and utilities, establish direct democracy electoral devices, and protect labor encompassed "nearly all of the demands that had defined Oklahoma's Progressive impulse."[24] Of course, that "impulse" was primarily a reaction against large corporations. But lost in all of Goble's description is a clear identification of who were the progressives. Kate Barnard led the " 'social justice' wing of the emerging Progressive impulse," according to Goble.[25] The labor unions and the Oklahoma Farmers Union pushed for their special interests, which were naturally antagonistic to the desires of huge businesses with control of large markets. But were the workers and farmers progressive in a more comprehensive sense? In other words, did they support almost all other progressive reforms? That question is not answered.

A few years after publishing *Progressive Oklahoma*, Goble more clearly assessed the purity of the state's progressive leaders in *Oklahoma Politics: A History*, which he coauthored with James R. Scales.[26] In this excellent state political history, Goble and Scales explained that the original "progressive" coalition of the constitutional convention did not fare well from 1907 to 1910. The first legislature did implement many new laws that amplified and reinforced the principal provisions of the constitution. However, as this happened, the coalition began crumbling. Alfalfa Bill Murray, presiding as the first speaker of the Oklahoma House of Representatives, began feuding with Kate Barnard and the labor unions over child labor legislation and other prolabor measures. The natural animosities between workers and farmers emerged. The progressives were not thoroughly united in their progressivism.[27]

By 1910, according to Goble and Scales, a much more important change took place. The "anticorporate" drive of early progressivism (meaning four years earlier) faded and gave way to "business" progressivism. Oklahoma's progressivism "was entering a metamorphosis." Goble and Scales wrote, "Increasingly, leadership was falling, if only by default, to aspiring businessmen and professionals who had balked at the shrill antibusiness tones of the constitution's drafters. . . . They rejected crude political appeals to class grievances in favor of the calm promotion of public morality and economic growth directed by men like themselves: dignified, respectable and—by definition—progressive."[28] The leader of this new movement, according to Goble and Scales, was Governor Lee Cruce, a "conservative" banker. If the authors are accurate, this was quite a metamorphosis. Original progressivism, which was adamantly anticorporate, gave way to business progressivism, which was just as adamantly procorporate. This inconsistency typifies the contradictions prevalent in many histories of progressivism. It was this type of confusion that led Peter G. Filene to argue that we need a reconceptualization and clearer terms.

These criticisms of other historians are not meant to be harsh, for I realize it is much easier to find fault with the work of others than with my own. I hasten to point out that my own previous efforts to define and describe progressivism have failed. I was vague and offered poor definitions in my article in *The Chronicles of Oklahoma* entitled "A Progressive from Oklahoma: Senator Robert Latham Owen, Jr.," and in my subsequent dissertation on Owen (1985).[29] Owen served in the U.S. Senate from 1907 to 1925 and became identified with many reforms labelled "progressive." In my works on Owen, I was guilty of the same oversimplification and vagueness that have plagued most writers who have dealt with progressivism. The remainder of this essay attempts to rectify those

past failings, and I hope it will bring clarity to a confusing topic. It
relies heavily on the works of those historians discussed above.

During the late nineteenth century Oklahoma experienced many
of the same trends and patterns of development that occurred
throughout much of the rest of the nation. Before 1890 the economy
of the United States grew dramatically. The building of railroads
throughout the country stimulated the iron and steel industry and
created a national transportation network, which allowed the formation of nationwide marketing systems. The severe depression of the
early and middle 1890s disrupted the otherwise steady growth, causing many Americans to question the emerging economic system. By
the late 1890s the economy revived and expanded with unparalleled
vigor. Enlightened by the lessons of the depression of 1893–96,
corporate managers sought stability through mergers and elimination of competition. This led to a remarkable consolidation
movement patterned after the earlier actions of Augustus Swift in
meat packing, James B. Duke in the tobacco industry, John D.
Rockefeller in oil, Andrew Carnegie in steel, and others. Using both
vertical and horizontal integration, dozens of companies combined
and expanded at the turn of the century. In 1897 only 12 large combinations existed, capitalized at about one billion dollars, but by
1903 the number of large corporations had risen to 305, capitalized
at about seven billion dollars.[30]

As the new business combinations came to dominate the economy, many Americans began worrying about the tremendous power
and influence of the large corporations. However, the obvious effectiveness of the organizational methods of large companies caused all
kinds of interest groups to copy the corporate formula of organizing.
Bankers, several varieties of small businessmen, farmers, workers,
women's club advocates, and others rushed to form new associations or cooperatives to promote their positions. Some organizations, such as the American Federation of Labor, the American
Medical Association, and the American Bar Association already
existed by 1890, but in the last decade of the nineteenth century
and the first decade of the twentieth, these older groups revitalized and expanded their membership dramatically. Thus, similar to
the rise of the great corporations, various groups combined and

cooperated en masse to bring about change and promote their interests.[31]

The national changes in the economy profoundly affected Oklahoma at a time when the state underwent its greatest growth in population and development. In 1890 the combined population of Oklahoma Territory and Indian Territory numbered 258,657; by 1910 the state had grown to 1,657,155. In percentage of growth Oklahoma far surpassed any other state or territory during the period, and with an increase of almost 1.4 million the Sooner State ranked fourth in total numerical growth (behind New York, Pennsylvania, and California).[32]

Whether entering Oklahoma Territory during its various land runs or migrating inconspicuously into Indian Territory, the flood of newcomers brought tremendous economic and social change to Oklahoma. Cities and farms sprang up everywhere as farmers, businessmen, merchants, and miners arrived. In Indian Territory thousands of the newcomers were landless tenant farmers who leased land from prominent Indians. But regardless of occupation, these settlers caused Oklahoma to develop faster than any state or territory from 1890 to 1910.[33]

Like the trends throughout the nation at that time, these newcomers began forming cooperatives, combinations, and interest groups. While developers built many new railroads, four large companies began consolidating many of the smaller tracks and would soon control most of Oklahoma's railroad network.[34] Early in 1902 a group of coal operators—most of whom were affiliated with the railroads—created the Consolidated McAlester Coal Company. This corporation, fully owned by the combination of operators, marketed coal and managed credit for most of Oklahoma's coal companies, thereby replacing the less efficient and more costly independent commission agents who had marketed their coal in the past.[35] Also, at the turn of the century, developers began mining the tremendous lead and zinc deposits of northeastern Oklahoma. Most local producers of lead and zinc immediately joined an effective producers association that had been formed earlier in the adjacent fields in Kansas and Missouri.[36] Outside of mining, businessmen, merchants, and town boosters who had already formed local boards of commerce throughout the Twin Territories met in 1905 to form the Federation of Commercial Clubs of Oklahoma.[37] Thus, as was the case nationally, Oklahoma businesses consolidated, unified, and combined to control markets and influence opinion.

Professional associations also thrived in Oklahoma during the same period. Bankers in Oklahoma Territory established an association in 1893, and their counterparts in Indian Territory formed one in 1901. The two groups cooperated and sometimes held joint meetings, finally merging formally in 1904. Members used the association to discuss common problems, to promote public policies advantageous to them, and to work on cutting costs for insurance, fixtures, and supplies.[38] At the same time, other older and more established professional groups increased their activities. The Indian Territory Medical Association, founded in 1881, and the Oklahoma Territorial Medical Association, founded in 1893, reactivated their organizations and pushed successfully for the establishment of the School of Medicine at the University of Oklahoma in 1900. The two territorial groups met in May 1906 to form the Oklahoma State Medical Association. All of this was happening just as the American Medical Association reorganized (1901) and dramatically increased its effectiveness nationwide.[39] Dentists formed associations in Oklahoma Territory in 1891 and in Indian Territory in 1903. These two groups met in 1907 to form the Oklahoma State Dental Association just in time to lobby the constitutional convention on provisions affecting dental licensing in the new state.[40]

In addition to organizations founded strictly for economic or professional advancement, several groups formed to provide moral and social uplift. The women of Indian Territory founded a branch of the Woman's Christian Temperance Union in 1888, followed by the creation of a sister organization in Oklahoma Territory in 1890. Both female and male advocates of prohibition joined the Oklahoma Anti-Saloon League after its creation in 1898.[41] But the abolition of liquor was not the only moral or social concern of early Oklahomans. In 1898 delegates from eleven women's social clubs created the Oklahoma and Indian Territory Federation of Women's Clubs, which included eighty clubs by 1905. The federation accomplished much of its impressive agenda: establishment of public libraries, formation of public kindergartens, and creation of parks, gardens, and other city beautification projects. As statehood approached, the federation advocated provisions in the constitution to ensure a humane juvenile justice system and to restrict child labor.[42]

Although most women who belonged to the federation were well-to-do and from prominent families in their communities, an unmarried woman without wealth—Kate Barnard—surpassed all others in effecting social changes. Born in Kansas in 1875, Barnard's mother died when the girl was only two years old. With her father, Kate went to Oklahoma Territory when it first opened to settlement and ultimately moved to a deteriorating neighborhood in southern Oklahoma City. After graduating from St. Joseph's School there in 1903 and working about a year as a stenographer, Barnard began her social work as head of the United Provident Association, a charitable organization that collected clothing and other items for the city's poor. Soon Barnard attended conferences and seminars on caring for the needy, including a stay at the prominent Graham Taylor's Chicago School of Civics and Philanthropy. Influenced by a more activist view of social work, Barnard concluded that the poor could not be saved unless their economic opportunities improved. In 1905 she organized a local unit of the Women's International Union Label League and began aiding and promoting labor organization and activism. Most importantly, she attacked child labor with passion. As statehood approached, Barnard allied her crusade with the labor unions and the powerful Farmers' Educational and Cooperative Union. And these two interest groups profoundly influenced the writing of the Oklahoma Constitution.[43]

Territorial farmers, because of their numbers, wielded the most clout of any economic or demographic group in the emerging state. During the early 1890s they formed local farmers' alliances, which were affiliated with similar alliances in Texas and were part of a nationwide movement. Organized as local units in both territories, these groups established local cooperatives to store grain, gin cotton, purchase supplies in bulk, and influence politicians. Nationally, the alliance movement led to the formation of the Populist party, and, after that party's failure, the alliances rapidly disbanded.[44] Nonetheless, farmers remained an important economic and political force in the Twin Territories. They influenced legislation in Oklahoma Territory, as evidenced by a law in 1901 that established a territorial board of agriculture and that established county farmers' institutes to educate and enlighten farmers.[45]

Generally, farmers preferred more practical, direct improvements in their economic well-being. In western Oklahoma Territory they flocked to meetings to endorse the use of irrigation funds under the Newlands Reclamation Act, which the U.S. Congress passed in 1902.[46] Also, farmers organized local "Good Roads" clubs throughout the Twin Territories to promote an efficient transportation system in the rural areas.[47] But the most important self-help effort emerged in 1903 when the Farmers' Educational and Cooperative Union began organizing in the territories. Begun the previous year in Texas, this new organization grew to a membership of more than thirty thousand in the territories when all of the local clubs combined in 1905 to form the Farmers' Educational and Cooperative Union of Indiahoma. Like the farmers' alliances of the previous decade, the farmers' union sought economic advantages for its members through cooperatives to save on crop storage costs, through unified crop withholding to increase prices, and through direct political action. The farmers' union generally represented the more prosperous farmers, and the members looked to emerging leaders, such as Alfalfa Bill Murray, to guide them into the new state's political arena.[48]

In 1906 and 1907 the farmers' union influenced the constitutional convention dramatically. That success came largely as a result of the farmers' cooperation with organized labor. Industrial workers first organized in the 1890s when territorial railroad employees joined the American Railway Union and when coal miners enlisted in the Noble Order of the Knights of Labor. After these two unions failed, their members organized new unions in the Twin Territories. The railroad workers joined one of four different railroad brotherhoods, and beginning in 1898 the miners began organizing local units of the United Mine Workers of America. To achieve recognition in the bituminous fields of the Choctaw Nation, miners conducted a sporadic strike from 1899 to 1903, finally getting recognition in an agreement with regional coal operators.[49]

As the population grew, other unions appeared in the various new towns of the Twin Territories. Carpenters, printers, plasterers, plumbers, tinners, and various others organized trade associations.

This formation of unions culminated in the formation of the Twin Territories Federation of Labor in Lawton, Oklahoma Territory, in December 1903. Soon affiliated with the American Federation of Labor, this new group elected Peter Hanraty, a coal miner, as its president. The United Mine Workers dominated the organization, making up half of the Twin Territories Federation membership and providing 90 percent of its revenue.[50]

Much was happening in Oklahoma in the first decade of the twentieth century. The rapid formation of various organizations followed the national patterns, with events and activities in Oklahoma perhaps accelerated because of the rapid growth and the anticipation of statehood. Interest group organizers sought advantages in the new economic system and patterned their new combinations after the large corporations. Ironically, members of these interest groups often opposed the actions of those same large businesses that they emulated. The animosity toward big corporations was widespread, yet the consensus was as vague as it was universal. Few people defined "trusts," "monopolies," or the "special interests" with any precision. But virtually everyone agreed that these monsters existed. In the 1890s farmers and labor union members had pioneered the antagonism toward railroads and large companies. By the turn of the century, even small bankers, businessmen, and merchants throughout the hinterland of America began feeling threatened by large and usually distant economic powers. The bogey men varied. Small-town bankers feared Wall Street. Farmers feared both Wall Street and small-town bankers. Merchants in Oklahoma and Indian territories resented the economic control of Kansas City. Businessmen in Kansas City chafed at Chicago bankers and merchants who seemed to restrict their actions.[51]

Beginning about 1900, major magazines both catered to this emerging uneasiness and added to the discomfort with muckraking articles vividly depicting abuses of various businessmen and the corruption they caused in government. By about 1904 local newspapers and magazines throughout the country copied the national trend of muckraking and revealed that each state and each town faced similar problems.[52] The press in the Twin Territories joined the crusade. In 1906 alone, Oklahoma readers learned that the regional ice manufacturing "trust" and the southwestern lumber "trust" were gouging consumers with tremendous price increases. That same year, Oklahomans in both territories read about adulterated milk in Muskogee and about price rigging and bribery throughout Oklahoma Territory involving a large textbook manufacturer. Readers also learned about criminally negligent Rock Island Railroad officials who ignored complaints about a rickety temporary bridge on the Cimarron River near Dover. The bridge collapsed and killed one hundred passengers.[53]

As the press activated public opinion and as various interest groups organized to push their demands, a majority of Oklahomans sought to control the large economic interests that seemed to threaten them. The methods and tools were limited. A growing minority of Oklahomans sought fundamental structural changes through the Socialist party. They wanted to abandon the capitalistic economic system altogether. Most Oklahomans, however, desired more limited changes. Many wanted to break up true monopolies and forbid their existence. Others wanted to pass laws to punish the leaders of large corporations if they harmed the interests of the general public. Still others wanted to create governmental agencies to regulate both large and small corporations in order to prevent abuses. In Oklahoma, like much of the West, most voters desired more direct democracy to counteract the perceived domination of government by the large companies. The direct election of U.S. senators, direct primary elections, the initiative and referendum, and various other devices championed earlier by the Populist party would assure that the "people" would prevail over the ill-defined "special interests."[54] But opposition to the corporate villains provided only fleeting unity. When lawmakers contemplated real-life legislative actions, individual interest groups jockeyed to promote their own goals, often at the expense of erstwhile allies.

The first reform efforts occurred in August and September 1905 when several opportunistic leaders held a convention to organize Indian Territory as a state independent of its western neighbor. Among others, Charles N. Haskell, a railroad developer from Muskogee; Alfalfa Bill Murray, a farmer and attorney from the Chickasaw Nation; and Robert L. Owen, a mixed-blooded Cherokee lawyer from Muskogee, led the meetings. Aware that statehood separate from Oklahoma Territory would be virtually impossible, these leaders and others at the convention hoped their actions would enhance their political position when the real statehood process occurred. Astute and perceptive, the leaders of this dress rehearsal produced a constitution that embodied many of the concerns of the people. Calling the proposed state Sequoyah after the famed inventor of the Cherokee syllabary, the framers included several provisions designed to restrict large business enterprise. The Sequoyah Constitution provided for a strong corporation commission to regulate utilities and railroads; it outlawed price fixing, food adulteration, and unequal tax rates; and it sought to protect workers, women, and children.[55]

Voters in Indian Territory overwhelmingly endorsed the Sequoyah Constitution in November 1905, but Congress promptly rejected the document. Virtually every federal official insisted that Oklahoma Territory be part of the new state. Yet statehood was imminent. The Commission to the Five Civilized Tribes (popularly known as the Dawes Commission) had been laboring to allot land to the five tribes and was completing its work in 1906. Accordingly, in June, Congress passed the long-awaited Enabling Act authorizing joint statehood for the Twin Territories.

While the federal government prepared for an election of delegates to the constitutional convention, various interest groups planned strategy and took action to influence the outcome. Women's clubs sought to commit delegates to woman suffrage and to the abolition of child labor. The Anti-Saloon League, enthusiastic because of the Enabling Act's requirement for prohibition in the Indian Territory portion of the new state, marshaled forces to assure that all of Oklahoma would be "dry." Professional groups issued position statements and chose lobbyists to attend the convention. But the most effective political interest groups were the railroad brotherhoods, the Twin Territories Federation of Labor, and the Oklahoma Farmers Union. Representatives from all of these organizations met in a massive joint conference in August 1906 at Shawnee. Kate Barnard attended as a representative of the Women's International Union Label League. Delegates at this joint session forged the "Shawnee Demands," a list of goals that became a platform for many constitutional convention delegates and a blueprint for much of the constitution itself.[56]

Several of the Shawnee Demands reflected the widespread fear of large businesses. One of the provisions prohibited railroads from owning coal lands or mines of any kind; another demand called for a corporate tax commission with full power to inspect all corporate accounts; and one stipulation recommended a strong corporation commission to regulate railroads, insurance companies, pipelines, and all kinds of utilities. The coalition at Shawnee also endorsed the initiative, referendum, and recall; the direct primary; and the secret ballot. For labor, the Shawnee delegates wanted liberal workmen's compensation, an eight-hour work day for miners and government employees, an elected chief inspector for the mines, and an elected labor commissioner. For farmers, the participants advocated a liberal homestead and exemption law, a commissioner of agriculture, and the prohibition of gambling in farm products. Kate Barnard's influence could be seen in proposals to prohibit child labor in industry and to protect convicts from the contract labor system.[57]

The delegates at Shawnee represented a membership of union workers and farmers numbering more than fifty thousand—about one-fifth of the electorate. In addition to that number, many non-union workers, unaffiliated farmers, businessmen, and professionals also liked the Shawnee proposals to restrain the railroads, utilities, and other corporations. Not surprisingly, a large number of candidates for the constitutional convention endorsed part or all of the agenda, and a majority of them were elected. Generally, Republicans clung to the old issues of prosperity and the tariff and rejected the Shawnee Demands. Less restrained by old habits, Democrats embraced the platform. Partially as a result, 99 of the 112 positions for the convention went to Democrats in the elections held in September 1906.[58]

The constitutional convention fostered the political careers of several significant Democratic leaders. Alfalfa Bill Murray, who presided over the convention, later served as state speaker of the house, congressman, and governor. Pete Hanraty, the coal miner and union leader who was vice president of the convention, won the position of chief mine inspector after statehood. Robert L. Williams, who was a member of the powerful steering committee, later became the first chief justice of the Oklahoma Supreme Court and the third governor. Charles N. Haskell, the Democratic floor leader, won the governor's seat in 1907.

Meeting from November 1906 until March 1907, these men helped write a constitution along the lines of the Sequoyah Constitution and the Shawnee Demands. Delegates approved articles creating the initiative, the referendum, the secret ballot, and direct primaries; prolabor provisions establishing a commissioner of labor, a chief inspector of the mines, and an eight-hour work day in the mines and in government; and profarmer sections providing for a board of agriculture and liberal homestead exemptions. The new state constitution also included thorough regulation of various businesses under a strong corporation commission, an insurance commissioner, and a bank commissioner. The articles on taxation sought to make businesses pay their fair share. One article attempted to outlaw the creation of monopolies altogether, and another forbade alien ownership of real estate. Indicative of Kate Barnard's influence, the delegates prohibited child labor in industry and created the office of commissioner of charities and corrections—the only statewide elected office open to women. Reflecting widely held ethnocultural beliefs, the delegates wrote clauses segregating schools and defining the ''African'' race. Also, they not only established prohibition in the Indian Territory portion of the state, as the Enabling Act required, but they also submitted to the voters a concurrent constitutional amendment extending prohibition to all of the state.[59]

An urgent desire to control monopolies pervaded much of the debate on the most popular and urgent portions of the constitution. No one bothered to define a trust or a monopoly in a clear way. The delegates identified the Standard Oil Company as a member of the species of monopoly and attacked it with frequency. However, many delegates, including President Murray, conceded that corporate structure was necessary and that good corporations existed. Only businesses that restrained trade or crushed competitors unfairly should be punished and controlled. With Article V, Section 117, the delegates unburdened themselves of the responsibility of defining a monopoly by instructing the legislature to do so.[60]

Almost inexplicably, Republicans opposed the popular final prod-

uct of the convention. President Theodore Roosevelt, who had influenced the delegates to leave out comprehensive Jim Crow provisions, became angry because the constitution defined the "African" race and segregated the public schools. Roosevelt and
Attorney General Charles J. Bonaporte also condemned several of
the sections that restricted corporations. They forced the delegates
to make some changes, but Roosevelt continued to criticize the anticorporate character of the final version. After the completion of the
constitution, Roosevelt sent Secretary of War William Howard Taft,
the hand-picked successor to the presidency, to attack the largely
Democratic product. Visiting several towns in the late summer of
1907, Taft criticized especially the initiative, referendum, and other
devices of direct democracy. Ironically, in 1912, when the concept
of "progressivism" was popular, Roosevelt's Progressive party
embraced these same concepts that his administration had earlier
ridiculed. Yet others who called themselves progressives still
refused to convert to direct democracy. All of this again underscores
the hazards of accepting at face value the ambiguous ideology of
"progressivism."[61]

In the campaign for ratification of the constitution in 1907, the
Democratic opposition praised the popular direct electoral instruments. With equal passion, almost all Democrats also attacked the
trusts, monopolies, and big businesses. Each candidate labored to
depict himself as just one of the common people who disliked the
"corporate greed" of big businessmen. Haskell, who sought the
governor's post, outshone the rest. On one campaign stop he apolo-
gized for the absence of his wife. He explained, "She intended to
come, but at the last moment her work piled up on her and when I
left she was out in the backyard making soap."[62] He then berated
the idle rich even though Haskell in truth also had considerable
wealth.

Haskell, like other Democratic candidates, labored tirelessly to
convince voters that his opponents belonged to the predatory class.
In the primary campaign he accused Lee Cruce, an Ardmore banker
and Haskell's main rival, of charging customers a usurious interest
rate at his bank. Haskell also claimed that Cruce bitterly opposed the
sacred constitution. Both charges were false. Cruce had imposed the
usual standard fees of interest at his bank, and he early endorsed

the constitution, praising its provisions for direct democracy and against monopolies. Cruce did criticize the absence of comprehensive Jim Crow provisions and was lukewarm on prohibition, but he commended all other principal points.[63]

Virtually all other Democratic candidates for both minor and major offices hailed the constitution and its prevailing political ideas. Robert L. Owen, the leading candidate for the U.S. Senate, attacked Carnegie, Rockefeller, and the "trusts" with frequency and praised the constitution. His principal opponent in the eastern part of the state, Henry M. Furman, also spoke the same language, as did Thomas P. Gore, the leading senatorial candidate from western Oklahoma. At the secondary level of office seekers, attorney general candidate Charles West adopted a headline-grabbing, trust-busting stance that served him well for years. And the flamboyant, physically huge Jack Love won a seat on the Corporation Commission with a promise that he would "Make the Railroads Toe the Mark."[64]

The widespread condemnation of trusts was abstract and confusing at best, opportunistic and demagogic at worst. Many candidates, like Haskell, tried unfairly to label their competitors as evil allies of corporate criminals. But virtually all candidates had some old blemishes from their recent past if viewed up close. Haskell had been a leading railroad developer in Indian Territory. Like most railroad men, he often outfoxed stubborn landowners who refused to sell right-of-ways by waiting until night to build the line through the property of his sleeping victims. Also, along with other town developers, Haskell gained title to several town lots through fraud.[65] The future Senator Owen likewise accumulated vast amounts of property through highly questionable means. Both Owen and Haskell helped organize and direct the Muskogee Citizens' Alliance, a businessmen's group which attempted to crush the labor unions in that town in 1905. Within a year, candidates Owen and Haskell presented themselves as friends of labor unions.[66] Robert L. Williams hastily abandoned his legal practice representing railroads as the constitutional convention approached because he knew it might hurt him politically, yet at the convention he condemned those who associated with "corporate greed."[67] Over the next several years the Socialist party, criticizing local elites, often depicted Williams,

Owen, and Murray as landlords who grew rich off the labor of hapless tenant farmers.[68] Thus, only if the vague anticorporatism were applied in a very abstract way or at the national level could Oklahoma politicians avoid the taint of their own hypocrisy.

Opportunistic or not, Democratic politicians used the anticorporate imagery effectively. The Republicans accommodated them by taking the illogical position of opposing the ratification of the constitution but offering a slate of candidates to elect just in case it passed. The Democrats and the constitution won overwhelmingly in the general elections in September 1907. Four out of five congressional seats, all statewide offices, and a strong majority of the legislative posts (and therefore the two appointive U.S. Senate seats) went to Democrats.[69]

When the legislature met from December 1907 to May 1908, the Democratic majority took pains to reward labor, the interest group that embraced anticorporatism most avidly. The lawmakers enacted a safety code for miners, a health code for factories, and other similar measures. Also, they created the nation's first state-operated employment service; they forbade advertisements for recruiting strikebreakers; and they prohibited the blacklisting of workers. Reflecting a desire to control corporations, the legislators strengthened the powers of the Corporation Commission and imposed substantial taxes on utilities, mineral producers, and railroads. In the field of banking, lawmakers enacted stringent regulations and established a bank guarantee system that gained national attention and was copied by several other western states. Farmers, who had won some benefits in the constitution, made few major gains during the first session. Murray, who was the speaker, failed in his attempts to sell school lands to small farmers and in his efforts to adopt the Torrens system, a simplified method of verification of land titles supposedly beneficial to farmers. But the legislature did establish several small agricultural colleges around the state.[70]

Despite these successes, harmony did not always prevail among the advocates of anticorporatism. Legislators who represented the interests of labor clashed with leaders of the farm bloc during the first session. Kate Barnard, now commissioner of charities and corrections, continued her alliance with labor leaders, and they submitted a very strong child labor bill to tighten the restrictions found in the new constitution. Speaker Murray opposed the bill because it might have prohibited farmers from using children. Other profarmer representatives aligned with Murray, but they could not defeat the bill, which narrowly passed the house. Murray next appealed quickly to Governor Haskell, who obliged him and vetoed the act. The speaker then ordered Barnard to stop lobbying on the house floor and blocked a budget increase for her office. Outraged, Barnard persuaded her labor allies to condemn Murray as their enemy during their convention at Ardmore in July. Abstract anticorporate attacks on vague business interests had helped the farmer-labor coalition form. But the issue proved a weak glue in holding the farmers and workers together when their own tangible interests conflicted.[71]

Barnard stirred even more controversy when she tried to protect the property of young Indian orphans and mentally incompetent Indian adults. Her office continually publicized gross maladministration of the Indian estates. But her pleadings to help unfortunate Indians reaped only opposition. Almost every Oklahoma leader had consistently and emphatically demanded the removal of restrictions from the sale of all Indian allotments, which had been restricted to protect the Indians because of their ignorance of property values. In 1908, Oklahoma's congressional delegation won a partial victory with the passage of an act that allowed all mixed-bloods who were less than three-quarters Indian to sell part or all of their holdings.[72]

The issue of Indian lands demonstrated a major inconsistency in the logic used to attack large business interests. Critics accused corporate leaders of callously abusing farmers, workers, consumers, and other hapless common people. But many Oklahoma farmers, workers, and consumers unhesitatingly defrauded untutored Indians. Homegrown politicians seldom noted this hypocrisy, but a Chicago journalist observed, "In Wall Street they go after 'theirs' with the ticker and the seduction of stock certificates. In Oklahoma they seek the same thing with the abstract of the title men and the virgin soil. In Wall Street they shear the lambs and in Oklahoma they just take it away from the unsophisticated Indians."[73]

Similar to the issue of Indian lands, Governor Haskell's erratic oil and gas policies showed how the high principles of anticorporatism fell weakly before the power of local economic interests. Within minutes after taking the oath of office, Haskell ordered state and county officials to keep companies from extending their pipelines across the northern border of the state. The constitution required all companies to incorporate in Oklahoma before they could conduct business, and Haskell forbade all natural gas companies from exporting their products out of the state. He wanted all natural gas to remain in the state as an inducement for industries to locate there. Over the next several months, Haskell began changing his mind. Oklahoma had an excess of natural gas, causing home producers to call for outside markets.[74]

This change of position later embarrassed Haskell. In July 1908 he attended the Democratic national convention in Denver, where he publicly chastised Standard Oil Company. Back in Oklahoma, Attorney General West was filing suit to stop construction of a pipeline by the Prairie Oil and Gas Company, a subsidiary of the same dastardly Standard Oil. In a seeming contradiction, Haskell ordered West to drop the suit. Meanwhile, William Jennings Bryan, the Democratic presidential nominee, had chosen the Oklahoma governor as part of his inner circle. Haskell chaired the platform committee and was chosen treasurer of Bryan's campaign against Taft, the Republican nominee. Early in the campaign, editor William Randolph Hearst and President Roosevelt attacked Haskell as a hypocrite. They accused him of representing Standard Oil as an attorney in Ohio before he moved to Oklahoma. Moreover, they revealed that Haskell had blocked Attorney General West's lawsuit against Prairie Oil and Gas Company. Haskell argued that the pipelines offered the only chance for many independent oil men to market their products. But the opposition attacked with more allegations, forcing Haskell to resign from the campaign.[75]

Like Oklahoma politicians, even independent oil producers were ambivalent. They sometimes bitterly criticized the actions of Standard Oil and its branch companies. On other occasions, however, they supported the large corporations if it suited their purposes. As a consequence, Oklahoma's leaders often equivocated on issues involving oil production.[76]

Over time the old anticorporate issues lost their appeal. During the session of 1909, legislators did pass a few laws to protect workers and approved Kate Barnard's child labor bill, but lawmakers otherwise spent little time trying to restrict bad corporations or protect victims. Instead, they submitted a constitutional amendment requiring a literacy test for blacks, located several new state institutions, and squabbled over the location of the state capital. Perhaps the politicians perceived that all urgent anticorporate bills had passed in the first session. With such reforms seemingly spent, political leaders had turned their efforts to satisfying party needs or the interests of their communities.[77]

Ironically, as the effectiveness of anticorporatism declined in Oklahoma, national politicians began adopting the term *progressive* to attract voters who feared the vague enemy of big business. Before 1909 and 1910, *progressive* was used only in a broad sense and meant simply forward-looking or having to do with "progress." Americans overwhelmingly endorsed the conventional belief that the world was improving and developing into a better condition. Several writers had said Oklahoma's constitution was "progressive," but they meant the document contained the latest popular reforms and was the most forward-looking. They intended no specific ideological meaning.[78]

During 1909 and 1910 the word took on a new, but muddled, meaning. In those years several Republicans, primarily from the Midwest, began opposing many of the policies of their own party's leaders in the U.S. Congress. First, these rebellious Republicans called themselves "insurgents," but possibly in search of a label with more positive connotations, they appropriated the term *progressive*. The success of this label politically caused others to use it, and the varied meanings quickly emerged.[79]

Some Oklahoma politicians adopted the progressive label during the gubernatorial campaign of 1910. The Democrats, who had lost strength in the election of 1908, confidently expected to retain the governor's chair. Former Speaker Murray and former gubernatorial candidate Cruce immediately emerged as the two Democratic front-runners among four candidates. Although both claimed to be progressive, Murray told farmers that Cruce was their natural enemy because he was a banker and a tool of big business. Cruce denied this, of course, and praised the regulatory accomplishments of the constitutional convention and the legislature. Both leading Democrats endorsed prohibition and opposed woman suffrage. As the campaign progressed, the contest between Cruce and Murray hinged increasingly on the issue of race. Murray had helped exclude Jim Crow provisions from the constitution because President Roosevelt had threatened to reject the document if it had such stipulations. Cruce said this incident revealed Murray's insincerity on segregation and his sympathy toward blacks.[80]

Cruce won the primary election against Murray and two other weaker opponents and then faced Republican banker Joseph McNeal in the general campaign. Cruce used the same segregation issue against McNeal that he had against Murray. He also continued to rely on the old anticorporate tactics. He traveled throughout the coal mining districts, explaining that a vote for him was a vote for the continuation of the progressive accomplishments of the Haskell administration. Although Murray had criticized Cruce unfairly for being a banker, Cruce attacked fellow banker McNeal as a tool of railroads and corporations. McNeal had sometimes aided railroad officials when they protested the low rates imposed by the corporation commission. In Cruce's opinion, McNeal aided and abetted the enemy.[81]

Despite the anticorporate discourse, especially in the general election, Cruce and the legislature during his term did not go back to the anticorporate habits of the first legislature under Haskell. Enforcing segregation and prohibition laws seemed more important. Also, a ground swell of support for morality enforcement emerged in 1912 and 1913. Cruce accommodated these demands by endorsing more stringent Sunday "blue laws" and by sending the national guard to break up boxing matches and horse races, both of which were illegal in the state. The governor also tried to impose greater fiscal efficiency on government by suggesting the elimination of several educational institutions and by cutting the legislature back to fewer members. The reaction against these cost-cutting suggestions was immediate and strong. The legislature almost impeached the governor for his efforts.[82]

While Cruce and Oklahoma were preoccupied with blue laws and fiscal retrenchment, national politicians focused their energies on the anticorporate matters, culminating in the presidential election of 1912. In that contest retired President Roosevelt bolted the Republican party, when it refused him the nomination, and became the candidate of the hurriedly organized Progressive party, offering himself as the progressive alternative to supposedly nonprogressive President Taft. Adding to the confusion, Woodrow Wilson, governor of New Jersey, won the Democratic nomination and offered himself as a different kind of progressive.

For several years leading up to the climactic campaign of 1912, most of Oklahoma's delegation to the U.S. Congress used the imprecise language and imagery of anticorporatism to justify votes on various bills. The words and images fit the national issues just as poorly as they had state issues. For example, in 1909 Senator Owen became the leading national politician to advocate a cabinet-level department of health. He argued that, among other benefits, the department would eliminate the abuses of the patent medicine "trust." But opponents of the measure managed to conjure up antitrust arguments for their cause. They condemned the proposed department because it would become a tool of the American Medical Association, which was the "doctors' trust."[83]

Adroit politicians, whether from Oklahoma or elsewhere, managed to construct some anticorporate or progressive angle for their positions. Whether for or against a bill, they could produce a seemingly progressive rationale. Self-proclaimed progressives supported drug regulation, tariff revision, conservation, monetary reform, and several other issues. But other self-styled progressives opposed these same issues, often conjuring up the proper progressive or anticorporate image to fit their positions.

In 1913, while Oklahoma's U.S. congressional delegation struggled with national problems, politicians back in the state prepared for the upcoming elections in 1914. Robert L. Williams barely emerged victorious in his campaign for governor with the usual castigation of "special interests" and other vague villains. But increasingly, Oklahoma tenant farmers and workers became disillusioned with the tangible results of the early reforms. Many joined the Socialist party and through their votes relegated Williams's victory to a mere plurality. Soon the coming of war overwhelmed these concerns, and the old issues faded.[84]

Thus, in Oklahoma by 1914 the political imagery and terminology of progressivism had withered in strength. In fact, politicians had just started manufacturing the concept as the farmer-labor coalition was disintegrating about 1909. And historians have most often labeled this coalition as the essence of progressivism in Oklahoma. The unification was something of a fluke in the first place, because farmers and workers often had interests that conflicted. These interests, along with those of other pressure groups, created a political assortment too complex to reduce to the concept of progressivism. Politicians tried, though. As long as they attacked railroads, utilities, and vague trusts, they could hold a large portion of the constituency together. They could safely crusade for the "people" against the "special interests." If they favored one local interest group over another, however, they courted peril.

The vague and trendy terminology of anticorporatism at first unified voters and acted as a catalyst to effect many reforms that seldom lived up to expectations. In Oklahoma these changes came rapidly. After the initial surge in 1907 and 1908, conflicts quickly emerged, and the difficulty of making tough decisions became more apparent. As this happened, successful politicians turned to more conventional ethnocultural issues, such as prohibition and Jim Crow laws, or they pleased constituents by log-rolling to locate state institutions in their home districts. These trends should be understood, and the inconsistencies and complexities of the politicians and interest groups should be recognized. Telling the story of the era, with its rich variety and contradictions, is far more productive and insightful than trying to generalize using the inadequate concept of "progressivism."

NOTES

1. Robert L. Owen to Woodrow Wilson, Oct. 4, 1912, Series 2, Woodrow Wilson Papers, Manuscripts Division, Library of Congress, Washington, D.C., Microfilm Roll 31.

2. Charles N. Haskell to Woodrow Wilson, Mar. 24, 1913, Case File 389, Series 4, Woodrow Wilson Papers, Microfilm Roll 260.

3. The following brief review of the historiography of progressivism is not intended to be comprehensive. Among the best discussions of the subject are John D. Buenker, "The Progressive Era: A Search for a Synthesis," *Mid-America* 51 (July 1969): 175–93; Louis Galambos, "The Emerging Organizational Synthesis in Modern American History," *Business History* 44 (Autumn 1970): 279–90;

Richard L. McCormick, "The Discovery that Business Corrupts Politics: A Reappraisal of the Origins of Progressivism," *American Historical Review* 86 (Apr. 1981): 247–74; and David P. Thelen, "Social Tensions and the Origins of Progressivism," *Journal of American History* 56 (Sept. 1969): 323–41.

4. Benjamin P. De Witt, *The Progressive Movement: A Non-Partisan, Comprehensive Discussion of Current Tendencies in American Politics* (New York: Macmillan, 1915), 4–5.

5. See especially John D. Hicks, *The Populist Revolt: A History of the Farmer's Alliance and the People's Party* (Minneapolis: University of Minnesota Press, 1931); George E. Mowry, *The California Progressives* (Berkeley: University of California Press, 1951); and Russell B. Nye, *Midwestern Progressive Politics: A Historical Study of Its Origins and Development, 1870–1950* (East Lansing: Michigan State University Press, 1959).

6. Richard Hofstadter, *The American Political Tradition and the Men Who Made It* (New York: Alfred A. Knopf, 1948), 206–207, 230–31, 255–60; Richard Hofstadter, *The Age of Reform: From Bryan to F.D.R.* (New York: Alfred A. Knopf, 1955), 160–62, 213–32.

7. Samuel P. Hays, *Conversation and the Gospel of Efficiency: The Progressive Conservation Movement, 1890–1920* (Cambridge, Mass.: Harvard University Press, 1959), and *The Response to Industrialism, 1885–1914* (Chicago: University of Chicago Press, 1957).

8. Robert H. Wiebe, *The Search for Order, 1877–1920* (New York: Hill and Wang, 1967), and *Businessmen and Reform: A Study of the Progressive Movement* (Cambridge, Mass.: Harvard University Press, 1962).

9. Gabriel Kolko, *The Triumph of Conservatism: A Reinterpretation of American History, 1900–1916* (New York: Free Press of Glencoe, 1963); James Weinstein, *The Corporate Ideal in the Liberal State, 1900–1918* (Boston: Beacon Press, 1968).

10. J. Joseph Huthmacher, "Urban Liberalism and the Age of Reform," *Mississippi Valley Historical Review* 49 (Sept. 1962): 231–41; John D. Buenker, *Urban Liberalism and Progressive Reform* (New York: Charles Scribner's Sons, 1973); Irwin Yellowitz, *Labor and the Progressive Movement in New York State: 1897–1916* (Ithaca, N.Y.: Cornell University Press, 1965); David P. Thelen, *Robert M. La Follette and the Insurgent Spirit* (Boston: Little, Brown and Company, 1976); McCormick, "The Discovery that Business Corrupts Politics," 273–74.

11. Peter G. Filene, "An Obituary for the Progressive Movement," *American Quarterly* 22 (Spring 1970): 20–34.

12. Keith L. Bryant, Jr., *Alfalfa Bill Murray* (Norman: University of Oklahoma Press, 1968), 70.

13. Ibid., 71–72.

14. Ibid., vii–viii, 8–9, 21, 81–82.

15. Keith L. Bryant, Jr., "Kate Barnard, Organized Labor, and Social Justice in Oklahoma during the Progressive Era," *Journal of Southern History* 35 (May 1969): 145–64, and "Labor in Politics: The Oklahoma State Federation of Labor during the Age of Reform," *Labor History* 11 (Summer 1970): 259–76.

16. George O. Carney, "Oklahoma's United States House Delegation and Progressivism, 1901–1917" (Ph.D. diss., Oklahoma State University, 1972). See also George O. Carney, "Oklahoma's Territorial Delegates and Progressivism" *Chronicles of Oklahoma* 52 (Spring 1974): 38–51, and "Oklahoma's House Delegation in the Sixty-first Congress: Progressive or Conservative?" *Chronicles of Oklahoma* 44 (Summer 1977): 190–210.

17. Carney, "Oklahoma's House Delegation in the Sixty-first Congress," 190; Carney, "Oklahoma's Territorial Delegates and Progressivism," 38–39.

18. Carney, "Oklahoma's United States House Delegation and Progressivism," 301–24.

19. Ibid.

20. Rennard J. Strickland and James C. Thomas, "Most Sensibly Conservative and Safely Radical: Oklahoma's Constitutional Regulation of Economic Power, Land Ownership, and Corporate Monopoly," *Tulsa Law Journal* 9 (Fall 1973): 172.

21. Ibid., 169–70, 205–206, 208–17, 226–31.

22. Danney Goble, *Progressive Oklahoma: The Making of a New Kind of State* (Norman: University of Oklahoma Press, 1980).

23. Ibid., x.

24. Ibid., 214.

25. Ibid., 183.

26. James R. Scales and Danney Goble, *Oklahoma Politics: A History* (Norman: University of Oklahoma Press, 1982).

27. Ibid., 32–40.

28. Ibid., 52.

29. Kenny L. Brown, "A Progressive from Oklahoma: Senator Robert L. Owen, Jr.," *Chronicles of Oklahoma* 62 (Fall 1984): 232–65, and "Robert Latham Owen, Jr.: His Careers as an Indian Attorney and Progressive Senator" (Ph.D. diss., Oklahoma State University, 1985).

30. Alfred D. Chandler, Jr., "The Beginnings of 'Big Business' in American Industry," *Business History Review* 33 (Spring 1959): 1–15; Hays, *Response to Industrialism,* 43–58.

31. Hays, *Response to Industrialism,* 58–70; Wiebe, *Search for Order,* 111–32; Wiebe, *Businessmen and Reform,* 16–41.

32. U.S. Bureau of the Census, *Thirteenth Census of the United States Taken in the Year 1910: Population,* vol. 3 (Washington, D.C.: Government Printing Office, 1913), 461.

33. The best concise account of this influx of people is Douglas Hale, "The People of Oklahoma: Economics and Social Change," in *Oklahoma: New Views of the Forty-Sixth State,* ed. Anne Hodges Morgan and H. Wayne Morgan (Norman: University of Oklahoma Press, 1982), 31–51.

34. A good survey of railroad development is Donovan L. Hofsommer, ed., *Railroads in Oklahoma* (Oklahoma City: Oklahoma Historical Society, 1977).

35. I. C. Gunning, *When Coal Was King: Coal Mining Industry in the Choctaw Nation* (n.p.: Eastern Oklahoma Historical Society, 1975), 50–51.

36. Arrell M. Gibson, *Wilderness Bonanza: The Tri-State District of Missouri, Kansas, and Oklahoma* (Norman: University of Oklahoma Press, 1972), 175–78.

37. Orben J. Casey, "Governor Lee Cruce and His 'Righteous Crusade' " (Master's thesis, University of Oklahoma, 1972), 17.

38. James M. Smallwood, *An Oklahoma Adventure of Banks and Banking* (Norman: University of Oklahoma Press, 1979), 40–43, 47–50.

39. Mark R. Everett, *Medical Education in Oklahoma: The University of Oklahoma School of Medicine and Medical Center, 1900–1931* (Norman: University of Oklahoma Press, 1972), 21–23.

40. J. Stanley Clark, *Open Wider, Please: The Story of Dentistry in Oklahoma* (Norman: University of Oklahoma Press, 1955), 16–18, 59–60, 65–69.

41. Jimmie Lewis Franklin, *Born Sober: Prohibition in Oklahoma, 1907–1959* (Norman: University of Oklahoma Press, 1971), 6–9.

42. Susan L. Allen, "Progressive Spirit: The Oklahoma and Indian Territory Federation of Women's Clubs," *Chronicles of Oklahoma* 66 (Spring 1988): 4–19.

43. Bryant, "Kate Barnard," 145–53; Goble, *Progressive Oklahoma,* 183–86.

44. H. L. Meredith, "The 'Middle Way': The Farmer's Alliance in Indian Territory, 1889–1896," *Chronicles of Oklahoma* 47 (Winter 1969–70): 377–86; Goble, *Progressive Oklahoma,* 158–60.

45. Territory of Oklahoma, Board of Agriculture, *First Biennial Report of the Oklahoma Territorial Board of Agriculture, 1903–1905* (Guthrie, Okla.: State Capital Co., 1905), 5–9, 21–25, 189–90.

46. Ibid., 28–29; *Otter Valley News,* Nov. 17, 1904, p. 6; *Oklahoma Farmer,* Nov. 16, 1904, p. 8.

47. William P. Corbett, "Men, Mud, and Mules: The Good Roads Movement in Oklahoma, 1900–1910," *Chronicles of Oklahoma* 58 (Summer 1980): 133–37; Territory of Oklahoma, Board of Agriculture, *First Biennial Report,* 193–94; *Muskogee Times-Democrat,* Dec. 6, 1906, pp. 1, 8.

48. Goble, *Progressive Oklahoma,* 160–64.

49. Ibid., 145–52; Bryant, "Labor in Politics," 260; John Barnhill, "Triumph of Will: The Coal Strike of 1899–1903," *Chronicles of Oklahoma* 61 (Spring 1983): 80–95.

50. Bryant, "Labor in Politics," 261–62; Goble, *Progressive Oklahoma,* 151–53.

51. Wiebe, *Search for Order,* 45–54, 81–86, 105; Hays, *Response to Industrialism,* 140–43.

52. McCormick, "Discovery that Business Corrupts Politics," 259–64.

53. Goble, *Progressive Oklahoma,* 167–78.

54. For a discussion of the options for fighting "special interests" at the national level, see McCormick, "Discovery that Business Corrupts Politics," 270–74. On direct democracy, see Bertil L. Hanson, "Oklahoma's Experience with Direct Legislation," *Southwestern Social Science Quarterly* 47 (Dec. 1966), 263–64; and Lloyd Sponholtz, "The Initiative and Referendum: Direct Democracy in Perspective, 1898–1920," *American Studies* 14 (Fall 1973): 43–47.

55. Goble, *Progressive Oklahoma,* 190–94.

56. Goble, *Progressive Oklahoma,* 164–65, 180–81, 186; Bryant, "Labor in Politics," 264–66.

57. A complete listing of the Shawnee Demands can be found in an appendix in Goble, *Progressive Oklahoma,* 228–29.

58. Oklahoma, State Election Board, *Directory of Oklahoma, 1981* (Oklahoma City: State Election Board, 1981), 651–52; Bryant, "Labor in Politics," 263, 266–69; Goble, *Progressive Oklahoma,* 151, 161, 200–201.

59. Goble, *Progressive Oklahoma,* 213–20.

60. Strickland and Thomas, "Most Sensibly Conservative and Safely Radical," 190–205, 228–29.

61. Norbert R. Mahnken, "William Jennings Bryan in Oklahoma," *Nebraska History* 31 (Dec. 1950): 266–67; Goble, *Progressive Oklahoma,* 219–24; Bryant, *Alfalfa Bill Murray,* 67–70; John Morton Blum, *The Republican Roosevelt* (Cambridge, Mass.: Harvard University Press, 1954), 148; Henry F. Pringle, *Theodore Roosevelt: A Biography* (New York: Harcourt, Brace, & World, 1931), 381, 385, 390.

62. Quoted in Casey, "Governor Lee Cruce and His 'Righteous Crusade,'" 27.

63. Casey, "Governor Lee Cruce and His 'Righteous Crusade,'" 22–27.

64. Brown, "Senator Robert L. Owen, Jr.," 159–60; Alvin O. Turner, "The Regulation of the Oklahoma Oil Industry" (Ph.D. diss., Oklahoma State University, 1977), 52–53; Irvin Hurst, *The 46th Star: A History of Oklahoma's Constitutional Convention and Early Statehood* (Oklahoma City: Semco Color Press, 1957), 45, 63–64, 78, 112; Scales and Goble, *Oklahoma Politics,* 29, 38–39.

65. Angie Debo, *And Still the Waters Run: The Betrayal of the Five Civilized Tribes* (Princeton, N.J.: Princeton University Press, 1940), 203–204.

66. Brown, "Robert L. Owen, Jr.," 132–35, 138–42, 162; *Muskogee Daily Phoenix,* Apr. 22, 1905, p. 8; Apr. 28, 1905, p. 1; Sept. 27, 1908, p. 5; *Oklahoma City Times,* Sept. 30, 1908, p. 4.

67. Goble, *Progressive Oklahoma,* 195; Strickland and Thomas, "Most Sensibly Conservative and Safely Radical," 200–201.

68. Socialist Party of Oklahoma, *Platform and Campaign Book,* 1914 (n.p., 1914), 42–55 (a copy of this booklet is located in Socialist Party File, Vertical Files, Library, Oklahoma Historical Society, Oklahoma City); Garin Burbank, "The Political and Social Attitudes of Some Early Oklahoma Democrats," *Chronicles of Oklahoma* 52 (Winter 1974–75): 442–54; James R. Green, *Grass-Roots Socialism: Radical Movements in the Southwest, 1895–1943* (Baton Rouge: Louisiana State University Press, 1978), 313–51.

69. Scales and Goble, *Oklahoma Politics,* 30.

70. Bryant, *Alfalfa Bill Murray,* 77–80; Scales and Goble, *Oklahoma Politics,* 37–39.

71. Bryant, *Alfalfa Bill Murray,* 80–83.

72. Debo, *And Still the Waters Run,* 176–80, 184–92, 225–27, 238.

73. *Oklahoma City Times,* Aug. 15, 1908, p. 1.

74. Hurst, *46th Star,* 33–34, 78–79; Turner, "Regulation of the Oklahoma Oil Industry," 55–56.

75. Turner, "Regulation of the Oklahoma Oil Industry," 57–58; Hurst, *46th Star,* 78–87; Louis W. Koenig, *Bryan: A Political Biography of William Jennings Bryan* (New York: G. P. Putnam's Sons, 1971), 434–39, 451–52.

76. Turner, "Regulation of the Oklahoma Oil Industry," 57–59; David C. Boles, "The Prairie Oil & Gas Company, 1901–1911," *Chronicles of Oklahoma* 46 (Summer 1968): 189–200.

77. Suzanne Jones Crawford and Lynn R. Musslewhite, "Progressive Reform and Oklahoma Democrats: Kate Barnard versus Bill Murray," *Historian* 53 (Spring 1991): 487; Scales and Goble, *Oklahoma Politics,* 45–50.

78. Arthur S. Link and Richard L. McCormick, *Progressivism* (Arlington Heights, Ill.: Harlan Davidson, 1983), 1–2; *Kansas City Star,* June 20, 1907, as cited in H. Wayne Morgan and Anne Hodges Morgan, *Oklahoma: A Bicentennial History* (New York: W. W. Norton & Company, 1977), 90; *Oklahoma State Labor News,* Nov. 29, 1907, p. 1.

79. For a contemporary Oklahoman's analysis of the change from "insurgents" to "progressives," see the comments of Senator Owen in "Honest Government and How to Obtain It," *The City Club Bulletin* (Chicago, Illinois), Dec. 14, 1910, p. 412 (copy in Robert L. Owen File, Vertical Files, Library, Oklahoma Historical Society, Oklahoma City).

80. Casey, "Governor Lee Cruce and his 'Righteous Crusade,' " 43–45; Bryant, *Alfalfa Bill Murray,* 89–97.

81. Casey, "Governor Lee Cruce and his 'Righteous Crusade,' " 56–60.

82. Crawford and Musslewhite, "Progressive Reform and Oklahoma Democrats," 487–88; Casey, "Governor Lee Cruce and Law Enforcement," 435–60; Scales and Goble, *Oklahoma Politics,* 53–58.

83. Brown, "Senator Robert L. Owen, Jr.," 191–94; "Protecting the Health of the People," *Twentieth Century Magazine,* Aug. 1910, pp. 464–65.

84. Scales and Goble, *Oklahoma Politics,* 59–79.

4

KATE BARNARD, PROGRESSIVISM, AND THE WEST

Suzanne J. Crawford and Lynn R. Musslewhite

Suzanne J. Crawford and Lynn R. Musslewhite teach together at Cameron University in Lawton. They are working on a book on Kate Barnard. I heard them give an earlier version of the thorough and thoughtful essay which follows in a session entitled "Western Reformers in the Twentieth Century" at a meeting of the Western History Association in Wichita, Kansas, in October 1988 and knew immediately that it belonged in this volume.

In June 1907 delegates from throughout the United States convened in Minneapolis for the seventh annual meeting of the National Conference of Charities and Correction. This sedate, serious gathering of reform-minded people met to deliberate the social issues of early-twentieth-century America. A panoply of notables gave eloquent, refined discourses on various social problems that faced the nation. However, it was an unscheduled address by an obscure reformer from Oklahoma Territory which briefly mesmerized this cosmopolitan group.

A diminutive, demure-looking young woman described by the press as "sweet and dainty as a wildflower and as refreshing as an Oklahoma breeze," Kate Barnard had come to this convention for the purpose of winning its support for the newly drafted Oklahoma Constitution. President Roosevelt had reacted negatively to some of the innovative reforms included in that document. Fear of a presidential veto of the constitution had propelled Barnard to Minneapolis, and a determination to sway Roosevelt's response brought her to the rostrum. In a speech of "sentimentality and loose facts," she beseeched the delegates to use their influence to advance the cause of social justice in the West. She closed with a simple, plaintive plea, "Will you help us?" And help her they did. Telegrams demanding favorable action on the Oklahoma Constitution streamed into the offices of the president and members of Congress.[1]

The subsequent adoption of the Oklahoma Constitution with its "radical provisions" provided an unparalleled opportunity for social justice reform at the state level. Under the governance of this new constitution, Barnard became Oklahoma's first Commissioner of Charities and Corrections. Owing to her reform efforts as commissioner, Barnard received widespread recognition as one of the West's most prominent progressive leaders.[2]

Born in Nebraska, raised in Kansas and Oklahoma, Kate Barnard saw herself as a westerner who had lived an ordinary western girlhood. Her family shared many experiences and values with other western families. They were rootless homesteaders and land speculators, constantly seeking quick wealth and clinging to a belief that in the West individuals succeeded or failed according to their own determination and initiative. To Kate and other westerners their region was a place of new beginnings where possibilities seemed endless.

Her vision of the West as the place of opportunity merged with her quest to establish a society free of want and full of justice.[3] Although she anticipated that the West would become the scene of industrialization and urbanization, she wanted such development harnessed. The West could grow economically, yet escape the social problems of unemployment and poverty by learning from the mistakes of the East. Her self-identification as a westerner and her image of that region tempered Barnard's personal outlook, her reform ideology, and her political career.[4]

In reply to numerous letters of inquiry about jobs and conditions in the West, Barnard emphasized that westerners were different from people in the East. Easterners who came to the West and did not adopt western values and practices would fail. Over and over, Barnard patiently explained to easterners that they had misconceptions of the West and its people.[5] Westerners were not "a wild and wooly set who can only be managed by the use of fire-arms and the iron heel of power."[6] Furthermore, the time of economic windfalls had passed. There was no more free land. State jobs did not lie around waiting for someone from the East to latch onto them. To the contrary, westerners disliked having new eastern arrivals employed in state institutions. The practice of handing out jobs to newcomers reminded them of territorial days, when they had endured carpetbag rule.[7] Barnard admitted that this suspicion of easterners and their ways could backfire. Western legislatures sometimes balked at using eastern models for new state facilities, choosing instead to copy the outdated institutional forms of neighboring states. Moreover, distrust of outsiders had often led to the hiring of inexperienced westerners to manage state institutions.[8]

Yet Barnard argued that the West could profit from an infusion of energetic, enterprising eastern people and an infusion of dynamic, innovative eastern reform ideas. Although the West had a stronger potential for social perfectibility than the East, it could still benefit from the expertise of eastern progressives.[9] Westerners were more receptive to experimentation and expansion of services at the state level. They were not handicapped by precedents or hidebound tradition. Barnard herself criticized the eastern practice of appointing commissioners and boards of charities and rejoiced that the Oklahoma constitution made the office of commissioner of charities and corrections elective. She repeatedly stressed the freedom of action an elected commissioner had compared to appointed officials and called upon other western states to follow Oklahoma's lead.[10]

For much of her public career Barnard sought to enlarge the role of state government but not the role of the federal government. Like many westerners, she believed that the federal government had mismanaged territories and imposed rule by outsiders. The eastern-dominated federal government should not hold the western states and territories captive any longer.[11]

Because of these views, Barnard was sympathetic to the desires of Arizona and New Mexico to end their federal tutelage. The possibility of writing new state constitutions based upon the latest reform ideas and practices made these two territories fertile ground for progressivism. Barnard encouraged some of their leading men and women to emulate Oklahoma's reform example. In particular she emphasized the importance of creating a farm/labor bloc as a reform pressure group.[12] As well as campaigning in Arizona and New Mexico, Barnard worked for reform in the neighboring states of Kansas and Texas.[13]

In many respects Kate resembled other western leaders. Initially historians argued that progressive leaders in the West as well as the rest of the nation were urban, middle-class, well-educated, Republican Protestants from old American stock. That original portrait has not gone unchallenged, however. Historians found that in Washington and California prosperous farmers and labor leaders constituted part of the leadership echelon. In addition, most western reform leaders differed little from conservatives in matters of class, education, religion, or other characteristics.[14]

A representative of the social justice arm of western progressivism, Kate Barnard fits within the broader profile of western progressive leaders presented in more recent studies. A Catholic of Irish ancestry, Barnard did not come from the upper middle class. Her father was a frontier lawyer and surveyor who struggled to make his fortune by speculating in real estate while practicing his professions.[15] In spite of limited family income, she attained enough schooling to pass the territorial examination for a teaching certificate, and she became a rural school teacher in 1896.[16] Several years later she turned to stenography in hopes of enhancing her employment opportunities. A poor typist who reputedly was better at giving orders than taking them, Barnard was ill-suited for secretarial work.[17] Young, confident of her abilities, and ambitious, she wanted a vocation, not a job. She subsequently realized that charity work would allow her to do public good and at the same time support herself.

Barnard secured employment during the spring and summer of 1904 as part of the staff of the Oklahoma territorial exhibit at the Saint Louis World Fair. Convinced that this trip would be the intellectual opportunity of a lifetime, Barnard was ready to absorb whatever lessons the fair and Saint Louis had to offer. In particular, an educational exhibit she saw at the fair awakened her to the possibilities for philanthropic work.[18]

Barnard returned to Oklahoma City. The poverty and unemployment in her Reno Street neighborhood made a vivid impression on her. Children, in particular, attracted her attention. The sight of undernourished and poorly clad children galvanized her into action in the fall of 1905.[19] She sent out a call in a local newspaper for well-to-do Oklahomans to empty their attics and donate their discarded clothing to the poor. Volunteer workers and piles of clothing arrived haphazardly at the Barnard doorstep, much to the discomfort and displeasure of her father.[20] Assessing the pandemonium, Barnard concluded that charity work had to be organized in order to be effective. Individual spontaneous action would not suffice.[21]

Like other progressives, she first turned to a local volunteer organization, the United Provident Association. She revitalized and expanded the organization, converting it into a more successful vehicle for collecting and dispensing benevolence. To achieve economy and efficiency, the organization had already adopted a policy requiring donors to contribute a fixed annual amount to the association and to eschew giving directly to the needy. The association established which families should get relief and in what amounts. During Barnard's tenure as matron of the United Provident Association, the donor's monthly dues were raised, and the organization began to operate year-round. Within the year, donations had increased substantially, and the association could afford to pay its matron, Kate Barnard, a salary of fifty dollars per month as well as allow her to add staff.[22]

Yet she soon discovered that giving away "bisquits and buns," even in an efficient manner, hardly made a dent in the suffering of the urban poor. This recognition led her to cast about for ways to prevent poverty instead of merely alleviating it. Convinced that chronic unemployment, low wages, and deplorable working conditions explained much urban poverty, Barnard began to regard unionization as one way to attack these problems. Consequently, she helped found a local chapter of the Women's International Union Label League to promote the purchase of union-made products. Her introduction to the cause of unionism led her to become a prime mover behind the organization of a federal trade union that recruited unskilled laborers. Subsequently, she also found work for them repairing and constructing city streets, sewers, and water lines.[23]

Although organizing unions and finding employment for union members represented steps in the right direction, these efforts did not entirely solve the question of urban poverty. Nor did unionism provide the answer for the needs of the child, the deaf, the dumb, the blind, the insane, and the imprisoned. Creation of a more humane, just, prosperous society required social legislation, and legislation meant politics, an area with which Barnard was familiar.[24] Owing to her father's success as a local politician, she had become acquainted with politics early in life. Her interest had been strengthened by her appointments to clerical positions in the territorial legislature of Oklahoma. There she learned valuable lessons in the practice of partisan politics.[25] In turning to politics, Barnard traveled along the same path that other western progressives had trod, moving from private voluntary association to public political action.[26]

The acquisition of political power necessitated building political support. Using her labor connection, she fashioned a loyal following among the working class. In August 1906, representatives of the Twin Territories Federation of Labor, the railroad brotherhoods, and the Indiahoma Farmers Union converged upon the town of Shawnee. As a delegate from the Woman's International Union Label League, Barnard attended the Shawnee Convention. The black-haired, ninety-eight-pound bundle of grit delivered a rousing address at the night session. Her persuasiveness influenced the members of the convention to view favorably reforms in child labor and compulsory education. This convention chose a Joint Legislative Board, which it charged with the mission of drawing up a list of farm and labor demands it wanted included in the Oklahoma Constitution. Two of the board's demands were compulsory education and an end to child labor.[27]

In a manner reminiscent of the Farmers' Alliance, this Oklahoma farm/labor bloc sought endorsement of its reform agenda from all candidates running for election as delegates to the Oklahoma Constitutional Convention. The election results disclosed the success of this tactic; 70 of the 112 delegates elected had publicly endorsed the farm/labor demands.[28] For the most part these delegates to the constitutional convention kept their pledges. All but a few of the twenty-four demands were incorporated into the constitution of the new state; among those adopted were the provisions prohibiting child labor and requiring compulsory school attendance, reforms identified with Barnard. The delegates paid further homage to Barnard and her political influence by creating the office of commissioner of charities and corrections, the only statewide position for which women would be eligible. Barnard received the Democratic nomination for the office in 1907. The election results showed she had won her race hands down, garnering more votes than any other office seeker.[29]

During her two terms as state commissioner of charities and corrections, Barnard continued to strengthen her labor support by lobbying for a number of labor bills. She vigorously worked for the successful passage of laws for an eight-hour workday on all public projects, factory inspection, scaffolding to protect construction workers, prohibition of blacklists, safeguards for employees who worked in the vicinity of steam boilers, improved working conditions in coal mines, and a free state employment bureau.[30] Organized labor saluted Barnard's efforts on its behalf and gave her its support for the reforms sponsored by her department. Barnard's attempts to achieve more humane treatment for the insane, defective, delinquent, and criminal received the firm backing of organized labor.[31] Thus, in Oklahoma labor was an early recruit to the banner of reform. In comparison, labor in other western states was a latecomer to the reform standard.[32]

Barnard recognized that farm votes as well as labor votes had played an important part in bringing progressivism to Oklahoma, and she encouraged farm and labor leaders to maintain their political rapport. Yet despite her admonitions and exertions, the farm/labor coalition began to disintegrate in 1908. Although some of her reform program did not have the unstinting support of farmers, she continued to enjoy widespread popularity and managed to hold her political coalition together long enough to get several measures concerning children through the legislature.[33]

Like other western progressives, Barnard's concern for children stemmed from her firm belief that "the child of today is the citizen of tomorrow."[34] The well-being of Oklahoma's children required the adoption of laws to vitalize the constitutional provision prohibiting child labor and establishing compulsory education. Barnard stressed that these reforms would work in tandem, one reinforcing the other.[35] The compulsory education bill endorsed by the commissioner of charities and corrections was passed by the first session of the state legislature in 1908. This law required children between the ages of six and sixteen to attend a full school term each year. Owing to the insistence of farmers, the minimum term was set at three months instead of the six months Barnard had wanted, but, overall, Barnard was well satisfied with the new law because in addition to mandatory schooling, it provided for mothers' pensions. Although the concept of mothers' pensions did not originate with Barnard, Oklahoma became the first state to experiment with this form of relief. Under the Oklahoma provision, the state paid widowed mothers dependent upon the earnings of school-age children the equivalent of what each child would have earned during the school term. Family economic necessity would not force children out of the schoolroom and into the labor market.[36]

In contrast to the ease with which the compulsory education bill passed, Barnard's child labor measure encountered tough resistance in the Oklahoma House of Representatives. She contended that opposition to the child labor bill emanated from two sources, Republican legislators who represented the interest of urban businessmen and a clique of Democratic legislators led by Speaker of the House William H. Murray. Businessmen feared that a child labor law would prevent industrial development, and Murray and his followers feared that such a law would prevent children from working on family farms.[37] After an up-hill battle, Barnard was able to get the bill through the legislature at the eleventh hour only to have it vetoed by Governor Charles N. Haskell. In explaining his action, the governor declared that the bill was too extreme. In his opinion, prohibiting fifteen- and sixteen-year-olds from gainful employment after school would be detrimental to the children. These restrictions would stymie teenage initiative and encourage idleness.[38]

Barnard's child labor measure drew a friendlier response from the second session of the legislature and became a law in 1909. By lowering the age for employment from sixteen to fourteen, the law overcame the governor's earlier objection and received his approval. According to that law, Oklahoma's children were prohibited from working in any occupation that could injure them physically or morally.[39]

The need to save Oklahoma children also compelled the establishment of a juvenile court system and industrial training schools for delinquent and incorrigible children. Evincing a typically progressive view, Barnard argued that unfavorable environments forced children to commit crimes; hence, the environments, not the children, were responsible for juvenile offenses. The malleable character of a child could be transformed in the proper kind of setting. Therefore, juvenile offenders should not be treated the same as adult offenders. In 1909, Barnard convinced the legislature to create a special court designed to improve the environment of youths needing legal supervision. This court would oversee the home life of neglected, abused, or delinquent children through the use of probation officers. If parents could not control their child, or if parents were incapable of providing their child with wholesome surroundings, the juvenile judge could send the child to the state industrial school. There he or she would receive moral training, formal education, and trade instruction.[40]

Barnard's efforts to reform the criminal justice system mirrored those of such western reformers as Ben Lindsey of Denver. His innovative ideas about juvenile courts, sentencing, and probation and parole influenced a number of states, including Oklahoma, to follow the example of Colorado.[41]

Barnard was also involved in the progressive effort to ensure better treatment for adult offenders. After muckraking exposés revealed the brutality and economic exploitation practiced in many prisons, crusades for humane treatment of prisoners swept through several western states. Kansas, Oregon, Arizona, and California as well as Oklahoma attempted to correct the worst of these abuses. Barnard's 1908 inspection of the Kansas state penitentiary, where Oklahoma prisoners were incarcerated, horrified her. Subsequent investigations, with their revelations of water cures, cribs, sexual perversion, and economic exploitation of prisoners, further confirmed Barnard's opinion of state prisons.[42] Characterizing most state prisons as obsolete, expensive, and unjust, she seized the opportunity to create a modern, humane, and effective structure in Oklahoma. For assistance she turned to penal experts throughout the nation.

Drawing ideas and help from prominent penologists and prison superintendents, Barnard pressed for the creation of a three-tier prison system. Besides training schools for incorrigible children, the system should include a reformatory for first-time offenders aged sixteen to twenty-five and a penitentiary for older or habitual criminals. At each level, attempts should be made to cure the criminal by firm but clement treatment, vocational training, and moral instruction. Such a system could be run economically by having convicts produce goods for use in other state institutions while they learned vocational skills. Thus, prisoners would return to society equipped to avoid poverty, the source of most crime.[43]

In trying to bring her reforms to fruition, Barnard employed two techniques common to progressives: mobilization of public opinion and the utilization of professional expertise.[44] Even before she was elected to office, Barnard had formulated a plan to generate momentum for reform. She persuaded prominent progressive figures to write articles for the *Daily Oklahoman,* one of the territory's most influential newspapers. John Spargo, A. J. McKelway, Edwin Markham, Jane Addams, and others contributed articles to the paper in 1906.[45] To rally further public support, she launched letter-writing campaigns and organized voluntary, special-interest associations. During the constitutional convention she formed the Anti–Child Labor League of Oklahoma City to function as a pressure group, and after her election she established a state conference of charities and corrections to build support for reform among businessmen, professionals, and club women.[46] She invited a number of experts to draft model laws and to address the new state legislature on behalf of various reforms. At her invitation Dr. Samuel J. Barrows, president of the International Prison Congress, drafted bills, spoke before the Oklahoma legislature, and lobbied for prison reform. Ben Lindsey wrote a bill creating a model juvenile court system and lectured in Oklahoma on its behalf.[47] Barnard also enlisted the help of the Russell Sage Foundation to pay for importing experts.[48]

Although Barnard's personal outlook, reform ideology, and political career had much in common with her fellow western progressive leaders, she also exhibited marked differences. While there were other women reformers in the West during the progressive era, and some even held public office, Barnard was the only woman elected to a major state office. Not only did Barnard's gender distinguish her from other progressives who were elected to major state offices, but also the degree and longevity of her political support set her apart from other progressive officeholders. In both the 1907 and 1910 elections her voting totals outdistanced the totals of any candidate regardless of party affiliation. This continued high level of support is more remarkable in light of the refusal of Oklahomans to adopt woman suffrage.[49]

Unlike many women progressive leaders, Barnard did not endorse suffrage until late in her political career. She felt suffragists attached too much importance to winning the ballot, and she doubted their claim that women would make ideal voters. Although she believed that women could use the vote to protect themselves from economic exploitation, she did not believe that women would behave more ethically at the polls than men. Instead of women voters purifying politics, the vote would diminish the moral superiority of women. To substantiate her view she often referred to an election she had observed in Denver. In that election lower-class women were herded to the polls by ward bosses, but middle-class women abstained from voting. She also argued that when enough women demanded the vote, men would give it to them. Consequently, woman suffrage did not merit Barnard's time and attention. Other reforms were more pressing.[50]

The breadth of Barnard's reform interests and the sheer number of legislative reforms that she worked to achieve also differentiated her from her fellow western progressives. Barnard involved herself in virtually every social justice reform advocated during the era. During her career, she championed a panorama of child-centered reforms; prolabor legislation; women's rights other than suffrage; improvements in the treatment of convicts, the insane, and the handicapped; and measures for public health, urban planning, and conservation.

By 1914 her reform interests had come full circle. Her public life closed with a crusade that focused upon the need to protect children.

However, even here her reform concern differed from that of other western progressives, for the children whom she defended were not white but Indian. In advocating the safeguarding of the estates of Indian minors, Barnard broke new ground. Yet the tide of public indifference to Indian rights ran too strongly for her to turn it back. Increasingly poor health, severe rebukes from the Oklahoma legislature, and diminishing public support for reform forced her to retire from public office in 1915 before she won this battle. Despite her determination to continue her fight for Indian children after leaving office, Barnard sank into the sea of oblivion.

In electing Kate Barnard, Oklahomans became the first state constituency to put a woman in a major state office. As commissioner of charities and corrections, Barnard had the responsibility for both formulating and enforcing public policy. Not until 1916 when Montana voters elected Jeanette Rankin to Congress would another woman surpass Barnard's political achievements at the polls. Noteworthily, it was the West where women first made inroads into formal politics. Western states were not only the first to elect women to positions of power, but also the first to confer full suffrage rights on women. While Barnard for much of her career attached little significance to woman suffrage, she firmly believed that women as officeholders and private citizens had important contributions to make in politics and reform.

The fluidity of politics in the early statehood period made Oklahomans more susceptible to the call of reform and more likely to allocate some measure of political power to women. Barnard realized these possibilities and seized her chance. Consequently, she emerged as the leader for social justice reform in the new state, and for a time she was a powerful political force, recognized for her accomplishments not only within the state, but nationwide as well. Partly because of her efforts, the state legislature adopted the most comprehensive reform program of any western state of the era. Her crusades on behalf of children, laborers, prisoners, and other disadvantaged Oklahomans brought improvements in their conditions as well as greater hope for their futures.

Barnard also held office long enough to feel the shifting mood of Oklahoma politics as the cost of reforms, especially effective enforcement, outran the citizens' willingness to pay. Economy and retrenchment became the cry of Oklahoma voters. Reform would have to take a rear seat. Once one of the most celebrated western social justice progressives, Kate Barnard died in 1930, unwanted and unloved, a relic who had been consigned to obscurity.

NOTES

1. *The Minneapolis Journal,* June 14, 16, 1907; *Proceedings of the National Conference of Charities and Correction, 34th Session* (Indianapolis: Wm. B. Burford Press, 1907), 207–209; "The Minneapolis Conference," *Charities and the Commons,* July 18, 1907, 385–95; Kate Barnard, "Shaping the Destinies of the New State," *Proceedings of the National Conference of Charities and Correction, 35th Session* (Fort Wayne, Ind.: National Conference of Charities and Correction, 1908), 37–42.

2. A. J. McKelway, " 'Kate,' the 'Good Angel' of Oklahoma," *American Magazine* 66 (1908): 587–93; "An Oklahoma Woman Lobbyist," *World Today* 13 (1907): 965–66; " 'Kate' of Oklahoma," *The American Review of Reviews* 38 (1908): 493–94; " 'Miss Kate,' Livest Wire in Prison Reform, Visits Us," *New York Times,* December 8, 1912; Julian Leavitt, "The Man in the Cage," *American Magazine* 73 (1912): 533–44; Helen Christine Bennett, *American Women in Civic Work* (New York: Dodd, Mead and Co., 1915), 93–113; George P. Hunt, "An Appreciation of Miss Barnard," *Good Housekeeping* 55 (1912): 606–607.

3. Kate Barnard to Sarah Morgan, Mar. 20, 1909; Kate Barnard to Edith H. Clogston, Mar. 8, 1910; Kate Barnard to James E. Gibbons, Mar. 13, 1909, Charities and Corrections Collection, State Archives of Oklahoma, Oklahoma City (hereafter cited as C&C Coll.); Kate Barnard, "Oklahoma's Child Labor Laws," *Sturm's Oklahoma Magazine* 5 (1908): 42; *Proceedings of the Fourth Annual Meeting of the American Academy of Political Social Science,* 32 (1908): 175.

4. Kate Barnard to W. B. Baker, Feb. 15, 1909; Kate Barnard to Mrs. J. F. Sharp, Oct. 7, 1908, C&C Coll.; Barnard, "Shaping the Destinies," 36–38; Kate Barnard to L. J. Smith, Oct. 14, 1909, C&C Coll.; *Proceedings of the Fifth Meeting of the Governors of the States of the Union, 1912,* Richmond, Va., 151–54.

5. Kate Barnard to Eliza Egan, Dec. 6, 1909; Kate Barnard to Sarah Morgan, Mar. 20, 1909; Kate Barnard to L. H. Burton, Feb. 10, 1909; Kate Barnard to Marion Gray, Sept. 14, 1909; Kate Barnard to Dr. John S. Fulton, Aug. 26, 1908; Kate Barnard to Emily M. Woolfork, Nov. 21, 1910, C&C Coll.

6. Kate Barnard to Gustave A. Stryker, Jan. 12, 1910, C&C Coll.

7. Ibid.; Kate Barnard to Sarah Morgan, Mar. 20, 1909; Kate Barnard to Edith H. Clogston, Mar. 8, 1910; Kate Barnard to Marion Gray, Sept. 14, 1909, C&C Coll.

8. Kate Barnard to Mrs. A. B. Avery, May 3, 1909; Kate Barnard to Dr. James H. Kelley, Mar. 1, 1909; Kate Barnard to R. P. Wynne, July 13, 1909; Kate Barnard to E. B. Nelson, Oct. 9, 1909; Kate Barnard to Dr. H. H. Hart, Dec. 24, 1909, C&C Coll.

9. Kate Barnard to James E. Gibbons, Mar. 13, 1909; Kate Barnard to Sarah Morgan, Mar. 20, 1909, C&C Coll.; Barnard, "Shaping the Destinies," 41; Kate Barnard to L. H. Burton, Feb. 10, 1909; Kate Barnard to Mrs. M. C. Kersh, June 6, 1908; Kate Barnard to I. M. Putnam, Dec. 17, 1907; Kate Barnard to Bessie G. Davis, Dec. 31, 1909; Kate Barnard to Mrs. C. H. Fuller, Jan. 23, 1909; Kate Barnard to Henry Wolfer, Mar. 20, 1909, C&C Coll.

10. Kate Barnard to Huxley T. Flaugher, Mar. 24, 1910, C&C Coll.; Barnard, "Shaping the Destinies," 41; Kate Barnard to Dr. John S. Fulton, Aug. 26, 1908; Hobart Huson to J. L. Harbour, Nov. 6, 1908; Kate Barnard to John L. Green, Dec. 3, 1910, C&C Coll.

11. Kate Barnard to Edwin Markham, June 1, 1909; Kate Barnard to Marion Gray, Sept. 14, 1909, C&C Coll.

12. Kate Barnard to Mrs. Phillip N. Moore, July 18, 1910; Kate Barnard to Paul U. Kellogg, July 18, 1910; Kate Barnard to Mrs. Carus, Aug. 8, 1910; Kate Barnard to Samuel Gompers, Aug. 8, 1910; Kate Barnard to H. H. McCulloch, Jan. 4, 1910; Kate Barnard to C. S. Barrett, Aug. 10, 1910; Kate Barnard to Norman E. Mack, Dec. 7, 1909, C&C Coll.

13. Kate Barnard to Hon. S. H. Greeley, May 5, 1910; Kate Barnard to Mr. Urick, Feb. 7, 1910; Kate Barnard to Clara Dyar, Nov. 23, 1908; H. P. Hanson to Kate Barnard, July 5, 1910; Kate Barnard to D. F. Sutherland, Feb. 3, 1910; Kate Barnard to Samuel J. Barrows, Jan. 13, 1909; Kate Barnard to Lee Bowman, Dec. 15, 1908; Kate Barnard to William Allen White, Jan. 12, 1909; Kate Barnard to Lillian Wald, Oct. 12, 1910, C&C Coll.; Kate Barnard to Walter L. Fisher, Dec. 29, 1914, Fisher Collection, Library of Congress, Washington, D.C.; Hunt, "An Appreciation of Miss Barnard," 606–607.

14. George E. Mowry, *The California Progressives* (Berkeley: University of California Press, 1951), 86–102; William T. Kerr, Jr., "The Progressives of Washington, 1910–12," *Pacific Northwest Quarterly* 55 (1964): 16–27; John L. Shover, "The Progressives and the Working Class Vote in California," *Labor History* 10 (1969): 586–88; Wayne E. Fuller, "The Rural Roots of the Progressive Leaders," *Agricultural History* 42 (1968): 1–13; Michael Kazin, *Baron of Labor: The San Francisco Building Trades and Union Power in the Progressive Era* (Champaign: University of Illinois Press, 1987), chap. 6.

15. Kate Barnard, "Working for the Friendless," *The Independent* 63 (Nov. 28, 1907); Kate Barnard to L. H. Burton, Feb. 10, 1909, C&C Coll.; U.S. Department of Commerce, Bureau of the Census, *Twelfth Census of the United States, 1900,* Schedule No. I, Population, 12:16; Kate Barnard to Mrs. M. C. Kersh, June 6, 1908, C&C Coll.; *Oklahoma State Gazetteer and Business Directory* (G. W. McMiller, 1908), 23; *Oklahoma City and County Directory* (Oklahoma City: Western Directory Co., 1900), 4.

16. Kate Barnard to Mrs. C. H. Fuller, Jan. 23, 1909; Kate Barnard to Eliza Egan, Dec. 6, 1909; Kate Barnard to Bessie G. Davis, Dec. 31, 1909, C&C Coll.; Oklahoma, Oklahoma County Superintendent, "School Board Records," District Township 11, 14, 1896, 1897, 1898.

17. Kate Barnard to Bessie G. Davis, Dec. 31, 1909; C. Leonard Brown to

Kate Barnard, Dec. 12, 1908, C&C Coll.; Edith Copeland, "Three Things Hath Honor," unpublished manuscript, Edith Copeland Collection, Western History Collections, University of Oklahoma, Norman, 29–31.

18. *Daily Oklahoman,* May 1, 1904; Kate Barnard to Governor T. B. Ferguson, Feb. 9, 22, 1904.

19. Kate Barnard to Isabel Clingensmith, Mar. 26, 1909, C&C Coll.; Kate Barnard, "Working for the Friendless," 1307–1308.

20. *Daily Oklahoman,* Nov. 5, 1905; Kate Barnard to Mrs. S. G. Wilke, Nov. 20, 1909, C&C Coll.

21. Kate Barnard to Ethel Adams, May 29, 1909; Kate Barnard to John L. Green, Mar. 17, 1909, C&C Coll.

22. Kate Barnard to Mr. J. W. Haden, Jan. 22, 1910; Kate Barnard to John L. Green, Mar. 17, 1909; Kate Barnard to Mrs. S. B. Wilke, Nov. 20, 1909; Kate Barnard to Isabel Clingensmith, Mar. 26, 1909, C&C Coll.; *Daily Oklahoman,* May 26, June 7, Oct. 17, 1906.

23. Kate Barnard to Mrs. C. W. Kersh, June 6, 1908, C&C Coll.; Kate Barnard, "Working for the Friendless," 1308; Kate Barnard to Ethel Adams, May 29, 1909; Kate Barnard to John L. Green, Mar. 17, 1909, C&C Coll.; American Federation of Labor, *List of Organizations Affiliated with the American Federation of Labor,* "Local Unions," George Meany Memorial Archives, Washington, D.C.

24. Barnard, "Oklahoma's Child Labor Laws," 42–43; Kate Barnard to Mr. C. H. Fuller, Jan. 23, 1909; Kate Barnard to Ethel Adams, May 29, 1909, C&C Coll.

25. Kate Barnard to Mary B. Eakins, Oct. 1, 1908, C&C Coll.; Oklahoma, House, Journal of the House, *Proceedings of the Seventh Legislative Assembly of the Territory of Oklahoma* (Guthrie, Okla. Terr.: State Capitol Company, 1903), 51; Oklahoma, Oklahoma County, Board of County Commissioners, "Election Records," Book 2:100, 297; Book 3:112, 274; Oklahoma, Territorial Council, Journal of the Council, *Proceedings of the Eighth Legislative Assembly of the Territory of Oklahoma* (Guthrie, Okla. Terr.: State Capitol Company, 1905), 13.

26. For examples from California, Colorado, and Washington, see Kevin Starr, *Inventing the Dream: California through the Progressive Era* (New York: Oxford University Press, 1985), 236, 255; Mowry, *California Progressives,* 62–88; Fred Greenbaum, *Fighting Progressive: A Biography of Edward P. Costigan* (Washington, D.C.: Public Affairs Press, 1971), 17; Lee F. Pendergrass, "The Formation of a Municipal Reform Movement: The Municipal League of Seattle," *Pacific Northwest Quarterly* 66 (1975): 13–14.

27. Joint Legislative Board of the Farmer's Union, Federation of Labor, and Railway Organizations, "Demands," Peter Hanraty Collection, Western History Collections (hereafter cited as Hanraty Coll.); *Shawnee Herald,* Aug. 23, 1906, *Norman Transcript,* Sept. 20, 1906; Kate Barnard to Mrs. M. C. Kersh, June 6, 1908, C&C Coll.; Kate Barnard to Mrs. C. H. Fuller, Jan. 23, 1909; Laura Corder to Kate Barnard, Jan. 28, 1909; C&C Coll.

28. Kate Barnard to Samuel Gompers, Oct. 11, 1909; Kate Barnard to Mrs.

C. H. Fuller, Jan. 23, 1909, C&C Coll.; James R. Scales and Danney Goble, *Oklahoma Politics: A History* (Norman: University of Oklahoma Press, 1982), 21; Danney Goble, *Progressive Oklahoma: The Making of a New Kind of State* (Norman: University of Oklahoma Press, 1980), 197.

29. Oklahoma, State Constitution, Article 6, Section 27, "Commissioner of Charities and Corrections"; Oklahoma, State Election Board, *Directory of Oklahoma, 1981,* 670, 674–75; Barnard, "Shaping the Destinies," 39; Kate Barnard to Mrs. C. H. Fuller, Jan. 23, 1909, C&C Coll.; Barnard, "Oklahoma's Child Labor Laws," 43; Kate Barnard to Samuel Gompers, Oct. 11, 1909; Kate Barnard to Ethel Adams, May 29, 1909, C&C Coll.

30. Kate Barnard to Lilah Lindsay, Aug. 19, 1908; Kate Barnard to E. J. Westbrook, June 1, 1908; Kate Barnard to the Guthrie Trades Assembly, Oct.19, 1909, C&C Coll.

31. Kate Barnard to S. H. Greeley, May 5, 1910; Kate Barnard to J. Luther Langston, Aug. 10, 1908, C&C Coll.; Oklahoma State Federation of Labor, *Proceedings of the Fifth Annual Convention, 1908,* 18–19, 24–25; Oklahoma State Federation of Labor, *Proceedings of the Joint Legislative Committee, 1914,* 12; Henry Fleck to Kate Barnard, Aug. 22, 1910, C&C Coll.; Oklahoma State Federation of Labor, *Report of the Legislative Committee, 1907–08,* 15–16.

32. For discussions of the role of labor in progressive reform in California, see Kazin, *Baron of Labor;* Alexander Saxton, "San Francisco Labor and the Populist and Progressive Insurgencies," *Pacific Historical Review* 34 (1965): 433–39; Shover, "The Progressives and the Working Class Vote"; Michael Paul Rogin and John L. Shover, *Political Change in California: Critical Elections and Social Movements, 1890–1966,* Contributions in American History No. 5 (Westport, Conn.: Greenwood Publishing Corporation, 1970), chaps. 2, 3.

33. Kate Barnard to J. Luther Langston, Aug. 10, 1908; Kate Barnard to C. Schayze, July 18, 1910; Kate Barnard to J. A. West, July 23, 1908; Kate Barnard to Guthrie Trades Assembly, Oct. 19, 1909, C&C Coll.; Scales and Goble, *Oklahoma Politics,* 42–43, 45.

34. Kate Barnard to William Lair, May 17, 1909, C&C Coll.

35. Kate Barnard to Mrs. Cora Davis Thompson, Nov. 5, 1908; Kate Barnard to Mrs. E. E. Lamoreaux, May 4, 1910, C&C Coll.

36. Kate Barnard to Lilah Lindsay, Aug. 19, 1908; Kate Barnard to David Harris, Jan. 26, 1910; Hobart Huson to Grace Tanneyhill, Feb. 10, 1910, C&C Coll.; Susan Tiffin, *In Whose Best Interest? Child Welfare Reform in the Progressive Era* (Westport, Conn.: Greenwood Press, 1982), 122; Oklahoma, State Legislature, *Session Laws of 1907–1908,* Chap. 34, Article I, "Compulsory Education," 393–95.

37. Kate Barnard to Owen R. Lovejoy, Nov. 9, 1908; Kate Barnard to Cyrus Northrop, Nov. 11, 1908; Kate Barnard to Mrs. J. F. Sharp, Oct. 7, 1908, C&C Coll.; Scales and Goble, *Oklahoma Politics,* 43; William H. Murray, *Memoirs of Governor Murray and True History of Oklahoma,* Vol. 2 (Boston: Meador Publishing Company, 1945), 122.

38. Kate Barnard to Mrs. J. F. Sharp, Oct. 7, 1908; Kate Barnard to Lilah Lindsay, Aug. 19, 1908; William Franklin to Governor Charles W. Haskell, June 20, 1908, C&C Coll.

39. Oklahoma, State Legislature, *Session Laws of 1909*, Chap. 34, Article I, "Child Labor," 629–34; Hobart Huson to Arthur P. Kellogg, Mar. 4, 1909; Kate Barnard to the Speaker and the House of Representatives, Feb. 23, 1909; Kate Barnard to C. G. Jones, Feb. 17, 1909, C&C Coll.

40. Kate Barnard to Huxley T. Flaugher, Mar. 24, 1910; Kate Barnard to Roy E. Stafford, June 12, 1908; Kate Barnard to William Lair, May 17, 1909, C&C Coll.; Oklahoma, State Legislature, *Session Laws, 1909*, Chap. 14, Article VIII, "Juvenile Courts," 185; Kate Barnard to Mrs. Finis Bentley, May 10, 1910, C&C Coll.

41. D'Ann Campbell, "Judge Ben Lindsey and the Juvenile Court Movement," *Arizona and the West* 18 (1976): 5–20; Charles Larsen, *The Good Fight: The Life and Times of Ben B. Lindsey* (Chicago: Quadrangle Books, 1972); Charles N. Glaab, "The Failure of North Dakota Progressivism," *Mid-America* 39 (1957): 205–209; Pendergrass, "The Formation of a Municipal Reform Movement," 18; Martha S. Bradley, "Reclamation of Young Citizens: Reform of Utah's Juvenile Legal System, 1888–1910," *Utah Historical Quarterly* 51 (1983): 328–45.

42. Starr, *Inventing the Dream*, 220–21, 255; "Prison Reform in Arizona," *Charities and the Commons*, June 22, 1907, p. 334; John Conley, "Beyond Legislative Acts," *Public Historian* 3 (1981): 26–32; Kate Barnard, *First Annual Report of the Department of Charities and Corrections* (Guthrie, Okla.: The Leader Printing Company, 1908), 4–16; Kate Barnard to Dr. Gid Brece, Dec. 30, 1908; Kate Barnard to Ben R. Breezley, Jan, 13, 1909; Kate Barnard to Lewis E. Palmer, Mar. 5, 1909; Kate Barnard to Mrs. Edgar Orton, Apr. 19, 1909, C&C Coll.; H. R. Houghen, "Kate Barnard and the Kansas Penitentiary Scandal, 1908–1909," *Journal of the West* 17 (Jan. 1978): 9–18.

43. Kate Barnard to Talmage L. Smith, Oct. 15, 1909; Kate Barnard to Hon. C. N. Haskell, Feb. 23, 1909, C&C Coll.

44. Richard L. McCormick, "Progressivism: A Contemporary Reassessment," in McCormick, *The Party Period and Public Policy: American Politics from the Age of Jackson to the Progressive Era* (New York: Oxford University Press, 1986), 283–85; Martin J. Schiesl, *The Politics of Efficiency: Municipal Administration and Reform in America: 1880–1920* (Berkeley: University of California Press, 1977), 3–24; Arthur S. Link and Richard L. McCormick, *Progressivism* (Arlington Heights, Ill.: Harlan Davidson, 1983), 67–72; John C. Burnham, "Essay," in John D. Buenker et al., *Progressivism* (Cambridge, Mass.: Schenkman Books, 1977), 18–22.

45. *Daily Oklahoman*, Oct. 21, Nov. 11, Dec. 16, 1906; Kate Barnard to Hon. Edwin Markham, June 1, 1909; Hobart Huson to Editor, *Times Democrat* (New Orleans), Mar. 11, 1909, C&C Coll.

46. Kate Barnard to Mrs. Wealthy Wilson, Apr. 12, 1910; Kate Barnard to S. C. Heyman, Jan. 10, 1910; Kate Barnard to Bishop Theophile Meerschaert, Apr. 13, 1908, C&C Coll.

47. Paul Kellogg to Kate Barnard, Jan. 23, 1908; Kate Barnard to Samuel Barrows, Dec. 23, 1907; Apr. 14, 1908; Jan. 21, 1909; C&C Coll.; Kate Barnard to Ben Lindsey, Oct. 17, Nov. 3, 1907, Lindsey Collection, Manuscripts Division, Library of Congress, Washington, D.C.

48. Kate Barnard to Hon. R. L. Owen, Dec. 21, 1907; John M. Glenn to Kate Barnard, Nov. 20, 1907; Jan. 12, 1908; Kate Barnard to Mrs. J. F. Sharp, Oct. 7, 1908; Kate Barnard to Amy Woods, Apr. 27, 1909, C&C Coll.

49. Kate Barnard to Norman E. Mack, Dec. 7, 1909; Kate Barnard to Dr. W. E. Settle, July 12, 23, 1910; Kate Barnard to Alex H. Polson, Apr. 3, 1909; Kate Barnard to Mrs. L. B. Snider, June 19, 1909; Kate Barnard to Della Packard, Feb. 10, 1909; Kate Barnard to Mrs. L. W. Cole, May 9, 1910, C&C Coll.; *Directory of Oklahoma, 1981,* 670, 674–75.

50. Kate Barnard to Willie Sutherland, Nov. 5, 1910; Kate Barnard to Alex H. Polson, Apr. 3, 1909; Kate Barnard to Dr. Carter, Feb. 4, 1910, C&C Coll.

5

"IN DEATH YOU SHALL NOT WEAR IT EITHER":

The Persecution of Mennonite Pacifists in Oklahoma

Marvin E. Kroeker

The reception of immigrant groups in Oklahoma, obviously, was not always positive. Marvin E. Kroeker, professor and chair of the Department of History at East Central University, recounts the treatment of one such minority in the essay which follows. The story is made more interesting—and validated—by Kroeker's inclusion of his own personal experience and perspective.

Oklahoma's colorful history is tarnished by a record of bigotry, prejudice, and intolerance toward minorities, particularly Native Americans and African Americans. Although ignored by early historians, the main features of this seamy aspect of the state's history are by now generally known. There is at least one other sordid chapter in Oklahoma history that still remains to be told: the persecution of Mennonite conscientious objectors to war. Oklahomans—historians and nonhistorians alike—are generally unaware of the scope and intensity of the oppression of this German ethnic group during the periods of war. This essay seeks to at least partially fill this void by examining the relations between this small nonconformist group and the larger Oklahoma society during World Wars I and II.

Mennonites were among the first non-Indians to settle in western Oklahoma, first as missionaries to the Cheyenne and Arapaho, and then as homesteaders. By 1914 there were at least forty-four Mennonite church communities located in the state. That number includes communities of the Amish, who are historically identified with Mennonites. There were also non-Mennonite German and German-Russian settlements scattered throughout Oklahoma, especially in the western half of the state.[1]

It was during World War I that Oklahomans first began to turn against the Germans, whom they called "Krauts," in their midst. And when they discovered that the reclusive Mennonites were not only German but also pacifists, the antagonism increased. Once President Woodrow Wilson decided to take the country into war in 1917, he worked mightily to convince the American people that the heretofore ignoble European conflict was now, in fact, a "just war" worthy of total support. To aid the administration in selling the war, Wilson established a propaganda bureau, euphemistically called the Committee on Public Information. Its head, George Creel, inspired the creation of local and state Councils of Defense to whip up patriotism and encourage all-out support for the war effort, including the draft and bond drives. Unfortunately, in Oklahoma the self-appointed council members operated as extralegal snooping committees who targeted Germans for abuse and sought to enforce their own versions of loyalty and patriotism.[2]

One of the largest concentrations of German-speaking citizens in Oklahoma was found in Washita County. The main religious and commercial center of the German-Russian Mennonites in that area was my hometown of Korn. In 1918 superpatriots prevailed in getting the town's name Anglicized to Corn. In like fashion the German town of Kiel in Kingfisher County was made Loyal. To have an Oklahoma community named Bismark was also considered wrong, so in 1918 this McCurtain County town was made Wright.[3]

Renaming towns was one thing. Much more serious was the effort through terror and intimidation to change the religion and culture of the German-speaking Mennonites. Councils of Defense hounded and harassed them for using the German language in

worship services and for their adherence to a fundamental
Anabaptist/Mennonite principle of opposition to war. Most of the
Oklahoma Mennonites had left Tsarist Russia forty years earlier
because of threatened restrictions on both the use of German and
exemption from military service. They had come to America for a
freedom of religion that federal and state officials had assured them
included military exemptions and the right to worship in any lan-
gauge. But in 1918 self-proclaimed defenders of the American way
marched into a Mennonite church near Fairview and ordered all services, including prayers, be conducted in English. Notices were
posted on church doors declaring: "GOD ALMIGHTY UNDER-
STANDS THE AMERICAN LANGUAGE. Address HIM only in
that Tongue."

The patriotic frenzy went beyond mere threats. A General Conference Mennonite church was burned to the ground near Inola in
northeastern Oklahoma. Two months later the barn which the congregation was temporarily using for worship services was likewise
destroyed. A Mennonite Brethren church in Inola was also scorched
to the ground, apparently by a patriotic arsonist. The free exercise
of religion was becoming costly in the Sooner State. One Inola
Mennonite was forcibly abducted and held for several days because
he had failed to buy war bonds. This action may have been encouraged by a statement released by the Oklahoma attorney general declaring that the failure to buy liberty bonds was against the
law. John Jantzen, a conscientious objector subject to the draft, was
warned about a possible lynching if he refused to cooperate. Because of the hostile atmosphere, he and his father, Franz Jantzen,
a lay Mennonite Brethren minister, left Inola under the cover of
darkness and made their way to Kansas City, where they boarded a
train to Canada. Eventually other members of the family joined
them, never to return to live in Oklahoma again.[4]

Henry Reimer, a Mennonite Brethren farmer living near Collinsville, nearly lost his life at the hands of a lynch mob. This came two
weeks after he vocally protested the closing of a German Bible
school by order of the local Council of Defense. He also removed a
picture of an American flag that members of the council placed in
the front window of his home with instructions that it be displayed
until the end of the war. When neighbors reported the removal of the

flag, two members of the Council of Defense placed Reimer under arrest and had him locked in the Collinsville jail. On the night of April 19, 1918, a mob of fifty men overpowered the jailers and took Reimer to an armory building, where they prepared to hang him. A double electric cord was wrapped around his neck and the other end attached to a basketball goal. He was forced to kiss every star on the flag, and then the chair on which he was standing was kicked out from under him. While his writhing, unconscious body was swinging back and forth, a courageous assistant chief of police intervened and saved his life. It was noted that this hanging was very similar to a fatal lynching of a German in Collinsville, Illinois, earlier in 1918. The Illinois story had been reprinted in the *Collinsville* (Oklahoma) *Star* under the headline "WARNING."

From a Tulsa jail, Reimer denied that he was guilty of disloyalty or any crime. "My neighbors," he said, "have taunted me so much that I cannot help but say things sometimes." He believed that because of his poor English his statements in the heat of emotion must have been misunderstood. Despite his plea, he was charged in federal court with contempt, disloyalty, and obstructing the draft by endeavoring to incite to disobedience.

Tensions in Collinsville eased somewhat following a community meeting where Mennonite spokesmen were present. At this meeting, the Tulsa county attorney delivered a blunt speech explaining the kind of behavior he expected from the Germans. This was followed by an inflammatory harangue against Germans by a man who claimed to represent the Oklahoma governor's office. Peter C. Hiebert, a Mennonite educator from Hillsboro, Kansas, was then allowed to speak to the crowd. He explained that Mennonite opposition to the war was based on religious convictions and not feelings of disloyalty to the United States or feelings of loyalty to Germany. In fact, he said, Mennonite Brethren were of Dutch origin, and those living in the area were either born in Russia, a country on the side of the Allies against Germany, or were descendants of immigrants from Russia. The chairman of the Council of Defense thanked Hiebert for his presentation, and the local newspaper editorialized that the meeting "showed our people that those Germans are loyal to America and are willing to do their 'bit.' " Henry Reimer was soon released from jail, but did not immediately dare return to Collinsville. Instead, he went to live with relatives in the Corn area.[5]

Although charges were filed against the victims of violence, apparently there were never any charges filed by law enforcement officials against anyone for the perpetration of such acts. A local sheriff at Inola did offer to track down the church arsonists with the help of bloodhounds owned by Mennonite farmers. The Mennonites kindly declined the offer. Mennonite teachings opposed the initiation of lawsuits. Thus, to paraphrase Dr. Johnson, patriotism apparently was a safe refuge for the scoundrels who engaged in such illegal activities in Oklahoma.

All Oklahoma Germans were suspect. *Harlow's Weekly* branded the teaching of German a "traitorous act," and Cordell outlawed the use of German within its city limits. In 1919 the Oklahoma legislature passed an English-only law that prohibited the use of any foreign language in the first eight grades. Local pressure forced a private Mennonite German school near Bessie to close its doors. Yellow paint was smeared on many Mennonite homes. Although all Germans, no matter what their religious persuasion, faced harassment and violence, the scope and intensity of the hostility against Mennonites throughout the United States during the Great War led Fred Luebke, historian of Germans in America, to conclude that they were "the most grievously abused of any German culture group in the United States."[6] And probably nowhere in America were they more grievously treated than in Oklahoma. But Mennonites on the home front fared better than their drafted sons.

The draft law of May 18, 1917, included an exemption provision for conscientious objectors (COs) who were members of recognized Peace Churches, but stated that "no person so exempted shall be exempted from service in any capacity that the President shall declare to be noncombatant."[7] If James Madison's views had prevailed in 1789, religious pacifists would have had a constitutional right *not* to bear arms. His original version of what came to be the Second Amendment to the Constitution read: "The right of the people to keep and bear arms shall not be infringed; a well-armed and well-regulated militia being the best security of a free country; but no person religiously scrupulous of bearing arms shall be compelled to render military service in person." The House of Representatives passed the amendment; however, the Senate eliminated the CO clause. Thus the legal status of the CO is derived as a matter of legislative privilege rather than a constitutional right.[8]

Unlike Madison, President Wilson seemed to have little concern for the scruples of religious objectors. In a Flag Day speech he called the peace advocates traitors and schemers. It was ten months before he issued any orders describing the type of noncombatant service pacifists would be required to perform. In the meantime, Secretary of War Newton Baker advised concerned Mennonite leaders that their young men must register and report to military camps when called. But he assured them that there was no need to worry. "We will take care of your boys," he promised.[9] Oklahoma Mennonites complied in good faith, only to discover to their dismay what Baker apparently had in mind when he said he would "take care" of them. Once in camp under military law and discipline, army officers did their best to knock pacifism out of them and pressured them to accept full military service. It did not work. Despite suffering serious consequences, few Mennonites buckled under.[10]

Most Oklahoma Mennonites were sent to Fort Travis, Texas, carrying with them documents verifying that they were COs and that they were to do only noncombatant service. Instead, they were mustered into service like any other recruit, ordered to wear the uniform, drill, and swear the military oath. The failure to comply resulted in a general court-martial for 45 COs stationed at Fort Travis. All were found guilty of failure to follow orders and sentenced to life imprisonment at Fort Leavenworth, Kansas. The commanding officer reduced the penalty to twenty-five years at hard labor. By December 1918 there were 150 Mennonite COs jailed at Fort Leavenworth; 35 came from Oklahoma, more than from any other state. Twelve of the Oklahomans came from Washita County. Henry Reimer, whose father had survived the lynching at Collinsville, was among those detained at Fort Leavenworth. The men remained incarcerated until freed by a general amnesty after the end of the war. At that time, the Oklahoma state legislature passed a resolution strongly condemning the amnesty decree.[11]

John Klaasen, a member of the Herold Mennonite Church near Corn, died of influenza while imprisoned at Fort Leavenworth. He had been sentenced for refusing to wear a uniform, a compromise he said his conscience would not allow him to make. This occurred despite the fact that Secretary Baker on September 25, 1917, had directed that Mennonites should not be forced "to wear uniforms as the question of raiment is one of the tenets of their religious faith." The army, displaying utter contempt for his conscientious stand, dressed his body in a uniform before sending it home for burial. When the flag-draped casket arrived in Cordell, the boy's father, Rev. Michael Klaasen, removed the flag and dressed his son in civilian clothes before interment. Speaking as if his son could still hear him, the distraught father told him, "In your life you did not wear the uniform, so in death you shall not wear it either." Religious convictions had earlier led the Klaasen family from the Ukraine to Central Asia, and then later to the United States. Now, because of the intense hostility stirred up over his actions, and fearing for his life, Klaasen fled to Canada. Half of his congregation soon followed.[12]

How can one explain the martial quality of Oklahoma patriotism? Why was there so much hostility toward religionists who, in the words of Oliver Wendell Holmes, "believe more than some of us do in the teachings of the Sermon on the Mount"?[13] How could a group that refuses to kill be considered a danger to the security of the state or nation? The pietistic and clannish Mennonites were so clearly identifiable that no honest observer could possibly have associated them with Socialists or the draft resisters that were involved in the notorious Green Corn Rebellion. The idea that Mennonites had Socialist leanings was and is preposterous. At that very time, 1917–18, they were receiving news that the radical Socialists in Russia were furiously destroying Mennonite lives and property.[14]

There were few voices raised in behalf of reason and tolerance during the war. And fewer still in defense of conscientious objection to war. The churches, from conservative fundamentalist types to mainliners, fervently endorsed Wilson's call to arms. They had long forgotten that the early Christians had staunchly refused to participate in war.[15] Those who believed in the "Just War" doctrine, as did President Wilson, an ardent Presbyterian, rationalized the war as a necessary crusade to preserve Christian civilization. In Oklahoma the churches seemingly followed the theology of warmongers like Theodore Roosevelt and Billy Sunday. God and country came to be closely entwined. The historic Peace Churches—Mennonite, Church of the Brethren, and Society of Friends—were few in number in the state and did not proselytize. Nor did they make a concerted effort to explain their religious views to the general public. Individual members who sought to articulate their beliefs at times were inept. For example, one Mennonite recruit who had trouble with the English language explained his responsibilities to the government on the basis of the scriptural injunction, "Give to the Kaiser what the Kaiser's is, and to God what God's is."[16] Most Oklahomans were totally ignorant of the Anabaptist theology of nonresistance and the Mennonite denomination's four-hundred-year history of adherence to beliefs, no matter the cost. Thus there was no understanding or appreciation of the nonconformist stand taken by these religious objectors to war. In Oklahoma the only true test of loyalty was the willingness to fight for one's country. This, in a sense, had also become a sacred creed—a tenet of civil religion. Conscientious objectors, therefore, were slackers, cowards, disloyal, and anti-American. And since the Mennonites were also perceived to be representatives of what was then popularly referred to as the "horrible race of Huns," they, more than other Germans, bore the brunt of the persecution during the war.

Another factor may have contributed to the anti-Mennonite sentiment in Oklahoma: they were nonconformists in a frontier region where that characteristic was disdained. The frontier historian Ray A. Billington noted that "in the West social cohesiveness, standardized behavior, and restrictive limitations on individual freedom" were common. On the frontier the community spirit was so prevailing "that no one dared express individuality; people lived and dressed and thought exactly alike. . . . Amidst the anonymity of a city, a person might dare to be different; amidst the intimacy of the frontier, he did not."[17] Available evidence appears to show that Mennonites living in the western states were under more duress than those living east of the Mississippi, with Oklahoma being the most inhospitable and Kansas, Montana, and South Dakota not far behind. The large Mennonite concentrations in Pennsylvania experienced little violence or hostility. Local draft boards, unlike those in the western states, were generous with agricultural exemptions and placed few men into military camps.[18]

The Mennonite historian C. Henry Smith characterized the typical CO as "willing to do any kind of work, in the danger zone or out, if its purpose was to save life rather than to destroy it, if it was not connected with the military establishment. He was neither a coward nor a slacker; he chose the hard road of loyalty to his convictions rather than the easy one of compromise. He was made of the same stuff as that of his forefathers who some hundreds of years earlier went to the martyr's stake by the thousands rather than to surrender religious beliefs which they thought to be right."[19]

One of the few prominent Americans to plead for the respect of conscience was Harlan F. Stone, dean of the Columbia Law School and later Chief Justice of the Supreme Court. As a member of the army's board of inquiry during World War I, he studied the problems of COs in the military. "It is easy but undiscriminating and shallow," he wrote, "to denounce the conscientious objector as a coward and slacker." He expressed the belief that "Many . . . are muddle-headed and inconsistent in their theories of life . . . but their evident sincerity and willingness to suffer to the end rather than to yield up their cherished illusion make impossible the wholesale condemnation of the conscientious objector as a coward and a slacker." Stone believed that if it was the country's political theory "that the ultimate end of the state is the highest good of its citizens, both morals and sound policy require that the state should not violate the conscience of the individual." American history "gives confirmation to the view that liberty of conscience has a moral and social value which makes it worthy of preservation at the hands of the state. So deep in its significance and vital, indeed, is it to the integrity of man's moral and spiritual nature that nothing short of the self-preservation of the state should warrant its violation; and it may well be questioned whether the state which preserves its life by a settled policy of violation of the conscience of the individual will not in fact ultimately lose it by the process."[20]

The hostilities, confrontations, and tensions of the war period had effects on Mennonites that carried over into the 1920s and 1930s. The younger generation became more inclined to become "Americanized." It was more comfortable to coexist with "English" neighbors if one's Germanness and Mennonitism were played down. The second-generation syndrome also came into play as many sought to cut themselves off from their immigrant past and melt into the mainstream. Also, the emphasis on nonresistance was neglected in some Mennonite churches as acculturation accelerated.

In 1940, Europe was again at war, and Congress once again debated a draft bill. Fortunately for religious pacifists, key officials in the Franklin D. Roosevelt administration were in sympathy with Chief Justice Stone's enlightened view that in a democracy the government should not coerce action in opposition to conscience. Also by that time both military and government officials were in agreement with Peace Church representatives that the arrangements for objectors had been badly handled during World War I. Thus when Mennonite, Quaker, and Brethren delegates met with government officials they found them more willing to listen to their proposals regarding government service in wartime. Like other concerned Americans, Oklahoma Mennonites were appalled by the strident nationalism and military aggressions of Hitler and Mussolini. If the United States became engulfed in another war, how could they avoid the "yellow slacker" image of World War I? How could they demonstrate their loyalty and patriotism without resorting to arms? What they desperately needed was a moral equivalent to war. In a meeting with President Roosevelt on January 10, 1940, Peace Church representatives presented him with copies of their creeds on the issue of war and a statement of concern should a draft be reinstituted. They requested advance discussions by church and government officials "regarding procedures for handling conscientious objectors and types of sevice which might be provided." They stressed the importance of alternative nonmilitary work directed by civilians. The churchmen came away from this cordial meeting convinced that the affable president agreed with them. Actually FDR would devote precious little time to this subject thereafter.[21]

The concerted lobbying efforts of the Peace Churches paid off. Using the British National Service Act as a model, their spokesmen were successful in getting an alternative civilian service feature written into the Burke-Wadsworth conscription bill. The act also broadened the category of conscientious objectors to include any individual who by "religious training and belief" was opposed to participation in war. They sought but failed to gain a Quaker-pushed proposal for complete exemption for those with religious convictions against all forms of compulsory service. Finally, the law had a provision for conscientious objectors who were willing to go into the army to perform noncombatant duty.[22]

The recognition of CO rights in the Burke-Wadsworth Act, or Selective Training and Service Act of 1940, led to the Civilian Public Service (CPS) program, a remarkable experiment in church-state relations in the United States. A National Service Board for Religious Objectors was established to work with the government in devising the CPS program. If certified by local draft boards, COs would be assigned to civilian work designated by the president to be of "national importance." Under the provisions, COs received no pay, dependent families received no allowances, and upon completion of service there would be no government benefits. When General Lewis B. Hershey was named head of the Selective Service System, he was also assigned general jurisdiction over CPS, although the law called for a civilian director. This was never challenged by the Peace Churches, indicating that they were generally satisfied with his administration.

CPS was initially patterned after the Civilian Conservation Corps that had been instituted during the Great Depression. Thus most of the early CO draftees were assigned to camps in the western part of the country to work on a variety of conservation projects. President Roosevelt had some qualms about approving this kind of service, declaring that it was too easy, but he was finally persuaded to authorize it. However, he shocked everyone when he insisted that the program be financed entirely by the Peace Churches, not the government as had been agreed to by his own administration planners. CPS work assignments were gradually expanded to include service in mental hospitals, dairy improvements, medical experiments, and community projects in Puerto Rico. Some COs who volunteered to serve as human "guinea pigs" in medical experiments were infected with such diseases as hepatitis and polio (one man died in this experiment), and others underwent experiments testing the results of hunger and starvation.[23]

Most of the COs from Oklahoma worked in state mental hospitals or on conservation projects. Appalled by the snake-pit conditions found in most "insane asylums," the Mennonite denomination after the war established four institutions for the care and treatment of the mentally ill—a direct result of its participation in that phase of CPS.[24]

County draft boards in Oklahoma were reluctant to honor requests for CO classification. Mennonite registrants in Garfield, Washita, and Major counties often faced hostile interrogation when called upon to defend their religious convictions on nonresistance. A favorite question that invariably came up was, "What would you do if someone entered your home to rape and murder your mother? Would you use force to protect her?" If rejected for CO classification by the local board, a registrant had the right of appeal to an Appeal Board. The Appeal Board referred the case to the Justice Department for review, investigation if desired, and a recommendation. A final appeal could be made to the president.[25] The largest number of CO classification appeals of any county in the United States originated in Major County, Oklahoma. In most cases, the Appeal Board overturned the negative rulings of the Oklahoma draft boards.

Not only was the CO classification difficult to obtain from local boards in Oklahoma, but the mere fact of registering as an objector to war could also cost one his job. One of my friends in Fairview was fired from his teaching position when word got out that he was a registered "yellow CO." When Marvin Hein of Fairview entered CPS, the local American Legion post voted to demand the return of a first-place trophy awarded to him in a state oratory contest sponsored by the organization. The secretary of the post later confessed that because he had opposed this decision he "forgot" to inform Hein of the Legion's demand.

Not all Mennonites conscribe to the tenet of nonparticipation in the military. Although the official stance of all Mennonite and Amish branches is Christian pacifism, most congregations leave the issue up to the individual and his conscience. In some families, brothers chose different roads. My oldest brother chose to accept noncombatant service in the army. Serving in a communications unit, he participated in the Normandy invasion and accompanied the First Army into Germany, gaining a Purple Heart and a Bronze Star in the process. Another brother chose the nonmilitary option and was assigned to work in a mental hospital in Pennsylvania for the duration. It took no less courage, given the prevailing attitudes in

Oklahoma, for my pacifist brother to choose CPS work than for the other brother to put on the uniform. I also had a sister who joined the Army Nursing Corps. As a family we managed to accept and respect each other's views and choices. Occasionally the war-peace issue led to conflicts and splits within church communities. Being taunted or shunned in one's home church or community could be the most painful of all experiences.

Records show that 45.9 percent of the Mennonites drafted in the United States served in the CPS; 14.5 percent accepted noncombatant work in the army; and 39.6 percent took regular military service. The figures for Oklahoma Mennonites probably paralleled the nationwide percentages. Between 1940 and 1947, according to a Selective Service System publication, the total number of Mennonite assignees to CPS was 4,610, by far the highest number of any denomination. The Church of the Brethren was second in the number of adherents in CPS, with a total of 1,468. The Society of Friends was third with 902.[26] These figures make it clear, contrary to common belief, that the Quaker group is no longer the major pacifist body in America. That designation belongs to the Mennonites.

In Oklahoma during the war period there were 1,511 conscientious objectors on the rosters of local draft boards. This figure includes both those registering for noncombatant service in the military (1A0) and those registering for work in CPS (4-E). The total for the nation was 52,354, with Oklahoma ranking eleventh in the number of CO registrants by states. Although the 1,511 Oklahoma registrants represented only 0.27 percent of the total number of state registrants, only 9 draft boards out of 105 did not have any objectors on their rolls. Not all registrants were inducted into service. Of those COs actually inducted, 11,950 went into CPS and an estimated 25,000 went into the army to perform noncombatant duty.[27]

Approximately 65 percent of the COs in CPS came from the historic Peace Churches, with the remainder coming from well over one hundred different religious groups. The Selective Service director reported that he had no concern about the boys from the Peace Churches because he was convinced that they honestly were willing to give their own lives and in good faith were unwilling to contribute "to the taking of somebody else's life." Although he admitted to some concern about some other objectors (primarily Jehovah's

Witnesses), he testified that the CO provision in the law was "administered in such a way as not to become an invitation to mere slackers."[28]

The general scorn and hostility faced by CO registrants spilled over to their families and, not infrequently, to the larger Mennonite community. Throughout their history Mennonites have been referred to as *die Stillen im Lande* (the quiet of the land). As a high-school-aged student in Corn during World War II, I came to understand why my Mennonite forebears had tended to be so quiet and withdrawn from the world. It was much more secure to stay within one's own like-minded group. I noticed that my friends and I began to play it very safe with "outsiders" or "English" people. We tried to hide our German Mennonite connections and avoided discussing anything that might lead to questions about our attitudes toward war or the draft. It was not easy. Although Corn was only a small village, everyone in Oklahoma seemed to know it was a Mennonite center or some kind of German community. And once identified as being from Corn, the first question usually was, "Are you a CO?" Actually, as in World War I, just being an ethnic German or German-Russian was enough to make you a suspect in the eyes of some. I had an advantage over some of my Corn friends. My parents' farm was located on the eastern fringe of the Mennonite community, which put us on the rural Colony mail route. Thus, instead of revealing that I came from Corn, I could honestly tell nosey people in Weatherford, Clinton, or Cordell that I came from Route 2, Colony, thereby steering any conversation toward Indians, John Seger, or fishing holes in Cobb Creek. A former resident of the Fairview community reported that she never talked about her two brothers who were in CPS while she attended the Fairview Public School. It was my generation that deliberately lost the use of the German language, except for the Low German vernacular (Plattdeutsch), which was retained longer. (Such folly on my part proved costly when I entered graduate school and found that I had to pass two foreign language proficiency exams. It took a year of study and two attempts before I managed to pass the German test, ironically administered by a professor with a Mennonite background).

There was some tension between Corn and Bessie, a German-Russian non-Mennonite community west of Corn. Since most of the

Bessie settlers were Catholic or Lutheran, the Mennonites would have little to do with them. And the Bessie citizens made it clear that they did not want to be lumped together with the German pacifists on the other side of the Washita River.

The anti-German and anti-CO sentiments also resulted in various acts of discrimination against Mennonite folk. For example, the wartime shortage of rubber resulted in the rationing of tires. Priorities were established and county boards were appointed to administer the rationing program. Mennonite farmers in the Corn community, including my father, found it virtually impossible to get authorization from the board in Cordell to replace worn-out tires on their farm vehicles. After several unsuccessful attempts, my father unexpectedly received notice that a permit had been granted. We found out the reason later. Our mail carrier, a non-Mennonite from Colony, had vociferously informed the board that Mr. Kroeker had a son overseas in the army and that he deserved better treatment. The permit was then granted forthwith.

Acts of abuse and intimidation against Mennonites were not uncommon after the United States entered the war, although apparently they were not as numerous as in World War I. The splashing of yellow paint on barns and houses was a frequent occurrence in Mennonite communities throughout Oklahoma. A Cordell lawyer was threatened by a mob and a brick was thrown through his office window because he handled draft appeals for Mennonites.[29] The hostility of the merchants in this county seat was so obvious that many Washita County Mennonites stopped trading there, going to Clinton or Weatherford instead. Merchants there were either more tolerant or more astute; at any rate, they were happy to have the business.

The *Daily Oklahoman* carried several objective and rather positive stories about the Corn Germans during the war, but E. K. Gaylord, the bombastic and jingoistic editor, held no truck with nonconformist thought. Dr. E. F. Webber, a prominent radio preacher in Oklahoma City, created a brief statewide furor when he announced that he had received information about what he considered to be a dangerous pro-Hitler element in Corn. An investigation revealed that a harmless and somewhat eccentric resident in that community had written a letter to Webber complaining about his strident, nationalistic, and anti-German "preaching." There was also an unfounded rumor that the Ladies' Sewing Circle in the Corn Mennonite Brethren Church was secretly preparing bandages and other medical supplies for the Nazi armies.

The Oklahoma American Legion provided another example of Oklahoma's unique brand of patriotism. In late 1942 the state legionnaires passed a resolution calling for the repeal of the conscientious objector provisions in the Conscription Act of 1940 and for subjecting all draftees to military service. W. F. Rogers, Jr., department commander, and Milt Phillips, department adjutant, forwarded the resolution to Senator Elmer Thomas with a request that he introduce a repeal bill in Congress. On January 11, 1943, the Democratic senator from Lawton complied, apparently without consulting either the Roosevelt administration or the Department of War.[30]

The Senate Military Affairs Committee held hearings on S. 352 on February 17, 1943, with the chairman, Senator Robert Reynolds of North Carolina, presiding. Senator Thomas appeared briefly before the committee to submit the resolution adopted by the Oklahoma American Legion and to urge members to give it their "full attention." Senator Reynolds entered into the record thirty-four letters, some with multiple signatures, that the committee had received on S. 352. All opposed repeal.[31]

Selective Service Director Lewis B. Hershey and Lieutenant Colonel W. D. Partlow, Jr., representing the War Department, testified in opposition to the Thomas bill. Hershey told the committee that the National Convention of the American Legion had rejected a similar resolution, killing it in committee. He disputed the contention of the Oklahoma Legion that its resolution represented the views of a large number of Legion departments, since no other state had taken similar action. In fact, the state American Legion of New Jersey had passed a resolution endorsing the assignment of COs to a veteran's hospital in their state. This invitation was probably prompted by the positive reports on the service of COs in the New Jersey state mental institution. Veterans' organizations in Maine, New Hampshire, and Vermont had also approved the use of these men.[32] Responding to questions about the CPS programs, General Hershey stated that his department was "rather proud" of the work record of the COs in the conservation camps, hospitals, public health facilities, and "especially the parachute project" (Smoke Jumpers) to fight forest fires which he had only recently authorized. An aide to General Hershey elaborated on seven experimental health projects in which seventy-five CO volunteers served as guinea pigs in experiments with lice infestation, freezing temperatures, and high-altitude simulation tests.[33]

The director believed that these kinds of work activities were much better than putting pacifists in jail, where he believed most of them would end up if the Thomas bill passed. Lieutenant Colonel Partlow agreed that the CPS arrangement should remain in force even though the War Department did not endorse the principle of conscientious objection to war. Forcing these kinds of men into military service, he said, would cause nothing but trouble for the army. Furthermore, the repeal bill would also cancel the noncombatant service provisions with which the army was quite satisfied. Most of the noncombatants provided good service in the medical corps, he reported.[34]

Senators Mon C. Wallgren, Washington State, and Chan Gurney, South Dakota, found it hard to believe that the COs received no pay for their service and that there were no provisions for dependents' allowances. Several times Wallgren raised the question of no pay, and he added the observation: "You are treating these fellows worse than the Japs [sic]."[35] Hershey defended the no-pay policy. If COs were paid, "It would destory the best public relations." Furthermore, they did not want pay for service, seeing the lack of pay as evidence of their willingness to sacrifice during the war. "I do not believe any of the Mennonite Church members . . . would accept any money," he said.[36] Hershey realized that conscientious objection was a volatile issue in some quarters, and as the administrator of CPS he was very concerned about public relations. In concluding his testimony before the committee, Hershey explained his philosophy on the best way to deal with the pacifists and also revealed why his department refrained from publicizing some of the work assignments he had just described: "The conscientious objector, by my theory, is best handled if no one hears of him. It is a solution and therefore, if we would publicize these many good things, you would get a current of other things, and therefore it is best to leave it alone.''[37] This view had some merit if applied to those parts of the country where little was heard about COs. In Oklahoma where there was considerable negative publicity, a more positive and objective portrayal of the COs and the CPS program by General Hershey, or other public officials, would have been helpful. Such a portrayal certainly did not come from Senator Thomas, who did not even bother to attend the hearings long enough to hear Hershey's testimony. As for his repeal bill, it died in committee.

At the end of World War II, Mennonite leaders raised the question, "If involuntary service during wartime had some redeeming social value, why not voluntary service as a witness during peacetime?" As a result, scores of Oklahoma Mennonite youth volunteered for humanitarian work in this country; others contributed their skills for two to three years in underdeveloped nations, working through the Mennonite Central Committee organization called PAX (Latin for "peace"). This program was similar to the popular Peace Corps later established by the John F. Kennedy administration.

In 1948, one year after the World War II draft law had expired, Congress acceded to President Harry S Truman's request and reinstated the draft. In what must be considered one of the greater wonders of the twentieth century, the new law provided complete deferment for the CO. When the Korean War began, Congress, with vociferous help from those normally antagonistic to pacifists, woke up to what it had done. The 1951 draft law ended the deferment policy and reinstated civilian service provisions for religious objectors but not the conservation camp system. Thus during America's wars in Korea and Vietnam, alternative service "contributing to the maintenance of the national health, safety and interest" has been the government's policy on conscientious objectors. This time around, neither Congress, Selective Service, nor Mennonites opposed payment for COs. Apparently the Mennonite position was, "Working in a helping profession—with or without pay—is a worthy service if done in the name of Christ." Almost all were assigned to mental hospitals, where they received the prevailing wage.[38]

During the McCarthy era in the 1950s some Sooner elements continued to behave in a manner that reinforced Oklahoma's image as perhaps the most intolerant state in the Union. During that period of

hysteria about communism, the Oklahoma legislature passed a stringent loyalty oath that required all state employees not only to swear
that they had no Communist leanings but also that they would be
willing to bear arms in defense of the country. This again put tremendous social and economic pressure on those with religious
scruples against participation in war. A history professor with a
Quaker background at the University of Oklahoma refused to sign
the oath and went without pay until the loyalty oath was struck down
as unconstitutional by the courts. The loyalty oath prompted me to
leave the state in 1951 to begin my teaching career elsewhere.

Although the tar, brush, and yellow paint may not have been put
away forever in Oklahoma, the frequency of their use subsided after
the 1950s. Some jobs were still threatened and lost; classification
appeals were still necessary at times (Jerry Penner, an Oklahoma
Panhandle Mennonite, at great financial and emotional cost was
forced to go to the Supreme Court to secure his CO classification
during the Vietnam conflict); and taunts, harassment, and other
shameful treatment have still occurred. Generally speaking, however, greater tolerance has been manifested. Societal changes
contributed to this. Mainline denominations have adopted ''peace-
making'' resolutions and programs, and studies of Anabaptism are
markedly increasing in theological schools. Nuclear pacifists
abound; Oklahoma Presbyterians in Indian Nations Presbytery
endorsed the Nuclear Freeze Resolution in 1982. During the Vietnam War, conscientious objection was embraced by growing
numbers of young people as a way of demonstrating their opposition
to national policy in prosecuting that bloody conflict. They helped
draw fire away from the more traditional pacifists. Unfortunately, in
the minds of militant Oklahomans peace came to be a dirty word,
almost synonymous with communism. Although much more willing
to work ecumenically than in the past, Mennonites tend to look
askance at selective pacifism or any type of pacifism not based on
Christian religious training and belief. Indeed, they prefer the term
nonresistance to *pacifism*.

Ethnic German and German-Russian Mennonites in Oklahoma
are now enjoying a period of cordial relationships with their fellow
citizens. Their reputation for compassion, humanitarian work, and
volunteerism is widely recognized and acclaimed. Whenever a natu-

ral disaster strikes the state, Mennonites are only a step behind. With mops, hammers, and saws, they come to clean up, repair, and rebuild, demonstrating their commitment to serving humankind— be it in war or in peace. Seen in this context, their peace witness is now more tolerated than perhaps at any other time since *die Stillen im Lande* arrived in Oklahoma. If the Mennonite past is prologue, this will probably last until the next war breaks out.

NOTES

1. Marvin E. Kroeker, " 'Die Stillen im Lande': Mennonites in the Oklahoma Land Rushes," *Chronicles of Oklahoma* 68, no. 1 (Spring 1989). See also Douglas Hale, *The Germans from Russia in Oklahoma* (Norman: University of Oklahoma Press, 1980); and Richard C. Rohrs, *The Germans in Oklahoma* (Norman: University of Oklahoma Press, 1980).

2. James W. Fowler, "Tar and Feather Patriotism: The Suppression of Dissent in Oklahoma during World War One," *Chronicles of Oklahoma* 56, no. 4 (Winter 1978–79), 422.

3. Kent Ruth, *Oklahoma Travel Handbook* (Norman: University of Oklahoma Press, 1977), 78, 146, 250.

4. Dean Kroeker, "Eden: Tried by Fire," in *Growing Faith: General Conference Mennonites in Oklahoma,* ed. Wilma McKee (Newton, Kans.: Faith and Life Press, 1988), 77–78; *The Collinsville Star,* Apr. 20, 1918; Wesley Prieb to author, Nov. 20, 1991.

5. *Muskogee Daily Phoenix,* Apr. 20, 21, 1918; Wesley Prieb, *Peter C. Hiebert* (Hillsboro, Kans.: Center for Mennonite Brethren Studies, 1990), 49–51; David Reimer interview with author, Mar. 18, 1993.

6. Rohrs, *Germans in Oklahoma,* 46–47; Frederick C. Luebke, *Bonds of Loyalty: German Americans and World War I* (DeKalb: Northern Illinois University Press, 1974), xv.

7. U.S. Congress, *Public Law No. 12,* 65th Cong., 1st sess.

8. Albert N. Keim and Grant M. Stoltzfus, *The Politics of Conscience: The Historic Peace Churches and America at War, 1917–1955* (Scottsdale, Pa.: Herald Press, 1988), 25.

9. Ibid., 39–40.

10. David Haury, *Prairie People: A History of the Western District Conference* (Newton, Kans.: Faith and Life Press, 1981), 201–202; James C. Juhnke, *A People of Two Kingdoms* (Newton, Kans.: Faith and Life Press, 1975), 100–102; James C. Juhnke, *Vision, Doctrine, War: Mennonite Identity and Organization in America, 1890–1930* (Scottsdale, Pa.: Herald Press, 1989), 234.

11. Juhnke, *Vision, Doctrine, War,* 236, 240; Robert R. Coon, "Being a Peace Church Makes a Difference," in *Growing Faith,* ed. McKee, 152; J. D. Mininger, *Religious C. O.'s Imprisoned at the Disciplinary Barracks, Ft. Leavenworth, Kansas* (Kansas City, Mo.: N.p., 1919).

12. Coon, "Being a Peace Church," 153; H. C. Peterson and Gilbert C. Fite, *Opponents of War, 1917–1918* (Madison: University of Wisconsin Press, 1957), 124.

13. Quoted in Keim and Stoltzfus, *Politics of Conscience,* 9.

14. H. Wayne Morgan and Anne Hodges Morgan, in their *Oklahoma: A History* (New York: W. W. Norton & Co., 1948), 101–102, assert: "Most Germans suspected of disloyalty were of Mennonite or Brethren congregations with pacifist or Socialist leanings."

15. See Jean-Michel Hornus, *It is Not Lawful for Me to Fight: Early Christian Attitudes toward War, Violence, and the State* (Scottsdale, Pa.: Herald Press, 1980).

16. Juhnke, *Vision, Doctrine, War,* 232.

17. Ray A. Billington, "Frontier Democracy: Social Aspects," in George Rogers Taylor, ed., *The Turner Thesis Concerning the Role of the Frontier in American History,* 3rd ed. (Lexington, Mass.: D.C. Heath, 1972), 166–67.

18. Juhnke, *Vision, Doctrine, War,* 237; C. Henry Smith, *Smith's Story of the Mennonites* (Newton, Kans.: Faith and Life Press, 1981), 549.

19. Smith, *Smith's Story,* 547.

20. Neal M. Wherry, *Conscientious Objection,* Special Monograph No. 11, Vol. 1 (Washington, D.C.: Selective Service System, 1950), 64–65.

21. Ibid., 69–70; Keim and Stoltzfus, *Politics and Conscience,* 76–77.

22. Keim and Stoltzfus, *Politics and Conscience,* 93–102.

23. Ibid., 109–12; Smith, *Smith's Story,* 553. For a detailed look at CPS, see Melvin Gingerich, *Service for Peace* (Scottsdale, Pa.: Herald Press, 1949).

24. Smith, *Smith's Story,* 554.

25. Wherry, *Conscientious Objection,* 123–24.

26. Ibid., 317–19; J. A. Toews, *A History of the M.B. Church* (Hillsboro, Kans.: Mennonite Brethren Publishing House, 1975), 350–51.

27. Wherry, *Conscientious Objection,* 314–17.

28. Ibid., 326; U.S. Congress, Senate, *Hearing Before the Committee on Military Affairs United States Senate on S. 315 and S. 675,* 78th Cong., 1st sess., 1943, p. 15.

29. Coon, "Being a Peace Church," 155.

30. Wherry, *Conscientious Objection,* 87–88.

31. U.S. Congress, Senate, *Hearing on S. 315,* pp. 2–3.

32. Ibid., 16, 22.

33. Ibid., 19, 23.

34. Ibid., 23–25.

35. Ibid., 17.

36. Ibid., 20.

37. Ibid., 23.

38. Keim and Stoltzfus, *Politics and Conscience,* 132–34, 139, 145.

6

SHE NEVER WEAKENED:

The Heroism of Freda Ameringer

John Thompson

John Thompson is the author of the book Closing the Frontier: Radical Response in Oklahoma, 1889–1923, *which was published by the University of Oklahoma Press and won the Robert C. Atherton Prize from the Western History Association in 1988. He is currently working on a biography of Oklahoma City District Attorney Curtis Harris to be entitled* River of Fire: Curtis Harris vs. the Sixties. *In this essay, he tells the story of Freda Hogan Ameringer, who was married (in 1930) to the person often considered Oklahoma's leading Socialist, Oscar Ameringer; but, as Thompson makes clear, she made quite a contribution to the state's history in her own right as well.*

Oklahoma is a young state where young historians have the opportunity to come into contact with pioneers who were "present at creation" of the state of Oklahoma. Many scholars have come under the spell of historical figures who have greatly influenced their academic careers. Freda Ameringer had such an influence on me.

With the death of Freda Ameringer in 1988, a month before her ninety-sixth birthday, Oklahoma lost one of the bravest, wisest, and most determined crusaders in our history. Freda Ameringer was prominent in the rise of the Socialist party, the antiwar movement during World War I, the New Deal, the defeat of antilabor "right-to-work'' legislation, the Civil Rights movement, and the good fight for the Equal Rights Amendment, and she lived to admire Jesse Jackson and the Rainbow Coalition.

Freda frequently quoted her late husband, Oscar, whose autobiography culminated with the words, ''It's a great life—If you don't weaken!'' Freda never weakened. Her intellect, curiosity, humor, and commitment remained steadfast. Almost until the end of her life, she studied the *Washington Post Weekly,* the *Journal Record,* and (reluctantly) the *Daily Oklahoman,* and she would diagnose local and global developments with unique insights. Freda rehabilitated a broken shoulder, which was the result of a near fatal stroke at age ninety-three, so that she could get back to her typewriter. Freda observed that one thing that kept her alive was her desire to vote for Jesse Jackson for president and thus affirm the continuity of the democratic struggle that was her life's work.

In 1983 the University of Oklahoma Press reissued Oscar Ameringer's *If You Don't Weaken.* During an editorial session, James R. Green, who is one of the nation's top experts in early-twentieth-century history, and I tried to dissuade Freda on one seemingly minor point. Jim and I assumed that her memory was flawed on that detail, and we were dismayed by her stubbornness. Finally, Freda lost her patience and gave a ten-minute lecture, reinterpreting our discipline for us and demonstrating that we and most of our profession had misread this aspect of American labor history. I should add that Freda was the best editor involved with the project. After watching her teach us upstarts a few tricks of the trade, I teased her about wanting to go to work for the *Wall Street Journal,* which was opening a new plant in Oklahoma City. Freda laughed and acknowledged that she could teach them a few lessons.

Everyone who knew Freda had multiple stories illustrating her determination and wit. My favorites were of her polite but firm dealings with William (''Alfalfa Bill'') Murray and Senator Robert S. Kerr. Murray, the eccentric who inexplicably betrayed his progressive inclinations and became a vicious racist, anti-Semite, and Red-baiter, was a customer of Freda's at the *Leader* Press. (''And he was none too quick in paying his bills,'' Freda noted cryptically.) One day Murray offered to trade two of his books for one of Oscar's. Freda replied, ''I'll do it for old times sake, Governor, but you are getting the best of the bargain.'' Murray chuckled and replied, ''You are undoubtedly right. You are undoubtedly right.''

Freda said that she was temperamentally predisposed to radical-ism but that she eventually learned to work within the system. When she brought Eleanor Roosevelt to Oklahoma City to promote an effort to help inner-city children, Freda let others with more respect-ably moderate politics take the credit. When problems arose, however, as they did when Senator Kerr balked at buying a ticket, Freda took charge. Freda's friends can easily imagine her stern voice as she dealt with the situation, ''Senator Kerr, how would it sound if the senior senator showed disrespect to the President's widow?'' Kerr promptly donated ten dollars.

The following is a hybrid, a personal essay as well as an analysis of Oklahoma's cultural and political history. I hope that it will stim-ulate further discussion of our state's social history and fond memories in the people who knew and loved Freda Hogan Ameringer.

I

''It's a damned great life, if you don't weaken.''
(Freda Ameringer's paraphrase
of Oscar Ameringer)

Surveying the written legacy of Freda Ameringer's life was intellec-tually and emotionally confusing. My friend's archives included documentary evidence of the extreme political repression which destroyed her beloved Socialist party.[1] They also included House Concurrent Resolution 561, in which the Oklahoma legislature ''Commend(ed) Mrs. Freda Ameringer for her many contributions as a journalist; congratulating her for her numerous accom-plishments.''[2]

When surveying her files, I would read a personal note to Freda from Eugene V. Debs, the Socialist party's presidential candidate who was incarcerated for opposing World War I. Then I would read a handwritten thank you from Stanley Draper, manager of the Okla-homa City Chamber of Commerce. In 1919, Freda wrote Theodore Debs, brother of Eugene Debs, regarding their efforts to free Debs from federal prison, ''The war was too much without the incarceration of our comrades. . . . It would be easy to lose my socialist faith and become a raving anarchist."[3] In 1969 she persuasively spoke out for the Girl Scout camp "Cookieland."[4]

A more dispassionate historical analysis of Freda Ameringer lends insights into the nature of socialism and liberalism in Oklahoma. The lives of Freda Ameringer; her father, Dan Hogan; and Oscar Ameringer provide a case study into the political history of Oklahoma.

It would be easy to describe her political life as the story of a young zealot who abandoned her socialism as she matured into a liberal. Such an interpretation would fit nicely with the historical school that is still dominant in Oklahoma. Freda knew that mainstream historians would interpret her career in such a manner. Consequently, she explicitly and forcefully, in print and verbally, repudiated such a demeaning view of her work and the work of her comrades.

During the 1950s, American historians succumbed to the understandable, though myopic, tendency to dismiss radical political movements as primitive precursors to the modern liberal consensus. According to this theory, American Populists and Socialists were bigoted and atavistic rebels who could not come to grips with the modern world. Socialists did not survive, hence they were wrong.

This ethnocentric fallacy has been largely repudiated by social scientists. Unfortunately, Oklahoma historians still tend to dismiss radical political ideologies such as socialism as aberrant and immature. Even contemporary historians such as Wayne Morgan have lumped socialism with populism and the Ku Klux Klan as legacies of "modernization." The assumption was that Oklahoma could never produce a "real" Socialist movement. Obviously, the thousands of Oklahomans who voted Socialist did not understand modern politics.[5]

Freda Ameringer, however, came of age during the golden age of socialism in Oklahoma. She helped create a humanitarian, populistic, and intellectually sophisticated grass roots movement committed to racial and social justice. Her story should be remembered by any person who has struggled to balance his or her idealism with the dictates of political "reality."

II

"Industry of the People, By the People, and For the People."
(Oscar Ameringer's definition
of Industrial Democracy)

Freda Ameringer was born in 1892 in the coal mining town of Huntington, Arkansas. Among Freda's earliest memories were the "barbarism of the small town funeral." She frequently recounted how, "In your youth, you stood at a mine top, time after time, and saw charred bodies brought to the surface, weeping families huddled about."[6]

Freda's paternal grandmother, Alice Wiley, a daughter of a slaveholder and a Confederate Army officer, was an abolitionist from Mississippi. Freda recounted her grandmother's dedication to education as a means of changing society: "In her [grandmother's] backwoods home there had been more books than in all other homes combined for miles around. . . . It was the lack of educational advantages for her children which grieved her most. However, these children inherited her love of books and the passion for learning."[7]

Freda's father, Dan Hogan, and her mother, Lottie Yowell, created an environment that was equally stimulating and dedicated to social change. "Dan Hogan," wrote James Green, "published two Socialist newspapers and ran for state office several times. His daughter grew up working as a 'girl Friday' in the newspaper office, canvasing for her father's Socialist campaigns and listening to the stories she heard from visitors like Mother Jones and Eugene Debs. She was raised on Southwestern socialism."[8]

Freda was especially impressed that local coal miners, despite a life of exploitation and poverty, were drawn to "Shakespeare, Dickens, and other classics." She wrote, "Many a young miner boy or girl owes his first taste for good reading to that little frame office [her father's law office]." She also remembered that "Perhaps because they work alone . . . miners are good clear thinkers, and generous to a fault." Coal miners continually visited the office "to read newspapers, magazines and books Papa always had around—and to talk."[9]

Lottie Hogan also taught Freda values of neighborliness that were common in Huntington. Freda wrote, "My earliest memories of my Mother are seeing her prepare food—a kettle of soup, a chicken baked or stewed—for a sick neighbor." Freda also praised her mother's "solicitude of others, her interest in her community" and her mother's "going from door to door to collect dimes and quarters to provide for a family overtaken by misfortune." In numerous editorials and in personal conversations, Freda mentioned her mother's cooking and concern for neighbors as well as her love of plants and nature.[10] During the 1970s and 80s Freda, the feminist, recognized that her praise of her mother's domestic skills sounded sexist, but she often asserted that an appreciation of her mother's household abilities and neighborliness contributed to her socialism.

Another characteristic that Lottie Hogan shared with her community was her devout Christianity. Freda's father, on the other hand, was a skeptic, even if he was a pleasant one. "When the minister and his wife came to Sunday dinner," Freda reminisced, "Papa was the perfect host and when admonished about his need to be saved he reminded the minister that the unbelieving husband is sanctified by the believing wife."[11]

Dan Hogan brought this tolerant affability to his socialism. One of Freda's anecdotes exemplified his good-natured class consciousness: "Passing the cemetery once, Papa remarked how superior those resting beneath handsome monuments must feel to those whose resting place was marked by a simple tablet."[12]

Hogan was such a popular figure that he ran a strong gubernatorial campaign in 1914, the year when most Socialists saw a temporary drop in their support. That year, Hogan received 10,434 votes for governor of Arkansas. James Green determined that Hogan and Fred Holt of Oklahoma were "probably the only Socialist gubernatorial candidates in the country to poll more voters in 1914, than Debs [the Socialist presidential candidate] polled in 1912."[13]

Dan Hogan could be defiant, and he was willing to risk violence in extreme cases of self-defense. In 1914, coal miners were engaged in a bitter strike against the Bache-Denman Company and its armed guards when they heard of the Ludlow Massacre, in which thirteen miners and miners' family members were killed by the Colorado state militia. "Dan Hogan and his daughter Freda, who were prominent socialists in the area," wrote James Green, "addressed a large meeting of miners and their supporters." It was alleged that strike leaders on the platform with the Hogans threatened to "arm every miner in the Hartford Valley." Soon after, a crowd of one thousand engaged in "several clashes" with company guards, who were subsequently "routed." Green wrote: "An American flag was then hoisted over the mine tipple along with a banner which read: 'This Is Union Country.' "[14]

The key to Dan Hogan, however, was his perseverance. Freda described this quality saying, "I saw my father in about every environment—flushed with success or discouraged in the face of what seemed to be hopeless odds, addressing the applauding or hostile crowds, with good friends or bitter enemies. And he was always himself, always determined in his stand. And it was good to stand by his side."[15]

Never were the stands taken by Freda's father and mother more courageous than when they stood for racial justice. Freda was strongly influenced by her father's defenses of black defendants in capital cases. She frequently told the story of her father's saving the life of a black girl and how he and Lottie defied social norms by bringing the girl home to spend the night. After another case a young and penniless black defendant promised to repay Dan Hogan as soon as she was able for saving her life. Decades later she located Freda's father and paid her bill.[16]

At the age of sixteen, Freda began work with her father at the *Huntington Herald,* learning a full range of journalistic and organizational skills. Freda campaigned actively for woman suffrage. Freda worked as secretary of the Arkansas Socialist party, and she served on the Socialist party's national Women's Committee. Above all Freda "knew the Socialist rank and file and she knew the perilous world of publishing a radical newspaper in the Southwest."[17]

In 1917, Freda moved to Oklahoma, "where the schools were better," to assist Oscar Ameringer in organizing the Oklahoma Socialist party. Freda and Oscar made a great team. She was a salesperson without peer, and he was the charismatic leader of one of the strongest Socialist movements in American history.

Oscar Ameringer, the "Mark Twain of American socialism,"

brought an indefatigable wit and imagination to his lifelong campaign for social justice. James Green, the premier scholar of American Socialist history, attributed Ameringer's success as an organizer to his profound understanding of his adopted country. Green wrote that "Ameringer discovered industrial unionism, Jeffersonian democracy, and Mark Twain's humor before he studied Marxism. . . . He learned that Americans, for all their individualism, knew the value of solidarity, that they liked to hear someone who knew how to make fun of the rich and powerful."[18]

Oscar formulated a homegrown Marxism which he called "Industrial Democracy," or "Industry of the people, by the people, and for the people." He adjusted orthodox Socialist tenets to the conditions and the culture of Oklahoma. Ameringer stood firm against the temptation to gain temporary advantage by supporting "Jim Crow," or the American entry into World War I, and he kept the party neutral on religious issues.[19]

An awareness of Freda's, Dan Hogan's and Oscar Ameringer's Socialist ideology is important in interpreting the history of American political radicalism as well as Oklahoma history. The Hogans and Ameringers played a soothing role, trying to prevent sectarian divisions between Socialists. David Shannon summarized the varying leftist approaches. Moderates such as Victor Berger and Sidney Hillman placed more emphasis on orthodox political efforts, and they were more willing to compromise (Victor Berger even supported segregation as a necessary cost of political success). Daniel De Leon, William ("Big Bill") Haywood, and members of the Industrial Workers of the World (IWW) scorned electoral politics and were willing to engage in "direct action" to undermine capitalism.

In recent years, a cottage industry of historians categorizing the various Socialist beliefs of radical leaders has prospered. My reading of the Ameringers' socialism is that it was closest to that of Eugene V. Debs, who advocated "Industrial unionism in the economic field and militant Socialist agitation in the political field." A slightly different interpretation has been presented by James Green, who characterized Ameringer as a "Social democrat" and a "gradualist."[20]

Under either interpretation, Oscar's and Freda's socialism was squarely within the center of American Marxism, but they were often thought to be excessively moderate by Socialists in the radical state of Oklahoma. Their good relations with moderates like Berger and Hillman raised eyebrows of Oklahoma Socialists, who often leaned towards the stridency of Haywood and the IWW. Moreover, Oscar's unwillingness to use violence, except in clear cases of self-defense, was thought to be timid. Oscar, however, disarmed his critics with self-deprecating wit. Oscar said that there were two types of Socialists, "Red" Socialists and "Yellow" Socialists. Ameringer admitted to being a "Yellow" Socialist.[21]

Ameringer's "yellow" approach was a product of his ideals, his pragmatism, and his firsthand experience with "agent provocateurs." During the bitter New Orleans brewery workers' strike of 1907, Ameringer repeatedly vetoed calls for violence. Ameringer learned later that the leading advocate of deadly force was a Pinkerton detective who had a history of infiltrating union leadership and initiating violence that discredited labor.[22] (It is noteworthy that the personable Ameringer gained that important piece of intelligence by conversing with an opponent who he perceived to be honest and worthy.)

III

"This land shall not be sold forever, for this land is mine: and ye are sojourners with me."

(Leviticus 25:23 as quoted
in the Oklahoma Renters' Union creed)

In 1912, Eugene V. Debs, the Socialist candidate for president, received 16 percent of the vote in Oklahoma. Two years later, 21 percent of Oklahomans voted Socialist. In 1911, Ameringer received 23 percent of the vote in a three-way race for mayor of Oklahoma City. With the entry of the United States into the war in 1917, however, Socialists were subjected to political repression unsurpassed in American history. In 1918, Oscar came within a few hundred votes of being elected to Congress (in Wisconsin), and yet he barely escaped indictment for his antiwar writings.[23]

The destruction of the Oklahoma Socialist party was accomplished, in part, when "Red" Socialists ignored Oscar's counsel.

During the summer of 1917, a group of Socialist tenant farmers invited Ameringer to a clandestine meeting to plan the violent overthrow of capitalism. Ameringer told these naïve radicals:

From what I know about conspiracy, I wouldn't be in the least surprised if one of these informers was in this room right now. So for his benefit, and for that of the party at the receiving end of the dictaphone hidden behind some object in this room, here is where I stand: I am convinced beyond the slightest shadow of a doubt that the American people did not want this war. . . . I believe this war was foisted on the American people by their lying press, politicians, warmongers and munitions manufacturers. . . . But now that the gory die is cast, the only thing any of us can do is to work for a speedy peace through all the legal and constitutional means still open to us.[24]

The wisdom of Ameringer's patience was proven to be correct. The "Reds" initiated the infamous Green Corn Rebellion in Hughes and Seminole counties. One thousand radical farmers were defeated in their attempt to march on Washington, D.C. It should be noted that one of the more intense advocates of violence, who perhaps was an agent provocateur, later appeared as a key witness for the prosecution of the rebels.[25]

The ultimate defeat of antiwar Socialists should not overshadow the creativity of their efforts. Oscar, Dan Hogan, and Freda began publishing the *Daily Leader* in 1917, when left-wing publications were banned from the U.S. postal service. James Green has observed that publishing the *Leader* seemed to be foolhardy. Freda told Green that many of her comrades thought, "Well, we just ought to oil the machinery and wait until the conflagration is over." Freda was undeterred, however, because, "when you have a dream and a vision, your spirits get the necessary life."[26]

In 1917 and 1918, Freda shuttled between Oklahoma and Milwaukee, improvising creative political strategies. Oscar was especially eloquent in recounting the efforts of Freda, "[a 96-pound] slip of an Arkansas girl . . . trying to stop the World War." While working in Milwaukee, "we installed her near one of the main branches of the Milwaukee post office, where she carried on her subversive activity as our underground depository of whatever mail our friends among the postal employees could snitch.''[27]

Back in Oklahoma, Freda became the chief fundraiser for the *Leader* as well as the Milwaukee party. Repression faced by Oklahomans was even worse than that encountered by German-American Socialists in Wisconsin. Gangs of vigilantes criss-crossed rural Oklahoma, coercing farmers to purchase Liberty Bonds. Those who refused to buy bonds, and thus lend financial support to a war that they opposed, were beaten, tarred, and feathered.[28]

Freda recognized that the independent, strong-willed farmers who had been bullied into buying those ''Marks of Cain'' were embarrassed about being intimidated. Consequently, Freda was able to talk them into donating their Liberty Bonds. Oscar described the precarious financial condition of the *Leader* Press and Freda's imaginative efforts to save it:

Under these circumstances any sane businessman or firm would have welcomed bankruptcy with open arms. But worldsavers are not good businessmen, which may explain why they have outlived so many sets of cool, calculating businessmen. . . . We used to hand out two to three thousand dollars in pay checks three minutes before noon, Saturdays (banks closed at twelve on Saturdays), and then frantically rush for the already cranked Ford in a wild scramble to get the money in the bank before it opened at nine o'clock Monday morning. . . . My companion in these wild sallies was Freda. . . . If there was still a Liberty Bond at large, she knew exactly where it was.[29]

At the end of one of those sallies, wrote Oscar, Freda saved the newspaper by soliciting a donation from a farmer in Medford named Fred. ''Fred didn't even have a dollar in the bank. [But Fred said] 'Over there right under the floor, in a tin box, let's see what I can find for you, Comrades.' What Comrade Fred dug out was the missing thousand dollars. The world was saved for seven days more.'' Oscar then described his coworker Freda: ''Toward three, Sunday morning, with Freda sleeping exhausted on the back seat, I drove into Oklahoma City. I thought of the many good people and also of the still more numerous crooked people who were accusing us in those days of keeping going by means of Moscow gold. It was gold that kept us going, all right: gold smelted in the crucible of a noble ideal and by the fire of faith. But it didn't come from Moscow.''

IV

"The art by which politicians obtain campaign contributions from the rich and votes from the poor on the pretext of protecting each from the other."

(Oscar Ameringer's
definition of politics)

Despite violence, economic discrimination, censorship, and electoral fraud, Socialists recovered from the challenge of World War I and led a progressive coalition which resulted in the election of John C. (''Our Jack'') Walton as governor in 1922. The Walton administration was a failure, and the Socialist party disappeared.[30]

The manner in which Socialists met their final defeat, through betrayal by Walton, made their losses especially bitter. Even so, both Oscar and Freda responded with humor. Oscar used the experience to formulate his definition of politics, as quoted above.[31]

The Walton debacle also gave Freda a bittersweet anecdote which she frequently used to illustrate the need for education in a democracy. When the Socialists broke with Walton (which happened early in his administration), Freda's father printed a passage from Robert Browning in the *Leader:* ''Just for a handful of silver he left us, Just for a riband to stick in his coat.'' When Walton read the headline, he commanded his secretary, ''Go find out who this son-of-a-bitch Browning is and give him some sort of job that will close his mouth.''[32]

During the 1920s, Freda and Oscar Ameringer witnessed the near total collapse of political radicalism in Oklahoma. A major reason for the defeat of leftist alternatives was bitter conflicts within the Socialist movement. Oscar Ameringer and Dan Hogan unsuccessfully sought to prevent divisiveness. Dan Hogan told the 1919 Socialist party congress that Americans should ''give unqualified support to Soviet Russia,'' but he counseled against applying ''Russian methods for Americans.'' In his classic study of the failure of socialism in America, James Weinstein blamed the decline of the left on sectarian conflicts. Weinstein bemoaned the fact that "large sections of the Party had already done what Hogan warned against."[33]

Ameringer presented a similar interpretation of the fall of the Socialist party. Oscar, however, phrased his explanation in a more colloquial manner, writing that the movement broke into "right wings, left wings and winglets of wings, and most of them attached to dead birds."[34]

The defeat of socialism was doubly bitter because it was part of the destruction of the entire spectrum of political progressivism in Oklahoma. In *Closing the Frontier,* I recounted the rise of three varieties of radical thought which grew out of the Oklahoma frontier. The sober conclusion of my analysis was: "Within a generation three sets of political alliances failed in their attempt to challenge the capitalists' approach to building a new society. The fact that the Populists, the Socialists, and the neopopulists were crushed, dispersed, and, for the most part, forgotten should not, however, tarnish the memory of their brief battle. Oklahomans who are especially nostalgic for the prairies and the hills as they were before their exploitation, should also remember the political cultures that were sacrificed."[35]

Such a pessimistic analysis must be considered within the context of the euphoria of Socialists in frontier Oklahoma. Oscar Ameringer had joked previously that pessimistic Socialists, who had been called "impossiblists," had doubted that the "cooperative commonwealth" could be established in Oklahoma before 1916. Even if the Ameringers and their comrades had not transformed the world, their efforts in the dark days of the 1920s and '30s were impressive by any other comparison. During that period Freda and Oscar built remarkable careers as Socialist journalists and as troubleshooting reformers. Both efforts cast light on the constructive nature of Oklahoma socialism.

In 1931, the *Oklahoma Leader* changed its name to the *American Guardian.* For the next seventeen years Oscar edited the nationally and internationally respected newspaper. Most of the fifty-six thousand subscribers of the *American Guardian* lived outside of Oklahoma, and its editorial policy reflected their concerns.[36]

The respect which the *Leader* and the *American Guardian* earned was insufficient by itself to insure the profitability of the *Leader* Press. From 1922 to 1931, the press survived by printing the *Illinois Miner*. Oscar edited the *Miner* and wrote a column of political satire under the nom de plume of "Adam Coaldigger." "Of course the *Illinois Miner* crusaded for the new social order," wrote Oscar, "but we did it without employing the stock phrases of Marxism. Such strange words as 'proletariat,' 'bourgeoisie,' and the rest of the old-line socialist patter never appeared in this American-language labor paper."[37]

When the antisocialist John L. Lewis gained control of the Illinois Miners Union, Ameringer's contract was canceled. Freda and her father were able to make up for that loss by establishing a weekly controlled-circulation local newspaper, the *Oklahoma City Advertiser*.[38]

The *Advertiser* provided "timely commercial advertising and information" to the community. It began as a four-page periodical containing over 80 percent advertising. Although the *Advertiser* could hardly be described as Socialist, it was an innovation designed to break the stranglehold of monopoly journalism which characterized the nation, and especially Oklahoma. The first editions were delivered at no cost within a relatively small geographical area. By 1933, the *Advertiser* had forty thousand paid subscribers.[39]

While Oscar's *American Guardian* concentrated on national and international issues from a Socialist perspective, the *Advertiser* analyzed local politics from a liberal perspective. In 1933, the *Advertiser* initiated a muckraking series, "The History of Oklahoma Natural Gas Co."[40] In 1935 it helped lead the unsuccessful fight against the probusiness terms of the proposed twenty-five-year franchise of the utility. Other progressive issues championed by the *Advertiser* during the 1930s included reform of higher education, the protection of veterans' benefits, and affordable health-care insurance. The *Advertiser's* other articles ranged from political humor and book and theater reviews to local sports and "Mrs. Hogan's Home Recipes," written by Freda's mother.[41]

The *Advertiser* should not be considered a major break from the Ameringers' earlier socialism. Their earlier success had been based, in large part, in flexibility and a respect for the concerns of their constituencies. Moreover, the *Advertiser* promoted small business while condemning monopoly. Its good-humored and innovative support of small businessmen was consistent with the logic that Oscar had once employed in persuading a crowd in Clinton, Oklahoma, which was largely comprised of members of the Ku Klux Klan, to vote unanimously that they, not Ameringer, were crazy. He had pointed out that small farmers who voted Socialist were the natural allies of small businessmen. The merchants then agreed that they were crazy to support the Klan in terrorizing farmers and thus driving their business to mail-order firms like Sears.[42]

When explaining the strategy and operation of the *Advertiser* to the typesetter's union, Freda attributed the newspaper's philosophy to that of Sidney Hillman, a family friend and the Socialist president of the Amalgamated Clothing Workers. Hillman's union "recognized a community of interests (of workers) with employers . . . going so far as to send its engineers and experts to ferret out waste and inefficiency." Organized labor could better create prosperity because, "We [union members] come from thrifty families, brought up to make jelly from apple peelings and cores. . . . Where are the cores and peelings we might save in our operation by working more closely together? Those on the job are in a better position than any one else to see leaks, waste, which might be stopped."[43]

The issue was more than efficiency, however. Freda never surrendered to the "bread and butter" unionism of John L. Lewis, who limited labor's efforts to increasing wages and benefits. Freda was committed to the early radical, often Socialist, organized labor of the early years whose goal was peace and justice. Freda acknowledged that by the 1930s economic repression and political realities made it foolhardy to advocate a "cooperative commonwealth," but she argued that labor could best help itself by remembering: "Early trade unionists had a vision for those who would come after them. . . . As they labored to build up their own miserable standards of living, for the right to call their souls their own, they still found time to work for free public schools and libraries. . . . I am one who believes that the best answer to attempted brainwashing against unions is the performance of unions themselves in their community's affairs."[44]

A few years later, when unions were even more besieged, Freda summarized her sense of the mission of organized labor: "Our

children's children and those who come after them will either be
grateful for our foresight or face harder problems. . . . A labor
movement which gives consideration and support to community
needs may better expect the community's understanding of its own
problems and aims."[45]

Although Freda and Oscar were best described as Debsian socialists, more radical than reformers like Sidney Hillman and Victor
Berger, though more moderate than Bill Haywood and the Industrial
Workers of the World, the pragmatic aspects of their ideology inevitably led to compromise and reformism. Given the poor status of
socialism today, debates over "how socialist was the socialism of
the Ameringers?" are not especially pressing. Any analysis of their
activities in the 1930s, though, must make a stab at addressing such
a question. Moreover, in numerous personal conversations Freda
told me of the distress she felt when it was suggested that her socialism had evolved into liberalism.

Freda spent a great deal of effort debating the mixture of socialism and reformism in her and Oscar's ideologies. Freda said that she
had been more radical than Oscar during the heyday of Oklahoma
socialism. During the New Deal, however, they switched.

Oscar once participated in an agricultural relocation project,
under the auspices of the New Deal's Resettlement Administration,
which resulted in little except Oscar's hilarious account of governmental bureaucracy. Oscar wrote, "What right had I, an old Red, to
scorn red tape?" Even so, the "alphabet soup" of New Deal paperwork got the best of his resettlement effort, and only one hundred
families were benefited.[46]

A second reason why Freda came to be supportive of Roosevelt
was the role of Eleanor Roosevelt in raising the consciousness of her
husband, Franklin. A division of labor evolved in Oscar's and
Freda's careers, with Oscar concentrating on national and international debates and Freda concentrating on winning local campaigns.
Freda needed respectable allies, and Eleanor Roosevelt was ideal.

Oscar, however, grew increasingly preoccupied with opposition
to war. Oscar, whose German heritage and personal loss during
World War I (his son was gassed and left shell-shocked during the
battle of the Argonne Forest) made him irrevocably antiwar, condemned nazism, communism, and Roosevelt's efforts to lead

America into World War II. (In the last issue of the *American Guardian* dated December 15, 1941, Ameringer acknowledged that war was the only way to defeat Hitler.)[47]

Oklahoma socialism during its golden age was a grassroots movement, growing from the state's frontier culture. The Socialist leadership merely harnessed and organized that indigenous ideology. During the 1930s Oklahoma continued to produce a variety of homegrown leftwing political efforts, but they never came close to victory. During the Great Depression, which James Green has called "the Indian Summer of Oklahoma Socialism," the effectiveness of the left was the result not of a strong organization, but of the personal charisma and contacts of the Ameringers.

In retrospect, the influence of the Ameringers, who no longer represented a potent political party, is remarkable. For example, the Southern Tenant Farmers' Union (STFU), which with the help of Eleanor Roosevelt was to become the key to protecting the interests of southern sharecroppers, was inspired by Oscar's writing. (H. L. Mitchell, the cofounder of the STFU, decided to organize tenants while reading Ameringer's Renters' Union creed while sitting in his outhouse.)[48]

The power of the Ameringers' words and ideas were reinforced by their network of personal contacts. The Ameringers' colleagues included Carl Sandburg, Edward R. Murrow, Supreme Court Justice Louis Brandeis, Roger Baldwin, Carry McWilliams, Eleanor Roosevelt, and others.[49]

Freda's and Oscar's personal influences were prolonged by their willingness to subordinate political differences to their genuine love of their neighbors, even their enemies. Despite the extreme antipathy of Edward K. Gaylord, owner of the *Daily Oklahoman,* to progressivism of any type, the Ameringers remained on good personal terms with the newspaper's staff. One day when Gaylord was out of town a senior editor smuggled Oscar into the office, and Ameringer spent the afternoon holding the staff spellbound with hilarious anecdotes.[50] Another senior editor of the *Oklahoman* found himself abandoned by his friends when he delayed medical treatment for his daughter because of his beliefs in Christian Science. (He eventually relented and brought his daughter to the doctor, but because of the delay, she died. His fellow church members spurned

him for relenting, while his other friends attacked him for sacrific-
ing his daughter.) Oscar was one of the few persons who did not
condemn the editor, and he wrote his bitter enemy a kind personal
note.[51]

During the early 1940s Oscar was slowed by illness, and he died
in 1943. Perhaps the most telling tribute to Oscar's charm and compassion was the eulogy in the *Daily Oklahoman,* "He Hated No
Man." In response to Oscar's compassion, Luther Harrison, the
conservative editor of the *Daily Oklahoman,* wrote, "Probably the
man did not even know how to hate a human being."[52]

V

"Step by step, the longest march can be won."
(Freda Ameringer's reason for a campaign
for an Oklahoma City earnings tax.)

James Green wrote of Freda's career after Oscar's death:

Oscar's widow Freda who shared his quality of humor, carried on the
struggle. She continued to operate the *Leader-Guardian* plant as the last
union print shop in town until 1972. She published the *Advertiser* until
1968 and made it a curious blend of commercial advertising and progressive editorializing, a "kind of community conscience" for Oklahoma City,
as she put it. The socialist Party was no longer a "sort of home," as it had
been, but she became very active in women's clubs and in the YWCA, the
only place blacks and whites could meet together in Oklahoma City for
many years. She was a founder of the Urban League in 1946, and worked
with the organization "in the early hard days." She views her civil rights
work as a continuation of Oscar's fight in 1910 against the grandfather
clause amendment. Freda Ameringer was also a leader of a civic club effort
to create more public parks in the city, a reform she was committed to by
the Milwaukee socialists.[53]

With Oscar's death, Freda continued their effort to subordinate
political conflict to personal compassion as well as her side of their
division of labor, which resulted in Freda concentrating on local
issues. For the next forty years Freda subordinated her disappoint-

ment with the failure of socialism by waging relentless campaigns to improve the quality of life in Oklahoma.

During the next four decades Freda was known primarily as a "liberal." It could be argued, however, that liberalism in post–World War II Oklahoma was more unpopular than Marxism was in frontier Oklahoma. It was not as dangerous to be a liberal in modern Oklahoma as it was to be a Socialist in the state's early years, but it was more lonely. Early Socialists faced repression because of the popularity and potency of their message, while modern liberals were ignored because of their small numbers and lack of influence.

Freda loved to philosophize about her socialism and the limits of liberalism, but she did not let those theoretical concerns interfere with her effectiveness. She explained her persistence with wry humor. "The late Charles Beard, noted American historian, threatened to resign from the human race," mused Freda, challenging cynics to provide a better alternative to her pragmatism.[54] In a more serious editorial Freda quoted Martin Luther: "If I knew the world would end tomorrow, I would still plant my apple tree."[55]

Among the "apple trees" that Freda helped plant were the Oklahoma City Pilot Club, which raised one hundred thousand dollars (in 1946 dollars) to serve forty-five hundred inner-city children; the Willard Neighborhood Center and eight other community centers for children of the slums that were immortalized in Carry McWilliams's *Ill Fairs the Land;* and the Oklahoma City Urban League and YWCA. Freda was especially committed to the United Way ("the only thing on which I agree with E. K. Gaylord"), UNICEF (the United Nations Children's Educational Fund), the Oklahoma County Library, and the Unitarian Church. These efforts won her the honor of the *Woman's Home Companion* "Clubwoman of the Year" in 1956.[56]

Most of these institutions were relatively uncontroversial, even in postwar Oklahoma, which featured an influential "lunatic" right. Freda did not shrink from more unpopular battles, however. Her commentaries were frequently devoted to praising the United Nations, the Supreme Court while Earl Warren was Chief Justice, President Lyndon Johnson's War on Poverty, local antipoverty efforts and the tax increases required to pay for them, and nuclear disarmament. Freda saw no value in needlessly antagonizing community leaders, but she never "hid her lamp under a bushel."[57]

While the vast majority of her editorials were conciliatory, Freda never ducked a fight. During the key political disputes of postwar Oklahoma, Freda's background in radical politics should have been clear to a sensitive reader. The *Advertiser* editorialized fervently for desegregation and against "right to work" and the urban renewal efforts advocated by the Oklahoma City Chamber of Commerce, while she supported slum clearance efforts designed with the help of the community.[58]

I was particularly interested in Freda's editorials on urban renewal because, during the 1980s, she and I had engaged in a prolonged debate over the revitalization of downtown Oklahoma City. Freda agreed with my complaints regarding the city's power structure, but she supported a compromise effort to rebuild a downtown cultural center. While studying Freda's archives I learned for the first time of her support for slum clearance efforts designed with the help of the community, which faced the opposition of the Chamber of Commerce. Freda sought to divert money from "bricks and mortar" redevelopment to public transportation. She wrote, "Let us not be content with fixing up down town for our pride and edification; but move on to programs for the benefit of everyone."[59]

Freda's most passionate campaign during her "liberal" period was her opposition to the *Daily Oklahoman* and its owner, E. K. Gaylord. Freda was a professional newspaperwoman who was "grieved" by the rise of newspaper monopolies and the resulting collapse of journalistic integrity. "We need to recognize new evidence," wrote Freda, "that daily newspapers except in extremely rare instances . . . are 'money machines' and look elsewhere for inspiration and leadership."[60]

As contemporary Oklahomans will attest, the damage caused by monopolies in journalism has been severe in Oklahoma City, with the dominance of the Oklahoma Publishing Company (OPUBCO) and WKY television and radio, which were also owned by Edward K. Gaylord. Today's Oklahomans would enjoy spunky *Advertiser* editorial statements such as the following: "The monopoly of daily newspapers at Fourth and Broadway [*The Daily Oklahoman* and the *Oklahoma City Times*] hit a new low." Friends and foes of Gaylord, wrote Freda, were equally dismayed "by the almost daily waves of nausea these [Gaylord's] editorials loose [which] were unpalatable alike to many in the camps of both the 'ins' and 'outs.' ''[61]

In another editorial Freda employed mockery, referring to "Mr. Gaylord's statement that he had been a registered Democrat for— was it 39 years or am I confusing the time period with Jack Benny's age?"[62]

Freda was further outraged when the *Oklahoman* called for a return to one of the more disgusting features of "Jim Crow" segregation. In a page one editorial, Freda wrote, "The editorial in *The Sunday Oklahoman*, 'Illiteracy at the Polls,' is worthy of Governor Wallace's staunchest segregationist supporters. . . . The *Oklahoman* editorial, of course, was for the prime purpose of heaping the same condemnation on President Johnson's administration that they have so relished from the days of Franklin D. Roosevelt. They just don't like administrations which are concerned with plain justice."[63]

Freda's wit was at its bitter peak in 1958 when Gaylord broke the typesetters' union at OPUBCO and discharged long-term employees. Freda wrote, "It would be interesting also to know why it has taken such an astute gentleman [Gaylord] so many years to know what wolves in sheep's clothing these pressmen are. For some of them were in the company's employ no less than 40 years. Too bad Gaylord never had time to see the movie *You Can't Take It With You*. Maybe it will be rerun on his T.V. station this summer."[64]

In 1962, Freda adopted a similar approach in countering one of Gaylord's frequent unsolicited sermons on Oklahoma's flaws, which he believed required an undiluted dose of capitalism. Freda wrote that Gaylord, the "Missionary to the savage Democrats of Oklahoma . . . made a gillion million bucks during 55 years of Democratic maladministration. . . . No telling what he could have accomplished if the Democrats hadn't been around holding him back."[65]

It must be remembered that Freda did not spare William Atkinson, owner of the *Oklahoma Journal*, which provided some competition to OPUBCO during the 1960s and '70s. Freda editorialized, "Mr. Atkinson has shopping centers, lumber yards, and real estate holdings. As for his policies, what are they?"[66]

A progressive resident of Oklahoma City who rereads the *Adver-tiser's* front-page editorials does so with joy that his city once had a person who dared to challenge the *Daily Oklahoman* and the conservative business elite. A historian must read those editorials in a more rigorous manner, however. A social scientist trying to be objective must question whether a distinctive legacy of early Oklahoma's Marxism was displayed in the *Advertiser*. Such a cold-hearted academician must reach an ambiguous conclusion.

A reader who did not know of Freda's Socialist past might conclude, with some justification, that the *Advertiser* was no more than a respectably progressive newspaper and that it occasionally fell short of being very liberal. For example, the *Advertiser* opposed the Vietnam War from an early date, but it was reluctant to attack Lyndon Johnson for fear that such criticism would provide support for Richard Nixon. Freda's praise of liberals such as Fred Harris and Mike Monroney was barely distinguishable from her commendations of Robert S. Kerr. A careful reader would note that she often tried to distance herself from Senator Kerr, but she must have known that her reservations about Oklahoma's senior senator would be missed by the average subscriber.[67]

Freda's desire to accentuate the positive was noticed by her fellow journalists, and even conservative newspapermen called her to task for it. Such attacks severely strained Freda's policy of concentrating on constructive efforts. One such jab, by Walter Harrison, led to an unprecedented counterattack. Harrison criticized Freda for shrinking from her Socialist past and losing the "guts" which Oscar and Dan Hogan always exhibited. Historians should be thankful for Harrison's challenge, because it forced Freda to put her personal feelings into print. Considering private conversations in which Freda had forcefully restated her faith in socialism and her frustration at having to work within the system to achieve results, I was not surprised to read her response to Harrison's nitpicking. Freda wrote: "To borrow Mr. Harrison's inelegant word, men and women may differ in their idea of what constitutes guts. Does it flatter the male animal to think that we are less able? . . . And for all the equipment that Mr. Harrison implies for himself, I don't believe I would have done some of the things he has done."

At that, Freda recounted a number of journalistic abuses that Harrison rubber-stamped while he worked for OPUBCO. The most revealing passage in Freda's broadside was her account of Dan Hogan's and Oscar Ameringer's legendary persistence:

The truth is that both my father and Oscar were weary and sick at heart in their last days. It is true that many of their ideas had come to be incorporated into the laws of the land; if tedious illness had not sapped their strength they might have found more comfort in this fact; but each was tired from the long fight, each believed he saw war clouds of the future, perhaps wars so devastating as to wipe out civilization itself. If mankind everywhere preferred to listen and follow the Walter Harrisons and the *Daily Oklahomans* what could they do?[68]

A historian reading such an exchange and recognizing the pragmatic yet idealistic nature of Oklahoma Socialists must also recognize other links of the *Advertiser* with Freda's radical past. Although the *Advertiser* was discrete, it was "radical" in the sense that Freda's editorials always returned to the "roots" of an issue. Her proclamations were uncompromising on the need for a humanistic education for all; the need to protect nature and to create gardens, parks, and other refuges for the human spirit; and a steadfast commitment to peace and justice. Occasionally Freda would offer a bit of political history, as she did when she compared Martin Luther King to her comrade, Eugene V. Debs.[69]

Freda justified her journalism of joy by quoting Robert Hutchins: "Politics is something more than power. It is the business of learning together how to achieve freedom, justice and the common good."[70] She recognized that her brand of politics, aimed at a revolutionary transformation of the human soul, was a slow process. Buried in an editorial supporting a library bond issue was a statement of her pragmatic political philosophy: "Politics, no less than life, is full of compromise. . . . The give and take we are told is necessary." Even so, we need activists who "are more interested in sowing ideas than in victory." Freda was confident that "often in hard unfeeling soil the pioneer plants his seed, perhaps watering them with his own bitter tears. But the day may come when he or his children or his children's children see these trees blossom into wide acceptance. . . . These hardy souls . . . keep alive the faith and soul of peoples; important not of itself alone but to victories which stretch ahead in the future."[71]

The *Advertiser* survived until 1968. By that time Freda's educated activism had been superseded by the ahistorical "New Left" of the sixties. Freda retired in 1972, and the old *Leader* Press survived only as the *Journal Record,* a competent business newspaper. Freda found solace, however, that Oscar's, Dan's, and her *American Guardian* had been taken over by Norman Thomas's *Progressive* magazine, meaning that one of their journalistic adventures still operated.

VI

"Primed with wisdom from another time."
(John McCutcheon)

When I first met Freda in 1977, she was extremely helpful to scholars, especially young ones. Freda was typically candid, but she did distinguish between sympathetic historians who were "sort of McGovern-type liberals" and Socialists such as James Green, Neil Basen, and myself.

James Green was the historian who was best able to balance his admiration for Freda with the discipline required of a social scientist. For that reason, the conclusion of Green's preface to *If You Don't Weaken* must be repeated in whole:

At the age of ninety Freda Ameringer has not weakened in her commitment to justice and equality. She is an outspoken critic of the New Right and the arms race and a well-known advocate of equal rights for women and minorities. She hopes that this edition of *If You Don't Weaken* will acquaint new generations of readers with Oscar Ameringer and his legacy, believing that the values he fought for are more important today than ever before. It may be that times have changed since Oscar put his intelligence and wit to work for democratic labor unions, for governmental honesty and racial harmony, for world peace, and for a cooperative alternative to monopoly capitalism that would save the family farmer and allow workers to achieve industrial democracy. But Freda Ameringer believes that the crusades he helped to start still need finishing. Indeed, in our own troubled times, when hopes for social change have given way to cynicism and fatalism, it might be useful to remember the words of an old idealistic Socialist who never lost faith in the people of his adopted land. Oscar closed his story with this sermon: "Before settling the troubles of distant lands, settle your own. If war there must be, make it war to the knife against poverty, disease, and ignorance at home. . . . You alone of all the countries of the earth have neared the land of promise. See that your gifts are neither hoarded by greed nor wasted in conquest and war, but are honestly distributed for the good of all. Close your glorious arch of religious and political freedom with the keystone of industrial democracy, be the cost what it may. For economic autocracy and political democracy cannot dwell under the same roof."[72]

If Freda had her way, this essay would end at that point, with the beautiful words of Oscar Ameringer. Freda, however, deserves tribute for her own eloquent and unfailing voice.

Freda Ameringer helped build a Socialist movement of such surprising strength that historians have pretended that it was not real. Her political party was destroyed so completely that today's Oklahomans have forgotten it. After witnessing those two unbelievable historical events, Freda knew firsthand that radical change is always possible. And she never despaired of passing that wisdom to subsequent generations.

Freda Ameringer enjoyed the lyrics of John McCutcheon, a contemporary folksinger. Because of her failed hearing, she could not hear the music, but she saw some of Oscar in this troubadour of today. I would read McCutcheon's and other progressives' lyrics to Freda, who especially loved the reminder that talented young people were continuing the struggle for peace and justice.

McCutcheon's song, "Water from Another Time," is about his grandmother. McCutcheon sang of the lessons his grandmother would pass down to him as they used an old rusty pump that was "primed with water from another time." His grandmother taught him:

> You don't take much, but you gotta have some,
> The old ways help, the new ways come,
> Leave a little extra for the next in line,
> Gonna need a little water from another time.

By the final verse it is clear that future generations must be sustained by more than the natural resources which must be conserved and preserved. I will never forget reading to Freda the closing refrain,

> Though Grandpa's hands have gone to dust,
> and Grandma's pump reduced to rust,
> Their stories quench my soul and mind,
> Like water from another time.

NOTES

1. "Howat-Holt, Prosecutive, Trial and Vindication" file, Freda Ameringer Collection, Oklahoma City, Okla. See also Oscar Ameringer, *If You Don't Weaken* (Norman: University of Oklahoma Press, 1983), 354–69; James Green, *Grassroots Socialism: Radical Movements in the Southwest* (Baton Rouge: Louisiana State University Press, 1978), 345–95.

2. Oklahoma, House, Concurrent Resolution No. 561, 31st Leg., 2d sess., Feb. 14, 1968.

3. Personal inscription in *Eugene Debs and the Poets,* in Freda Ameringer papers.

4. Jody Huffstetler to Freda Ameringer, attached to "The Scouter," Nov., 1989, Freda Ameringer Collection. See also *Oklahoma City Advertiser,* Mar. 18, 1965.

5. Wayne C. Morgan, *Oklahoma: A Bicentennial History* (New York: W. W. Norton, 1977), 93–117.

6. Freda Ameringer, undated, untitled manuscript, Ameringer papers, p. 2; Kay Blake, "Freda Ameringer, Editor-Publisher of the *Oklahoma City Advertiser*" (Undergraduate thesis, University of Oklahoma, 1959), 2.

7. *Oklahoma City Advertiser,* Apr. 20, 1961.

8. James Green, "Introduction," in Ameringer, *If You Don't Weaken,* xl.

9. *American Guardian,* Jan. 2, 1954; *Oklahoma City Advertiser,* Nov. 19, 1954.

10. *Oklahoma City Advertiser,* Oct. 13, 1960.

11. Freda Ameringer, untitled manuscript, presentation to Unitarian Church, p. 4, Ameringer papers.

12. *Oklahoma City Advertiser,* June 2, 1966.

13. Green, *Grassroots Socialism,* 292.

14. Ibid., 283–84.

15. *American Guardian,* Jan. 25, 1935.

16. *Oklahoma City Advertiser,* June 21, 1952; May 7, Oct. 4, 1957.

17. Green, "Introduction," xl.

18. Ibid., xxiii.

19. Ibid., xxxv–xxxvi, xxxviii–xxxix; Green, *Grassroots Socialism,* 102–109.

20. David Shannon, *Socialist Party in America* (New York: MacMillan, 1955), 17–36; Green, *Grassroots Socialism,* 154, 164.

21. Ameringer, *If You Don't Weaken,* 352–54; Green, "Introduction," xxxv–xxxviii.

22. Ameringer, *If You Don't Weaken,* 203–204, 207.

23. Green, "Introduction," xxxviii; Green, *Grassroots Socialism,* 186.

24. Green, "Introduction," xxxix; Ameringer, *If You Don't Weaken,* 353–54.

25. Ameringer, *If You Don't Weaken,* 355.

26. Green, "Introduction," xl.

27. Ameringer, *If You Don't Weaken,* 325.

28. James Fowler, "Tar and Feather Patriotism," *Chronicles of Oklahoma* 56, no. 1 (Winter 1978–79): 402–29.

29. Ameringer, *If You Don't Weaken,* 362–64.

30. Green, "Introduction," xlii.

31. Ameringer, *If You Don't Weaken,* 393.

32. *Oklahoma City Advertiser,* Jan. 16, 1959; Ameringer, *If You Don't Weaken,* 390.

33. James Weinstein, *The Decline of Socialism in America* (New York: Monthly Review Press, 1967), 161–62, 180–86.

34. Ameringer, *If You Don't Weaken,* 459.

35. John Thompson, *Closing the Frontier: Radical Response in Oklahoma, 1889–1923* (Norman: University of Oklahoma Press, 1986), 226.

36. Ameringer, *If You Don't Weaken,* 390; Green, "Introduction," xliii; Green, *Grassroots Socialism,* 413; Prospectus, *American Guardian,* 1936.

37. Ameringer, *If You Don't Weaken,* 400.

38. Ira Greenberg, "History of the Oklahoma City Advertiser" (Undergraduate thesis, University of Oklahoma, 1941), 9, 13; Green, "Introduction," xliii.

39. Greenberg, "Oklahoma City Advertiser," 11–16.

40. Ibid., 19–22.

41. Ibid., 28–30. See also *Oklahoma City Advertiser,* Aug. 18, 1966.

42. Ameringer, *If You Don't Weaken,* 366–69.

43. Freda Ameringer, unpublished, undated manuscript, presentation for the International Typesetters Union, 2–3.

44. Ibid.

45. *Oklahoma City Advertiser,* Nov. 18, 1955.

46. Ameringer, *If You Don't Weaken,* 421–45. See also Oscar Ameringer, "No Thoroughfare to Utopia," *Reader's Digest,* July 1940, pp. 13–17.

47. *Daily Oklahoman,* Oct. 27, 1941; Green, "Introduction," xliv.

48. Green, *Grassroots Socialism,* 433–35; H. L. Mitchell to Donald Henderson, Aug. 12, 1936, Southern Union Tenant Farmers' Union papers, North Carolina State University.

49. Prospectus, *American Guardian,* 1936; *Oklahoma City Advertiser,* Oct. 8, 1954; Nov. 15, 1962; personal conversations.

50. Personal conversation.

51. Ibid.

52. *Daily Oklahoman,* quoted in *Oklahoma City Advertiser,* Jan. 23, 1959.

53. Green, "Introduction," xlv–xlvi.

54. *Oklahoma City Advertiser,* Nov. 10, 1966.

55. Ibid., Aug. 20, 1959.

56. Blake, "Freda Ameringer," 16–20; Jean Lipman Block, "The Club-woman of the Year," *Woman's Home Companion,* 1956, pp. 3–4, 6–11; Freda Ameringer, unpublished, undated manuscript, Ameringer Collection, *Oklahoma City Advertiser,* Feb. 19, Apr. 23, July 23, 1954; Oct. 25, 1962; July 1, 1965; Feb. 21, Apr. 4, Oct. 7, Nov. 14, 1963.

57. *Oklahoma City Advertiser,* Feb. 26, Apr. 30, Dec. 12, 1954; Feb. 14, June 6, Aug. 8, 26, Sept. 5, 1963; Mar. 4, 11, 1965.

58. Ibid., Feb. 26, May 7, 1954; Feb. 18, 1955; May 15, 1962; Nov. 21, 1963; Mar. 3, 1965.

59. Ibid., Mar. 10, 1966.

60. Ibid., Aug. 26, 1965.

61. Ibid., Apr. 6, 1961.

62. Ibid., June 7, 1962.

63. Ibid., Aug. 19, 1965.

64. Ibid., June 27, 1958.

65. Ibid., Nov. 1, 1962.

66. Ibid., Aug. 26, 1965.

67. Ibid., Jan. 6, Mar. 3, 1966.

68. Ibid., July 31, 1953; personal note from Walter Harrison, Aug. 1, 1953, is attached.

69. *Oklahoma City Advertiser,* May 7, 1954; Feb. 18, 1955; Oct. 19, 1961; Aug. 2, 1962.

70. Ibid., June 25, 1964.

71. Ibid., Aug. 4, 1964.

72. Green, "Introduction," xlvi–xlvii.

7

WOBBLIES IN THE OIL FIELDS:

The Suppression of the Industrial Workers of the World in Oklahoma

Nigel Sellars

Nigel Sellars is a candidate for the Ph.D. in history at the University of Oklahoma. It was while listening to Sellars deliver an earlier version of this paper at the 1988 meeting of the Oklahoma Association of Professional Historians at El Reno Junior College that I first conceived of the idea of putting together a collection of alternative views of Oklahoma history. Thank you, Nigel, for the idea and the paper.

The black-robed and hooded mob was waiting when the nine Tulsa police officers escorted the seventeen IWW prisoners from city hall, heading for the county jail. It was just before midnight, November 9, 1917. At the intersection of First Street and Boulder Avenue, the forty-odd Knights of Liberty halted the police and took control of the prisoners. The officers offered no resistance.[1]

The vigilantes bound the prisoners' arms and legs, then drove them to a secluded ravine near Irving Place on Tulsa's west side. There, by the light of fires and the headlights of automobiles, the Knights of Liberty stripped their captives to the waist, tied them to

129

a tree, and lashed them repeatedly with what one prisoner said was "a double piece of new rope, five-eighths or three-quarters hemp." With each whip stroke, the leader of the mob said, "In the name of the outraged women and children of Belgium."[2]

When they finished the whipping, the vigilantes applied hot tar and feathers to their victims' backs. The torture completed, the Knights of Liberty released their prisoners and drove them into the Osage Hills, firing rifles and pistols over their heads.[3]

With one act of mob violence the businessmen and police officers who comprised the Knights of Liberty used the patriotic fervor of the American entry into World War I to drive the Industrial Workers of the World and their affiliated Oil Workers Industrial Union from Mid-Continent oil fields of Tulsa. The probusiness and fiercely patriotic Tulsa newspapers cheered the whippings, and the action was widely condoned throughout the western states where the IWW was active. It was, as the *Tulsa Democrat* reported, "a party, a real American party."[4]

The Tulsa Outrage, as the union called it, and the Green Corn Rebellion, an ill-fated August 1917 tenant farmers' revolt organized by the IWW-inspired Working Class Union led by former union member H. H. ("Rube") Munson, marked the end of the union's influence on the last American frontier and foreshadowed the final defeat of America's native syndicalist movement. For even as the state's oilmen and landowners declared open warfare on the IWW, federal prosecutors began a series of "disloyalty" trials against the union for its supposed opposition to American entry into World War I. Those trials, culminating in the Chicago trial of the IWW's national leadership, eventually broke the union. But before oilmen, landowners, and U.S. attorneys drove them down, the Wobblies made their presence known in Oklahoma, especially among the oil workers of the Mid-Continent field.[5]

Formed in Chicago in June 1905, the Industrial Workers of the World grew out of several existing radical trade unions, including the Western Federation of Miners and the United Brotherhood of Railway Employees. These unions, as historian Paul Brissenden noted, believed the existing craft unions, controlled by the more conservative American Federation of Labor, had become increasingly powerless to achieve real benefits for American workers.[6]

As an antidote, the IWW espoused industrial unionism, a philosophy in which all workers within a single industry would belong to one union that would provide for craft autonomy locally, industrial autonomy internationally, and working class unity overall.[7] The one big union called for class struggle above all, with no affiliation to any political party and with control in the hands of the collective membership. Its goal was a general strike of all workers which would produce a socialist America.

But the IWW itself hardly demonstrated the solidarity it championed and underwent several factional splits. Eventually a Chicago faction, led by Western Federation of Miners Secretary William D. ("Big Bill") Haywood, gained the upper hand. Inspired by French syndicalists such as Georges Sorel, the Chicago faction called for direct action, including sabotage and work slowdowns, to settle labor disputes. The endorsement of sabotage proved a fatal mistake for the union. While the union meant sabotage to include anything from work slowdowns to failure to maintain needed equipment, most people assumed it meant violence.[8]

The factionalism proved costly, reducing the union from forty thousand members to only seven thousand by 1914.[9] But the IWW found renewed strength in the "floaters," native-born migratory workers from the western states, especially the Pacific Coast. These workers were also called "bindlestiffs" or "bundlestiffs" because they carried a blanket roll slung by a cord around their shoulders.[10] The bindlestiffs rode the rails looking for work, usually as harvest hands cutting and threshing wheat or picking hops, as lumberjacks, or, later, as roughnecks or pipeline workers in the oil fields of Oklahoma and Texas.

Oklahoma, as a new state, attracted men like the bindlestiffs. Like the Pacific Coast, much of the work in the state was seasonal. Farm laborers began the wheat harvest in northern Texas and southern Oklahoma and followed the ripening grain north through Kansas, Nebraska, and the Dakotas and into Canada. Oil workers "followed the oil" as oil field after oil field was drained of its reserves. Because these workers were migratory, they lacked many of the political rights of other citizens, especially the vote. One oil worker, in a Federal Writers' Project interview, said most were never in a town long enough to register to vote. Another said most

moved on after only a few weeks or months. A similar fate befell
tenant farmers, despite the best efforts of the Oklahoma Socialist
party. While most tenants could theoretically vote, their need to
seek a better deal kept them moving from area to area. To these
people, the IWW and its ideology of direct action at the point of production offered a way to gain a better life. As some tenant farmers
told IWW organizer Frank Little in 1912, they were attracted to the
IWW's ideas because they could not see how politicians—even
Socialist politicians—could administer the hoped-for cooperative
commonwealth.[11]

Initially the IWW had some difficulties organizing in the state.
Oklahoma City Local 230 existed at least as early as February 1906
and attempted to organize at least some of the state's coal miners.
The local appears short-lived, because by November of the same
year members of the Wichita local had asked the union's General
Executive Board for organizers to work with hotel and bakery workers in Oklahoma City. A handful of workers remained when Frank
Little came to Oklahoma City to organize a local in 1912. But Little
apparently had no success, nor did an attempt to form an oil workers' local in Tulsa two years later.[12]

But by 1917 the IWW-affiliated Agricultural Workers Organization (AWO) No. 400 had succeeded in organizing migrant harvest
workers from Oklahoma to Manitoba, Canada, and virtually controlled the labor market in the midwestern wheat belt with its
"2,000 mile long picket line." The largest union in the IWW
increased its influence when some Tulsa oil workers requested a
charter from the AWO in either December 1916 or January 1917.
The Tulsans become one of the first locals of the Oil Workers Industrial Union No. 450.[13] The Chicago headquarters appointed Arthur
Boose as the local's secretary.

Boose, known as the Old War Horse, was a veteran organizer
who worked among the Finnish iron miners in the Mesabi range of
northern Minnesota. He fled to Oklahoma after Minnesota authorities indicted him and four other Wobblies on a trumped-up murder
charge. Boose, under the name Arthur Fritz, was driving a team on
railroad construction jobs when the union's General Executive
Board told him to go to Tulsa.[14]

Under Boose's guidance, the local's members, although few in

number, began work in the Glen Pool and Cushing fields west of
Tulsa, both of which were part of the huge Mid-Continent field.
Almost immediately the union was perceived as a threat by Tulsa's
oil industry, predominantly controlled by the Standard Oil Company. Standard Oil owned Prairie Oil and Gas and Carter Oil, both
active in the state.[15] As novelist Upton Sinclair remarked, ''In Oklahoma, everything is Standard Oil.''[16]

Like most labor-intensive enterprises which rely on keeping
wages low to keep profits high, Oklahoma's petroleum industry
hated unions. The editor of the industry's *Oil and Gas Journal*
wrote with unbridled sarcasm of earlier organizing efforts by the
American Federation of Labor. He claimed that if oil companies
gave in to worker demands, they might as well ''plant flowers
around the derricks, put in swimming pools on the leases, and open
club rooms and other forms of amusement.''[17]

The sarcasm masked a painful truth: working conditions in Oklahoma oil camps were dreadful at best. Several Department of Mines
reports indicate they were unsanitary and both disease- and crime-
ridden.[18] But despite bad working conditions, there was no shortage
of workers. Then as now, migrant workers came to the oil field for
the good wages, not the working conditions. By 1917 the going
wage was was thirty-five to forty cents an hour for a ten- to twelve-
hour day. By comparison, harvest workers then earned $1.50 to
$2.50 a day, and some were paid in two bushels of wheat a day,
worth about fifty cents a bushel.[19]

Despite the good wages most oil workers received, the oil workers' union seems to have had early success, especially in organizing
pipeline workers and storage-tank builders. A miniature free-speech
fight, similar to those organized by the IWW in San Diego and Spokane, broke out on February 6, 1917, in Drumright. Three days
later Drumright authorities fined Boose twenty-five dollars and costs
for contempt, but he was released on bond. The *Drumright News*
estimated fifty Wobblies crowded into the small courtroom.[20]

Also in February, oil workers struck for higher wages in Vinita.
Drumright had its own union branch as of March 20, and by April,
New Wilson and Healdton also possessed locals. Sporadic strikes
followed throughout the year, including an August strike of twenty-
three workers, five of them Wobblies, in Hominy. The five lost their

jobs when the eighteen other workers returned to work.[21] In Tulsa, the Home Refining Company blamed the IWW for a wage strike at its refinery. The workers requested a fifteen-cent-an-hour raise to fifty cents an hour, a request which the company refused.[22] The local sheriff's office sent special deputies "to suppress any demonstration of a hostile nature."[23]

The tension between the oil workers' union and the oil companies rose throughout the summer, fed by press reports of radical actions elsewhere in the state and across the nation. While the American press as a whole did its best to attack the IWW and the leftist movement in general, the Oklahoma press and the Tulsa papers in particular were especially slavish. At its annual meeting in 1917, the Oklahoma Press Association sent a message to the Oklahoma congressional delegation, pledging its members' loyalty to the war effort.[24]

Oklahoma had more than its share of prowar violence, including the murders of several people who expressed antiwar sentiments and the burning of a German-owned building in Muskogee.[25] But fear of the IWW seemed the greatest spur to the zealots. Most officials apparently took to heart Arizona Senator Harry Ashurst's claims of German sponsorship of the IWW, whom he called "Imperial Wilhelm's Warriors."[26]

Ashurst's charge was ridiculous. The majority of the Wobblies were native-born Americans, and, unlike the Socialist party, the IWW took no stand against the war. In fact, about 95 percent of all union members registered with draft boards. Most Wobblies served when called up, although admittedly, some did so to foment antimilitarism from within.[27]

But the truth failed to stop John B. Meserve, a member of the Oklahoma Council of Defense, from claiming that the Wobblies had sent their most vigorous organizers to Tulsa "to destroy the waterworks and simultaneously place incendiary bombs in various parts of the city," or an Enid resident from saying that two million IWW members were plotting to overthrow the government.[28] The state's newspapers dutifully reported such rumors as fact, and the prowar sentiment thus generated proved an effective union-busting tool. The failure of the tenant farmers' revolt known as the Green Corn

Rebellion, with its tenuous IWW connections, only added fuel to the press's jingoism.

While the papers attacked the IWW, the Wobblies fought back with some "free press" action of their own. IWW stickers known as "silent agitators" soon became a familiar sight in Tulsa. The eye-catching gummed-label stickers urged workers to organize or "Slow Down. The hours are long, the pay is small, so take your time and buck 'em all." Others displayed the wooden shoe or the sabo-tabby cat, euphemisms for sabotage. Opponents said such stickers and flyers subverted the war effort. *Harlow's Weekly* printed an alleged IWW flyer which called for workers to join the IWW and refuse to be drafted.[29]

But the stickers were feeble responses to the virulent attacks of the *Tulsa World*. Of the three white, probusiness Tulsa papers—the *Times,* the *Democrat,* and the *World*—the *World* was the most pro–oil industry, prowar, racist, antiforeigner and antilabor. Its hatred for the IWW, which is repeatedly called "German bought and German controlled," was extreme, to say the least. An August 9, 1917, editorial suggested it was the *World* which linked the Green Corn Rebellion to the IWW and charged the Wobblies with being "nothing less than emissaries of the enemy seeking to cripple the energies of the nation by an attack from behind."[30]

When on October 29, 1917, a bomb exploded at the home of J. Edgar Pew, a manager for the Carter Oil Company, the *World* fired the first volley that would lead to the Tulsa Outrage. Its page-one headline cried, "I.W.W. Plot Breaks Prematurely in Blowing Up of Pew Residence," and citing "unimpeachable sources," the paper claimed the bomb was part of a general IWW conspiracy that included a general strike and destruction of property. A front-page message also called on 250 men to join the Tulsa Home Guards, a local militia intended to protect the city from German attack.[31]

Tulsa police arrested oil worker W. J. Powers for questioning four hours after the bombing. The *World* claimed that Powers was caught trying to leave town and that his denials that he was an IWW member only proved he was. The paper also claimed itself to be an IWW bomb target, citing four letters allegedly from the IWW which called for the "downfall of certain capitalist newspapers."[32]

On October 31 the paper, spurred on by a subsequent refinery explosion and by IWW-inspired oil workers' strikes in Texas and Louisiana, began endorsing vigilante actions against political radicals. Naturally, it reserved its harshest words for the IWW. The *World*'s editorial writer suggested either placing Wobblies in concentration camps or lynching them. "What is hemp worth now, the long foot?" the editorial asked.[33]

A week after the Pew bombing, on November 5, 1917, the Tulsa police, without a search warrant, raided the IWW offices in the New Fox Building on Brady Street. It was the third time in two months that the hall had been raided. On September 5, federal agents seized literature, letters, and the local's day book in one of a series of raids nationwide ordered by U.S. Attorney General A. Mitchell Palmer. The material taken later figured in indictments in Chicago and Wichita.[34]

The agents made no arrests on that September day, although they made up for it on September 28 when three federal agents attended one of Boose's educational talks in the Wobbly Hall and arrested him afterward. Boose later recalled that he was charged as a fugitive from the bogus Minnesota murder charge and "with almost every crime I had ever heard of, including lack of what is commonly called patriotism." The authorities extradited the Old War Horse to Chicago, where he joined Bill Haywood and 164 other Wobblies facing charges of conspiracy to obstruct the war effort.[35]

But while the two September 1917 raids were carried out by federal agents with a larger objective in mind, the November raid was clearly a local effort intended to destroy the oil workers' union once and for all. When E. M. Boyd, a pipeline worker who had replaced Boose as local secretary, told police the union paid rent for the hall and asked to see a warrant, an officer "replied he did not give a damn if we were paying rent for four places [as] they would search them whenever they felt like it." Even though police found no incriminating material, they arrested the eleven men present on vagrancy complaints and jailed them. A city judge placed the Wobblies under the highest bond permitted by state law. The vagrancy charge was patent nonsense, especially because one prisoner was a local printer and another was employed by a Tulsa plumber.[36]

The *World* proclaimed that war had been declared on the IWW, and a Tulsa police captain promised to arrest any men found loitering near the IWW offices and to send them back to jail again and again. They backed up the claim with an additional arrest on November 6.[37]

The twelve men were brought to trial on November 8, 1917 before Municipal Judge T. D. Evans, who was later Tulsa's mayor during the city's 1921 race riot. In a bizarre proceeding for a municipal vagrancy trial, prosecutors tried to learn the attitudes of the prisoners and defense witnesses toward the government and its war policies. Defense attorney Charles Richardson argued that city authorities failed to show any misconduct on the Wobblies' part. Richardson said the IWW was harassed because it was "the only fraternal society in the country which requires that every man, before being accepted, shall establish the fact that he is a bona fide worker and wage earner."[38] After five hours, Evans adjourned the trial until the next afternoon.

Disappointed at the lack of sensational information from the trial, the *World* unleashed its most virulent anti-IWW attack yet. The unsigned editorial, probably written by either Managing Editor Eugene Lorton or Senior Editor Glenn H. Congdon, was entitled "Get Out the Hemp." The editorial openly called for lynching Wobblies and claimed that "a knowledge of how to tie a knot that will stick might come in handy in a few days." The editorial writer justified the remarks by saying the IWW was an enemy of the country and threatened the production of petroleum needed for the war effort. In order to defeat Germany, true patriotic Americans had "to strangle the I.W.W.'s. Kill 'em just as you would kill any other kind of snake. Don't scotch 'em; kill 'em. And kill 'em dead. It is no time to waste money on trials and continuances like that. All that is necessary is the evidence and a firing squad. Probably the carpenters' union will contribute the timber for the coffins."[39]

When the trial resumed that day, the prosecutors rested their case solely on the fact that the defendants were IWW members. None of the men had criminal records, and police failed to tie them to the Pew bombing. In fact, one defendant, Bernard Johnson, had been in Tulsa only three days. However, when the trial ended at 10:30 P.M., Johnson was found guilty of not owning a Liberty Bond. The other eleven had previously agreed that the decision in his case would apply to them all. Then Judge Evans ordered five witnesses arrested, tried them, and found them guilty. All the men were fined one hundred dollars. In justifying his action, Evans said, "These are no ordinary times."[40]

The Knights of Liberty were waiting when the police led the men from the city jail. That prominent businessmen comprised the mob and had police cooperation seems indisputable. The police said they could not identify any mob member, but Boyd, the IWW secretary, in testimony to National Civil Liberties Bureau investigators, said the vigilantes provided police chief E. L. Lucas and a detective named Blaine with robes. Boyd said six of the prisoners knew both policemen quite well.[41] Haywood said the mob included members of the Tulsa Commercial Club, while a lieutenant in the Tulsa Home Guard admitted that the Knights of Liberty obtained their weapons from the guard's arsenal. As Deputy United States Marshal John Moran said, "You would be surprised at the prominent men in this town who were in this mob."[42]

The white Tulsa press received advanced notice. The *World*'s managing editor, Glenn Congdon, and his wife went along as spectators.[43] A *Tulsa Times* reporter said the Knights, resembling Ku Klux Klansmen, provided "a picturesque scene."[44]

The day after the floggings, the police continued their crackdown on the IWW, promising to arrest members as soon as they were discovered. When one of the seventeen prisoners was arrested in nearby Sand Springs, Tulsa police told the Sand Springs police chief to "turn him loose and tell him to keep going—away from Tulsa." The police also shut down the IWW hall on Brady Street, a fairly moot act, as the remaining oil workers' union members, obviously fearing for their safety, had fled to the IWW local in Augusta, Kansas, to regroup.[45]

Attacks on the IWW also continued in the press. Two days after the incident, the *World* praised the Knights of Liberty as a "patriotic body." It called on every citizen to keep an eye on his neighbor lest he show unpatriotic tendencies, a theme it continued throughout the month. The *Daily Oklahoman*, while calling the Tulsa act "a rather highhanded proceeding," also weighed in against the IWW, saying Wobbly "treason is common knowledge. The black treachery of it defies words." The editorial concluded that the state had trees, "rope in plenty and the will to use them."[46]

Newspapers did not limit their assaults to editorials. As the anti-IWW hostility spread to other communities, increasing numbers of news stories reported the events. On November 15, 1917, the Sapulpa police chief shot a man who attacked him with a knife. The sheriff claimed the man was a Wobbly.[47] Soon almost any incident, real or imagined, became the basis for attacking the IWW. The *Drumright Daily News* accused two men arrested in Okmulgee of being Wobblies and of possessing a "powerful alkaloid" poison for some unexplained nefarious antigovernment scheme.[48] On November 24, the *Tulsa World* accused the IWW of setting on fire a railroad station at Henryetta.[49] Not to be outdone, the Drumright paper on November 26 covered the front page with the headline "Frisco Flyer Speeds Into I.W.W. Trap of Death: Three Killed." The headline was based on a single paragraph in which officials speculated the IWW was to blame.[50] Although the wreck was actually caused by a metal children's toy placed on the tracks by some young boys, the *Daily News* declined to apologize, saying train wrecking was in harmony with IWW practices.[51]

The Tulsa crackdown continued with the December 28, 1917, arrest of Charles Krieger. Krieger, a Wobbly and a Philadelphia machinist, was accused of the Pew bombing. His October 1918 trial ended in a hung jury. Tulsa judge R. S. Cole quashed a second indictment in November 1918, but Krieger was bound over for trial again. After twenty-two months in jail, he was acquitted. The state's witnesses consisted of oil-company detectives and "stoolies" from Leavenworth. One informant broke down and admitted that federal authorities had offered him a pardon. Two others also testified they were offered pardons for their testimony.[52]

Other Oklahoma IWW prisoners were not so lucky. Arthur Boose, Rube Munson, Walter Reeder, and three other Oklahomans (including well-known Socialist orator Stanley J. Clark) were indicted in Chicago. Five others—Carl Schnell, Joseph Gresbach, E. M. Boyd, Wencil Francik, and Michael Sapper—were among twenty-six union members convicted in a Kansas City federal court of hindering the government's war programs. Most of the men shared prison cells in Leavenworth with the Wobblies indicted in Chicago and with those Working Class Union members such as long-time Oklahoma Socialist Tad Cumbie, convicted as a result of the Green Corn Rebellion. A 1921 court ruling freed Schnell, Gresbach, and Boyd.[53]

The Oklahoma legislature also joined fourteen other states in passing criminal syndicalism laws. The Oklahoma law, based on an Oregon statute, was clearly aimed at driving the IWW from the state.[54] The union did not have to be reminded of the law's purpose. "Everybody knows that these laws have been made and are intended to be used for the purpose of exterminating the I.W.W. and silencing radical agitators in general."[55]

By the time the law passed in 1919, what little threat the IWW posed to the entrenched powers in the state had vanished. But that did not stop Governor James A. B. Robertson from sending the National Guard to Drumright to halt a telephone operators' strike allegedly tied to the IWW and from using an alleged potential for IWW violence in order to declare martial law in six coal-producing counties during a nationwide miners' strike in November and December 1919. The use of the militia proved effective in breaking the strike, which the United Mine Workers had organized.[56]

By using fear of the IWW, conservative government and business interests found a fruitful means to shift the blame for economic strife from their own policies onto labor unions and on "conspiracies" of the IWW and Bolsheviks. They succeeded in effectively destroying the state's strong Socialist party and in placing even the ostensibly loyal American Federation of Labor on the defensive against a growing business campaign for the open shop and "100-percent Americanism." The alleged violence of the Wobblies thus became the means to thwart Oklahoma's native radical and reform movements and to render organized labor subservient to boosterism.

But the IWW in Oklahoma was by then a shadow of its former self. When a meatpackers' strike led by the AFL broke out in Oklahoma City in 1921, the Oklahoma County sheriff's department arrested the city's small Wobbly contingent and ordered them to leave the city, although they had nothing to do with the strike. By May 1923 the IWW threat was apparently so feeble that police arrested only two delegates to an Oklahoma convention of the Agricultural Workers Industrial Union on vagrancy charges. The last legacy of the IWW in Oklahoma was the Oklahoma City headquarters of the oil workers' union, but that, too, would vanish when the General Executive Board moved the headquarters to Chicago as part of a doctrinal dispute that would split the union in 1924. In Oklahoma, as across the nation, the combined might of federal prosecutors, the establishment press, police, and vigilantes had shaken the IWW "as a bulldog shakes an empty sack."[57]

NOTES

1. National Civil Liberties Bureau, "The 'Knights of Liberty' Mob and the IWW Prisoners at Tulsa, Oklahoma, November 9, 1917" (New York: NCLB, February, 1918), 6–7. (hereafter cited as "Knights of Liberty Mob").

2. Ibid.; *Tulsa Daily World,* Nov. 10, 1917.

3. "Knights of Liberty Mob," 7.

4. *Tulsa Democrat,* Nov. 11, 1917.

5. The origins of the term *Wobbly* are uncertain. It may simply have meant the IWW was considered unstable, or it may have referred to a "wobble" saw used by lumberjacks, many of whom were IWW members. The off-center saw wobbled and cut a groove wider than its own thickness. A legend attributes the term to a Chinese restaurant owner in British Columbia in 1912 who fed IWW members passing through. Before feeding them, he would ask, "Are you IWW?" but in his Cantonese-flavored English it came out as "Ah loo eye wobble wobble?" See Patrick Renshaw, *The Wobblies: The Story of Syndicalism in the United States* (New York: Doubleday, 1967), 133, and Bernard A. Weisberger, "Here Come the Wobblies!" *American Heritage* 18 (1967): 35.

6. Paul F. Brissenden, "The Launching of the Industrial Workers of the World," *University of California Publications in Economics* 4 (1913): 3.

7. Ibid., 6.

8. Paul F. Brissenden, *The I.W.W.: A Study in American Syndicalism,* Columbia University Studies in History, Economics, and Public Law No. 193 (New York: Columbia University Press, 1920), 213–43. For most Wobblies, sabotage merely meant "to hit the employer in his vital part, his heart and soul, or in other words, his pocketbook" (from Walker C. Smith, "Sabotage, Its History, Philosophy and Function" [Spokane: Walker C. Smith, 1913], 8). For discussions of the meaning of sabotage and of the influence of European syndicalist ideas, see Mike Davis, "The Stop Watch and the Wooden Shoe: Scientific Management and the IWW," *Radical America* 9 (Jan.–Feb. 1975): 69–95; and Salvatore Salerno, *Red November, Black November: Culture and Community in the Industrial Workers of the World* (Albany: State University of New York Press, 1989). See especially Salerno's chap. 4, "The I.W.W. and the G.C.T.," for the syndicalist influence. Salerno also challenges the prevailing concept of IWW direct action deriving from the American frontier experience.

9. William Z. Foster, "Trade Union Progress and the I.W.W.," *The Toiler* 2 (July 1914): 7–8.

10. Charles Ashleigh, "The Floater," *International Socialist Review* 15 (July 1914): 35–36.

11. Charles Daugherty, *First Annual Report of the Commissioner of Labor, 1907,* quoted in *Oklahoma Labor Statistics,* Labor History Document R-7672, Oklahoma Historical Society, p. 3; "Take It Away, Cathead," and "The Roughneck," in Ned DeWitt, "Oil in Oklahoma" project of the Federal Writers Project, Box 43, Western History Collections, University of Oklahoma; Garin Burbank, *When Farmers Voted Red: The Gospel of Socialism in the Oklahoma Countryside, 1910–1924* (Westport, Conn.: Greenwood Press, 1976), 17; Covington Hall, "Labor Struggles in the Deep South" (unpublished typescript at Tulane University, New Orleans, La.; photocopy at Archives of Labor and Urban Affairs, Walter Reuther Library, Wayne State University, Detroit, Mich.), 218.

12. *Industrial Worker* (Joliet, Ill.), Feb. 1906, 7; *Industrial Union Bulletin,* Apr. 20, Nov. 2, 1907; Jan. 5, 1911; Feb. 22, 1912. A list of IWW locals in the Dec. 26, 1912, issue shows none in Oklahoma. *Oil and Gas Journal,* Apr. 23, 1914, p. 24; Apr. 30, 1914, p. 3.

13. Earl Bruce White, "*The United States* v. *C. W. Anderson et al.:* The Wichita Case, 1917–1919," in *At the Point of Production: The Local History of the I.W.W.,* ed. Joseph Conlin (Westport, Conn.: Greenwood Press, 1981), 143–64; Clayton R. Koppes, "The Kansas Trial of the I.W.W., 1917–1919," *Labor History* 16 (1975): 339–58.

14. Stewart H. Holbrook, "The Last of the Wobblies," in *Little Annie Oakley and Other Rugged People* (New York: Macmillan, 1948): 172–73.

15. White, "*U.S.* v. *Anderson,*" 144–45.

16. Upton Sinclair, *The Brass Check: A Study of American Journalism,* rev. ed. (Pasadena, Calif.: Sinclair, 1931), 241.

17. *Oil and Gas Journal,* Apr. 23, 1914.

18. William D. Haywood, *Bill Haywood's Book: The Autobiography of William D. Haywood* (New York: International Publishers, 1929), 296; Drue Deberry, "The Ethics of the Oklahoma Oil Boom, 1905–1929" (master's thesis, University of Oklahoma, 1976), 7.

19. Deberry, "Ethics," 9; James Morton Smith, "Criminal Syndicalism in Oklahoma: A History of the Law and Its Application" (master's thesis, University of Oklahoma, 1946), 32; E. F. Doree, "Gathering the Grain," *International Socialist Review* 15 (June 1915): 740; and Donald Green, "The Beginnings of Wheat Culture in Oklahoma," in *Rural Oklahoma,* ed. Donald Green (Oklahoma City: Oklahoma Historical Society, 1977), 60.

20. *Drumright Daily News,* Feb. 9, 1917.

21. Smith, "Criminal Syndicalism," 29.

22. Ibid.

23. *Drumright Daily News,* Nov. 2, 1917.

24. Virginia C. Pope, "The Green Corn Rebellion: A Case Study in Newspaper Self-Censorship" (master's thesis, Oklahoma A&M College, 1940), 37.

25. James Fowler, "Tar and Feather Patriotism: The Suppression of Dissent in Oklahoma During World War One," *Chronicles of Oklahoma* 56 (1978–79): 409.

26. H. F. Ashurst, "The I.W.W. Menace," *Congressional Record* 55 (1917): 6687.

27. Melvin Dubofsky, *We Shall Be All: A History of the Industrial Workers of the World* (Chicago: Quadrangle, 1969), 357.

28. Report of John Meserve to National Defense Council, Jan. 26, 1918, on "I.W.W. and Pro-German Activities in Tulsa," Council of National Defense Files, War Records Office, National Archives, Washington, D.C.; and *Seattle Call,* Oct. 2, 1917, both quoted in Horace C. Peterson and Gilbert C. Fite, *Opponents of War: 1917–1918* (Madison, Wis.: University of Wisconsin Press, 1957), 171.

29. Weisberger, "Here Come the Wobblies!" 89; *Harlow's Weekly,* June 6, 1917.

30. *Tulsa World,* Aug. 9, 1917.

31. Ibid., Oct. 30, 1917.

32. Ibid.

33. Ibid., Oct. 31, 1917.

34. *International Socialist Review* 18 (Sept. 1917): 208.

35. Holbrook, "Last of the Wobblies," 173.

36. "Knights of Liberty Mob," 4–5; "Tulsa, Nov. 9," *The Liberator* 1 (Apr. 1918): 17; *Tulsa World,* Nov. 6, 1917.

37. *Tulsa World,* Nov. 6, 1917.

38. Ibid., Nov. 7, 1917.

39. Ibid., Nov. 9, 1917.

40. "Knights of Liberty Mob," 14; Peterson and Fite, *Opponents of War,* 172–73; Scott Ellsworth, *Death in a Promised Land: The Tulsa Race Riot of 1921* (Baton Rouge: Louisiana State University Press, 1982), 30; *Tulsa World,* Nov. 10, 1917; *Tulsa Democrat,* Nov. 10, 1917; *Tulsa Times,* Nov. 10, 1917.

41. "Knights of Liberty Mob," 8–9.

42. Haywood, *Bill Haywood's Book,* 296; "Knights of Liberty Mob," 13–14.

43. "Knights of Liberty Mob," 10. Oddly, Congdon is misidentified as Conlin.

44. *Tulsa Times,* Nov. 10, 1917. The Klan comparison was probably no accident, and it would seem reasonable to believe many Knights of Liberty were also Klansmen. Donald Pickens suggests that the Knights were a forerunner of Tulsa's Klan, the only difference between them being that the "Knights of Liberty wore black, while the Ku Klux Klan used white sheets" (Donald L. Pickens, "The Principles and Programs of Oklahoma Socialism, 1900–1918" (master's thesis, University of Oklahoma, 1957), 83. Scott Ellsworth, in his Tulsa race riot study, noted that several estimates place Klan membership in Tulsa at about six thousand between 1915 and 1944, and Tulsa Klan No. 2 claimed thirty-two hundred members by 1921 (Ellsworth, *Death in a Promised Land,* 22, 124n.)

45. Ellsworth, *Death in a Promised Land,* 33; White, "*U.S.* v. *Anderson,*" 152.

46. *Daily Oklahoman,* Nov. 12, 1917.

47. *Tulsa World,* Nov. 16, 1917.

48. *Drumright Daily News,* Nov. 19, 1917.

49. *Tulsa World,* Nov. 24, 1917.

50. *Drumright Daily News,* Nov. 26, 1917.

51. Smith, ''Criminal Syndicalism,'' 34.

52. Ibid., 34–35; Peterson and Fite, *Opponents of War,* 176; Eugene Lyons, ''Tulsa: A Study in Oil,'' *One Big Union Monthly* 1 (Dec. 1919): 35–37.

53. White, ''*U.S.* v. *Anderson,*'' 157–59; *Daily Oklahoman,* June 13, 1921; Mrs. N. L. [Nannie] Phillips, ''I.W.W. Organization and Activities in Oklahoma,'' 7-page typescript, October 19, 1938, in Vertical Files, Oklahoma Historical Society Library, Oklahoma City, p. 7.

54. Peterson and Fite, *Opponents of War,* 18; Smith, ''Criminal Syndicalism,'' 42–47.

55. ''The Anti-Syndicalist Laws,'' *One Big Union Monthly* 1 (April 1919): 9. The law was not used until 1923 against Arthur Berg, an IWW organizer arrested near McAlester for possessing syndicalist literature. He was sentenced to ten years in the state penitentiary and fined five thousand dollars and court costs. Berg's conviction and that of Homer Wear, another Wobbly, were overturned by the state court of criminal appeals in 1925. See Smith, ''Criminal Syndicalism,'' 53–77.

56. *Drumright Derrick,* Sept. 25, 1919; Federal Writers Project, *Labor History of Oklahoma* (Oklahoma City: A. M. Van Horn, 1939), 58–59. Robertson seems obsessed with alleged IWW conspiracies, as indicated by the number of letters from investigators and labor spies in the coal fields, especially those from former Territorial Sheriff Chris Madsen and from National Guard intelligence officer John H. Cary. See the James A. B. Robertson Papers, Oklahoma State Archives, Oklahoma Department of Libraries, Oklahoma City, especially Box 11, folders 9 and 10.

57. Ellis Donham, ''Oklahoma Labor History'' (undated manuscript in vertical files, Oklahoma Historical Society), 37; *Daily Oklahoman,* May 20, 1923; *Oklahoma City Times,* May 21, 1923; IWW, *General Office Bulletin,* Mar. 1924, p. 29, copy in Archives of Labor and Urban Affairs, Walter Reuther Library, Wayne State University; William D. Haywood, ''Break the Conspiracy,'' *One Big Union Monthly* 1 (Dec. 1919): 7.

8

THE ROAD ONCE TAKEN:

Socialist Medicine in Southwestern Oklahoma

Alana Hughes

Alana Hughes is a student at the University of Tulsa and also employed by the Honors Program there. She did the research for the essay that follows under the supervision of Professor Danney Goble. A slightly different version was given at the 1990 meeting of the Oklahoma Historical Society in Lawton. Dealing as it does with a little-known alternative approach to medicine in one Oklahoma community, it is an excellent example of an alternative view of Oklahoma history.

The publication of Robert Wiebe's *The Search for Order* in 1967 gave historians a view of the process of reform in the early twentieth century. According to Wiebe, reform originated in the drive of professional groups who separately sought to rationalize their professions and collectively aimed to organize the entire society. Picked up by others, that thesis has been used to explain phenomena as diverse as the appearance of business corporations, the rise of universities, and the conservation crusade. Apparently, the Wiebe thesis has become something of a universal solvent in American history.[1]

What the thesis leaves out, however, is as important as what it includes. Focusing primarily upon Americans as producers, it ignores the equal reality that they also were consumers. The ''search for order'' usually turns out to be a search conducted by organized interest groups selfishly seeking not order but income. They did so not only at the expense of consumers but also at the expense of an older tradition of reform, which emphasized Americans' common plight as consumers and sought to address it through cooperative enterprise.[2]

Southwestern Oklahoma provides an object lesson in the differences between those two approaches. True to the Wiebe notion, medical practitioners (among others) organized there, among other places. As part of a network that ran from local and county medical societies to the nationwide American Medical Association, they had rationalized their profession by instituting demanding educational requirements enforced by state certification laws. One unquestioned result was a dramatic rise in physicians' status and income.

But southwestern Oklahoma was also home to a cooperative tradition even older than statehood. With its initial settlement it was a fertile ground for the cooperative gospel preached by Texas and Kansas followers of the Populist party. Later, it embraced the cooperative marketing and purchasing schemes backed by the Territorial Farmers' Educational and Cooperative Union. Later still, it elected to the state legislature and county courthouses certified Socialists committed to the "cooperative commonwealth."[3]

If those early dreams bore precious little fruit, neither did they die outright. In the late 1920s and the 1930s, southwestern Oklahoma did realize one specific form of cooperative enterprise. Farmers and others in Beckham County and surrounding counties combined to build a cooperative hospital, the Elk City Community Hospital. Owned by its consumers, that hospital symbolized the meaning of the cooperative vision. Its long battles fought in the state's courts and legislature against the organized medical profession also symbolized something else: the power—and the purpose—of organized medicine's definition of "order."

The man who stood in the arena for those battles was the hospital's founder, Dr. Michael Shadid. Born in Lebanon to a desperately poor family in 1882, Shadid emigrated to America at age sixteen. Like many Lebanese, he traveled his new country as a peddler, selling jewelry and linens from a satchel carried on one shoulder. The other shoulder bore a satchel of college textbooks, the matter for each night's reading and dreaming. Eventually Shadid's travels bore him to Texas's John Tarleton College, where he enrolled in the courses necessary for admission to medical school. So thorough had been his self-study that a year later he entered Washington University Medical School in Saint Louis. In little time he earned three precious documents: a medical diploma, a certificate of U.S. citizenship, and a membership card in the Socialist Party of America.[4]

In 1911, Shadid brought all three to the new state of Oklahoma. With him, too, were a wife and a daughter (the first of an eventual six children). He settled down to practice rural medicine among the large Shadid clan of western Oklahoma.

Shadid's kinsmen and countrymen helped make his new locale a home. So, too, did the political rebels that passed through the area. Socialists such as Oscar Ameringer, Dan Hogan, and Pat Nagle were more to his liking than were his professional colleagues. From farmers and others he learned that the patients traveled for miles to see doctors who did little more than prescribe a dose of salts or, depending on the wealth of the patient, an unnecessary operation. Some physicians confirmed those charges. One candidly informed him that he had removed the appendix of a farmer suffering from a minor stomach disorder "for a mule and a plow. My tenant farmer," he explained, "needs a mule and a plow, and that fellow didn't need his appendix."[5]

Such tales lost none of their meaning as Shadid's own practice grew. By the late 1920s, when he was nearing middle age, enjoying a comfortable patient load, and earning fifteen thousand dollars annually, he had become obsessed with the possibilities of cooperative medicine. Repeated experience with mercilessly acquisitive medicine made the social need clear. The example of the area's consumer-owned cotton gin cooperatives made the solution visible. If farmers could afford one hundred dollars to join a cotton gin, surely they could afford fifty dollars to build a hospital and annual fee to cover their families' entire costs for medical and surgical care.

The times were not propitious. Shadid launched his effort in October 1929, within weeks of America's greatest financial collapse. But his audience was well chosen. Shadid called together the most reform-minded farmers of Elk City. The group included many former members of the Socialist party who had given up on politics and had joined the powerful Farmers' Union to tackle their economic problems more directly. Shadid spoke to the group in the basement of the Carnegie Library, outlining his proposal for the people's own Community Health Association. Their low membership fees would build and maintain a member-owned hospital. There, all members would receive free or reduced cost for medical services, hospital stays, and prescriptions. Treating them would be a hospital staff of surgeons, specialist physicians, nurses, and even a dentist. Members would be eligible for life to receive a share in the benefits.

After only a few minutes, the local farmers announced that they were, as they said, "with you, Doc." Familiar with the organization of cooperatives, the farmers quickly formed committees and enlisted W. E. Hocker, president of the Farmers National Bank, as their trustee for the project. Hocker indicated his support of the hospital by joining the first to become shareholders at the cost of fifty dollars.[6]

By mid-1930 the hospital fund was on solid ground despite the financial upheaval caused by the Depression and the effects of local drought. The fund was solid enough to compel the farmers and Dr. Shadid to form a permanent organization with a constitution and an elected board of directors made up almost entirely of farmers. The board chose and purchased the hospital site. Construction on the first cooperative hospital in the United States began immediately.

Almost as quickly, the Beckham County Medical Society began a campaign to close the hospital before it could benefit the first member-patient. The local medical society threatened to revoke the licenses of doctors joining the staff of the Farmers' Union cooperative hospital. Concerned that they would lose patients and thereby continued financial support of their local for-profit hospitals, several members of the county medical society spread rumors to local businessmen that the hospital would fail and that Shadid would take it over for his own gain. The opposition made much of the fact that Dr. Shadid was foreign-born and a Socialist to boot.[7]

To the farmers interested in cooperative medicine, it mattered little that Shadid was Lebanese; many of them were "furriners," or first-generation Oklahoma farmers. They were ashamed neither of Shadid's origins nor of their own. Neither were they fearful of the bogeyman of socialism. Hard experience had left them unpersuaded of the absolute virtues of acquisitive capitalism. These farm families proved to be more tolerant and progressive than their city "betters."

That did not mean that individually they could put together the necessary capital, particularly as farm prices continued to drop with the Depression's spread. In December 1930 the construction work on the hospital stopped and new rumors flourished: "They never meant to build that hospital."[8]

Shadid sought assistance from the Farmers' Union. It was a justifiable alliance. Many of those who had purchased hospital memberships were also members of the Farmers' Union. And the Farmers' Union itself had been born out of the tradition of cooperativism and anticapitalism. Together Shadid and the union secured a loan for fifteen thousand dollars from the Great American Insurance Company, payable on completion of the hospital. The note was secured by a mortgage on the building. To that sum Shadid added ten thousand dollars of his own money, receiving a note from the board of directors. Within a few months they resumed building the hospital.

Depressed economics and a well-organized opposing faction aside, the two-story brick hospital was completed in 1931, and the dedication ceremonies included as speakers John Simpson of the Farmers' Union and Oscar Ameringer, the Mark Twain of southwestern socialism.[9]

Three thousand people attended that dedication of the pioneer hospital on Friday, August 15, 1931. The dedication of a hospital was not an uncommon event in Oklahoma; dedication of a hospital owned by two thousand families and managed in the interest of the owners was the first in the nation.

Dr. Michael Shadid explained that the purpose of the hospital was neither for the making of profits nor for charity. "A profit-making hospital by its very nature is designed not to heal but to bring a return on its investment." The hospital was dedicated to the service of its shareholders and to humanity. The ideals and cause of the hospital were the same as those of the cooperative movement: the cause of the people, the disinherited, and the poor. The cornerstone's simple inscription, borrowed from the biblical injunction of Galatians 6:2, seemed to capture it all: "Bear ye one another's burdens."[10]

The hospital was open and scarcely on its feet when the local medical association called in an ally with a powerful weapon. The state medical board began efforts to revoke Dr. Shadid's license to practice medicine and threatened other doctors with the same action if they accepted positions at Community Hospital. Tom Cheek, the newly elected president of the Farmers' Union, and his associate Zed Lawter took the matter to Governor William H. Murray.

Murray acted immediately, and the following week his personal journal, the *Blue Valley Farmer*, printed a message from the governor. Always sensitive to a popular cause—particularly one that pitted the "interests" against the "people"—Murray defined the issue in just those terms: "There is," he wrote, "an 'inner circle' of the medical association, as there is of various class organizations in the state. These 'inner circles' of doctors, lawyers, and dentists, and other class organizations undertake to regulate and control those who are not obedient to their wishes." The aging constitutionalist then offered his response:

I want to state that there is no danger of any doctor who may be employed in that hospital losing his license. . . . If the medical board attempts such conspiracy they will be dismissed by the Governor and prosecuted for such conspiracy under the laws as will any other doctor in any such conspiracy.

So this is notice to the doctors of the state, and all concerned, that the farmers in Beckham County who sought to organize for themselves a hospital for the treatment of their families have the legal constitutional right to do so, and will be protected to the limit by the Governor of Oklahoma, and any organization of more than three persons having for its purpose the destruction of the hospital, or its injury, or the taking away of the license of any physician in such hospital will, under the criminal law, be guilty of conspiracy, and will be prosecuted. . . .

The farmers of Beckham County are hereby guaranteed their rights, under the law, to continue.

Having spoken to the immediate problem, Alfalfa Bill returned to what he detected as the overriding issue: "This is not the first instance where the 'inner circle' have attempted even to thwart the execution of the laws. When I say the 'inner circle' I mean those in control of these several class organizations, not alone of the physicians, but of the lawyers, dentists, barbers, *et cetera*."[11]

Doubtlessly knowing that Murray's deeds would match his

words, the medical association quieted its assault. In fact, the Beckham County Medical Society disbanded. Nearly a year and a half later, however, it reappeared—with Dr. Michael Shadid no longer listed as a member. Unaffiliated with the local medical society, Shadid found it impossible to obtain malpractice insurance. But because Community Hospital needed him, he continued to practice. His only insurance was his patients' good will.[12]

The political threat temporarily had passed, but the hospital's economic challenge only worsened along with the surrounding economy. Many of the members were unable to pay their annual dues, and the hospital and its physicians were reduced to barter, exchanging medical care for chickens and vegetables. Presumably the nurses ate the poultry and produce, for their only pay was room and board at the facility.[13]

Even such cost-cutting measures, however, left the hospital operating at a loss. In January 1932, a vice-president of the Great American Insurance Company notified Shadid that he would be visiting and inspecting the hospital to determine that the company was not in danger of losing the fifteen-thousand dollar loan. Shadid took quick-thinking action:

> There was just one patient in the hospital when the telegram arrived, and I was afraid that unless the hospital looked reasonably busy we might not get the loan that had been arranged.
>
> I phoned my wife and asked her to send down any of the children who were at home, and two of them came running over. That wasn't enough, so I sent them back for some playmates and went out to collect a couple of friendly adults. I hurried them all into bed, and their clothes were barely whisked out of sight when the vice-president was announced. I showed him through the moderately busy hospital while my children and friends lay in bed, fairly splitting with suppressed laughter. . . . Later, people said that in addition to filling the beds with ringers, I had parked two old cars in front of the building to add to the effect, but I hadn't. I hadn't thought of it.[14]

The loan indeed was safe. Shadid admitted resorting to deception, but only because of his belief in the success of the hospital. His faith was not misplaced. The hospital, in fact, paid off the loan from the insurance company and the personal loan from Shadid. Physicians and other staff workers began drawing set but regular salaries. Paid memberships passed the two thousand mark. Despite the national economic depression, Community Hospital continued to grow, with expansion in 1934 and 1936. Membership sales improved as local farmers and townspeople saw the effects of their neighbors' involvement with cooperative medicine. No longer did residents of the rural Elk City community fear the economic disaster commonly associated with medical treatment. Instead, Dr. Shadid and his staff witnessed a different effect—the acceptance of preventive medicine. Patients were consulting the physicians at Community Hospital *before* they became seriously ill.[15]

Its financial struggle ended, the hospital's political battle reopened in 1936. Quickly the battlefield shifted from Beckham County to the state supreme court and, finally, to total war in the legislature.

Organized medicine opened fire. The state board of medical examiners officially commanded Shadid to defend his right to hold a medical license, citing charges of "unprofessional conduct." The complaint was not signed by a member of Shadid's profession, a qualified physician, but by a layman, a janitor employed by an opposing doctor. Retaining Gomer Smith, a liberal attorney from Oklahoma City, Shadid refused to appear before the board. In 1937 the case went before the state supreme court, where it lay unsettled until 1941, when it was referred back to the district court of Beckham County.

In February of that year, the Beckham County district courtroom was filled with five hundred spectators, many representing families who made up the membership of Community Hospital. At noon the group, attired in everything from faded overalls to pressed suits, cheered as Gomer Smith made a statement in behalf of Dr. Shadid and the hospital. Smith leveled the same charge as had Governor Murray: a conspiracy headed by western Oklahoma physicians was trying to hound Dr. Shadid and close the hospital. His best evidence was the complaint itself, one they had pressed upon an employee of their own hospital. "It looks to me like," Smith argued, "of all these 2,000 heads of families, these doctors could have found someone to say they'd been fleeced, besides one of their own janitors." His rhetoric aside, Smith went to the legal heart of his case: that the charges filed in 1936 against Shadid did not specify sufficiently the nature of the misconduct. Following Smith's summation, Judge

Lucius Babcock of Sayre granted a writ of prohibition barring the board of medical examiners from prosecuting the four-year-old charge of unprofessional conduct against Dr. Shadid.[16]

During the four years of awaiting the settlement of the case involving his medical license, Shadid was also battling organized medicine on the floor of the state legislature. The protracted legal battle and the issues it underscored had won the hospital some political friends in Depression-era Oklahoma. Some of those served in the legislature, where they presented bills written to provide legitimacy to the cooperative hospital. Early in the sixteenth assembly of the legislature those bills met opposition in both the house and the senate. One house committee killed an amendment to a relief bill that would allow cooperative hospitals, like all other hospitals, to receive state appropriations to defray the cost of providing medical services to indigents. Another bill, presented by two senators and twenty representatives, sought to amend the existing law governing the state board of medical examiners. One section would have removed much of the board's jurisdiction. It provided that the state board of medical examiners could not suspend the license of a physician or surgeon without a direct appeal from the board to the district court of the county involved. The term *unprofessional conduct* would no longer apply to doctors rendering medical service at the cooperative hospitals or those with prepayment plans. Another amendment, most disturbing to the opposition, authorized solicitation of cooperative memberships by paid agents.[17]

In the midst of the "most persistent professional battle ever seen in the Oklahoma legislature,"[18] House Speaker Leon Phillips announced that he wanted action on the bill. Action came forth, but the bill died in conference committee when the senate refused to accept technical house amendments. Representative Henry Worthington, the bill's champion, pronounced that the legislative requests of the farmer had been pushed aside to accept the program of "big business."

With the bill to legalize cooperative hospitals killed, the Farmers' Union sought an amendment to the state constitution. Drafted by former governor Murray, the amendment declared the license to practice the art of healing to be a property right—a right that could not be canceled without due process of law. It provided that no member of any medical profession could be disciplined for participation in connection with cooperative medical health services. The proposed amendment also clearly defined the right of cooperative hospitals to solicit memberships.[19]

More than sixty-six thousand Oklahomans signed the petition calling for the amendment. The secretary of state approved it, and, predictably, the county medical society, now abetted by the state society, questioned its validity. The matter went before the supreme court, and the petition received a favorable decision just in time to get the question on the November 1940 ballot.[20]

By a margin of nearly 84,000 votes, Oklahomans registered their support of cooperative medicine. In almost any previous election in state history, the 294,000 ''yes'' votes would have effected the change. But 1940 saw a bitterly contested presidential election as Franklin Roosevelt was seeking a precedent-shattering third term. Too many Sooner voters marked their ballots for FDR (or Wendell Willkie) and went home, dooming the question to death by the ''silent vote'' since it did not receive a majority of all votes cast.[21]

While the supporters and opponents of cooperative medicine had battled to earn a place on the 1940 ballot, the two had also met again in the legislature. At stake was a bill aimed at legalizing cooperative medical practices in Oklahoma. The bill spent several months dozing in a committee before House Floor Leader Murray Gibbons awakened it with a plan that indicated a reversal of the brother-in-law attitude held by the sixteenth legislature. Gibbons moved that another bill, one requiring annual registration of all physicians, be sent back to committee to add the features of the cooperative bill. Governor Leon Phillips voiced his support. Finally, the combined bill passed.[22]

After eleven years, the battle in the courts and on the floor of the legislature was over. The people of the Seventh District of Oklahoma showed their confidence in Shadid's ability by petitioning him to run for Congress. Seeing a chance to continue his appeal for cooperative medicine, he accepted.

The election campaign, with nine other candidates crowding the ballot, provided the opposition in western Oklahoma another opportunity to strike out at Dr. Shadid. Their zeal was fresh, but their charges were tired. This time these charges were not spread as rumor but declared as fact. Shadid kept track of many of the libels during the final weeks of the campaign. Every small town in the district had a different falsehood. Dr. Shadid was accused of being a Communist, an enemy spy, an atheist, a millionaire, a drunkard, and a murderer (he reportedly had drowned one of his daughters for marrying an American). It is doubtful that any congressional candidate in Oklahoma, if not America, has been called upon to defend himself against such a large number of lies.[23]

Strangely, the cooperative hospital was not attacked in the campaign; the opposition, still mainly doctors, used Shadid's foreign birth, communism, and socialism as weapons. Shadid did not go into this battle unarmed; the campaign showed the good humor that had sustained him through earlier battles and had won him a loyal following.

Shadid counted on the voters. What he did not count on was the strength of his political enemies. They convinced William Simpson, son of the former president of the Farmers' Union, to appeal to the district leaders, saying, "after all, the Farmers' Union cannot afford to support a foreigner for Congress." A good many of the farmers did vote for a foreigner, and Shadid finished as the runner-up among the ten candidates in the primary. He finished only seven thousand votes behind Sam Massingale, close enough that had the law at the time provided for a runoff election, he eventually might have won. After the defeat, the farmers told him, "Next time, Doc."

Next time came unexpectedly soon. Massingale died in office, and a special election was held to replace him. Shadid was defeated again, this time by fewer than five hundred votes. Shadid called for a recount, but his request was denied as Victor Wickersham took office to represent the Seventh District of Oklahoma.[24] Shadid decided not to pursue the matter, and for the first time since the hospital opened, he took a much needed vacation. He left two sons, Alex and Fred, both physicians, to handle matters at the hospital.

The two were badly overworked. The hospital was still having trouble acquiring doctors, surgeons, and technicians. Drawing upon the steadfast opposition of its state and county affiliates, the American Medical Association refused to accept Community Hospital or allow it to advertise in the national medical journals. The technicians' national organizations similarly refused to accept advertising from the hospital or to place those who worked for it on their national registries. To complicate matters, the war effort took its toll on the hospital staff.[25]

Every young doctor and surgeon was declared essential by the Office of Procurement and Assignment of Physicians. Dr. Shadid's oldest son, Alex, enlisted immediately after he was declared "available." The other Shadid son, Fred, took on alone his father's duties at the hospital. Without him the doors would close.

The senior Shadid launched a campaign to keep Fred at the hospital. He appealed to the state draft board, the Office of Procurement and Assignment of Physicians in Washington, D.C. and, finally, to Senator Claude Pepper of Florida, head of a subcommittee on education and labor. Senator Pepper later launched an investigation of the activities of the manpower commission with special reference to the Procurement and Assignment Service (P&AS).

Meanwhile, the members of the Beckham County draft board delayed completing the paperwork necessary to draft Dr. Fred Shadid. As a result of the investigation initiated by Senator Pepper, a go-between representative for the P&AS office investigated the situation in western Oklahoma and found that very few doctors remained and that Dr. Fred Shadid was, in fact, essential.[26]

In 1946, Dr. Michael Shadid stepped down from his long-term position as medical director of Community Hospital. The board of directors voted to replace him with Dr. Fred Shadid. Fred continued the special mission to its members that his father had given the hospital, while extending its services to the entire community. Postwar Oklahomans continued to join as members, and more turned to the hospital as fee-paying patients. One reason that they would turn to Community Hospital was its established and remarkable record of providing health care. No hospital within 120 miles matched the range of services of Elk City's Community Hospital. Those who took advantage of those services were entering a hospital that in a single year delivered 103 babies without even one incidence of maternal mortality. Even more impressive, over a thirteen-year span the hospital had not lost a single infant.[27]

One example of the hospital's steady willingness to accept the responsibility for the people's health also became an example of organized medicine's continuing irresponsible vindictiveness. In 1949 the hospital joined organized medicine in a new battle. This battle was fought not in the legislature or in the courtrooms, but in the polio isolation wards of the pediatric units of hospitals throughout the United States. At stake was not the livelihood nor the liability of professional physicians, but the lives of crippled children.

The National Foundation for Infantile Paralysis (the March of Dimes) sent Dr. Fred Shadid to Denver for training in the diagnosis and treatment of polio cases. Learning that, the local medical society reared back and threatened the hospital. Its members contacted the Oklahoma State Commission for Crippled Children and posed objection to recognition of Community Hospital. Without this recognition, neither state monies nor national charity funds would be available to any stricken children entering Community Hospital for polio treatment. By now doctors at Community Hospital were used to this vicious cycle, one that turned on wheels as predictable and as cold as those on the empty wheelchair of a fallen polio victim.

When the local newspapers published this story of continued reluctance to support Community Hospital, the Elk City Civic Council stepped in. Three women representing the council called on Dr. H. K. Speed, president of the Beckham County Medical Society. Their interview with Dr. Speed was printed in the Elk City papers and read in part:

Mrs. Ernest Mobley: What would be your attitude toward our having a polio isolation ward in Elk City?

Dr. Speed: We would be against it and wouldn't let it happen.

Mobley: Why does not the county medical society approve the Community hospital?

Dr. Speed: Because they are not recognized.

Mobley: By whom?

Dr. Speed: By the county society.

Mobley: That is you. Why don't you recognize them?

Dr. Speed: If I were to tell you all the details, I'd be sued for damages.

Mobley: If you tell the truth you can't be sued. You don't libel anyone with the truth.

Dr. Speed: If you were men, I'd throw you out. I left the door open, but you wouldn't take the hint.

The newspaper's readers fully understood the hint and knew how to counter it. The papers carrying the interview were barely on the stands when the citizens—farmers and businessmen, housewives, and mothers—began a fundraising campaign of their own. This was not a march of dimes, but a march of dollars to finance aid to polio victims at their community hospital. The county chairman for the polio drive informed the national foundation of the plan and stated that the next national drive in that region would be futile. It was a dramatic statement perhaps, but by now the Elk City Community Hospital and its battles had received national attention if not support. The national foundation had little reason to doubt that these independent southwestern Oklahomans would, indeed, bear their neighbors' burdens. Within days the national foundation pledged its financial support. In this battle the hospital would not fight alone.

Almost overnight the most severe polio epidemic in Oklahoma's history struck. In all of southwestern Oklahoma there was only one hospital prepared for the crisis. The wards of Community Hospital were filled, and the staff that Dr. Fred Shadid had trained worked around the clock to care for the polio victims.[28]

A year later, in 1950, the warfare between Community Hospital and the medical society reached its final battle. The hospital filed a $300,000 lawsuit against the Beckham County Medical Society, alleging violation of the common law of conspiracy and Oklahoma's antitrust statutes. These were precisely the same charges that old Alfalfa Bill Murray had leveled twenty years earlier. Backing them now was the evidence of two decades of the society's efforts to impair the hospital's operations, its physicians' status, and its constituents' health.

In 1952, the Beckham County Medical Society surrendered and agreed to add the hospital's doctors to its membership roll. In exchange, the hospital dropped the suit and allowed the society's doctors access to the region's most advanced medical facility, the same one that the society had tried to destroy for twenty years.[29]

Ironically, the hospital was eventually destroyed, but the fatal blow came not from physicians but from efforts to provide decent health care collectively. The spread of private insurance lured those with money away from the cooperative scheme and into private programs such as Blue Cross and Blue Shield. Oklahoma's expanding public welfare system began to help the poorest with their physicians' and hospital bills. The needy and the elderly who required Social Security's support became eligible for that agency's Medicaid or Medicare programs. For all of those reasons, in 1964 the Elk City hospital ended its experiment in cooperative medicine to become municipally owned and operate on a fee-for-service basis.[30]

At their best, the programs that finally killed the hospital upheld the idea of providing dependable, affordable health care. Nonetheless, the hospital had served its purpose. During times when there seemed to be no escape from medical inequality in rural Oklahoma, the cooperative system had provided competent services. It had done so without acquiring mortgaged farms or exchanging the people's dignity for the professional's search for order. Those who know and contemplate its history can understand that it was not professionals who were responsible for reform but the people themselves who dragged the professionals kicking and screaming toward public responsibility.

NOTES

1. Wiebe, *The Search for Order, 1877–1920* (New York: Hill and Wang, 1967); Alfred P. Chandler, *The Visible Hand: The Managerial Revolution in American Business* (Cambridge, Mass.: Belknap Press, 1977); Burton J. Bledstein, *The Culture of Professionalism: The Middle Class and the Development of Higher Education in America* (New York: Norton, 1976); Samuel P. Hays, *Conservation and the Gospel of Efficiency: The Progressive Conservation Movement, 1890–1920* (Boston: Harvard University Press, 1959).

2. David P. Thelen, *The New Citizenship: Origins of Progressivism in Wisconsin, 1885–1900* (Columbia: University of Missouri Press, 1972); David P. Thelen, *Paths of Resistance, Tradition and Dignity in Industrializing Missouri* (New York: Oxford University Press, 1986); Lawrence Goodwyn, *Democratic Promise: The Populist Moment in America* (New York: Oxford University Press, 1976).

3. Worth Robert Miller, *Oklahoma Populism: A History of the People's Party in Oklahoma* (Norman: University of Oklahoma Press, 1987); Danney Goble, *Pro-*

gressive Oklahoma: The Making of a New Kind of State (Norman: University of Oklahoma Press, 1980); James R. Green, *Grass Roots Socialism: Radical Movements in the Southwest* (Baton Rouge: Louisiana State University Press, 1977).

4. Michael A. Shadid, *A Doctor for the People* (New York: Vanguard Press, 1939); *Vici Beacon,* letter to the editor from playwright Sari Scott, May 29, 1945; Fred Shadid, *Co-Op Hospital: The First Rural HMO* (California: unpublished, 1988); Green, *Grass Roots Socialism.*

5. McAlister Coleman, one of Ameringer's "comrades," provides the introduction and explanation of Shadid's early experiences with the medical practice in rural Oklahoma in Michael A. Shadid, *Doctors for Today and Tomorrow* (New York: Cooperative League of the U.S.A., 1947); Michael A. Shadid, *Crusading Doctor: My Fight for Cooperative Medicine* (New York: Vanguard Press, 1946).

6. Coleman introduction in M. Shadid, *Doctors for Today,* ix; M. Shadid, *Doctor for the People,* 113–18. The first elected board of directors included as members Paul Peeler, chair; A. J. McKenney; S. C. Thompson; C. A. Gassner; J. W. Cain; Jesse M. Barber; W. A. Hostetler; Harry Luther; Arthur A. Hill; E. F. Luthy; and Earl Green.

7. M. Shadid, *Doctor for the People,* 119–29; Fred Shadid, *Co-Op Hospital,* 3; *American Guardian,* Apr. 16, 1937, p. 1; Coleman, introduction in M. Shadid, *Doctors for Today,* x.

8. M. Shadid, *Doctor for the People,* 121.

9. Ibid., 122; Ameringer's wit and principles are both well recorded in *If You Don't Weaken: The Autobiography of Oscar Ameringer* (New York: H. Holt and Company, 1940). Ameringer's newspaper, *The American Guardian,* followed the community hospital and its battles for several years.

10. Fred Shadid, *Co-Op Hospital,* 3; *American Guardian,* Aug. 21, 1931, p. 1.

11. M. Shadid, *Doctor for the People,* 129–33.

12. Coleman, introduction in M. Shadid, *Doctors for Today,* x–xi.

13. Fred Shadid, *Co-Op Hospital,* 3.

14. M. Shadid, *Doctor for the People,* 140–42.

15. Ibid., 144; Fred Shadid, *Co-Op Hospital,* 4.

16. Coleman, introduction in M. Shadid, *Doctors for Today,* xii–xiii; Charles Saulsberry, "Medical Board is Barred from Trying Shadid," *Daily Oklahoman,* Feb. 11, 1941, p. 1.

17. M. Shadid, *Doctor for the People,* 167–68; *Harlow's Weekly,* Jan. 9, 1937, p. 16; *Harlow's Weekly,* Feb. 6, 1937, p. 8.

18. *Harlow's Weekly,* May 8, 1937, p. 10.

19. Ibid., May 16, 1937, p. 7, and June 12, 1937, pp. 5–6.

20. *American Guardian,* May 6, 1938, p. 3.

21. Oklahoma State Election Board, *Directory of Oklahoma, 1977* (Oklahoma City: State Election Board, 1977), 648.

22. *Harlow's Weekly,* Apr. 15, 1939, p. 16.

23. M. Shadid, *Crusading Doctor,* 231–32.

24. Coleman, introduction in M. Shadid, *Doctors for Today,* xx; *Elk City Journal,* Mar. 27, 1941, p. 1; Fred Shadid, *Co-Op Hospital,* 13.

25. Fred Shadid, *Co-Op Hospital,* 17–19; Civil Action No. 11211, filed in the Beckham County District Court, Aug. 28, 1950.

26. M. Shadid, *Doctor for the People,* 282–96.

27. Fred Shadid, *Co-Op Hospital,* 17; J. D. Ratcliff, "Co-op Hospital," *Colliers,* July 31, 1943, pp. 25–27.

28. M. Shadid, *Crusading Doctor,* 262–65; Civil Action Suit No. 11211.

29. Fred Shadid, *Co-Op Hospital,* 21–24. This represents the out-of-court settlement and agreement with nine propositions agreed to by both parties on Apr. 22, 1952.

30. Interview with former medical director Dr. B. Sugarman, Elk City, Okla., Apr. 1989.

9

WOODY GUTHRIE:
The Oklahoma Years, 1912–1929
Harry Menig

"Damn communist." So said one item of graffiti on the remaining walls of Woody Guthrie's dilapidated old house in Okemah, Oklahoma, in 1980.[1] Perhaps the survival of that kind of attitude toward Guthrie helps to explain why he is given two pages in a major recent U.S. history textbook but is not yet in the Oklahoma Hall of Fame and is not even mentioned in some major Oklahoma history textbooks.[2] Harry Menig, in the following article from the Chronicles of Oklahoma *in 1975, does an excellent job of relating Guthrie to his Oklahoma roots.*

During World War II, the people of Okemah, Oklahoma, received a letter written on the Atlantic Ocean. The message came from an experienced merchant seaman, a man who knew the perils of German U-boat torpedoes. He was homesick; his name was Woody Guthrie. Alone at sea, a one-time Dust Bowl refugee, a folksinger, cartoonist and journalist, he reminisced: "There is a look and a smell about your smoking timbers that even is good away out here." Guthrie also had a message for his hometown folks, a message he implied would be good peacetime

"Woody Guthrie: The Oklahoma Years, 1912–1929," by Harry Menig, first appeared in *The Chronicles of Oklahoma* 53, no. 2 (Summer 1975): 239–65. Copyright 1975. Reprinted from *The Chronicles of Oklahoma* (Oklahoma City: Oklahoma Historical Society, 1975) with permission.

conduct. "Men of all kinds and all colors," he observed, "fight here side by side."[3] If the war, any war, can teach a lesson, it would be the lesson Guthrie observed at sea: that petty differences must be laid aside in time of extreme national emergency.

More than ten years had passed since Guthrie left his birthplace, yet in his letter he recalled the good as well as the bad times. His mind must have been filled with mixed memories: his mother's songs; his father's wealth and status; the town alive with cotton wagons, crowds, music and animals; the black harmonica players; the Indian stickball games and corn dances; the seven room house burning; the tornado; his sister's death; his mother's illness; his father's failure; the lynching and shooting of blacks; the drunkenness and free-wheeling boom-town days; and the town's death.

Guthrie's letter was more than a story with a moral; it was a simple observation with a plea for a very complicated hope for better conditions for all people. He never forgot his origins, never gave up the desire that all people might begin to live in harmony. His experiences in Okemah from 1912 to 1929 do not only recreate a social history but they also indicate that what he learned as a young boy influenced him for the rest of his life. His work and the memories people have of him is in itself [sic] an exciting account of a unique period in Oklahoma history and culture.

Guthrie's talents had their beginning in both his home and the small pioneer town of Okemah. As a balladeer, cartoonist and journalist, he found an amazing amount of resource material for his autobiography and for his history of American life. From his mother, Nora Belle Tanner Guthrie, the daughter of one of Oklahoma's first log-cabin school teachers, he learned music and a deep respect for family love and unity. Charles Edward Guthrie, Woody's father, gave to him a sense of humor, a politician's mind and a journalist's eye. Okemah was, in a sense, Woody Guthrie's foster parent. From its people he learned music, charity, hatred, violence, but most of all, a sense of "getting along"—a need for self-survival through cooperation. In later life, he combined his musician's ear with his reporter's eye to point out, and sometimes to protest, the unfair conditions which forced many people to live unsatisfactory, unnatural lives. He himself was once left homeless and parentless because of the fates of health and weather. He never forgot the love his parents once gave to him, and he later transferred this love to all mankind; common men with a common goal became his children and he became their father spokesman.

Guthrie's own parents provided their children, Roy, Clara and Woody with a warm and loving home. The land investments of Guthrie's father allowed the family to live without fear of want; luxuries were at their demand; they needed only to sign the Guthrie name. Money, in early Oklahoma, however, was not easily earned, and Guthrie's mother had to pay a high price for the niceties of small-town pioneer life. The price was worry, for his father was in the uncertain land-trading business.[4]

At first Woody Guthrie's mother was able to compensate for her husband's uncertain occupation, for they had a new home and a growing family in a growing town. The house, built about 1912, the year of Woody's birth, according to him, had seven rooms and cost between seven and eight thousand dollars. "I remember a bright yellow outside—a blurred haze of a dark inside," he recalled. The ample money his father was able to share with his family obviously made his mother happy. "Mama could sign a check for any amount, buy every little thing that her eye liked the looks of," Guthrie wrote.[5] He understood that his father's money set him apart from the typical Oklahoman. "I wasn't in the class of people John Steinbeck calls the Okies," he said. "My dad was worth forty-thousand dollars."[6] While his father could give his family anything they "liked the looks of," his mother was not the ambitious type. In fact, she was quite the opposite, wanting only a stable and comfortable life, something she had known as a young girl. Guthrie claimed his grandmother, Mrs. Lee Tanner, once described his mother to him and declared: "She went to my little school house where I taught over on the Deep Fork River and she read her books and got her lessons, and she helped me mark and grade the papers. She liked pretty music and she sang songs and played her own chords on the piano."[7] Guthrie's love for his mother was described by Mrs. V. K. Chowning of Okemah as "deep devotion."[8] Obviously she taught him more than a love for nice things; the ballads he learned from her were mixed with love for his family. Her influence, he said, took hold at a very early age. On the porch of their seven-room home, he claimed he composed his first song:

> Listen to the music,
> Music, music;
> Listen to the music,
> Music band.

Fortunately, Guthrie's mother had more to offer him and his older brother Roy and older sister Clara than music. Her strength of character and fortitude came to the children in the same words of Ma Joad in John Steinbeck's *The Grapes of Wrath*. Guthrie's mother told him: "We love your papa, and if anything tries to hurt him and make him bad and mean, we'll fight it, won't we? . . . We're not the scared people Woody." Unfortunately, what she thought her family could unite against and fight was impossible odds. Guthrie, in his youth, showed his devotion by offering a simple solution for family peace. He wrote: "If ever single livin' one of 'em would all git together an' git rid of them mean, bad politics, they'd all feel lots better, an' wouldn't fight each other so much, and that'd make my mama feel better."[9]

The new Guthrie home with all the luxuries could not hide the fact that Guthrie's father was part of a rough era, when landownership changed rapidly. The hostility of Guthrie's mother toward this rough way of life is remembered by many Okemah people. "She was often spiteful," recalled Mrs. Chowning. "One day, when she was mad at Charlie, she took all the furniture out of their house and piled it up on the front yard." As Guthrie's father grew in popularity, the townspeople grew in curiosity of the family. The personality of Guthrie's mother became public property, and as her worrying turned to depression, and the depression to a total nervous breakdown, town gossip grew stronger.[10]

To have a father who was popular was to young Guthrie a rare gift. In spite of the devotion he held for his mother, he could not help cherishing his father's tales of the day's land dealings. At night, Guthrie claimed, after his father "would ride in on the horse," he would sit on his father's knee and listen to "who he was fighting and why, and all about it." If Guthrie was devoted to his mother, it was obvious that he idolized his father. "Papa was a man of brimstone and hot fire in his mind and in his fists," he recalled, "and was known all over that section of the state as the champion of

all the fist fighters."[11] His admiration of his father was obviously
more folklore than fact, and evidently a boy's wish for a hero-
father. Regardless of the myth, Guthrie's mother could not help but
be upset over her husband's own "tall tales," for she knew he had
other abilities which did not necessitate fist fighting. Guthrie never
had to choose between his parents' ideals, for fate decided the issue.
Nevertheless, he, like his mother, presented an equally half-true
image of his father.

Guthrie's father was more than a fist fighter; he was a prominent
Oklahoma Democrat, and thus commanded much respect and public
scrutiny. A closer view of Guthrie's father reveals Woody's heritage
as well as his background, first gained from affluence and status and
later from deprivation and anonymity.

Guthrie's father loved his family, worked for them, gave them
what they needed and fought hard for them. "He was a cowboy,"
recalled Mrs. Chowning, "who came in here from Texas."[12] The
cowboy and fist fighting image, however, is only a partial truth.
Guthrie's father was more than a folk hero, for he was what is commonly referred to as a self-made man. In Okemah, in the early days
of Oklahoma statehood, times were comparatively primitive, and
the Old West still prevailed. Nevertheless, the *Okemah Ledger,* the
town's weekly newspaper, was stocked with investment and insurance advertisements. The people of Okemah were urged to invest
and protect their possessions; "Did You Ever Stop and Think" ran
one advertisement for fire insurance. The advertisement appeared
beside an article written by Guthrie's father titled "A Baby Defined," in which he wrote that he was "as happy as a lobster" over
the birth of Woody.[13]

The first years of the life of Guthrie's father in Okemah were
promising. He was elected to the office of Court Clerk, serving as
the first clerk in Okfuskee County shortly after statehood.[14] From
1907 to 1912 he was laying the foundation for a well-established
homelife for his family. By 1912, the year of Woody's birth, he was
becoming better known and at the same time more community
minded. Early in the year, he was concerned with the unclaimed
land ownership question. Being a national election year, emotions
normally ran high when various speakers came to Okemah to pro-
pose a variety of solutions to the major questions in Oklahoma:

who would get the unclaimed land and how would it be sold? One Socialist party speaker, named Thurman, particularly aggravated Guthrie's father, for he seemed to provoke something very close to his life—individual rights, private ownership and enterprise. Woody's father, who owned much of the land and many buildings in Okemah, was understandably concerned when Thurman suggested that the Federal government intervene to take possession in solving the ownership question, and the speech provoked a two-column full-page response from Guthrie's father.

The article, titled "Evasive, Shifting and Inconsistent: A Careful Diagnosis of the Socialist and Anti-Christian Speech Made in this City on Christmas Day by Agitator Thurman," revealed an abiding belief in individual rather than state right to ownership. Guthrie's father attacked the logic of Thurman's argument by pointing out his inconsistent suggestions: that the Federal government should take possession, and the failure of state government to offer viable solutions. To Guthrie's father, Thurman's argument was "Wishy-washy, slippery, and dangerous." He distrusted government intervention on a large-scale basis. "I have always been taught," he wrote, "that socialism meant majority rule. This would look like it meant Bossism." He concluded his counter argument to Thurman's plea for "purer" government through socialism with a Henry David Thoreau type statement which he directed to his neighbors: "No body of men can establish pure government unless that body of men are pure in themselves."

The political persuasion of Guthrie's father was tied to his concept of private enterprise; however, this article, plus several others, indicate his belief in a grass-roots government. As a family man in a small pioneer town, he found it necessary to protect his own rights as a land owner. Woody Guthrie would later adopt this type of thinking through his support of President Franklin Delano Roosevelt's Works Progress Administration and then in his support of the Congress of Industrial Organizations. Guthrie's belief that individual rights could be maintained by group solidarity was inherent in his father's writings. Guthrie's father concluded his argument with a touch of stylistic satire and a serious approach to the facts. He spurned Thurman with "Ta, ta, Doc Rev Socialist Windjammer" and then pointed out in a serious tone that the Socialist party had not provided the working man with as many benefits as the two million member American Federation of Labor.[15]

The political thinking of Guthrie's father gave to Woody the belief that solutions to governmental problems could be solved through established and accepted channels. The Democratic party to Guthrie's father was best suited to handle issues, as it was a well established and actively working organization. However, the common people were a part of this party, and Guthrie's father, and Woody himself, never lost sight of an individual's power within a large system. Most evident in the writings of Woody's father is his constant reference to the people of Okemah. As a family man with active political aspirations and significant financial operations, he was quick to identify himself with the middle class people of Okemah. In July, 1912, the *Okemah Ledger* was alive with the Guthries. In the same issue announcing the birth of Woody, his father was listed with D. W. Scully of Padan, Oklahoma, and Tom Hall of Okfuskee, Oklahoma, as candidates for the office of County Assessor. The birth announcement added to the political career of Woody's father, for it portrayed him as a respectable family man and a commoner: "Mr. and Mrs. C. E. Guthrie are the proud parents of an eight pound democrat boy that arrived at the new home Sunday afternoon. In another column of this issue will be found an article by Charlie on the baby question that we think is mighty clever."

By combining the political career of Guthrie's father with news of his homelife, the Guthrie family became more public than ever. In addition, the common man image of Guthrie's father was further strengthened in his own essay titled "A Baby Defined":

It is a well established rule of nature that current events, to a certain extent, constitute the basis of current topics. The rule being strictly applied in my case, it has been my great pleasure to devote both time and thought to a systematic search for the best definition of a baby.

After devouring . . . many volumes of the latest and most up to date works which deal with the theories of Creation, Evolution, and the origin of the Family; brushing away the cob webs to gain entrance to the antiquated libraries of our ancestors, I have finally succeeded in finding a definition. I have selected . . . one given in England in the hope of receiving a prize which had been offered by a London newspaper.

"A baby—a tiny feather from the wing of love dropped into the sacred lap of motherhood; an inhabitant of Lapland; a padlock on the chains of life; a curious bud of uncertain blossom; . . . the morning caller, the noonday crawler; midnight bawler; . . . the latest edition of humanity of which every couple think they possess the finest copy. . . ."

I concur in the definition as given, and trust it will meet with the approbation of our splendid populace which is composed of real homebuilders. To say the least, I am as happy as a lobster.[16]

No matter how colloquial, no matter how witty Guthrie's father attempted to be, his readers could not help realize that he was a well-read and talented man whose interests took him beyond the hardships of frontier life; yet he could apply his learning to a celebrated but simple occasion—the birth of his son Woody. To compliment the good citizens of Okemah as a town of "real homebuilders" was a politician's effort to win his public. When Guthrie's father was appointed as "Temporary Secretary" to the "Permanent Wilson-Marshall Club" of Okfuskee County, it was evident that he had won some support. Thus, Guthrie can be seen as a product of his father's career more than in name only.[17]

Guthrie's father attempted to give his family what they needed, but his political aspirations were often the cause of family disunity. Like many ardent politicians, he was unable to leave his work at the office. As public figures, the Guthries enjoyed only a short-lived reign of public approval. The rumors, probably half spread out of jealousy, concerning Guthrie's mother grew as his father grew in popularity. The small town of Okemah, like many small towns, was high on gossip. Guthrie, with a touch of satire, described Okemah as "Just another one of those little towns. I guess, about a thousand or so people, where everybody knows everybody else; . . . Everybody had something to say about something or somebody and you usually knew almost word for word what it was going to be about before you heard them say it." When tragedy hit the Guthrie family, a family already in the news, rumors could not be curtailed. One day, the new seven-room home mysteriously burned to the ground, leaving no evidence of the cause of the catastrophe. The result, however, was recorded by Guthrie who claimed one of his friends told him, "Kids say your mama got mad an' set her brand new house on fire, an' burnt ever' thin' plumb up." While his mother's discontent with her husband's fist fighting life helped spread these rumors, the real catastrophe came in the ironic fact that Guthrie's father had no fire insurance. In a sense, his only investment was the family; while the new house burned, destroying all the "nice things" the Guthries tried to live as a united family.[18]

Guthrie's father attempted to regain the family's trust and self-respect when he bought another house for about $1,000. Constructed to last forever, it was a two story structure: the first floor was made of stone and built into the side of a hill, while the second story was made of wood with an overhanging front porch. The view from the porch was for the young Guthrie a lookout; from there he watched the trains go by and the wagons come into town from the nearby farms. "He used to sit out on that front porch a lot," recalled Mrs. Chowning. "It was the only place he could find some peace and quiet from his hectic homelife," she continued. "Okemah" Guthrie wrote, means "Town on a hill" in Creek. For him, the new home offered a view of Okemah in action, and to some extent, became a symbol of his homelife and hometown.[19]

Luckily for Guthrie, he was at an age when the family house burning catastrophe could not take its total effect. The older Guthries, however, realized the importance of the disaster. While the children, Roy and Clara, lost most of their toys, Guthrie's mother lost the one thing she could offer her family—strength and security. All complained of the darkness, the dampness and the general drabness of the new home; it did not compare to the seven-room home that had burned. Guthrie's mother, unfortunately, never had a chance to fully recover after losing her home. Guthrie described what was to become a common scene. In the new house she was washing the dishes when Clara shouted at her: "Mama, look! You're draining the dishes without a drain pan! The water's dripping like a great big . . . river . . . down. . . . And then Clara looked over the hot water reservoir on the wood stove and nobody in the house saw what she saw. Her eyes flared open when she seen that her mama wasn't listening, just washing the dishes clean in the scalding water."[20] Nevertheless, Guthrie's father continued his efforts to regain position and prosperity in Okemah. Guthrie also found other things to do when the family was having a hard time.

Guthrie's spirit was undamaged. Instead, he began to observe and take part in the activities of Okemah. A typical scene that Woody might have seen from the porch was the cotton wagons coming to town: "The white strings of new cotton bales and a whole lot of men and women and kids riding into town on wagons piled double-sideboard full of cotton," Guthrie remembered, "driving under the funny shed at the gin, driving back home again on loads of cotton seed." This farming town, he claimed, had a population before the big oil boom of approximately 1,500. On a typical Saturday at this time "all the farming people'd come in," Guthrie stated, "they'd have a trades-day, buy a new buggy, box of tobacco, or a new pair of button down shoes." While the parents were buying and selling, the children would enjoy the monkeys down at Moomaw's Drug Store. There, where the owner kept his monkeys in a cage in the window, the children gathered to wait for the big escape. The monkeys, being curious, would get out of their cages and climb on top of the brown stone building, where they watched business activity.[21]

On Saturday night, Guthrie would participate in the various traveling carnivals and minstrel shows that came to town. The Dubinsky Tent Show was one such opportunity for this young man to witness magical tricks, singing comedians and Robert Ripley type freak shows. If the town had a particularly exciting evening, the local drunks provided some sleeping citizens with impromptu versions of "In the Good Old Summer Time" or "Sweet Adeline."

On Sunday, for those who had the strength, many found it fun to visit the Fort Smith and Western Railroad platform to watch the incoming and outgoing trains. The Fort Smith and Western line had opened its service to Okemah in 1903 and the novelty of train watching was still fresh during this time; people were interested in seeing who and what came into Okemah. The Broadway Hotel and Dexter House also sent their hacks to carry back the new people and fresh supplies. Okemah was in the pre–oil boom stage.[22]

As Okemah prepared for the oil boom, the Guthries attempted in vain to recover their normal homelife. Their new house was not fitted to their personalities; it was cold as stone; they were warm with life. For one time, and only one time, a disaster seemed to work for and not against the Guthrie family. A tornado struck Okemah around 1917, taking with it a large part of their home. Guthrie described the results. The house "stood there without a roof. It looked like a fort that had lost a hard battle. Rock walls partly caved in by flying wreckage and by the push of the twister. Our back screen door jerked off its hinges and wrapped around the trunk of my walnut tree."[23] The Guthries celebrated this disaster. Though Woody's father had lost more money, he was able to find a better house on the more fashionable north Ninth Street section of Okemah. Guthrie's mother believed she could regain some of her warmth and strength in this new home, and the family was able to reunite for a short time and begin to share in the oil boom times.

During the following five years, between 1918 and 1922, Okemah experienced an oil boom never to be equalled. These years for the Guthries were a mixture of success and failure. Guthrie's father was, by 1922, at the summit of his political career. The *Okemah Ledger* announced that he was a Democratic candidate for the Oklahoma Corporation Commission, claiming that he had "active working organizations in twenty-six counties of the state." The announcement, also stating that his new headquarters was located in Oklahoma City, Oklahoma, was accompanied by a photograph of Guthrie's father in a well-tailored business suit. He appeared stylish, healthy and youthful. A month later, the *Okemah Ledger* reported that he "feels sure of winning the state nomination."[24] Though his political aspirations were strong and he appeared youthful and expressed confidence, his homelife had worsened both personally and financially. Instead of being "happy as a lobster" over the birth of his son, Guthrie's father was silent over the death of his daughter Clara, then aged fourteen.

Guthrie's mother barely had time to recover from the house burning and tornado disasters when Clara was killed as the result of burns received after a kerosene stove exploded. Her depression over this tragedy was self-consuming, a condition from which she never fully recovered. Guthrie described her condition: "She got careless with her appearance. She let herself run down. She walked around over the town; looking and thinking and crying. The doctor called it insanity and let it go at that. She lost control of the muscles of her face."[25] Though Guthrie's father was unable to regain the nice things—the house, the part-time maid, the car—he never stopped trying. His mother, unfortunately, was never able to combat her illness. Her breakdown this time certainly aided the gossip seekers.

Believing that these depressions were inherited, many Okemah residents thought Clara had committed suicide. ''She did it to spite her mother,'' one Okemah resident recalled the gossip. Such talk would damage any politician's career, and though Guthrie's father was positive politically, he never again held a public office in Okemah, and he lost the race for the Oklahoma Corporation Commission.[26]

While the Guthries were suffering, Woody adopted his father's positive thinking. As a young boy in a booming town, he easily absorbed the ever present excitement in Okemah. The serious and depressing family problems undoubtedly caused him to seek some relief and pleasure in activities in the town. Guthrie showed a great deal of influence from his father when he described a rock war. According to Woody, the ''new'' oil boom children had no ''say so'' in how ''the gang'' was run. Like his father, Woody took the ''new'' kids' side. Guthrie described this gang as a mini-society with elected officials from president to sheriff to outlaws. ''We had to have someone to throw in the jail,'' an empty piano box, he explained. Beyond the humor, however, was Guthrie's implicit concept that government could work for everyone if it were run by honest men who contributed on equal terms. His father's ideals of individual ownership and his belief in the good of the American Federation of Labor were not far removed from young Guthrie's early thought.

Okemah itself offered Guthrie more than rock wars. After 1918 the town began to change from an agricultural entrepot to a banking and investment center. The question on everyone's mind was no longer the land itself, but what was under it, as oil had been discovered in large quantities. Guthrie found excitement in the town rather than in his home. He stated that his family did not share in the oil boom profits; with a laugh, Guthrie said, ''No, we got the grease, we didn't get no oil.''[27] Guthrie and the town were excited when newspaper headlines told of the promising influx: ''The Oil Derricks Come Marching on in Okfuskee County; Okemah Well Making 500 Barrels—Pipeline Being Laid; [and] Magnolia Pipeline Soon to be Extended to Okemah.''[28] His description of the beginning boom indicates the zest of the people: ''Trains whistled into our town a hundred coaches long. Men drove their heavy wagons by the score down to pull up alongside of the cars, and skidded the big engines. . . . They unloaded the railroad cars, and loaded and tugged a blue jillion different kinds of funny looking gadgets out into the field. And then it seemed like all on one day, the solid-tired trucks come into the country, making such a road that it made your back teeth rattle.''

As Guthrie found himself more a part of this rapid transformation, he described it as a sordid carnival atmosphere. He gave a dim view of the types of oil production people to first come to Okemah: ''The first people to hit town was the big builders, cement men, carpenters, teamskinners, wild tribes of horse traders and gypsy wagons loaded full, and wheels breaking down; crooked gamblers, pimps, whores, dope fiends, and peddlers, stray musicians and street singers, preachers cussing about love and begging for tips on the street corner. Indians in dirty loud clothes chanting along the sidewalks with their kids crawling and playing in the filth and grime underfoot.''[29] According to Guthrie, the population of Okemah increased about five times during this period, going from the original 1,000 to nearly 5,000. Some Okemah residents recalled what this increase did to the settlement. ''You would see tents around town,'' said Mrs. Chowning, ''where some men would sleep in the day and others would sleep at night.'' From this change, Guthrie gained both positive and negative reinforcement. His parents were also influenced, and their money often was mismanaged. ''The children,'' recalled one observer of the Guthries, ''always had expensive toys, but necessities were scarce.'' When Guthrie became more dependent on Okemah for his education and livelihood, he discovered that the town was equally, if not more guilty of mismanagement than his mother and father. The oil discovered beneath Okemah's soil was not the only thing to be revealed. The saying that excessive wealth breeds greed and greed breeds violence was proved in Okemah's oil boom. The long held racial hatred of the community soon exploded with a force equal to any oil gusher.[30]

Violence soon became an intricate part of the oil boom. After a hard day's rigging and drilling, oilfield workers and those feeding off the fast and easy money came to town for a night's entertainment. Gambling, drinking and prostitution were undoubtedly prime pastimes. Guthrie described an election night in oil-boom Okemah: ''A board was all lit up, and the different names of the men that was running for office was painted on it. One column would be, say, 'Frank Smith for Sheriff,' and the next 'John Wolkes.' One column would say 'Fistfights' and another column would read 'Gangfights.' A man would come out every hour during the night and write 'Precinct Number Two, for Sheriff Frank Smith, three votes, John Wilkes four, Fistfights four, Gangfights none.' "[31]

Throughout the oil boom, the *Okemah Ledger* in numerous brief accounts reported the activities of the town's less respectable citizens. Lawlessness became a common topic, as reported in its headlines: "Three Men Hold Up Okfuskee Storekeeper; Sheriff Finds Buried Still and Whiskey; Pleads Guilty to Whiskey Offence; [and] Gamblers and Choc Seller Arrested."[32]

The culmination of the fist fighting days of Guthrie's father had come. Though this new violence in Okemah may have been exciting to young Guthrie, it was of a different calibre than the earlier tales of political fisticuffs. The new violence was definitely non-political. The times were such that making money became an end in itself, and the best confidence man often became the richest. During this time, while an early teen-ager, Guthrie donned his father's business suit and attempted to make his own way in the bustling town. As a businessman, however, Guthrie was not as successful as his father. He described his short career as a root beer salesman in a concession stand. Guthrie was instructed by his boss, however, to sell on request the little bottles under the counter. Curious to taste the "rot gut," he sampled one of the bottles. "When I woke up," Guthrie claimed, "I was out of a job." His next venture was in the newspaper business, this time as a street-corner newspaperboy. Guthrie soon discovered that oil-boom workers either could not or would not read the news. He realized, though, that if anything were made to look like something, especially something exciting, it would sell. Guthrie's procedure was both profitable and humorous. He would sell all his papers to the local drunks who would roam Okemah's Main Street, shouting out humorous headlines young Guthrie had composed himself. Unfortunately local officials were not totally pleased with this fun business venture. Guthrie described the results: "I spent sixty cents for twenty more papers at the drugstore. 'Listen,' the paper man was telling me, 'th' sheriff is gettin' mighty sore at you. Every night there's three or four drunks walkin' up and down th' streets with about twenty papers yelling out some goofy headlines!' '' Guthrie replied: "Business is business."[33] Fortunately, Guthrie never became a cold-hearted business man; if the oil boom taught him anything, it was that within any system that operates with acts of violence, and the confidence game, some must win and some must lose. The losers, the blacks and Indians of the town, became Guthrie's prime interest in later Okemah years and in the years that followed after he left his birthplace.

The racial scene of Okemah had its foundation before Guthrie's birth. What he witnessed was a result of years of growing discontent between the races. The *Okemah Ledger* once boasted of the town's near total whiteness. In 1911, the year before Guthrie's birth, the school census was reported as 555 white students and 1 black student. The fact was celebrated by calling Okemah "a banner white town." At the end of the school year, however, the boasting had changed to fear after two blacks, Laura and L. D. Nelson, were lynched six miles north of town on a bridge over the North Canadian River. They were hanged for shooting George Loney, a local rancher, who reportedly caught them in the act of cattle rustling. The fear in the minds of Okemah whites was a result of rumors of black retribution by "sacking and burning" the town.[34] By Guthrie's time, during and after the oil boom, the general feeling toward blacks in Okemah was distrust and fear. Guthrie undoubtedly heard many versions of the lynch-night scene, and he likewise felt the discomfort between the races in the town.[35]

The oil boom was indirectly responsible for some racial tension, for the population of Okemah had increased not only in number but also in racial distribution. Guthrie claimed the town was made up of "one-quarter negro, one-quarter Indian, and one-half white." When asked how they got along, he replied, "No, not what I'd call equal terms. There's been a lot of shooting scrapes and fights. They have some crazy way of looking at the colored situation."[36] The "crazy way" of the white population often involved violence or the threat of violence as the only solution. For the black and Indian in Okemah, hostility was a way of life. Because they were generally not allowed to share directly in the oil boom, they often resorted to taking their share. Again *Okemah Ledger* headlines told the story: "Two Negroes in Jail on Horse Stealing Charge; [and] Indian

Caught Stealing Weapons from Sheriff's Office.''[37] Fearful of a minority uprising, white retribution was often serious. In a simple case of chicken stealing, "one Negro," Shirley Watson, was tried for the crime. She was sentenced to one year of imprisonment at a trial held approximately one year after the thievery. On the date of the crime, January 22, 1921, her accomplice, Felix Moaning, also a black, had been shot and killed, "caught in the act."[38]

The culmination of Okemah's racial tension came on July 5, 1922, when a group of white-sheeted men paraded in open cars down the main street of the town. A newspaper reporter claimed that the parade plus the $50.00 charitable donation made in the name of the Ku Klux Klan a week before proved its existence in Okfuskee County.[39] The parade was undoubtedly the Klan's warning to the local blacks.

The town had changed from the quiet farming community of Woody's early years. The Guthries themselves had experienced an equally radical transformation. While the oil boom gave Guthrie's father promise of a new and more powerful political office as Oklahoma Corporation Commissioner, the increase in violence and hatred heightened his wife's worry. The Guthries, according to Woody, in order to start fresh and give his mother a change of environment, moved to Oklahoma City in 1923. Guthrie's account of their stay of nearly a year is not specific, but it reveals that his father was unable to find satisfactory employment. Guthrie also made no comment concerning politics; his father's political career had evidently lost its initial promise. Nevertheless, the Guthries returned to Okemah in 1924, hoping to start a business in the new motorcycle industry. Woody's uncle, Leonard Tanner, had convinced his father of going into business with him as a motorcycle dealer in Okemah. When Tanner was suddenly killed, the Guthries once again lost an opportunity to regain their livelihood and status. The town could offer little for the family, for the oil boom was declining. Guthrie described the results:

I bumped along. Drug along. Maybe that old man was right. I looked in at the lobby of the Broadway Hotel. Nobody. I looked through the plate glass of Bill Bailey's pool hall. Just a long row of brass spittoons there by their self in the dark. I looked in at the Yellow Dog bootleg joint. Shelves shot all to pieces. I looked in the window of a grocery store at a clerk with glasses on playing a fast game of solitaire. Weeds and grass in the door of this garage? Always was a big bunch of men hanging around there. Nobody running to and out of the Monkey Oil Drug Store. They even took the monkey and the cage from out in front. Benches, benches. All whittled and cut to pieces. Men must not have much to do but just hump around and whittle on benches. Nobody even sweeps up the shavings.[40]

Guthrie's description revealed the havoc of overuse. The "grab-it-all" philosophy had almost turned Okemah into a ghost town, and it would take time for it to recover some of its economic vitality. The Guthries, however, never had a chance to recoup financially. Woody's mother soon worsened and the doctor's advice was followed. She was sent to the Central State Hospital in Norman, Oklahoma, leaving Guthrie's father as the sole head of the household. He alone could not provide the security the Guthrie children needed. Ironically, Guthrie's father was the victim of another mysterious fire which nearly took his life shortly after his wife's commitment. Woody supplied the gossip this time: "I always will think he done it on purpose. He lost all his money; he lost his hog ranch; he used to raise the best pure bred hogs in the whole country. He felt like he was doing something good. Working hard." Though Guthrie's father did not die from his burns, he went to Pampa, Texas, to recover at his sister's farm. The children were adopted by the town, although Woody never chose any particular family as a permanent address.[41] He was completely on his own for the first time. In the next several years in Okemah, he would learn a great deal.

Because it had become an Okemah custom to talk about the Guthries, the children then became the center of attention. Woody, who found himself on his own, lived in the old "gang" house and became a junk collector. "We had an old wagon," recalled his partner, Colonel Martin, "which we built ourselves. We didn't do it too well for we had two big wheels in front and two little wheels in back so all the weight went on the old Jenny. We'd haul our junk and sell it out at Mark's Junk Yard here in town."[42] People began to pity the sight of Guthrie in quest of money. "Woody was a mess," recalled Mrs. Chowning, who first took an interest in him when he began to live on his own. "He used to come to my back door," she said, "and sing a song. We'd have coffee or tea together." For a short time Guthrie was the concern of the more respectable families of Okemah. Mrs. Chowning could have influenced the youth's decision to join the Boy's Glee Club in high school, for she was as early as 1922 one of the directors for the Glee Club theater productions.[43]

In school Guthrie was an unusual student. "He used to go to school early because no one was at home," recalled Mrs. Dorothy Dill of Okemah. "He'd draw funny pictures on the blackboard," she went on, "and all the other students would try to get there early to see what Woody drew." On one occasion he drew a picture of two stick figures running past a fire hydrant with a city in the background. On the lower left hand corner, Guthrie wrote his name in large capital letters. Once proud that his mother could sign her name for social purposes, it was as if Woody now signed his name for attention, a reminder that the Guthrie name still had promise of being respected again.

Guthrie's formal education, though not complete, offered him many opportunities to perform in public. "He was a little showman, a natural performer," one friend recalled. "The teacher never had to tell Woody what to do," Mrs. Dill said, "he'd just get up and begin to sing and dance." Others recalled Guthrie's in-town performances. Whenever money was needed for school functions, the students would borrow the Dosseys' wagon and Guthrie would sing and dance on it while others passed the hat. Martin remembered Woody's "ebony bones" which he ordered by mail: "They were about eight inches long and he would rub them together to get music and he would do a jig dance." Even those who remembered him in less than favorable terms admitted his unusual talents. "When we bigger boys went out for football and basketball," J. O. Smith said, "Woody would carry the water. He was a little wirey haired fellow always under foot, always making some kind of music in the back of the classroom."[44]

Though Guthrie performed more than he studied, and spent more time on the street than in the classroom, he found some time for high school academics and activities. The structure and discipline required in high school was likely too much for the parentless boy. In English, Guthrie did barely "C" work for a three year average, while in algebra his grade was closer to the "B" level. Guthrie

made up this low grade in English by participation on the staff of
Panther, the high school newspaper, and as a member of the Publications Club, which was the yearbook committee. These activities
were undoubtedly more suited to him than a structured classroom.
Nevertheless, typing, like algebra, was easy for Guthrie, and an
"A" was his reward. Geography, too, posed no problems for him,
for another "A" was added to his record. In ancient and modern
history, he did near "B" level work as a total average. Guthrie's
only failure came in psychology.[45] As in English, his own personality and past experiences were probably in conflict with preconceived
theories. Guthrie had learned that fate, not psychology, was the
determining factor in life. It was wiser for him to base theories on
the facts of life rather than to create dreams.

School could not give Guthrie enough, for he had lost his family
and Okemah's oil boom excitement also had died. However, his
memories of lost wealth, status and love were rejuvenated through
his close contacts with the two minorities of Okemah, the blacks and
Indians. Guthrie found in them a deep respect for their openly
expressed cultures. "Woody never missed an Indian stickball game
or the annual Corn Dance," said Mrs. Chowning. "Those stickball
games," she continued, "were worse than bull fights. They'd just
get out there and practically kill one another." Guthrie, who relished in excitement, found a new cause for violence and celebration.
He must have been close to the Indians, for according to Mrs.
Chowning, "you had to be invited to attend their annual Corn
Dance."[46]

The blacks of Okemah, however, became Guthrie's prime interest. From them he not only learned music but also discovered the
blues, a way of expressing want, need and loneliness. He confessed
his love for the Negroes: "Ever since I was a kid . . . I've always
found time to stop and talk to those colored people because I found
them to be full of jokes [and] . . . wisdom. . . . I learned how to play
the French harp off a boy shining shoes down there. I was about fifteen or sixteen years old. He was playing the railroad blues. Every
day he'd play one; it was the same title over and over; he'd im-
provise. I never hardly pass an Indian or Negro—I learned to like
them."[47] Guthrie "learned to like them" because they too could
express in music the feeling he had already developed about life—

that poverty, deprivation, injustice and loneliness were often un-avoidable. People were victims of these fates.

By 1940, shortly before Guthrie wrote his message of hope to the people of his hometown, he recalled what Okemah had taught him. By 1929, the year his high school transcript was mailed to Pampa, Texas, Guthrie already had seen what the American public was to witness in the Great Depression. The Dust Bowl had worsened Oklahoma's plight, and Guthrie found the rhythm of sadness in Negro music to be a perfect expression of those hard economic times. He described the feeling of this music: "The blues is plain ole being lonesome." He remembered his Oklahoma years. "People where I come from are lonesome for a job, lonesome for spending money, lonesome for drinking whiskey." The conditions of the blues, Guthrie pointed out, were "Being out of work, being lonesome, being in jail." To him the blues was [sic] "a complaint, a lament, something wrong when you look around."[48] The lonesome sound of the black harmonica player's "railroad blues" which Guthrie heard as a young boy in Okemah later became his song for all people. The trains which the people of Okemah enthusiastically observed were now leaving, taking with them a good part of the town's spirit.

Guthrie's experiences in Okemah would have been sufficient cause for him to become a cynic: the numerous fires, his mother's illness and his early struggles for self-survival. Surprisingly, however, he maintained a spirit of hope. This spirit was taken directly from his Oklahoma years. His mother's message to her children to "fight for our Papa" became for Guthrie a cause to fight for all people who suffer from hard times. His hope was ever present, and Okemah was always on his mind.

Guthrie's parents attempted to provide him with a comfortable homelife and a middle class way of life. This influence later found expression in Guthrie's many songs for and about children. His "Riding in My Car," for instance, presents a typical scene of a child asking his father to go for a car ride. Guthrie delighted young audiences in this ballad with his car motor and honking horn sounds. In most of his children songs, a warm and loving homelife was presented. After the car ride, in this hypothetical home, the father might sing a lullaby such as "Grassy Grass Grass" in which, with-

out guitar accompaniment, Guthrie tapped out the rhythm in repeated phrases such as:

> Grassey grass grass,
> Tree tree tree,
> Leafie leaf leaf,
> One two three.[49]

Secure in bed in a loving home the children would sleep. Guthrie's
early years were quite similar.

A man must by necessity earn a living. On a more serious level,
Guthrie showed the influence of his father's journalistic and political mind. His father had always presented himself, and others had
always thought of him, as a common man with broad backgrounds
and interests. Though an ardent politician, he always considered his
family, and had "down to earth values." Fate unfortunately denied
Guthrie's father the ultimate success he strove for all his life. The
common man, dispossessed of his home, became Woody Guthrie's
theme.

Oklahoma's Dust Bowl offered Guthrie a tremendous source for
trying this idea. After he left Okemah in 1929, he spent several
years in Texas living once again with his father. In the early 1930s
Guthrie hit the road for California, which he initially considered as
the "land of milk and honey." By 1940, however, he had learned
that California was not the promised land. His advice to would-be
Okies—those who had migrated from Oklahoma to California—
was to stay at home and work for better conditions within their
native state. He warned Oklahomans of the half-truths spread by
popular singer Jimmie Rodgers who in "California Blues" claimed
that in California people could "sleep out every night" and drink
water that tastes "like cherry wine." Guthrie registered his advice
to the would-be Okies in his own ballad "Do Re Me":

> Well if you want to buy a home or farm,
> That can't do nobody harm,
> Or take your vacation by the mountains or the sea,
> Don't swap your old cow for a car,
> You'd better stay right where you are;
> Well you'd better take this little tip from me,

> Cause I look through the want-ads every day,
> And the headlines on the papers always say oh . . .
> If you ain't got the Do Re Mi, boys, (repeat)
> Well you better go back to beautiful Texas, Oklahoma,
> Georgia, Kansas, Tennessee.[50]

For a victim of the Dust Bowl, to stay in Oklahoma was often impossible. Guthrie offered the homeless sharecropper two alternatives to leaving. Both choices were based on his father's teachings: to stay and fight with your fists, or to stay and work through the system. The two most popular ballads by Guthrie, "Pretty Boy Floyd" and "Tom Joad," reflect these alternatives for the common man. In the ballads, Pretty Boy Floyd was an outlaw while Tom Joad joined the unions for a common cause. Both ballads reflect the extremes of Guthrie's personality and Oklahoma experience.

In "Pretty Boy Floyd," the common man, Charles "Pretty Boy" Floyd, encountered the evil deputy sheriff who, using "vulgar words of language," indirectly insults Floyd's wife. The conflict, Guthrie explained, was over a new ruling in town: "They had made a new ruling since Pretty Boy had been to town about the week before about tying your horses—automobiles was getting pretty big about that time." Floyd was a true gentleman and, to protect his lady's honor, grabbed a log chain. "And in the fight that followed he laid that deputy down." Although the deputy had drawn his gun, Floyd was forced to escape to "the trees and timbers on that North Canadian River's shore." From that point on, Guthrie claimed, Floyd became an outlaw because the story of the deputy's death began to grow. Guthrie describes a typical rumor concerning Charles Floyd: "He was worse than quintuplets, with three guns in each hand an a whole bunch more in his pocket."

Woody made "Pretty Boy" Floyd into a twentieth century Robin Hood. Floyd, though an outlaw, is open, direct and honest to himself. He will rob the banks which have robbed the good farmers. His method was a "Wild West" expression:

> Now as through this world I ramble,
> I've seen lots of funny men,
> Some will rob you with a six gun,
> And some with a fountain pen.

Guthrie gave Floyd a peculiar quality. Floyd loved the homesteader much as Guthrie's father praised the "real home-builders." In the ballad, Floyd would "come to beg a meal" from a farmer, and "leave a thousand dollar bill" underneath the napkin as a thank you note. Guthrie claimed that "You'll never see an outlaw drive a family from their home."[51] Like Guthrie's father, Floyd was forced to live a life determined much by chance and circumstance. He was not afraid to fight for his rights and therefore had to pay the price. The ballad, "Pretty Boy Floyd," had an unusual appeal because, unlike a "Jesse James" type ballad, "Pretty Boy Floyd" does not end in a shoot-out with the law winning. Instead, Floyd would, it was implied, continue to live outside the system and at the same time contribute to the needy farmers. As the Guthries tried to live on, as Woody continued to hope, so does the message of "Pretty Boy Floyd."

The outlaw motif was considerably softened in "Tom Joad," a ballad based upon the movie version of John Steinbeck's *The Grapes of Wrath*. The Joads, a family united around Ma Joad, were a family of dispossessed sharecroppers. Guthrie idealized the two heroes of this ballad, Preacher Casey and Tom Joad, by making their message impossible to reject. Guthrie transferred his own mother's teachings when Tom Joad, a probable self-portrait, speaks:

> Wherever little children are hungry and cry!
> Wherever people ain't free;
> Wherever men are fightin' for their rights,
> That's where I'm a gonna be, Ma,
> That's where I'm a gonna be.

Though Tom Joad joined the organized unions, he did so for a human cause. He would, it was assumed, attempt to create a purer way of life by becoming more socially aware of people's needs. Guthrie, who once fought for the "new kids" because they had no "say so" in how "the gang" was run, now fought for the "new men" who again "had no say so" in how the nation and their lives were run.[52]

Guthrie's concern with the Dust Bowl refugees found expression through two other ballads, "I'm a Jolly Banker" and "Willy Rogers Highway." In both ballads, Woody reflected his father's belief in private rather than governmental ownership of land and homes. In both cases, Guthrie protested the conditions of the Oklahoman by casting blame on a "mysteriously" evil or totally ineffective Federal government. Both ballads were quite satiric in tone with a reminder of the "Ta, Ta, Doc Rev Socialist Windjammer" attitude of Guthrie's father.

In "I'm a Jolly Banker," the banker, named "Tom Pranker," acts according to his name:

> I safeguard the farmers, widows and orphans,
> I check up your shortage,
> And bring down your mortgage;
> I'll plaster your home with a furniture loan;
> If you show that you need it, I'll let you have credit,
> Just bring me back two, for the one I lent you;
> I'll come down and help you, I'll rake you I'll scalp you,
> I'm a Jolly Banker, Jolly Banker am I.

Guthrie, who once said, "business is business," was only a boy operating in an oil boom where money was plentiful. As a young man trying to get along, he found little room for a "Tom Pranker," a man who had no feeling or compassion. Pranker's only desire is for self-gain and greed. As a banker, Pranker stood as a symbol of the Federal government. Unlike an outlaw, the government could literally rob anyone with a fountain pen. Guthrie satirized the government, and at the same time proclaimed the natural innocence of the "widows, orphans and children."

In similar fashion, Guthrie satirized the Oklahoma hero, Will Rogers, in "Willy Rogers Highway." The tone of this ballad was definitely personal. Guthrie had a share of what was now dust and hunger. He opens his ballad with a direct challenge to Will Rogers:

> My Sixty-Six highway, this Will Rogers road,
> It's lined with jalopies just as far as I can see;
> Can you think up a joke, Will, for all o' these folks
> From New York town down to Los Angeles.

Guthrie continued this challenge in the remaining refrains. These lines reveal a more specific protest:

> Can you make up a joke that'll win them a job?
> Can you grin up a tale that'll feed my folks stranded?
> Did ye tickle Hoover enuf ta build us all houses?
> You hafta go back, Will, and tickle 'em again.[53]

The relief of humor which Rogers gave to the movie audiences of the 1930s seemed insufficient to Guthrie. Although Guthrie had a well-developed sense of humor, he could not find reason to laugh at such Rogers films as *David Harum,* in which Rogers played a hard dealing but golden hearted banker. In the movie, Rogers was no "Tom Pranker." Instead, he gave the widow her mortgage, paid in full as a Christmas Day present.[54] For Guthrie, the hometown banker as portrayed in this film did not exist. In times of need, Guthrie wanted workable solutions, not charity.

Guthrie found a solution to the needs of economically depressed Americans in the growing labor unions. The defense Guthrie's father gave to the American Federation of Labor in 1912 became in Guthrie a personal campaign. In 1940, he returned to Oklahoma to work for the Oklahoma City local union of the Congress of Industrial Organizations. The oilfield workers were on strike for better conditions and Guthrie performed at several of their union rallies. Working for Bob and Ina Wood, he composed his most noted union ballad, "Union Maid." In it Guthrie presents a picture of a working woman, a woman who is not afraid:

> There once was a union maid, She never was afraid,
> Of goons and ginks and company finks,
> And the deputy sheriffs that made the raid.

The union maid, however, was also strong because she has a family united for a common cause:

> Get you a man who's a Union man,
> And join the Ladies Auxiliary,
> Married life ain't hard,
> When you got a union card.[55]

Guthrie saw promise in a union of people working for better conditions. During their Okemah years, the Guthries had never found the rewards of a united effort, for fire, wind and death removed their opportunities.

For Guthrie, the family unit was the basis for strength in fighting injustice. Guthrie, like his father, warned people against the dangers of political bossism, and both Guthries called for united action on the part of Americans to fight side by side for a common cause.

Guthrie left Oklahoma in 1929, but his stay in Pampa, Texas, was short lived, and in the mid-1930s he made the trek westward to California with thousands of Dust Bowl refugees. Like the others, whom Steinbeck called ''Anonymous People,'' Guthrie took his Oklahoma heritage; however, unlike the others, he was a talented singer, writer and personality. Guthrie's Oklahoma years served him in two principal ways. He learned many native American ballads from his mother which gave to him a deep respect for American cultural history as recorded through song, and most important, he realized that poverty was only a matter of circumstance. His own deprivations plus the misery he saw around him enabled Guthrie to empathize with his fellow man. From his father, however, Guthrie found inspiration and hope. Also like his father, Guthrie believed in the rights of the common man. Stated simply, Guthrie's contribution to American thought was based on three basic ideals. The right of the common man to seek and maintain ownership of private property was foremost in Guthrie's thought. Ideally expressed, this right would find culmination in a small self-sufficient farm. In addition Guthrie believed in the sanctity of a strong family unit. He maintained that a strong family was a basic means of achieving social reform. The family unit would provide a sense of love and security, protecting the common man from the often inhumane corporate structures. Guthrie's third principle was directly inherited from his Oklahoma experience. With the end of the Okemah oil boom and the beginning of the catastrophic Dust Bowl and Great Depression, Guthrie witnessed the downfall of the common man. His belief in the right of every man to earn a living without fear or degradation served him as a guiding principle from the 1930s until his death in 1967.

The later works of Guthrie, when analyzed in terms of his three major beliefs, reveal that he never forsook his Oklahoma cultural heritage. The observant historian can find in the life and works of

Guthrie a unique approach to American history in turmoil. Guthrie's interpretations of the Dust Bowl, the Great Depression, the development of the labor unions, World War II and the McCarthy Era are to a great extent from an Oklahoma point of view. As America changed from an agricultural to an industrial society, Guthrie attempted to remind Americans that the agrarian love for a home, a family and a job were still worth preserving. Through the ballad tradition, Guthrie fought a battle against the creation of a society devoid of human compassion. As a veteran of diverse economic periods in Oklahoma history from the Okemah oil boom to the Dust Bowl, Guthrie was able to give his messages of hope to all Americans.

NOTES

1. John Anderson, "Woody Guthrie's Memory Still Out of Tune," *Chicago Tribune,* May 5, 1980.

2. James Kirby Martin et al., *America and Its People:* vol. 2, *From 1865* (Glenview, Ill.: Scott, Foresman and Co., 1989), 778–79.

3. Woody Guthrie, "Letter to the People of Okemah," "Today" column, *Okemah Ledger,* n.d., Dorothy Dill's "Scrapbook," Okemah, Okla.

4. Woody Guthrie, "Interview of Alan Lomax," *Woody Guthrie: Library of Congress Recordings* (Washington, D.C., March 22, 1940), Side Number 1; Woody Guthrie, *Bound for Glory* (New York: E. P. Dutton, 1943), 39.

5. Ibid., 38, 39.

6. Guthrie, *Woody Guthrie: Library of Congress Recordings,* Side Number 1.

7. Guthrie, *Bound for Glory,* 72.

8. Interview, Mrs. V. K. Chowning, Okemah, Okla., June 27, 1973.

9. Guthrie, *Bound for Glory,* 38–39, 77.

10. Interview, Mrs. Chowning. The belief at the time was that Guthrie's mother could not stand the pressure of her husband's political career. The ups and downs involved in land trading and running for public office were assumed to be the cause of her deep depressions, resulting in her total mental breakdown. What was assumed to have been madness is now known to have been Huntington's Chorea, a hereditary nerve-degenerating disease. The facts known about her health, however, appear not to diminish the reactions people still have concerning the Guthrie family.

11. Guthrie, *Woody Guthrie: Library of Congress Recordings,* Side Number 1.

12. Interview, Mrs. Chowning.

13. *Okemah Ledger,* July 18, 1912, p. 2.

14. Guthrie, *Woody Guthrie: Library of Congress Recordings,* Side Number 1.

15. Interview, Col. Martin, Okemah, Okla., June 28, 1973; *Okemah Ledger,*

January 4, 1912, p. 1; Guthrie, *The Nearly Complete Collection of Woody Guthrie Folk Songs* (New York: Ludlow Music, 1963).

16. *Okemah Ledger,* July 18, 1912, pp. 5, 12.

17. Ibid., August 15, 1912, p. 1.

18. Guthrie, *Bound for Glory,* 37, 49; Guthrie, *Woody Guthrie: Library of Congress Recordings,* Side Number 1.

19. Interview, Mrs. Chowning; Guthrie, *Bound for Glory,* 44, 45–56.

20. Guthrie, *Bound for Glory,* 46.

21. Ibid., 41; Guthrie, *Woody Guthrie: Library of Congress Recordings,* Side Number 1; Interview, Col. and Mrs. Martin.

22. Interview, Mrs. Dorothy Dill, Okemah, Okla., June 27, 28, 1973; "Roy Martin Recalls Okemah," in Mrs. Dill's "Scrapbook."

23. Guthrie, *Bound for Glory,* 89.

24. *Okemah Ledger,* June 29, 1922, p. 1, and July 13, 1922, p. 1.

25. Guthrie, *Bound for Glory,* 133, 136.

26. Interview, Mrs. Chowning.

27. Guthrie, *Bound for Glory,* 116; Guthrie, *Woody Guthrie: Library of Congress Recordings,* Side Number 1.

28. *Okemah Ledger,* July 17, 1919, p. 1, February 23, 1922, p. 1, and March 2, 1922, p. 2.

29. Guthrie, *Bound for Glory,* 94, 96.

30. Guthrie, *Woody Guthrie: Library of Congress Recordings,* Side Number 1; Interview, Mrs. Chowning.

31. Guthrie, *Bound for Glory,* 96–97.

32. *Okemah Ledger,* February 23, 1922, p. 1.

33. Guthrie, *Bound for Glory,* 93–101; Guthrie, *Woody Guthrie: Library of Congress Recordings,* Side Number 1.

34. *Okemah Ledger,* March 7, 1912, p. 1; "Imaginations Run Wild in Okemah," *Okemah Ledger,* May 25, 1911, n.p.

35. Interview, Mrs. Dill; Mr. Glenn Dill, also present at the interview, disagreed with his wife concerning the lynching. Their reactions made the event seem as if it had happened yesterday.

36. Guthrie, *Woody Guthrie: Library of Congress Recordings,* Side Number 4.

37. *Okemah Ledger,* February 23, 1922, p. 1, and July 17, 1919, p. 1.

38. Ibid., January 12, 1922, p. 1.

39. Ibid., July 5, 1922, p. 1.

40. Guthrie, *Bound for Glory,* 138–47.

41. Ibid., 157; Guthrie, *Woody Guthrie: Library of Congress Recordings,* Side Number 1; Interview, Col. Martin.

42. Ibid.

43. Interview, Mrs. Chowning; *Okemah Ledger,* April 20, 1922, p. 1.

44. Interview, Mrs. Dill; Guthrie's drawing, Mrs. Dill's "Scrapbook"; Interviews, Col. Martin and J. O. Smith, Okemah, Okla., June 27, 28, 1973.

45. Guthrie, "Pupil's Record of High School Credits," Superintendent's Office, Public Schools, Okemah, Okla.

46. Interview, Mrs. Chowning.

47. Guthrie, *Woody Guthrie: Library of Congress Recordings,* Side Number 1.

48. Ibid.

49. Guthrie, "Grassey Grass Grass," *The Greatest Songs of Woody Guthrie,* Vanguard VSD-35, Side Number 2.

50. Guthrie, "Do Re Mi," *The Nearly Complete Collection of Woody Guthrie Folk Songs,* 66.

51. Guthrie, *Woody Guthrie: Library of Congress Recordings,* Side Number 3; Guthrie, *The Nearly Complete Collection of Woody Guthrie Folk Songs,* 86.

52. Ibid., 90; Guthrie, *Bound for Glory,* 116.

53. Guthrie, "Jolly Banker," on *Woody Guthrie: Library of Congress Recordings,* Side Number 3; Guthrie, "Willy Rogers Highway," *The Nearly Complete Collection of Woody Guthrie Folk Songs,* 126; Guthrie, *Bound for Glory,* 101.

54. *David Harum,* Will Rogers Memorial, Claremore, Oklahoma.

55. Pete Seeger, "Woody Guthrie, Songwriter," *Ramparts* (Nov. 30, 1968): 30; Guthrie, "Union Maid," *The Nearly Complete Collection of Woody Guthrie Folk Songs,* 94.

10

THE NEW DEAL COMES TO SHAWNEE

Dale E. Soden

No one doubts the importance of the New Deal either in the nation or in Oklahoma. Yet that phrase, "the New Deal," is so vague and impersonal, and its history at the national level so complex, that it is sometimes very hard for students to get a handle on. This article by Dale Soden, from the Chronicles of Oklahoma *in 1985, helps to make it comprehensible and concrete by localizing it to one Oklahoma community, Shawnee. Soden is now an associate professor of history at Whitworth College, Spokane, Washington.*

The New Deal, regarded by virtually all historians as the most celebrated American public works project, has been intensively analyzed at the national level. Franklin D. Roosevelt's leadership, congressional appropriations, psychological impact, and overall effectiveness have received close scrutiny from historians. In Oklahoma, while the experience of the Great Depression, and most notably the plight of the farmers, has received a great deal of study, the impact of specific New Deal programs has received relatively little attention. Danney Goble and

"The New Deal Comes to Shawnee," by Dale E. Soden, first appeared in *The Chronicles of Oklahoma* 63, no. 2 (Summer 1985): 116–25. Copyright 1985. Reprinted from *The Chronicles of Oklahoma* (Oklahoma City: Oklahoma Historical Society, 1985) with permission.

James R. Scales have highlighted the response of Oklahoma's governors, but otherwise very little is known about how the New Deal functioned at either the county or the city level. The most recent work on the impact of the New Deal in the West, by Richard Lowitt, touches on some dimensions of the New Deal in Oklahoma but does not explore its implementation in large cities or small towns.[1]

An excellent case study of specific New Deal programs in Oklahoma is the town of Shawnee. In 1929, at the time of the stock market crash, Shawnee had a reasonably diverse economy for a town of approximately 24,000. Settled after the land run of 1891, Shawnee was remarkably industrialized as well as being an agricultural trading center. The Choctaw Railroad, which later was absorbed by the Rock Island, had chosen Shawnee, in 1896, as the site of its southwestern regional repair shops. Employing about 1,000 workers, the shops provided a firm foundation for future growth. An iron foundry, garment factory, and the largest cotton seed oil mill in the Southwest added an additional base of blue collar work. Town fathers hoped Shawnee would outdistance Oklahoma City as the hub city for the central part of the state, but by 1910 it was clear that Shawnee would play a secondary role after coming in a distant third in the state-wide election to determine the state capital.

For the next decade the population and economy of Shawnee remained static while depending on existing industry. Then, in the 1920s the city benefitted substantially from the oil boom in the Greater Seminole Oil Field. Population increased significantly and the city experienced major growth in residential and commercial building. The one bleak spot beginning in the mid-1920s was in agriculture; the intrusion of the boll weevil, and declining prices, began to seriously hinder cotton production.[2]

The stock market crash of 1929 did not cause much immediate concern, but during the course of Herbert Hoover's term as president conditions began to deteriorate. By the summer of 1932 Shawnee residents were feeling the full brunt of the Depression. Typical of what the city faced was the announcement in July that the Red Cross could only provide for strict charity cases and that by November 1, funds would be completely expended.[3] In August, the county announced that $90,000 would have to be cut from the budget.[4] Throughout the fall of 1932 and the winter of 1933 city residents became painfully aware of the depth of the Depression. In October, 1932, the Shawnee Unemployment Association met and urged that jobs with public employers be reduced to six hours a day in order to provide new positions. Perhaps more ominous to those who remained employed in Shawnee was the commitment to the prevention of violence during the winter months. ''We realize that conditions will be serious in Shawnee this winter,'' one group's organizer was quoted as saying, ''and we are preparing to organize against any lawlessness that hunger and cold might cause.''[5]

Another indication of the extent of the problem was revealed when the Baptist rescue mission in town reported that between January 3 and May 1, 1933, they had served 36,633 meals.[6] The problems facing Shawnee during the Depression had escalated during the previous November when one of the three city banks, the Shawnee National, collapsed. Tom Steed, who later gained fame as one of Oklahoma's most distinguished congressmen, reflected much of the anguish in his column: ''The shock was great because the public generally had regarded this bank as so rock-ribbed that failure was impossible.''[7] While there were two other major banks in the city, which in 1933 seemed quite solvent, the demise of the Shawnee National shook the confidence of the community rather deeply.

What was apparent to most residents was that new leadership was required; while Franklin Roosevelt's nomination was not met with universal assent, in part because Oklahoma's William ''Alfalfa Bill'' Murray had made an unsuccessful bid for the nomination, at least the Shawnee press began to rally around Roosevelt as the election approached. After Roosevelt's success in November, public optimism began to increase prior to the March inaugural. Then, with Roosevelt's inauguration, the editor of the *Shawnee Times Record* expressed open adulation: ''America's new deal went into effect Saturday noon. Already there has been more action than the Republican administration displayed during its entire four years. Not once has [*sic*] the new leaders appealed to the people of the country to be patient and to 'wait for the prosperity just around the corner.' ''[8]

By the summer of 1933 the effects of Roosevelt's legislative initiatives were beginning to make an impact. The acreage reduction that resulted from the Agricultural Adjustment Act was being favor-

ably received in the Shawnee press, and by October there was great
hope that cotton prices would go higher.[9] The National Recovery
Act, promoted by the Blue Eagle campaign, was greeted with great
enthusiasm. In a telegram to the Chamber of Commerce, Roosevelt
asked that the program get underway immediately. "The public will
be asked to renew its war time patriotism and support only those
who join in this program," said a local reporter who had seen the
telegram. "It is estimated that at least a third of the unemployment in the nation will be wiped out almost overnight as a result
of the program."[10] A number of local merchants announced they
were raising wages, and two local businessmen were appointed
to the state committees of the NRA.[11] By August 4 it was reported
that nearly 100 percent of the community had signed up for the
program.[12]

One aspect of Roosevelt's "100 days" revealed how severe the
Depression was for Shawnee. As a result of the bank holiday and
examination, the State National Bank needed to be closed and then
reorganized. Throughout August and September, Shawnee residents
were promised that the bank would reopen shortly, only to be told
later that continued problems remained unsolved. In fact the bank
was not reopened until January 6, 1934, as American National
Bank.

If the bank holiday reinforced the sense that problems were not
susceptible to the quick fix, Shawnee residents by October of 1933
were less enthusiastic about the NRA. "The novelty is beginning to
wear out, the first thrill of excitement is dying down, and the people
are wanting to be shown," reported one local newspaper. "Millions
of workers are confronted with the unpleasent [sic] spectacle of rising prices unaccompanied by comparable increases in their earning
capacity."[13] In later October and November, criticism began surfac-
ing regarding the inability of the government to raise cotton prices.
Farmers "believe the AAA has failed to aid them; have watched
their purchasing power, in many instances, go sharply on down
while other prices went on up sharply. The administration is frankly
worried as the farmstrike movement grows."[14]

Shawnee residents received much more favorably the relief measures that were a part of the New Deal. The most striking aspect of
Shawnee's experience with the New Deal was the wide variety of

projects which seemed tailored to Shawnee's particular circumstances. The intensity of Shawnee's organization relative to the nationally funded relief programs was indicated in the fact that the first Public Works Administration project in the state was the rebuilding of Jefferson school in Shawnee, which had been previously damaged by a tornado. Groundbreaking occurred the week of October 6, 1933. "In celebration of the event, a gigantic parade was held . . . in which 5,000 school children participated."[15] In November it was reported that 500 men were employed in Civil Works Administration (CWA) projects in the city. Most worked on the flood district project. "There was not a loafer on the job," said one reporter. "They talked to me as they worked. They are accomplishing something in the way of added improvements."[16]

When the Shawnee Chamber of Commerce published its yearly report in March, 1934, extensive attention was paid to the impact of the CWA in the first year. When the program was started, 12,000 people in the county signed up, and of these applicants, 3,500 were employed at one time or another. Each worker averaged between five and six dependents, which meant that CWA funds were feeding an estimated 13,000 to 15,000 people.[17]

Shawnee's CWA projects in early 1934 included the building of a rock wall and two huge gates for the Fairview cemetery. The cemetery streets were graveled and the entire cemetery refurbished. The laying of sewer lines also was a major priority in 1934. "Six thousand feet of sanitary pipe has [sic] been placed throughout the southern part of the city, most of which is situated in the Negro settlement heretofore financially unable to solve its sanitation problems because of prohibitive bond issues."[18] Funds were provided for a "colored park" as well. It is interesting to note that in a Jim Crow city black areas were not totally neglected; still there seemed no systematic attempt to apportion funds. While it is difficult to project, it is doubtful that sewage problem would have been addressed in this section of the city without the New Deal and the infusion of federal capital.[19]

Elsewhere in Shawnee, a dozen city blocks were provided with storm sewers; thirty-six miles of graveled roads were built; and thirty blocks of city streets were paved with asphalt. Every school was "repainted, refinished, its plumbing and electrical equipment rehabilitated and roofs repaired," said the report. "The city fire stations, the city hall and other public offices also have undergone extensive redecorating and repairs."[20]

The relief work in Shawnee was divided into primarily two categories: the first consisted of a variety of local short term projects that were designed either to promote quick employment or satisfy a social need; the second was designed to provide much more substantial public buildings or facilities. In 1985 most of these facilities were still in use, nearly fifty years after their completion. None of the projects, however, were designed to provide long-term structural employment.

The Federal Emergency Relief Association (FERA) directed the efforts of the short-term projects. For example, the survival needs of families received the highest priority. Relief workers found "whole families with measles and some with pneumonia who had no food in their houses." To meet this problem, the agency authorized 282 grocery orders and 1,111 commissary orders for the distribution of flour, butter, meat, and coal.[21] The concern for overall health conditions in the city was prominent. In 1935 a sanitary and general health project was funded at a cost of $9,000. The project employed thirty-five men, two nurses, and two sanitary inspectors. Its purpose was to clean city alleys, parks, and vacant lots, while providing typhoid and diphtheria immunization for school children.[22] This particular effort expanded so that carpenters, cement finishers, and laborers were employed making sanitary toilets.[23] To raise public awareness of the need, the local press reported that between 1922 and 1935, 50,750 infants had died in Oklahoma, and county officials argued that 75 percent of the deaths were the result of unsanitary conditions.[24]

Other FERA projects included the hiring of playground supervisors, asphalt unloading, school repairs, and even book mending at the library. The FERA established a sewing room which provided employment for thirty to forty women making clothing for the needy. There also was a garden project and a cannery for the use of Shawnee residents. And later, the Works Progress Administration sponsored quilting and hobby development for underprivileged persons. Additional funds were provided for what was described as a music project. Student nurses were also given training, and expenditures were approved for the support of housekeepers for the ill and elderly.[25]

Local farmers also received short-term aid from the Federal Emergency Relief Association. The summer of 1934 was drouth-stricken, and it was reported that close to 300 farmers besieged the local FERA Agency for help. In response, the FERA bought 275 head of cattle for the purpose of either putting them on pasture, using the meat for distribution to needy families, or fattening the cattle to be resold.[26] Longer-term aid for farmers came mostly from the Civilian Conservation Corps; officials from the Corps worked with Pottawatomie County farmers on the benefits of contour plowing and other erosion-fighting techniques.[27]

The second category of projects, on the long-term capital improvements, came under the umbrellas of the Works Progress Administration (WPA), the Civil Works Administration (CWA), and Public Works Administration (PWA). These projects, completed between 1935 and 1940, provided Shawnee with a number of significant public structures which were all in use in 1985. The construction of the county courthouse was one of the most important symbols of the New Deal in Shawnee. Bonds had been voted in December, 1933, and were supplemented with over $70,000 from a PWA grant. Construction began in the summer of 1934, and the building was ready for occupation by the end of June, 1935. City fathers orchestrated a rousing celebration in which Governor E. W. Marland and an estimated 25,000 people visited Shawnee to help dedicate the courthouse during a pioneer days celebration.[28]

During the late 1930s, the city benefitted from a number of street resurfacing and paving projects of which the most unusual involved Oklahoma Baptist University. The institution's historian recalled that the university president, John W. Raley, temporarily donated a piece of land to the city in order to avoid violation of the Baptist separation of church and state. The city proceeded to pave an oval street through the university, then gave the land back to the university.[29]

There were a number of other major projects which had long-lasting benefits for the city. A municipal auditorium was constructed in Woodland Park. Containing a gymnasium that could be converted into a state, the auditorium was finished in 1937. Woodland Park also was the site of the construction of a new swimming pool and bath house. Costing approximately $50,000, the pool was still Shawnee's major municipally-owned pool in 1985. In conjunction with the high school, a football stadium was built in 1936 and 1937. Seating 4,000 spectators, the stadium still served the school in 1985. In addition, funds were provided for tennis courts and wading pools in other parks around the city. One project that provided significant long-term benefit was the development of the Deer Creek water supply. An earthen dam was built on Deer Creek, nine miles west of Shawnee, and a reservoir that covered 1,320 acres was created. On July 22, 1937, Shawnee celebrated these projects with a downtown parade, a dinner in the park, and a city-wide social event by the new pool which was marked by a bathing beauty contest sponsored by local merchants.[30]

This heady momentum was slowed during the summer of 1937 following a number of cutbacks in New Deal programs. There was a 25 percent reduction in the number of people employed as funds were slashed state-wide.[31] Over the next few years the only major projects to be funded were the remodeling and rebuilding of Washington and Franklin elementary schools.

NOTES

1. Cecil Turner, "Oklahoma's New Deal: Program and Reaction" (M.A. thesis, University of Oklahoma, 1963); Danney Goble and James R. Scales, *Oklahoma Politics: A History* (Norman: University of Oklahoma Press, 1983); Richard Lowitt, *The New Deal in the West* (Bloomington: Indiana University Press, 1984). An assessment of the impact of the New Deal on Pittsburgh's machine politics can be found in Bruce Stave, *The New Deal and the Last Hurrah* (Pittsburgh: University of Pittsburgh Press, 1970).

2. John Fortson, *Pottawatomie County and What Has Come of It* (Shawnee: Pottawatomie County Historical Society, 1936); Ernestine Gravely, "Fifty Years Ago in Shawnee and Pottawatomie County," *Chronicles of Oklahoma* 31, no. 4 (Winter 1953–54): 381–91.

3. *Shawnee* (Oklahoma) *Times-Record,* July 15, 1932, p. 1.

4. Ibid., Aug. 5, 1932, p. 1.

5. Ibid., Oct. 21, 1932, p. 1.

6. Ibid., May 26, 1933, p. 1.

7. Ibid., Nov. 18, 1932, p. 1.

8. Ibid., Mar. 10, 1933, p. 2.

9. "Shawnee Chamber of Commerce Report," Mar. 1934, p. 6 (located in files of *Shawnee News Star*); *Shawnee Times-Record,* July 21, 1933, p. 1.

10. *Shawnee Times-Record,* July 28, 1933, p. 1.

11. "Shawnee Chamber of Commerce Report"; *Shawnee Times-Record,* July 28, 1933, p. 1.

12. *Shawnee Times-Record,* Aug. 4, 1933, p. 1.

13. Ibid., Oct. 6, 1933.

14. Ibid., Nov. 10, 1933, p. 3.

15. "Shawnee Chamber of Commerce Report," 3; *Shawnee Times-Record,* Oct. 13, 1933, p. 1.

16. *Shawnee Times-Record,* Nov. 24, 1933, p. 1.

17. "Shawnee Chamber of Commerce Report," 4.

18. Ibid.

19. The "colored park" is among the list of projects in the "Index to Oklahoma WPA Projects 1935–1942, Pottawatomie County," Box T 935–55, Oklahoma State Archives, Oklahoma Department of Libraries, Oklahoma City.

20. "Shawnee Chamber of Commerce Report," 4.

21. *Shawnee Times-Record,* Mar. 15, 1934, p. 1.

22. *Shawnee American,* Aug. 23, 1935, p. 1.

23. Ibid., Oct. 25, 1935, p. 1.

24. Ibid., Dec. 20, 1935, p. 4.

25. *Shawnee Times-Record,* Apr. 20, 1934, p. 2; Apr. 27, 1934, p. 1; May 25, 1934, p. 1.

26. Ibid., Aug. 31, 1934, p. 2.

27. Ibid., Nov. 23, 1934, p. 1; Mar. 29, 1935, p. 1.

28. Ibid., July 5, 1935, p. 1.

29. Eunice Short interview, Oct. 18, 1984.

30. *Shawnee American,* July 23, 1937, p. 1; Kenneth Abernathy interview, Feb. 15, 1984.

31. Ibid., June 11, 1937, p. 1. Summaries of the various projects and their expenditures were made. These records can be found in the Government Documents section of the Oklahoma State University Library, Stillwater, Oklahoma, under the title, "U.S. Works Progress Administration. Oklahoma. United States Community Improvement Appraisal Report. State of Oklahoma, Department of Government. (1938) #12 Shawnee."

11

THE SOCIAL GOSPEL OF NICHOLAS COMFORT

Bob Cottrell

Bob Cottrell claims appropriately, in the following 1984 article from the Chronicles of Oklahoma, *that Nicholas Comfort "steadfastly held to his democratic and libertarian ideals. Thus, he unerringly followed the tradition of the homegrown radicalism of the Southwest." But Cottrell also reports that Comfort was "condemned as a 'red,' subjected to bitter criticism, and investigated by the House Un-American Activities Committee and a state legislative inquiry seeking to ferret out communism in Oklahoma public schools." It has sometimes been quite unpopular in Oklahoma to express the very same ideals that have their roots in the state's radical tradition. It would appear that the state, or at least much of its populace, has forgotten—or chosen to ignore—its roots. Cottrell is an associate professor of history at California State University, Chico.*

Nick was always in trouble of some kind. . . . Lord how he used to speak up. . . . He was brimming over with Godly mischief. It would be a mistake to say that Nick was brave . . . he simply was not afraid of anything.

Ken Lowe, 1961

At one point during the 1930s, members of the Ku Klux Klan, attired in their white robes, ventured near the University of Oklahoma campus in Norman. Directly across from the educational institution, they left their infamous brand, a fiery cross. Shortly thereafter, Nicholas Comfort, Presbyterian minister and Dean of the University of Oklahoma School of Religion, drove with a friend to Oklahoma City to talk with the state leader, or Grand Dragon, of the KKK. Seated near the Klan chieftain, Comfort simply informed him that the actions of the hooded organization were wrong, and that even had they been proper, "he had no authority to behave the way he did." The churchman and his compatriot left after the ten minute encounter.[1]

The man who challenged the KKK because of strong personal and religious convictions, Nicholas Comfort, was an individual who became embroiled in the political and social affairs of the University of Oklahoma and the state of Oklahoma for over three decades. Comfort continually spoke out on controversial issues involving the liberties of political dissidents, the civil rights of racial minorities, economic inequality, and American militarism. Because of his writings and other activities, he was condemned as a "red," subjected to bitter criticism, and investigated by the House Un-American Activities Committee and a state legislative inquiry seeking to ferret out Communisim in Oklahoma public schools. Comfort also was a much defended man, admired by many in the Norman community and throughout Oklahoma for his "great personal integrity," "moral courage," "great generosity and sympathy," and uncompromising advocacy of deeply-held principles.[2]

Born in Brookston, Texas, on May 1, 1884, to a family of tenant farmers, this latter-day religious rebel grew up in an atmosphere of impoverishment. Young Nicholas's mother died shortly after his birth, and his father was frequently mired in debt. Working on plantations until he was seventeen, Nicholas moved with his father to Oklahoma in 1901. Boasting few material possessions, they staked a claim to land near Lawton. Because of his parent's illness, the son cleared the acreage and built a house.[3]

Plugging away at a series of jobs, Nicholas had obtained only a first grade education by his twenty-first birthday. But encouraged by the example of a young Indian woman who had returned from college to aid her people, Nick Comfort went back to school. He began a lengthy process of education which culminated with the attainment of three degrees, including a masters of science in theology. While studying, Comfort met and married Estern Ellen Oke of White-

house, Ohio, and helped to support a growing family through
teaching and ministerial work.[4]

The Social Gospel movement, which emerged during the late
nineteenth century and called for clergymen to help correct societal
ills, appealed to Comfort at an early stage of his career. An indication of his propensity to challenge the status quo and champion
underdogs, paralleling the actions of Social Gospel leaders, occurred while he was an instructor at Kansas City University. In 1912
his employers bemoaned the young professor's purported encouragement of student complaints of unsanitary living conditions and
his unwillingness to be a "team player." A 1917 letter from a friend
jokingly addressed to "Dear Heretic," indicated an awareness of
Comfort's belief that the church should confront social, economic,
and religious questions.[5]

Pacifism appealed to certain adherents of the Social Gospel, but
Nick Comfort entered military service in November, 1917, requested a commission as a chaplain which was never granted, and
completed his tour in the United States. His reaction to the military
and to American participation in World War I rapidly developed
into sharp disapproval. Comfort worked with the World Alliance
For International Friendship Through the Churches in an effort to
support the League of Nations and ratification of the Treaty of Ver-
sailles. Like many of his fellow countrymen, he soon felt betrayed
by the inadequacy of "the war to end all wars," and by the failure
of the treaty to resolve strife among the belligerents.[6]

Hoping to discover if he still desired to teach the young people of
his native region, Comfort accepted an appointment in the spring of
1919 as an instructor of philosophy and religion at Trinity College
in Tehuacan, Texas. He left the University of Chicago where he was
studying philosophy under James Hayden Tufts, and had completed
all residential work for a doctorate. The following year, Comfort
asserted his intention to devote his life to building the church in the
rural Southwest. Frequently in conflict with the views of fundamentalists throughout his career, the theologian at that time lambasted
those who failed to support needed change while exhorting instead a
return to "Holy Ghost revivals" or "Old Time Religion." He
declared that the cry of "sad and crushed" tenant children should be

heeded, or white slavery would certainly increase. Should a choice arise between church doctrine and the impoverished young, Comfort indicated that he would unequivocally side with the latter. Furthermore, like a true advocate of the Social Gospel, he charged that to redeem the world required making it a finer place to live in, that moral, social, political, and many other ideas condemned as "new fangled" must be employed.[7]

Believing further educational preparation was essential, Comfort enrolled at the famed Union Theological Seminary in New York City, and received his M.S.T. degree in 1923. He then attended the graduate school of Columbia University, working with John Dewey, but departed in 1924 to become pastor of the Presbyterian students at the University of Oklahoma.[8]

Shortly after arriving in Norman, Nick Comfort became involved with community and state social and political affairs. In July, 1925, he asked the president of the State Federation of Labor to speak at a Rotary Club meeting which he was chairing. The minister mentioned his desire to have the labor position presented to the club, whose members included professionals and businessmen. Comfort stated that most of these individuals were of rural stock, but had apparently "forgotten the block from which they were hewn." Nick's desire to challenge barriers involving class, race, religion, and nationality, and to promote the "brotherhood of man," was also displayed by his support for the religious activities of the Y.W.C.A. He deemed it essential to apply Christian principles to all existing problems, whether social or commercial, national or international.[9]

Because of a belief that public academic establishments offered inadequate religious instruction, Comfort joined with others to establish the Oklahoma School of Religion in 1927. Although [the school was] not directly affiliated with the University of Oklahoma, college credit was granted for course work completed at the school. Prior to 1930, Comfort served on the faculty of the School of Religion as a representative of the Presbyterian Church, and as director of the institution. At that date, Nick requested interdenominational support for the school, so that he could become Dean of the Oklahoma School of Religion, and not just act as the representative of a single church.[10] His long tenure in that position proved to be a highly controversial one because of the unequivocal stands he took on charged issues of the period.

Among the most praised and the most condemned of Comfort's actions involved his participation with the inter-war peace movement. By the mid-1920s, the protest movement against war and militarism began to attract increasing attention from Nick Comfort. He communicated with the famed pacifist leaders and his fellow ministers, Kirby Page and John Nevin Sayre. A letter from Page congratulated Comfort for having organized at the University of Oklahoma a group affiliated with the pacifist Fellowship of Reconciliation, a leading force in the anti-war ranks.[11]

Comfort, in turn, declared his support for the activities of Sayre and indicated his wonderment at the latter's work. The Norman pastor wrote that militarism was potent, but that a determined group at the university always supported efforts for a "creative peace." Sayre responded by sending additional information from the Committee on Militarism in Education, along with a speech by Ross A. Collins, chairman of the House Subcommittee on Army Appropriations, which scorned material waste by the armed forces.[12]

Members of the era's peace movement attacked military training in public institutions, and Comfort berated the influence of the military at the University of Oklahoma. As a participant at the Oklahoma Synod of Presbyterian Churches held in Muskogee in November, 1930, he backed a resolution damning compulsory military training in the state's public schools; Comfort believed that the measure would indicate the importance of "the military situation" in Oklahoma. He later asserted that to terminate such training would require a strong stance by the public, and stated that "lovers of peace" should intensify their efforts to obtain "disarmament in education."[13]

Owing to his controversial stands on peace, economic woes, and race, the Presbyterian minister encountered both considerable praise and criticism during his first years in Norman. Some backed Comfort and the Oklahoma School of Religion. The Vice President and General Manager of the Oklahoma Gas and Electric Company, J. P. Owens, wrote to the chairman of the Phillips Petroleum Company, L. E. Phillips, in 1930, soliciting support for the School of Religion, which would supposedly serve as an antidote for the "various schools of materialistic thought . . . rampant in the United States." Owens indicated that religious bodies would provide "the foundation stone of our social order," and should thus be assisted by individuals with "large property interests."

Most defenders of the iconoclastic clergyman cheered Comfort's stand as a "liberal Christian" who challenged fundamentalist ideas. A colleague credited Comfort with having done more than any churchman or educator at the University of Oklahoma to oppose the fundamentalist tenets that were popular in the state. Others, however, belittled Comfort and asserted that he belonged "to the devil." In late 1931, fundamentalist pastor, C. F. Stealey, attacked Dean Comfort and the Oklahoma School of Religion for "modernistic teaching." The secretary of the school's board of trustees responded, stating that Comfort, "one of the most Christlike men in Oklahoma," required no defense. Nevertheless, Nick's invitation to Norman Thomas to speak at a Faculty Club luncheon, along with other activities, rapidly resulted in the Norman minister's condemnation as a "red."[14]

Strife continued to afflict Comfort as his concern with social and political affairs intensified during the turbulent 1930s. With the American economy entrapped in the midst of the Great Depression, and with an international conflagration approaching, Comfort used three arenas to convey his ideas to the broad public. Beginning in September, 1935, he contributed a weekly column, "This Is Your Life," to the *Oklahoma Daily,* the campus newspaper. As he noted in his yearly report to the trustees of the Oklahoma School of Religion, Comfort believed that his editorials brought each week, "new friends, and new foes." He deemed it delightful to receive such high praise one week and such unrestrained invectives immediately thereafter. Significantly, this ambivalence emanated from the University of Oklahoma Board of Regents to school janitors, from nearly all Norman churches, and from many individuals throughout the state.[15]

In 1936 the Dean of the Oklahoma School of Religion helped establish the Norman Forum in an attempt to bring controversial speakers to the community. While plans evolved to create the forum, a Comfort-led group convened with President W. B. Bizzell of the University of Oklahoma to analyze the merits of the proposal. Comfort called public discussion essential while Bizzell worried about the reprobation that the university might receive. When the administrator suggested formation of a dinner club as an alternative, Comfort bristled that the university was "dying on the vine because it overnurtured the innocuous." Comfort's argument prevailed.[16]

Pacifists and socialists were among the speakers who addressed the Norman Forum, thus again encircling a Comfort-associated organization with controversy. In response to a letter requesting more information about the forum, Nick exclaimed that it was designed to uphold "our fundamental American traditions." He felt that noted speakers and lively topics would help awaken the people to the benefits of their democratic institutions and to an awareness that these "must be cultivated if we are to endure."[17]

Comfort utilized his *Oklahoma Daily* column and his position as president of the Norman Forum to further the peace movement which flourished and then dissipated during the 1930s. By the middle of the decade, a student peace movement had emerged on the nation's college and university campuses. Although originating later in Norman than in many other areas, the anti-war movement appeared at the University of Oklahoma by the spring of 1936. The university administration allowed a thirty-minute "strike for peace" in April of that year, and another during the following spring. The 1937 gathering probably served as the high point of the anti-war effort at the University of Oklahoma as 2,000 students congregated at a peace rally, and 200 signed a petition requiring a vote by the American people to obtain a declaration of war. Encouraged by the Nye Committee report concerning American entrance into World War I, Comfort told the crowd that the proponents of war dared not to tell the American populace the true reasons for possible involvement in the worsening international crisis. He declared that the American public would refuse to fight if they were given proper information. Comfort decried munitions-makers as "dollar-chasers," and stated that to oppose them signified a challenge to militarism. He proposed that three of every ten dollars allocated for military expenditures be used to promote peace, and postulated that "then we won't need the other $7 very long."[18]

Like many left-of-center during the height of the depression decade, Comfort believed that the drives for peace and social justice were inseparable. Thus, his *Oklahoma Daily* pieces not only riveted upon the issue of war and peace, but upon the economic holocaust caused by the worldwide depression. While the extensive dislocations engendered by the country's worst economic crisis abounded, Nick Comfort eloquently related the resulting deprivation. Because of this, he was often castigated as a proponent of class antagonism. Yet he repeatedly remarked that the very impoverishment of so many in a land of plenty, and the apparent selfishness of those at the top of the economic ladder, were the guiding forces in causing class consciousness and possible class warfare. Comfort recognized that "the downtrodden of the world" were becoming more perceptive and vocal than before. And unless conditions were ameliorated, he felt that the masses would confront "their oppressors" with force. He feared that such revolutionary action would produce wanton brutality and violence as had occurred during the Russian and Mexican revolutions, and as was brewing in the lands of China and India.[19]

Comfort warned that the recent calls for radical change in America were not the result of foreign agitation but were bred by real problems. He wrote: "The depression like a hypo put the causes of mass uprisings into the blood stream of our underprivileged classes." He believed that because of their continued destitution, the American poor were finally becoming cognizant of class realities, and he adjudged Franklin D. Roosevelt's New Deal attempts to alleviate the situation as only temporary palliatives which were doomed to failure. Unless something were done for the permanent relief of the suffering millions, they would be driven by sheer desperation toward "brute force and pillage." At such a time, in his opinion, every American would be forced to support or oppose them.[20]

The dominance of business interests, Comfort argued, was the root of the grave economic and social ailments of the United States. He wrote that the nation had become "a businessman's civilization," and that giant corporations were spreading "their tentacles" into all aspects of the American state. He called the wealthy "the real masters of our country," and warned that a plutocracy could not be formed or maintained through democratic means, that an economic elite always employed force as protection against the downtrodden.[21]

Reverend Comfort charged that the wealthy were buttressed by repression and militarism. He stated that evidently the American "ruling class" no longer considered economic pressure sufficient protection for its riches, and was endeavoring to abrogate civil liberties "as never before." He believed that those who attempted to focus attention upon "economic evils" and who agitated for necessary reform were slandered. Teachers were required to take oaths of allegiance, and were scared to speak out on controversial issues. He also pointed out that public figures who favored municipal ownership of utilities were confronted by opposing forces which were backed by great monetary resources.[22]

The wealthy and military leaders were linked, dependent upon one another, Comfort analyzed. This connection purportedly resulted in the profusion of the "tentacles" of the military, "octopus-like," over the entire country. Comfort condemned this development and the perceived glorification of military arms and "the military spirit." He denounced "the orgy of flag-waving and emotional superpatriotic prejudice" evidenced on armistice day. Viewing the international situation in the mid-1930s, he warned that the civilized world was preparing for an upcoming "holocaust of slaughter." He wondered how long the peaceful masses would continue to allow the "maniacal militarists" to lead them to destroy each other, in order that world markets and the control of raw materials might be retained. Comfort remarked that war had never resolved any problems, and he remembered "the last orgy of sacrifice" which had taken place during the first world war. The pastor exclaimed that the division of Christian peoples into "mere national cults, or insipid sects" lacking world vision, helped to feed the militaristic tide. He wrote that individuals should discard their hypocritical ways, and either disavow worship of "the Christ child" or work to create a social order where children would not be guided "to slaughter as He was by the militarists."[23]

To counteract what he considered militarism, Comfort called for a new mode of patriotism which would assist in the construction of an American nation that required no defense. Not an absolute pacifist, he declared that defense of one's homeland was not questioned. But the molding of a "fair and righteous" state that none would fear or want to destroy, was the vision Comfort held. To produce this ideal land, military funding should be used for peace propaganda, students should be required to take peace courses, peace advocates should be made heroes, peace societies should be formed. With these developments, "mankind's natural love of peace might blossom as a rose instead of being smothered as it now is."[24]

To help instill the peace spirit, he believed that the public lauding of the military and militarism should end. Those who declared war would be required to man the war front and remain stationed there until the conflict terminated or until they perished. Conscription should begin with the elderly. No profit would be allowed from the war effort and all would be compelled to work for the nation's goals during the period of hostilities. Military pensions would be abolished and all the money previously so targeted would be used for the oldest and the neediest Americans. Finally, "all the tinsel" should be removed from the professional warriors; when not drilling or practicing, they would perform such essential tasks as street sanitation, garbage removal, and road construction. When soldiers died, they would be buried without "pomp or glory," just as other useful citizens were.[25]

Viewing the growing attempts to increase military expenditures, Comfort feared that such legislative action would inevitably lead to American involvement in a world war. He argued that the only way for the United States to remain apart from the international battleground was to keep American possessions and citizens away from the arena of conflict.[26]

The minister also opposed his nation's involvement in military action because of the loss of civil liberties and democratic freedoms which he believed inevitably ensued during wartime. He warned that democracy and militarism were diametrically opposed. Condemning those who declared that America required a first class dictatorship, he charged that "self-styled patriots" who urged suppression of dissenters were the real enemies, more so than the Japanese, Russians, or Germans. A greater danger resided in the fact that their means "destroyed the very things that have made our nation possible."[27]

Attempts at the University of Oklahoma to prevent the establishment of a student chapter of the Veterans of Future Wars, an anti-
war organization, and the presentation of two works by Clifford
Odets, the left wing playwright, alarmed Nick Comfort. He asserted
that fundamental rights, including those protected by the first ten
amendments, were involved. Comfort chided the many who apparently were willing to abrogate certain freedoms from the
university community. He stated that attempts to ban ''outside
influences'' would require removal of the Reserve Officer Training
Corps (R.O.T.C.) and its buildings, various university properties,
and such groups as the Young Democrats, Young Republicans,
Y.M.C.A., Y.W.C.A., and Phi Beta Kappa. The removal of so-
called ''outside influences'' from the campus he adjudged impossible. Also, he believed that an academic institution depended upon
discussion of pertinent issues to fulfill its role in society. For example, an analysis of whether the United States should enter a war was
a vital question which he believed should be considered by all who
were concerned with the national welfare. Political and economic
considerations were the foundation of the state, and students needed
to confront such queries. Furthermore, he stated that the right to
hold any beliefs or to sponsor any political party or program, as long
as no legislative enactment was ignored, involved fundamental
American principles.[28]
Comfort thus sharply attacked what he considered economic in-
equities and militarism, both of which he viewed as antithetical to
democracy. The perils to democratic ideals and institutions deeply
troubled Comfort as he, notwithstanding allegations to the contrary,
believed strongly in the American democratic system. He declared
that political democracy could not operate in isolation but required
''intellectual, social, economic, and religious democracy'' to prevent its dissipation. He wrote that democracy was not just a theory,
but rather ''a way of living'' that demanded continual reaffirmation
and the exercise of America's leading source of power—the ballot
box. All institutions including the state and the church should be
subordinated to ''human welfare.'' As democracy and the concept
of class were directly contradictory, the people needed to demand
economic democracy, needed to engage in a protracted struggle or
face loss of political freedom. Comfort concluded that ''economic

autocracy and political democracy'' were engaged in ''a struggle to the death.'' He roared that economic slavery must be ended, that employers and workers together must establish labor conditions, and that the aged, the infirm, the unemployed must be cared for.[29]

Religion and the various churches should perform progressive roles, Comfort indicated, to support the American democratic ethos, social betterment, and peace. He remarked that the New Testament was ''the magna charta of democracy.'' Religionists should see Christianity ''as it really is, a brotherly way of living.'' Comfort warned that the religious must relinquish the sword, for weapons only brought ''spiritual death to the wielder as truly as physical death to the victim.'' Violence only bred ''political and economic suicide.'' Once people recognized this, a great stride would be made toward the elimination of ''modern mass murder.''[30]

Additionally, Comfort exhorted the church to disavow its claim to omnipotence. ''Religious imperialism'' must not be preached anymore. This was essential because of what he considered the longstanding church support for the American military presence in foreign lands which helped to remind ''the natives'' that they ''would do well to respect the missionaries.''[31]

Comfort encountered a trying period from 1938 to 1941 due in part to his continued advocacy of the Social Gospel and noninterventionism in spite of the heightened fascist push and the demise of the Popular Front alliance of liberals and leftists following the Nazi-Soviet Pact. His outspoken and controversial stands upon leading issues of the times produced bitter opposition and the sharpest attacks yet directed against him and the Oklahoma School of Religion.

While many left-of-center activists began to concentrate their attention upon the worsening international situation, Comfort retained his focus upon social and economic concerns in Oklahoma and the Southwest. He discussed the deplorable conditions in the black district of Shawnee, stating that more than 1,000 people lived in huts and shacks, some comprised of boxes. The average weekly income of the black families was less than two dollars. He charged that unconstitutional but ''inhuman segregation laws'' kept the people entrapped in dilapidated living conditions.[32]

Declaring that if Jesus were present he would be aiding his ''suffering and dying'' children, Comfort termed interracial committees essential, and he participated in the initial Southern Conference on Human Welfare held in Birmingham, Alabama, in the fall of 1938. There, the Norman minister guided an unsuccessful battle against racial segregation in the organization. Members of the gathering discussed the deep-rooted economic ailments of the South, and Comfort encouraged cooperation between various groups which desired change. "Labor, farm, civil liberties and government, housing, race relations and suffrage,'' he stated were related concerns.[33]

In late January, 1939, State Representative Tom Kight of Claremore criticized Nicholas Comfort and the Oklahoma School of Religion because of the dean's participation at the Birmingham convention. During a public hearing at the state capitol concerning a criminal syndicalism measure which he had proposed, the state legislator claimed that the school was ''communistic'' and he alleged that radicals were attempting to augment their influence by infiltrating churches. Challenging the Kight charges, Comfort demanded an open meeting to attempt to publicly vindicate the Oklahoma School of Religion from the red smear. Kight refused to convene such a hearing, and the newly elected governor, Leon Phillips, quickly berated the teaching of Communism or nazism in the state's public schools and called for a university investigation.[34]

In his correspondence with Kight, Comfort accused the Claremore representative of either ignorantly or maliciously trying to destroy the Oklahoma School of Religion with slanderous remarks. Comfort asserted that Kight could not cloud the issue by discussing something ''as tame'' as the involvement with the Southern Conference for Human Welfare.[35]

Friends, former students, and allies lent moral support to Nick and his institution. An editorial in the *Oklahoma Daily* stated that many in Norman were ''laughing out loud'' at Kight's charges. The editorial writer declared that the university and Norman communities recognized that Nick Comfort had probably done more than any other Oklahoman ''to encourage liberal thought.'' Furthermore, in the eyes of his supporters, the educator was one of the few individuals who supported freedom of speech even for his opponents. The success of the Norman Forum was largely attributed to Comfort, and he was praised for his courageous proposal for teacher's pensions and for his aid in protecting oppressed minorities. The editorial indicated that the University of Oklahoma faculty included several liberals, but that unlike Comfort, few "would risk their necks." The essay concluded with the observations that the churchman quickly spoke out when he saw injustice develop, that he was a preserver of democracy, and an instructor of Christian ethics in the classroom.[36]

A letter addressed to Comfort blasted the "Ism-Witch Hunt" of Governor Phillips and the "inquisition" of State Representative Kight. The writer believed that the two public officials apparently supported the activities of the House Un-American Activities Committee, as did those who desired to besmirch "all progressives and forward movements." Elizabeth Irwin, fired from her Oklahoma City teaching post because of her political views, wrote to encourage Comfort.[37]

Perhaps influenced by the condemnation of him on the right, Comfort sharply castigated an American Nazi Party conclave in New York City. In his weekly article, he declared that while he had always defended civil liberties, the open avowal of armed insurrection against the American government by the Nazis betrayed all democratic principles. He believed that they were active rebels and should be treated as such. To counteract them necessitated a large educational campaign, and a recognition of the deficiencies in the American economic, political, and social order.[38]

Following a speech which he delivered before the Oklahoma Youth Legislature in the State Capitol on January 9, 1940, Comfort again encountered strident criticism. In his talk, he warned that the greatest danger to democratic processes emanated from those who repeatedly employed "constitutional shiboleths [sic] but by their actions trample the constitution into the dust." Comfort denounced the attempt to exclude blacks and Communists from the Youth Legislature, a development which had resulted in division of the organization. He stated that despite his disagreement with the political desires of the Communists, he felt obligated to defend their constitutional right to express their ideas and program. He also asserted that blacks resided in this nation "through no fault of their own," and that racial discrimination contradicted American ideals and the concept of the brotherhood of man. Comfort wrote that a condemnation of Hitler's anti-Semitic persecution was insincere if "such flagrant racial discrimination" was allowed within Oklahoma.[39]

Because of this address and previous actions, Comfort was roundly censured by American Legion members who demanded his dismissal as chaplain of the Oklahoma Central State Hospital, a post he had held for more than fourteen years. The commander of the state chapter of the Legion, Dr. A. B. Rivers of Okmulgee, avowed that national unity was essential and that "no good American citizen" could "bosom a Communist in one hand and uphold the constitution of America in the other." He proceeded to assail Comfort as a Communist. After the minister once again demanded proof of the charge or a public apology, Rivers retorted that he had never accused Comfort of being a Communist but refused the request for either a debate or a retraction. Despite the disavowal of the Communist allegation, a letter from the deputy adjutant of the Legion to a high school principal reflected the thinking of certain members of the organization. The writer indicated that it was "disgusting" to realize that a supposed pedagogue "places his racial desires above his desires to train young people and then it is more disgusting to see them hide behind 'Democracy' to do this. Typically Communist." He suggested that more instruction be directed toward young "colored children" concerning "citizenship, rather than try to put them under Communist and other such influences by prating about racial equality."[40]

In his own defense, Comfort stated that his political, social, and religious tenets were "an open book" for all Oklahomans. Comfort proudly declared that he had always fought, "without fear or favor to anyone" for what he deemed proper, and would continue to do so. Such a stance, he recognized, had produced powerful antagonists, including certain Legion members.[41]

The *Oklahoma Daily* continued to support Comfort, but on February 28, the State Board removed him from his hospital position. The board cleared Comfort of the Communist charges, but reasoned that as the hospital cared for veterans and was aided by the Legion, the wishes of the organization had to be heeded. The following day, Comfort thanked the board for acknowledging that he was not a Communist and disclosed that he would no longer contest the ouster, refusing "to fight force with force." But he warned that the Legion was crippling democratic freedoms in the state.[42]

In a final salvo Comfort wrote to Rivers, bemoaning what he considered undemocratic and anti-American activities of the Legion concerning the dismissal. Comfort asked whether the inability to confront one's accusers and the lack of substantive evidence for the accusation did not violate democratic ideals. He called for the Legion to admit its bigotry and "wilful denial of brotherhood, justice, and constitutional rights to man." He castigated the organization's incitement of students to employ a "Red hunt" at Oklahoma A & M College. Comfort queried why the Legionnaires considered themselves privileged to dictate material to be discussed in public schools and on public platforms, and he wondered how their "desired dictatorship differed from those of Stalin and Hitler."[43]

As had occurred the previous year, sustenance for the pastor came from across the state. One writer claimed that the American Legion had become as closed-minded and bigoted as the Klan. Another letter compared Comfort's troubles with the crucifixion of Jesus and the poisoning of Socrates, and deplored the "witch-hunts" that made it more dangerous for citizens to think, and even more perilous to express their thoughts. Students at the University of Oklahoma circulated a petition to demonstrate their indignation at the treatment of Comfort.[44]

His adherence to the evaporating peace movement and his bitter denunciation of the American mobilization effort for possible entrance into the world war produced still more difficulties for the minister. Unlike many American liberals and leftists, Comfort remained a non-interventionist, despite augmented fascist aggression and success. Believing that the governments of England and France were little more democratic than the regime in Germany, he retained his conviction that the United States should remain aloof from the fighting. He considered these European states to be imperialistic, oppressive, and brutal, and he wrote that "they fattened on the blood of crushed people." Consequently, he stated that no aid should be granted to any European power. Rather, the United States should strive to aid the masses in all lands by engaging in direct contact with the people themselves. Responding to such analyses, a "foreign born patriot" termed Comfort's failure to extol the preparedness program an insult to all "red blooded" Americans. This writer asked: "If you don't like the country why don't you leave or are you one of the fifth columnists running at large." He also charged that Comfort had disgraced education.[45]

On May 19, 1940, as the Roosevelt military defense program continued to face heavy criticism, Comfort published a column in the *Oklahoma Daily* which condemned what he termed "a fit of hysteria" concerning an imminent threat to the nation. The minister declared that Germany would never attack the United States, and that his country was well armed for defensive purposes. He considered the air force to be the best element for protection, and indicated that moneys spent on the other branches of the armed forces were funds "poured into a rathole." Comfort argued that in spite of opposition, the United States would furnish the Allied powers with matériel, and should work to support "the democratic ideal" in the Western Hemisphere.[46]

The reaction to this editorial, which was penned at a time when the Nazi blitzkrieg was sweeping across Europe, was rapid and hostile. Governor Phillips angrily stated that the school paper should drop the Comfort column. Comfort answered that if the governor favored such tactics, "then he should go over and join Hitler." Nancy Royal, editor-elect of the *Oklahoma Daily,* revealed that she would confer with Dean Comfort concerning whether the column would be continued. President Bizzell suggested that Comfort limit the column to religious matters, but the latter refused to submit to censorship. While the 1937 *Sooner Yearbook* had been dedicated to Nick Comfort, the changed mood on the University of Oklahoma campus was demonstrated by the decision to drop the "This Is Your Life" [*sic*] column.[47]

Over the next few months, Comfort intensified his support for the faltering anti-war movement and for civil liberties. He served as a sponsor for the Committee to Keep America Out of the War and the Declaration Against Conscription, which warned that a peacetime draft "smacks of totalitarianism." Because he had been incorrectly listed on the national brochures as Dean of the University of Oklahoma, Comfort wrote to the organizations requesting that the mistake be rectified. He asserted that the university administration was "highly militaristic" and was sharply opposed to his position, and that a pervasive statewide resentment against his stand existed; therefore, it was highly unfair that he be associated with the academic institution. Comfort was also affiliated with the Committee on Militarism in Education and supported the Emergency Peace Mobilization which declared that strict neutrality provided the best defense, and urged members to guard the rights of labor, religious groups, and racial minorities, and civil liberties in general, and to support social reform.[48]

In early October of 1940 Comfort manifested his interest in the formation of an Oklahoma Committee on Civil Liberties to record abuses of political rights. Several recent developments in the state had demonstrated to him the need for such an organization. After writing a letter to his congressman urging opposition to a conscription bill, Professor Streeter Stuart had been dismissed from Southeastern State College. Through employment of a seldom used criminal syndicalism measure, eighteen persons had been convicted because of affiliation with the Communist Party. Their anti-military positions had caused over 200 members of the Jehovah's Witnesses to be arrested, and the American Legion had petitioned the courts to take three children from their parents after the youngsters had been expelled from school for failing to salute the American flag.[49]

On October 19, 1940, investigators of the Dies' House Un-American Activities Committee congregated in Oklahoma City and questioned Nicholas Comfort and two other ministers concerning their political views. When an interrogator attempted to moralize about the impropriety of a liberal "sticking his neck" out at the present time, Comfort exclaimed: "Young man, it's a shame to see a nice fellow [such] as you working for such a rotten boss like Martin Dies." The three churchmen issued a paper claiming that the Dies' committee call was "trumped up" and was designed to intimidate or stigmatize those individuals who attempted to uphold constitutional freedoms and democratic processes during a time of great international and national crises.[50]

Shortly thereafter, six faculty members, directly or indirectly affiliated with the University of Oklahoma, including Comfort, called for the creation of a state civil rights' committee at an upcoming conference on constitutional liberties. The pastor's old antagonist, Governor Phillips, asserted that the professors had no business dealing with such an organization, that they were employed to teach and should not become involved with issues that did not concern them. He remarked that the six individuals were "apparently sadly misinformed," and that perhaps there was insufficient work "to do down there in Norman." Despite the protestations of the governor, the six participated in the conference, which resulted in the establishment of the Oklahoma Federation For Constitutional Rights. Dr. A. B. Adams, Dean of the College of Business Administration, quickly acclaimed that such a move against the American government should not be tolerated.[51]

Undoubtedly at least in partial response to the actions of the new organization, the state legislature in early 1941 initiated an investigation into "all subversive activities at the University of Oklahoma." Among those called before the "Little Dies' Committee" was a now familiar figure at legislative investigations, Nicholas Comfort. Friends who remembered that trying period avowed that the Norman pastor "was completely unawed" by the proceedings. While waiting to testify at this inquiry, Nick Comfort "lay upon a table and slept the sleep of the just." In fact, he had to be awakened to undergo the interrogation. One individual reminisced that when Nick actually appeared before the investigators, "he was so plain-spoken that the hearing became a comedy." Comfort declared that he was a prime instigator in the creation of the Oklahoma Federation, and condemned what he considered the unjust arrests of Communists and the dismissal of Professor Stuart. The Oklahoma chapter of the Ku Klux Klan proceeded to attack the civil liberties' organization and cited Comfort as among the Federation's supporters.[52]

In May, 1941, the Oklahoma Senate's "Little Dies' Committee" report recommended the dismissal of Maurice Halperin of the Department of Modern Languages, and proclaimed that the Oklahoma Federation For Constitutional Rights had been devised by outside, subversive elements. The Oklahoma Federation responded by accusing the committee of anti-Semitic behavior in its questioning of Halperin. The Federation claimed that the attempt to dismiss the professor was without evidence, a demonstration of "dictatorial procedure" and an indication of "religious and racial intolerance."

The organization questioned why the state legislators considered themselves too royal for criticism levied by the public which had elected them. When the committee proposed the disassociation of the Oklahoma School of Religion from the University of Oklahoma, President Bizzell defended the institution as "one of the most satisfactory in the country."[53]

Having overcome repeated public investigations, Comfort soon was jolted by the Japanese attack on Pearl Harbor in December, 1941, which was followed by an American declaration of war. For some time, Nick generally refrained from commenting on the international arena, thus paralleling the course followed by many of the remaining segments of the peace movement. Perhaps significantly, his daughter Elizabeth was photographed with a group of university students who were listening intently to an organizer calling for the defense of the rights of conscientious objectors.[54]

Despite the general disintegration of the prewar peace movement, a pacifist element remained opposed to their nations' participation in the conflict, and American churchmen were among the antiwar leaders who urged protection of civil liberties. Many conscientious objectors were placed in Civilian Public Service camps during the war, where they gradually developed the concept of Gandhi-like resistance, or satyagraha, to effect social change, a practice that would be extensively employed by radical and reform groups through the post-war era.[55]

Ever prior to December 7, 1941, Nick Comfort had praised the Gandhian movement. Lauding the Indian pacifist as "one of the half-dozen supermen of all time," he declared that Gandhi was employing the finest principles which religion could offer. The practice of satyagraha reportedly gave the world its finest example "of the practicability of the Sermon on the Mount," as it supposedly eradicated violence and thus abolished war. Comfort stated that such a movement would one day be adapted to American democratic procedures, and that then democracy would move toward "the development of the fullest life for the greatest number that any government has yet afforded."[56]

As the world war exploded, Comfort remained committed to social improvement, visiting Japanese relocation centers and fighting for a program of teacher retirement in Oklahoma. Ineligible for such benefits, as he was an instructor at a private institution, Comfort nevertheless believed deeply in the worth of a free public school system, and he served as president of the Oklahoma Association for Teachers Retirement, traveling around the state to organize groups which would promote necessary legislation. In 1942 voters supported creation of a teacher retirement system in Oklahoma.[57]

Still desirous of a forum through which he could express his ideas throughout the state, Nick Comfort helped establish the *Oklahoma Journal of Religion* in January, 1944. In its pages, editor Comfort again affirmed that a brotherhood of man existed beyond the false barriers of class, wealth, learning, and nationality. He editorialized that cooperation was essential for progress. He wrote that those who challenged the status quo were denounced, murdered, imprisoned, or crucified. Along with the quiet ones who determinedly fought for good causes, however, they had guided the path "from darkness to light."[58]

Looking ahead to the postwar world, Comfort proclaimed that major domestic and international dilemmas would have to be confronted. Condemning segregation and anti-Semitism, the minister exhorted that these ills, along with "German Jew-baiting" and "Jap jingoism," must be contested. On the world front, Comfort predicted that the United States, Soviet Russia, and England would determine the course of the postwar period. He believed that the Russians were not "land hungry," and that the Soviet Union had been the nation most committed to creating world peace. He felt that the communist state was engaged in a concerted effort to improve the condition of its masses, and that while Americans might not approve of certain aspects of the Soviet program, a peaceful world order would best allow for positive transformations. Comfort feared that Britain would attempt to resubjugate its old colonial empire, a development which he felt should be prevented by the Soviet Union and the United States. He believed that the principles of freedom and democracy were best represented in his own land, and that America would possess its greatest opportunity as a leader during the upcoming peacetime. He argued that the United States should work for progress and reform and not repeat the isolationist stance of the post–World War I years.[59]

As the war neared a close, Comfort received a blistering letter which reproved him for his sympathetic attitude toward "RED MARXIST RUSSIA," the "hellish land of rape, murder, pestilence, and the vicious creed of KARL MARX—RELIGION IS THE OPIUM OF THE PEOPLE." Comfort's foe told him to go live in the Soviet Union, and declared that "the Reds" were busy achieving control in America while men were "being slaughtered by the millions for LIBERTY and CHRIST." The agitated letter writer warned that some "twenty million Republicans" felt as he did about "this Red Russian menace" to the nation, and were determined to check university instruction. The message was signed "An irate listener, and an AMERICAN who believes in the DEMOCRACY OF GEORGE WASHINGTON AND THOMAS JEFFERSON and not in the hellish Economic tribulation and philosophy of Karl Marx!"[60]

Postwar America failed to usher in the harmony and social progress which Comfort desired as the seeds of a Red scare quickly appeared. Because of inadequate funding, which was undoubtedly attributable to the prevailing political atmosphere, Comfort's controversial Oklahoma School of Religion shut down in 1947. The fundamentalist element in Oklahoma's Protestant churches also contributed to the demise of the School of Religion. Yet friends acknowledged that had the dean weakened his highly principled stands, money for his institution would have been available. Comfort, however, "was never willing to compromise or to do or say things he did not believe in," and he refused to avoid contentious issues.[61]

The political concerns of Nick Comfort continued unabated, and in early 1948, he helped write the state constitution for the Progressive Party. Revolving around the candidacy of Roosevelt's former vice-president, Henry Wallace, the Progressive Party attacked the cold warrior policies of Harry Truman, condemned the mounting infringement of political liberties, and urged expansion of social reform measures. In the summer of 1948, Nick served as a delegate at the party's founding convention in Philadelphia. Decimated by malicious claims of being a Communist, Wallace's own fumblings, and the leftward tilt of Truman prior to election day, the party vote proved highly disappointing. The charge of Communist domination of the party proved disastrous, and by September of the following year, Comfort seemed to feel the accusation was justified. Renouncing his membership in a public letter, Comfort declared that both Communists and Roman Catholics possessed "a loyalty center outside the United States" that frequently overrode their allegiance to this nation, and that they often advocated any means to achieve their goals. Comfort stated that he was "unalterably opposed to totalitarianism in all its forms," and affirmed that he possessed "no sympathy with Communist tactics," which he called "so stupid" as to hold little attraction for thoughtful individuals. Additionally, he exclaimed: "The Communists' appeal to force is contrary to all that I hold dear. Their appeal to class struggle is a denial of my concept of the brotherhood of man." Comfort affirmed that nevertheless, he would continue to defend the liberties of all groups.[62]

The Red Scare tactics of Senator Joseph McCarthy, which gathered full force during the 1950s, appeared to only indirectly bother the semi-retired Comfort. As McCarthy whipped up his anti-Communist campaign, Nick received a latter [sic] from a friend who warned that America would likely suffer setbacks in Germany and China because Americans did not believe strongly enough in democracy. The correspondence charged that the American people had become "intellectual witch hunters trying to determine what people think," and that if Jesus ventured to the United States, McCarthy would proclaim him a Communist. The writer continued: "Guilt by association, without trial and without a chance to know who is your accuser seems to be the fashion nowadays." As the conflicts of the era worsened, several Oklahoma scientists were compelled to discuss their dealings with Nick Comfort.[63]

Comfort now spent the bulk of his time on a farm located fifteen miles from Norman. The Comforts had sold their city residence, and had purchased the farm in May, 1948. In September, 1955, Nick Comfort suffered a stroke which left him paralyzed on the right side. One close compatriot remembered that Comfort loved physical activity, and that illness "broke his spirit." The Comforts soon moved to Rochester, Minnesota to be near their daughter, who was a physician, and the Mayo Clinic. On March 27, 1956, Nicholas Comfort died of a stroke.[64]

At a memorial service in Norman on April 29, allies and colleagues remembered Nick. They praised his convictions and ideals, proclaimed him "an uncommon man" and a true democrat, termed him fearless and "a devoted patriot" who truly loved the indigenous radical spirit of Oklahoma. The eulogists lauded his real friendship, great energy and "magnificent freedom of mind," and described him as "untamed," a prophet, a giant, an individual. Many expressed their admiration for his belief in the Christian brotherhood, and one long-time friend declared that "Nick was a devoted churchman who came remarkably near to practicing what he preached." Nearly a quarter of a century after his death, another friend fondly remembered that Comfort "loved his fellow man," and "wanted to fight for all his principles. That was his whole life."[65]

The concept of the Social Gospel, [. . . by which] men of the church utilized their pulpits to aid social reform, best encapsulates the philosophy of this Presbyterian pastor and educator, Nicholas Comfort. Comfort strove to further civil liberties, civil rights, economic betterment, and peace. He considered civil liberties as the cornerstone of the American democratic system, and continually defended the rights of castigated political and religious dissidents. Protection of the civil rights of racial minorities he deemed an essential part of the quest to create the brotherhood of man. Yet political freedoms alone were incomplete, Comfort argued, without corresponding economic rights, and thus he called for a certain degree of redistribution of wealth to aid the most impoverished. Consistently, he warned that American democracy and his envisioned brotherhood of man could never exist in a militaristic state; consequently, he dedicated long hours for the peace movement.

Because of his ideas and actions, this proponent of the Social Gospel, like so many other American reformers and radicals of his era, confronted considerable opposition and criticism. Working in a state with an increasingly conservative political environment and a continuing fundamentalist religious orientation, Nick Comfort challenged reactionary political and church doctrine. While he repeatedly endeavored to help effect the Christian brotherhood of man, Comfort was absurdly termed an instigator of class warfare, a subversive, and a "red."

Buttressed by his strongly held beliefs, Nick Comfort steadfastly held to his democratic and libertarian ideals. Thus, he unerringly followed the tradition of the homegrown radicalism of the Southwest.

NOTES

1. Ken Lowe, "Broken Images," July 30, 1961, Oklahoma School of Religion Collection, Western History Collections, University of Oklahoma, Norman, Oklahoma, p. 2 (hereinafter referred to as OSORC), index.

2. Elizabeth Delatore, interview, Nov. 15, 1979; Winifred Johnston, interview, Nov. 16, 1979.

3. Winifred Johnston, "The Book and the Author," in *Christ Without Armor: Uncensored Essays on the Democratic Way,* ed. E. N. Comfort (Norman, Okla.: Cooperative Books, 1940), 2.

4. Ibid.; Untitled biographical sketch, OSORC, index.

5. C. Roland Marchand, *The American Peace Movement and Social Reform, 1898–1918* (Princeton, N.J.: Princeton University Press, 1972); Paul A. Carter, *The Decline and Revival of the Social Gospel: Social and Political Liberalism in American Protestant Churches, 1920–1940* (Ithaca, N.Y.: Cornell University Press, 1956); Robert Moats Miller, *American Protestantism and Social Issues, 1919–1939* (Chapel Hill: University of North Carolina Press, 1958); D. S. Stephens to Nicholas Comfort, July 15, 1912, and Arch McClure to Comfort, Jan. 25, 1917, III, Miscellaneous and Personal Correspondence of E. N. Comfort, OSORC.

6. Miller, *American Protestantism,* 7, 8, 317–44; Donald B. Meyer, *The Protestant Search for Political Realism, 1919–1941* (Berkeley: University of California Press, 1960), 349–403; Merle Curti, *Peace or War: The American Struggle, 1636–1936* (New York: W. W. Norton & Company, 1936), 247, 255–56, 291, 299; Charles Chatfield, *For Peace and Justice: Pacifism in America, 1914–1941* (Boston: Beacon Press, 1973); Charles DeBenedetti, *The Peace Reform in American History* (Bloomington: Indiana University Press, 1980), 90–200; Reference letter from E. W. Hart, Aug. 13, 1918; Ea. Brown to Comfort, Aug. 10, 1918; William P. Meirell et al. to Comfort, Apr. 5, 1920, III, Miscellaneous and Personal Correspondence of E. N. Comfort, OSORC.

7. Biographical sketch, p. 2, OSORC (index); Comfort to A. J. Green, Sept. 28, 1920, III, Miscellaneous and Personal Correspondence of E. N. Comfort, OSORC.

8. Biographical sketch, p. 2, OSORC (index).

9. Comfort to President, State Federation of Labor, Oklahoma, July 16, 1925, XXVI, Personal Correspondence of E. N. Comfort, S, OSORC; Comfort, "Y.W.C.A. Religious Activities, 1926–1927," IV, Publicity, OSORC.

10. Ray Gittinger, *The University of Oklahoma, 1892–1942* (Norman: University of Oklahoma Press, 1942), 228–30.

11. Chatfield, *For Peace;* DeBenedetti, *The Peace Reform,* 108–37; Kirby

Page to Comfort, Feb. 9, 1925, XXV, Personal Correspondence of E. N. Comfort, P, OSORC.

12. Comfort to John Nevin Sayre, May 23, 1929, XXVI, Personal Correspondence of E. N. Comfort, S-second, OSORC.

13. Chatfield, *For Peace,* 152–56; DeBenedetti, *The Peace Reform,* 119; Comfort to Tucker P. Smith, Nov. 17, 1930; Comfort to Rev. F. M. Sheldon, Mar. 2, 1931; Comfort to Smith, Mar. 2, 1931; Comfort to Smith, Nov. 17, 1930, XXVI, Personal Correspondence of E. N. Comfort, S-second, OSORC.

14. J. F. Owens to L. E. Phillips, May 26, 1930, V, Norman Forum, OSORC; Fessenden A. Nichols to Comfort, November 30, 1931; Nichols to Comfort, July 19, 1931; Rev. Robert A. McCulloch to Comfort, Dec. 1, 1931; Comfort to Nichols, Dec. 3, 1931; Comfort to Carl Magee, May 27, 1932, XXV, Personal Correspondence of E. N. Comfort, N, M, and Mc, OSORC; Rev. F. M. Sheldon, "Defender Not Necessary, Is Pastor's View," *Daily Oklahoman,* Dec. 6, 1971, p. A-17; John B. Thompson, "A Personal Appreciation," p. 10, OSORC (index).

15. Comfort, "Dean's Report, June 1, 1935, to Nov. 2, 1936," II, National Intercollegiate Christian Council, OSORC.

16. Cortez A. M. Ewing, "Nick Comfort's Attitude Toward Public Affairs," p. 5, Apr. 29, 1956, OSORC (index).

17. Comfort to Mr. Lay, Dec. 28, 1936, III, Miscellaneous and Personal Correspondence of E. N. Comfort, OSORC.

18. Patti McGill Peterson, "Student Organizations and the Antiwar Movement in America, 1900–1960," in *Peace Movements in America,* ed. Charles Chatfield (New York: Schocken Books, 1973), 122–26; Chatfield, *For Peace,* 259–61, 271–73, 295–96; DeBenedetti, *Peace Reform,* 126–27, 131; "Peace Meeting Will Be Held This Morning," *Oklahoma Daily,* Apr. 22, 1939, p. 1; "Peace Group to Petition for Vote on Declarations of War," *Oklahoma Daily,* Apr. 23, 1937, p. 1; "Peace Day Is Peaceful on Campus," *Oklahoma Daily,* Apr. 28, 1938, p. 1.

19. Comfort, "So This Is Life," *Oklahoma Daily,* Jan. 19, 1936, p. 1.

20. Ibid.

21. Ibid., 1–2.

22. Ibid., 2.

23. Ibid., Jan. 19, Nov. 8, 1936; Dec. 19, 1937.

24. Ibid., Nov. 8, 1936, p. 1.

25. Ibid.

26. Ibid., Sept. 19, 1937, p. 1.

27. Ibid., Dec. 6, 1936; Sept. 18, 1938.

28. Ibid., Mar. 22, 1936, p. 1.

29. Ibid., Feb. 16, May 24, 1936; July 9, Sept. 18, 1938.

30. Ibid., Mar. 8, 29, 1936.

31. Ibid., Oct. 4, 11, 1936.

32. Milton Cantor, *The Divided Left: American Radicalism, 1900–1975* (New York: Hill and Wang, 1978), 144, 146; John Diggins, *The American Left in the Twentieth Century* (New York: Harcourt Brace Jovanovich, 1973), 135–36; Comfort, "So This Is Life," *Oklahoma Daily,* Oct. 2, 1938, p. 1.

33. Comfort, "So This Is Life," *Oklahoma Daily,* Oct. 2, 1938, p. 1; "Oklahoma Develops New Race Attitude," *Harlow's Weekly,* Nov. 26, 1938, p. 3.

34. "Comfort and Kight Call Truce until Conference," *Oklahoma Daily,* Jan. 27, 1939, p. 1; Comfort to Kight, Jan. 27, 1939, p. 1.

35. Comfort to Kight, Jan. 31, 1939, I, Re—Comfort Investigation, OSORC.

36. Ruth Robinson, "Word for Comfort," *Oklahoma Daily,* Jan. 27, 1939, p. 1.

37. W. G. Lewis to Comfort, Jan. 29, 1939; Elizabeth Irwin to Comfort, Feb. 1, 1939, I, Re—Comfort Investigation, OSORC.

38. Comfort, "So This Is Life," *Oklahoma Daily,* Feb. 26, 1939, pp. 1–2.

39. Comfort, *Christ,* 14–19.

40. "Local Legion to Check in Red Squabble," *Norman Transcript,* Feb. 25, 1940, p. 1; "Rivers Says Comfort Not Called Red," *Oklahoma Daily,* Feb. 24, 1940, p. 1; Milt Phillips to M. M. Figa, Jan. 23, 1940, Comfort to Dr. A. B. Rivers, February 17, 1940, I, Re—Comfort Investigation, OSORC.

41. Comfort to State Legislature, n.d., I, Re—Comfort Investigation, OSORC.

42. "Comfort Is Ousted By State Board," *Norman Transcript,* Feb. 29, 1940, p. 1; "Comfort Will Not Continue Ouster Fight," *Norman Transcript,* Mar. 1, 1940, p. 1.

43. Comfort to Rivers, n.d., I, Oklahoma Youth Legislature, OSORC.

44. Guy A. Lackey to Comfort, March 3, 1940, I, Re—Comfort Investigation, OSORC; "Petition Hits Removal of Nick Comfort," *Oklahoma Daily,* Mar. 6, 1940, p. 1.

45. Cantor. *Divided Left,* 147–49; DeBenedetti, *Peace Reform,* 132–37; Comfort, *Christ,* 24–27, 30–32; "A foreign born patriot" to Comfort, n.d., I, Re—Comfort Investigation, OSORC.

46. Comfort, *Christ,* 32–34.

47. "Governor Phillips Renews Attack on Dean Comfort," *Norman Transcript,* May 20, 1940, p. 1; "Nick Comfort Irks Phillips Through Column," *Oklahoma Daily,* May 21, 1940, p. 1; "Dean Refuses to Be Muzzled," *Tulsa Tribune,* May 24, 1940, in I, Re—Comfort Investigation, OSORC; *1937 Sooner Yearbook,* 3.

48. Comfort to Jack McMichael, July 19, 1940; Comfort to Edwin C. Johnson, July 19, 1940, I, Peace Organizations—National Council for Peace Mobilization; Committee on Militarism in Education to Comfort, July 12, 1940, I, Peace Organizations; OSORC.

49. Comfort to Ben L. Morrison, Oct. 1, 1940, I, Oklahoma Committee on Constitutional Rights, OSORC; "Communists and Negroes First Victims," *Action Bulletin,* Oct. 26, 1940, in I, Re—Comfort Investigation, OSORC.

50. "Ministers Quizzed By Dies Group," *Daily Oklahoman,* Oct. 20, 1940, p. 1; "Three Pastors Change Dies Call Trumped Up," ibid., " 'Smear' Attack Charged By Presbyterian Pastors," *Norman Transcript,* Oct. 20, 1940, pp. 1–2.

51. "Six Faculty Members on Rights Group," *Oklahoma Daily,* Nov. 10, 1940, p. 1; "Phillips Raps Six Profs In Rights Group," ibid., Nov. 13, 1940, p. 1;

"Six Profs To Attend Civil Rights Parley," ibid., Nov. 15, 1940, p. 1; "Rights Are Wronged In Hot Parley,"; ibid., Nov. 16, 1940, p. 1; "Adams Flays Subversive Actions," ibid., Nov. 19, 1940, p. 1.

52. "Regents Give Full Support To Red Hunt," Norman Transcript, Feb. 4, 1941, p. 1; Ewing, "Nick Comfort's Attitude," ibid., Feb. 11, 1941, p. 4; Lowe, "Broken Images," ibid., p. 2; "Three O.U. Students Are Ejected From Senate," ibid., pp. 1, 6.

53. "Ouster of Halperin Is Urged," Norman Transcript, May 8, 1941, p. 1; "Demand for Ouster of Halperin Is Denounced," Oklahoma Daily, May 9, 1941, p. 1; "School of Religion Connection Is Slight," Norman Transcript, May 9, 1941, p. 1.

54. Lawrence S. Wittner, Rebels Against War: The American Peace Movement, 1941–1960 (New York: Columbia University Press, 1969), 34, 36–37; Photograph of Elizabeth Comfort and other students sitting with David White, Fellowship of Reconciliation southwest secretary, Oklahoma Daily, Dec. 12, 1941, p. 2.

55. Wittner, Rebels, 40–124; DeBenedetti, Peace Reform, 138–40.

56. Comfort, Christ, 43–45.

57. Thompson, "Personal Appreciation," 10; Ewing, "Nick Comfort's Attitude," 6–7.

58. Comfort, "Christian Citizenship," Oklahoma Journal of Religion, Feb. 1944, p. 2; Comfort, "The Sense of What Is Important," ibid., Apr. 1944, p. 1.

59. Comfort, "Let's Get Our Heads Together and Pour Our Hearts Out to Each Other," ibid., Apr. 1944, pp. 1–2; Comfort, "Looking Ahead," ibid., June 1944, p. 1.

60. "An irate listener" to Comfort, Mar. 5, 1945, pp. 1–2, III, Miscellaneous and Personal Correspondence of E. N. Comfort, OSORC.

61. Athan Theoharis, Seeds of Repression: Harry S. Truman and Origins of McCarthyism (New York: Quadrangle, 1971); David Caute, The Great Fear: The Anti-Communist Purge under Truman and Eisenhower (New York: Simon and Schuster, 1979); Bibliographical sketch, p. 4, OSORC (index); Interview with Delatore.

62. Lawrence Lader, Power on the Left: American Radical Movements since 1946 (New York: W. W. Norton and Company, 1979), 33–37, 49–55; Karl M. Schmidt, Henry A. Wallace: Quixotic Crusade, 1948 (Syracuse: Syracuse University Press, 1960); Curtis MacDougall, Gideon's Army, 3 vols. (New York: Marzani and Munsell, 1965); Comfort to Mary Morgan, Sept. 12, 1949, pp. 1–2, I, Progressive Party, OSORC.

63. Caute, Great Fear; Fred J. Cook, The Nightmare Decade: The Life and Times of Joe McCarthy and the Senate (Lexington: University of Kentucky Press, 1970); Frank Milton Sheldon to Comfort, Apr. 3, 1950, III, Miscellaneous and Personal Correspondence of E. N. Comfort, OSORC; Dr. J. Rud Nielsen, untitled eulogy, p. 8, April 29, 1956, OSORC (index).

64. Biographical sketch, p. 4, OSORC (index); Interview with Delatore; "Rev. E. N. Comfort Dies of Stroke in Minnesota," Norman Transcript, Mar. 28, 1956, p. 1.

65. John F. Bender, "Tribute to Dean E. N. Comfort," p. 5, April 29, 1956, OSORC (index); Ewing, "Nick Comfort's Attitude," 4–5; Thompson, "Personal Appreciation, 10–12; Nielsen, untitled eulogy, 7; Mitchell S. Epperson, "A Tribute to Nick Comfort," p. 9, April 29, 1956, OSORC (index); Lowe, "Broken Images," 2; Interview with Dora McFarland, Nov. 15, 1979.

12

BEHOLD THE WALLS

Clara Luper

*Clara Luper was born in a rural area of Okfuskee County and went on to
earn degrees at Langston University and the University of Oklahoma. Her
book* Behold the Walls *was a moving personal account of her days as advisor to the Oklahoma City National Association for the Advancement of
Colored People Youth Council. In one part of the book she wrote a series
of letters to her country, including this one: "Dear America: This morning, James Arthur Edwards started singing from the 'Shores of Tripoli.'
Listen, we are waiting. Waiting for a hamburger, and in that hamburger,
the whole essence of Democracy lies. Your citizen, Clara Luper." Indeed.
It is sometimes hard for youth today who didn't live through it to see the
significance of the civil rights movement. Personal accounts, like the following story of the successful sit-ins at Katz Drug Store and Luper's
relationship with Mrs. John A. Brown, should help.*

CHAPTER I

The same group of NAACP Youth Council members had congregated at my house located at 1819 N.E. Park in Oklahoma City,
Oklahoma. It was August 19, 1958. The long hot summer's heat
seemed endurable in the small five-room, white frame house, but
the mosquitoes were in complete control outside and the youngsters

"Behold the Walls," by Clara Luper, first appeared in *Behold the Walls*. Reprinted with
permission, Jim Wire, Oklahoma City, 1979.

remained inside where they, with sweat on their faces, held their weekly meetings. Gwendolyn Fuller, president of the Council, was presiding. Ruth Tolliver and I were in the kitchen preparing grape Kool-aid and lunch meat sandwiches.

There was no advisor–youth council membership relationship then. It was a far deeper feeling that I had for the NAACP Youth Council members. I had watched them grow up from infancy. I had seen their minds develop and the values which they would carry through their lives change. I knew their parents and knew how much their parents loved them. I knew how unpopular it was to have your children involved in the NAACP Youth Council activities. It was even more difficult to get adults involved in the Council.

This was not the first NAACP Youth Council to operate in Oklahoma City. Mrs. Lucille McClendon had worked untiringly with a group some years before. Non-participation and non-support had spelled doom for the youth council. Through the leadership of John B. White and the insistence of Mr. and Mrs. D. J. Diggs and others, I had decided to take over the responsibility of reorganizing the Oklahoma City NAACP Youth Council. The fact that I was teaching American history at Dunjee High School in Spencer, Oklahoma and was a member of the Fifth Street Baptist Church furnished me with an ample number of young people who would become the nucleus of the Youth Council. William Miles, a student from Dunjee School, had been elected as the first president.

Each year at school, I'd present plays during Negro History Week, as it was called then. In 1957, I presented "Brother President," the story of Martin Luther King, Jr., and the non-violent techniques that were used to eliminate segregation in Montgomery, Alabama. The cast consisted of 26 students that were talented, ambitious and dedicated. The leading characters were William Miles, Joseph Hill and Maxine Dowdell. This play had filled the auditorium at Dunjee High School and drew tremendous turnouts all over the state.

In 1957, it was presented at the East 6th St. Christian Church, where Herbert Wright, the National Youth Director of NAACP, was in attendance. He was so impressed with the play that he invited me to present it in New York City at a "Salute to Young Freedom Fighters Rally." He agreed to pay the main characters' expenses;

however, I thoroughly understood the financial plight of the NAACP's national office and we worked out a compromise. We would raise the money for transportation, and he'd take care of our hotel and food bill in New York City.

Reverend J. S. Sykes, a very active C.M.E. minister, Mr. A. Willie James, the number-one NAACP membership writer, and Doc Williams, well-known bondsman and real estate dealer, helped me to raise $1,895.00 in order that we could make the trip. The Oklahoma City community responded rapidly and shared in our adventure.

The cast, most of whom had never been out of Oklahoma City, stopped in St. Louis for dinner and experienced their first integrated lunch counter service. This they continued to enjoy and appreciate on the trip. Words are inadequate to describe the expression and action of young people who, by tradition and custom, had been separated by the strong Visible Walls of segregation.

The group stayed at the Henry Hudson Hotel in New York City and the play was presented in both Manhattan and Harlem. The youth met freedom fighters from the south and the excitement and adventure of such a trip had a permanent effect on their lives.

In planning the trip, we decided to go the northern route and return by the southern route. On our return trip, we stopped in Washington, D.C. and visited the top historical spots including Arlington National Cemetery. As we stood in the Cemetery and watched the change-of-the-guard, each youth had an opportunity to think about Freedom. One asked, "What do you think would happen in this country if the Unknown Soldier's casket was opened and they would find out that he was black?" Joan Johnson said, "I don't know."

Barbara Posey, the secretary of the Youth Council, told the group that since all of these people had died for our freedom, we need to really get busy and do something for our country. Yes, these people, that are buried at Arlington Cemetery did all they could for freedom. I don't think the color of the unknown soldier's skin is important. I think it's what he did, and we have to do something.

Silently the group left Arlington Cemetery, after pledging that they'd do something for their country and loaded on the Greyhound bus. As the bus headed southward, the walls of segregation became so visible. In Nashville, Tennessee, the bus driver admitted that he did not know of any place where blacks could sit down and eat. So paper-sack lunches became the order of the day through Tennessee, Arkansas and into Oklahoma.

John White's words, "The Sooner State, The Sooner we get rid of segregation, the better off we'll be," were repeated continuously by the group. "True, you know segregation just doesn't fit in with my personality," Williams Miles said with a quick smile that faded back to a face of solemnity. The group applauded with loud outbursts of *"Freedom Now! Freedom Now!"*

Back in Oklahoma City, the group decided to break down segregation in public accommodations for all time and pay any price for it. "That will be our project—to eliminate segregation in public accommodations," the group said.

A strategy was worked out, where the public accommodations' owners and managers would be approached directly by a small delegation. There was never to be over three in the delegation and Mrs. Caroline Burkes, a stately freedom-loving white woman, was to accompany the groups on all occasions. This she did with a dedication that was followed up with letters and personal visits. This campaign was followed by a direct private approach to the city manager and city council which told the groups, "We are sorry, we do not have the power to interfere in private businesses. We don't tell the businessmen who to serve and they don't tell us how to run our city government." The campaign turned into a letter-writing campaign to churches—the white church leaders turned a deaf ear as their beautiful buildings stood as monuments to their dedication to Christianity. The black churches did not want to get involved at this time and told us that we could meet in their churches. They would take up a collection for us and make announcements concerning our worthwhile activities.

The meeting continued with a warm-up chanting rally. The group was chanting:

> We want to EAT—eat!
> We want to EAT—eat!
> NOW! NOW! NOW!
> We don't want any more excuses!

> We want to E-A-T—eat!
> We want to E-A-T—eat!
> NOW! NOW! NOW!

Gwendolyn Fuller leaned back in her chair and looked at the group as the singing and clapping grew louder and louder. Barbara Posey, the spokesman for the Public Accommodation Committee, made her report. "The owners of all public accommodations in Oklahoma City say they will not serve blacks. Now, what are we going to do?" Marilyn Luper spoke out: "I'll tell you, Barbara. I move that we go down to Katz Drug Store and sit down and drink a Coke." "I second the motion," said Areda Tolliver. The motion was carried unanimously by the group.

"When shall we go?" the group asked as if in a choir. "Gwen, let me tell you, you know that I made the motion to go, and I feel that I should have the privilege of deciding when we should go," said Marilyn Luper.

A silence fell over the meeting and after a few minutes with Marilyn staring into the future, she said, "Tonight is the time and as I read in Mr. Wisener's typing book, 'Now is the time for all good men to come to the aid of their party.'" "That doesn't mean that we will have to go tonight!" shouted Calvin.

A brother-sister debate occurred and in a high-toned voice, Calvin said, "Don't you ever think that I'm afraid to go!"

Barbara Posey said, "We have waited for over fifteen months, and Oklahoma has waited fifty years. Let's go down and wait in front of the manager so that people can see our problem."

Portwood Williams Jr. said, "The men in the NAACP Youth Council are ready to go right now and we are able to take care of any situation."

"We wouldn't doubt that," Gwendolyn said, and a bit of laughter sparkled in the air and echoed back into moments of silence.

Barbara Posey was recognized by the president, Gwendolyn Fuller, and she said, "We had better see what Mrs. Luper thinks. After all, she is the Youth Advisor."

I could feel the eyes of the members on me. I thought for a brief moment and traced the steps that we had taken. We had been *patient* and I saw in the children's eyes reflections of my restless childhood when I wanted to do something about a system that had paralyzed my movements and made me an outsider in my own country. Yet, these were children whose ages ranged from seven to fifteen years old.

I thought about my father who had died in 1957 in the Veteran's Hospital and who had never been able to sit down and eat a meal in a decent restaurant. I remembered how he used to tell us that someday he would take us to dinner and to parks and zoos. And when I asked him when was someday, he would always say, "Someday will be real soon," as tears ran down his cheeks. So my answer was, "Yes, tonight is the night. History compels us to go and let History alone be our final judge." We had another problem, we didn't have any transportation. Ruth Tolliver and I discussed the situation and decided to call three people that we knew wouldn't turn us down. Portwood Williams Sr., Lillian Oliver and Mary Pogue were selected.

I called Portwood Williams first. He lived in the next block. Mr. Williams was a talkative man with a sharp tongue, quick wit, and an adequate supply of words. He said, "I want to volunteer to drive car number one down to Katz Drug Store. My car is clean and ready. I don't blame you. I shined Mr. Charlie's shoes, and my mother washed Miss Ann's clothes. Now, I'm an upholsterer, the best in town, and my car is ready. I'll be there."

My next call was to Mrs. Lillian Oliver, a quiet, dignified, tall, school teacher and one who had served as an assistant NAACP Youth Council Advisor. I had known her since 1940 and through the years. We had been very close friends. I told her that I needed another car to take the NAACP youths down to Katz Drug Store. She didn't ask any questions. She said, "I'll be there in a few minutes. If you all are crazy enough to go, I'm crazy enough to take you!"

Lillian Oliver's cousin, Mrs. Grace Daniels, had related some of her experiences in Phoenix, Arizona, to the group and as I put the telephone down, I thought about Grace and how proud she would be of us. Lillian would have to call and tell her that we had started a direct-action campaign. I walked out on the porch where the kids were singing, "I want to be ready to sit for Freedom, just like John."

I hurried back into the house and called Mary Pogue, the mother of two of the youth. I knew that she would make me explain everything to her in detail . . . and she did! After I had finished, she said, "I'll be there in a few minutes."

I put the telephone down and heard it ring again. I had a feeling that it was my mother and I knew that it was not the proper time for me to tell her what we were going to do. I picked up the telephone and she said, "I just called to see if the NAACP Youth meeting was over." I said, "No, mother, it is not over. In fact, we are just beginning." She said, "Well, Clara, don't keep the kids up too late. You know tomorrow . . ." I said, "Yes, Mother, I'm going to take you downtown to eat for your birthday, which is only two days away." She said, "Clara, you aren't going to take me anywhere tomorrow. I'm not thinking about those white folks. What day is tomorrow, anyway? Well, Clara, we won't worry about it for tomorrow is just another day." I said, "Yes, Mama, tomorrow is just another day."

I rushed out of my house and on a still, hot, August night, August 19, 1958, we headed to Katz Drug Store in the heart of Oklahoma City. I went to the three cars and called the following names: Richard Brown, Elmer Edwards, Linda Pogue, Lana Pogue, Areda Tolliver, Calvin Luper, Marilyn Luper, Portwood Williams Jr., Lynzetta Jones, Gwendolyn Fuller, Alma Faye Posey, Barbara Posey, Goldie Battle and Betty Germany.

CHAPTER II

Are we ready to behold the walls, non-violently?

All the way downtown, I wondered if we were really ready for a non-violent war.

For eighteen months, the members of the NAACP Youth Council had been studying non-violence as a way of overcoming injustices. Basically, the doctrine of non-violence is rooted in the fundamental truth that whites are human. Being human, they will probably react with fear if they are threatened, but in the final analysis, they are likely to respond with good will. The white man's reaction may be one of surprise because we aren't answering injustices with injustices. He may then become angry because we are not. Then he may attempt to provoke us in a desperate attempt to try to incite us to violence.

He will become very suspicious and think that we are trying to make him do something that traditions and customs have taught him not to do. He recognizes that blacks are in the minority and that our belief in non-violence stems from weakness and therefore proceeds to take advantage of us. But gradually, if we have the tenacity to hold on to our non-violent approach, the white man will gain respect for us. We aren't defeating him, we'll be just removing his hostility and insecurities which will prepare him to function as a whole man in a Democratic Society.

Four basic rules had been used: First, we had defined our objective—to eliminate segregation in Public Accommodations. Second, we had to be honest. "Non-violence is not an approach to be used by hypocrites—honesty pays!" Third, you must love your enemy. "A doctrine as old as time, but as newsworthy as this hour's news story. You are to remember that you aren't up against a deep-eyed monster, you are up against a man who has been handed an overdose of segregation and who knows that segregation is wrong, yet he practices it. You are not to ridicule, humiliate, nor villify him at any time or in any way. Keep your goal in sight, you aren't out to defeat him, you are out to establish justice." Fourth, give the white man a way out. Non-violence demonstrates a kind of strength that shows up the weakness of injustices. Recognize that he has weaknesses and can be embarrassed for mistreating his brother. Find a way to let him participate in victory when it comes.

For over a year, the four strategic steps in non-violence had been used and had been reviewed over and over again.

The steps were investigation, negotiation, education and demonstration. Investigation: Get the facts. Make sure that an Injustice had been done. A non-violent approach will fail if it is based on false or shaky assumptions. Negotiation: Go to your opponent and put the case directly to him. It could be that a solution could be worked out and that there could be a grievance that we didn't know about. Let the opponent know that you are going to stand firm in order that you'll be ready to negotiate anywhere and anytime. Education: Make sure that the group is well informed on the *issues* and that men have always hated change, yet change must come. Demonstration: This is the final step only to be taken when all others have failed. Non-violent demonstration call[s] for discipline that is firm. Every provocation must be answered with continued good will. You must be ready for self-sacrifice that will leave no doubt as to your integrity, your dignity and your self-respect. Suffering is a part of the non-violent approach. It is to be endured, never inflicted. This approach will give you the *moral* victory upon which the eternal struggle for Freedom, Justice, and Equality can be won.

So non-violently, we were on our way to Katz Drug Store.

Katz Drug Store was located in the southwestern corner of Main and Robinson in downtown Oklahoma City. It was a center of activity with its first class pharmacy department, unique gifts, toys, and lunch counter. Blacks were permitted to shop freely in all parts of the store. They could order sandwiches and drinks to go. Orders were placed in a paper sack and were to be eaten in the streets.

This was the kind of wall that the older people should have undertaken years ago instead of financing this type of treatment. This was the kind of wall that the white Christians or the Jewish brothers should have fought. Maybe, this is the kind of battle that the atheist should have fought and now these thirteen little children could be enjoying an evening at home with their parents.

As I was thinking about what should have been done, Lana Pogue, the six-year-old daughter of Mr. and Mrs. Louis J. Pogue, grabbed my hand; and, we moved toward the counter. All of my life, I had wanted to sit at "those counters and drink a Coke or a Seven-Up." It really didn't matter which, but I had been taught that those seats were for "whites only." Blacks were to sweep around the seats, and keep them clean so whites could sit down. It didn't make any difference what kind of white person it was, thief, rapist, murderer, uneducated; the only requirement was that he or she be white. Unbathed, unshaven—it just didn't make any difference. Nor did it make any difference what kind of black you were, B.A. Degree Black, Dr. Black, Attorney Black, Rev. Black, M.A. Black, Ph.D. Black, rich Black, poor Black, young Black, old Black, pretty Black, ugly Black; you were not to sit down at any lunch counter to eat. We were all seated now in the "for whites only territory." The waitress suffered a quick psychological stroke and one said in a mean tone, "What do you all want?"

Barbara Posey spoke, "We'd like thirteen Cokes please."

"You may have them to go," the waitress nervously said.

"We'll drink them here," Barbara said as she placed a five dollar bill on the counter. The waitress nervously called for additional help.

Mr. Masoner, the red, frightened-faced manager, rushed over to me as if he were going to slap me and said, "Mrs. Luper, you know better than this. You know we don't serve colored folks at the counter."

I remained silent and looked him straight in the eyes as he nervously continued. "I don't see what's wrong with you colored folks—Mrs. Luper, you take these children out of here—this moment! This moment, I say." He yelled, "Did you hear me?"

"Thirteen Cokes, please," I said.

"Mrs. Luper, if you don't move these colored children, what do you think my white customers will say? You know better, Clara. I don't blame the children! I blame you. You are just a trouble maker."

He turned and rushed to the telephone and called the police. In a matter of minutes, we were surrounded by policemen of all sizes, with all kinds of facial expressions. The sergeant and the manager had a conference; additional conferences were called as different ranks of policemen entered. Their faces portrayed their feelings of resentment. The press arrived and I recognized Leonard Hanstein of Channel 9 with his camera and I sat silently as they threw him out and a whole crew of cameramen.

The whites that were seated at the counter got up, leaving their food unfinished on the table and emptied their hate terms into the air. Things such as "Niggers go home; who do they think they are? The nerve!" One man walked straight up to me and said, "Move, you black S.O.B." Others bent over to cough in my face and in the faces of the children. Linda Pogue was knocked off a seat; she smiled and sat back on the stool. Profanity flowed evenly and forcefully from the crowd. One elderly lady rushed over to me as fast as she could with her walking cane in her hand and yelled, "The nerve of the niggers trying to eat in our places. Who does Clara Luper think she is? She is nothing but a damned fool, the black thing."

I started to walk over and tell her that I was one of God's children and He had made me in His own image and if she didn't like how I looked, she was filing her complaint in the wrong department. She'd have to file it with the Creator. I'm the end product of His Creation and not the maker. Then, I realized her intellectual limitations and continued to watch the puzzled policemen and the frightened manager.

Tensions were building up as racial slurs continued to be thrown at us. Hamburgers, Cokes, malts, etc., remained in place as pushing, cursing, and "nigger," became the "order of the day."

As the news media attempted to interview us, the hostile crowd increased in number. Never before had I seen so many hostile, hard, hate-filled white faces. Lana, the six-year-old, said, "Why do they look so mean?"

I said, "Lana, their faces are as cold as Alaskan icycles."

As I sat quietly there that night, I prayed and remembered our non-violent philosophy. I pulled out what we called Martin Luther King's Non-Violent Plans and read them over and over:

First, resist the evil of segregation in a passive, non-violent way. We must refuse to cooperate with injustice; we shall not pay to be insulted. Segregation is an evil, it is contrary to the will of God, and when we support, or submit to segregation, we are condoning an evil. Every man has a right and a personal responsibility to ignore certain local laws, when they are contrary to the Constitution of the United States, no matter what the consequences are.

Number Two: Use the weapon of love in our everyday relations—violence must be avoided at all cost. We must not fight back, but we must resist peacefully and in a spirit of love. I mean the highest form of love—that love that seeketh nothing in return.

Number Three: We must mobilize for an all out fight for first-class citizenship—we must have leaders who live first-class citizenship as a symbol.

We must have slogans, for we will have to make these rights simple and understandable, so that they will filter into the hearts and the minds of people.

Fourth: We must get out the vote. The chief weapon of the Negro is the ballot. None of these other privileges will mean anything unless we also get the power of the ballot. We must vote and teach our children to vote.

Fifth: We must continue the legal legislative fight. We must continue our struggles in the courts, and above all things, we must remember to support the National Association for the Advancement of Colored People. We must ever keep in mind our major victories have come through the work of this great organization. At the same time we must support other organizations that are molding public opinion.

Sixth: The Church must be awakened to its responsibility. Religion is the chief avenue to the minds and the souls of the masses. The masses go to church; they listen to the minister; they have a great deal of respect for him. The minister, more than anyone else, has the ear of the people. The ministers must be awakened to their responsibilities, for the individual Negro must hold on to the one thing that has made them great, their "Spiritual genius." There is still hope, we must not give up, but we must push on.

Seventh: We must close the gap between the classes and the masses, for we are laboring to eliminate this existing evil. Therefore, it is imperative that the people—professionals, ministers, laborers, and all citizens—work together to achieve this freedom.

Last, but not least. We must be prepared. Whatever you choose for your life's work, do it well. We must prepare ourselves skillfully and intellectually to live in an integrated society. Whatever you as American citizens choose as your life's work, do it well. Do not be content with a job that is half done. Do your job so well that all the hosts of Heaven and earth will say, "Here lived a man that did his job as though God Almighty had called him at this particular moment in history to do it." Be not afraid, for God being with us is more than all of the world against us.

As I folded the paper, I looked up and saw a big burly policeman walking toward me. When he got within two feet of me, another officer called him to the telephone. I wondered why the policeman had to stand over us. We had no weapons and the only thing that we wanted was 13 Cokes that we had the money to pay for.

Amid the cursing, I remembered the words of Professor Watkins, my elementary principal and teacher in Hoffman, Oklahoma. He told us to "consider, always, consider the source."

There were some blacks entering the drug store. I saw some of the cooks and janitors. I opened my purse and wrote,

"When the time comes for cooking the food, blacks are all right;
When the time comes for washing the dishes, blacks are all right.
But when the time comes to sit down and eat, the blacks are all
wrong and that's not neat."

My daughter, Marilyn, walked over and pointed out a big, fat, mean-looking, white man, who walked over to me and said, "I can't understand it. You all didn't use to act this way; you all use to be so nice."

We remained silent and as he bumped into me, the police officers told him that he had to move on. An old white woman walked up to me and said, "If you don't get those little old poor ugly-looking children out of here, we are going to have a race riot. You just want to start some trouble." I remained silent. "Don't you know about the Tulsa race riots?" the woman asked.

I moved down to the south end of the counter, then back to the other end. This was repeated over and over. As I passed by Alma Faye Posey she burst out laughing and when I continued to look at her, she put her hands on the counter and pointed to a picture of a banana split.

It had been a long evening. Barbara, Gwen and I had a quick conference and we decided to leave without cracking a dent in the wall. Mr. Portwood Williams, Mrs. Lillian Oliver and Mrs. Mary Pogue were waiting. We loaded in our cars and left the hecklers, heckling.

We passed our first test. They pushed us, called us niggers and did everything, the group said.

"Look at me, I'm really a non-violent man," Richard Brown yelled. "Look at me. I can't believe it myself."

Small details of events were written out by Goldie Battle and it was not easy to make plans for the next day because of the large number of obscene telephone calls and threats that I was receiving. The call that really caught me unexpectedly came from a black man who would not tell me his name, but he told me how good the white folks had been to him and I was disgracing my race by taking those poor innocent children downtown.

"Sir, do you have any recommendation on what we can do to eat downtown?"

He said, "No, I do not."

Then I said, "I have one for you sir."

"Okay."

I said, "Sir, since the white folks are so good to you, where do you urinate when you are dressed up in your fine suit downtown?"

He said, "I take my can with me."

"Then, sir, I feel that it is time for you to go and empty your can."

Another black caller said that she was so embarrassed that she could hardly hold her head up. One black lady said she was working out in Nichols Hills and the lady told her to look and see what those people were doing. "Do you know them?" She said that she said *no*. She continued to do her work and when she got home she called me and I had never talked to my friend when she was in such a state of fright.

To my surprise, my mother and Mary Pogue came up to the house and explained to me all the dangers that I had gotten "all of us in." Mary had taken us downtown, but she said, "Oh! It was awful. Those people mean business. You should have heard the things that they were saying about you." The conversation continued and finally they went home.

As the crowd left my house, I hurried to bed, slept as soundly as a log. The robins reminded me that it was another day. The telephone started ringing, mostly hate calls. Then, Mary Pogue, my mother, Mrs. Pearl Chiles and Ruth Tolliver called. They were all saying, "Be careful, Clara—please, be careful."

As the calls continued to come in, I wondered if the kids would return. What are their parents saying? Will the parents be afraid of reprisals? Will there be violence today?

"Well," Reverend W. K. Jackson said in a sermon, "If you believe that you are right, go on and God will take care of you. Let His will be done."

I couldn't believe the kids were all back with new ones, including Edmund Atkins, Robert Lambeth, Elmer Smith, James Arthur Edwards, Carolyn Edwards, Henry Rolfe Jr., Leon Chandler, Willie Johnson, Arnetta Carmichael, Thomas Taylor, David Irving and Theresa Scruggs. Cars were lining up in front of my house. I had calls from Rolfe Funeral Home, Temple Funeral Home and McKay Funeral Home. They sent cars over to take the children downtown.

Blanche, the owner of Blanche's Drive-In, called to say, "Clara, I'll send some food and anything you need." We all started jumping up and down for truly, "This was the beginning, oh no, it was not the beginning, it was the continuation of man's desperate struggle to

be free and Oklahoma City would never be the same.'' I joined the
freedom band and we all began to sing:

> ''I want to be ready,
> I want to be ready,
> I want to be ready,
> To walk for freedom
> Just like John!''

In two days, the walls had fallen, not only at Katz in Oklahoma
City, but Katz billed as the world's leading cut-rate drug store
announced that its 38 outlets in Missouri, Oklahoma, Kansas and
Iowa would serve all people regardless of race, creed or color.

No longer could anyone go to Katz Drug Stores and say, ''Behold
the walls!''

. . .

Who are these white folks that do not want to eat with Blacks?
Where did they come from? Are these the people that Black people
raised their children? Are these the white boys and girls that Black
maids use to feed and take care of?

How long have Black maids been controlling white folks' homes
and kitchens? How ungrateful? Why, I would much rather eat at a
restaurant with a person, than to let him in my house, with all of my
valuables.

Something is drastically wrong here. What are the Black people
saying? Some are telling the whites that we are going ''too fast'' and
that we do not represent the majority of Blacks.

I know that those Blacks who aren't participating in the movement will be the first ones to eat in the restaurants, the first ones to
sleep in the hotels and the first and only ones to be placed ''by their
good white folks, on boards, commissions and in ''top paying
jobs.'' While those of us that are at John A. Brown's today will continue to be isolated from the fruits of Democracy.

I cannot continue to think about what's happening. I've got to
make something happen. I know what I'll do, I'll call John A.
Brown's and talk to Mrs. John A. Brown. She must be waiting for
me to call her.

I called and received the same response that I received in 1957, 1958, 1959 and 1960.

Okay if Mrs. John A. Brown doesn't want to talk to me, I sure do not want to see her. We have nothing in common anyway. I still can't understand Mrs. John A. Brown, however. She has never had us arrested in her store, and we have not discriminated against her with our sit-in techniques—maybe—oh—I just can't understand her. There is only one thing that I am sure of—if she doesn't want to see me, I DO NOT want to see her.

Mrs. John A. Brown was the Wall and the sit-ins and boycott continued with John A. Brown's as the main target.

In 1961, I received an emergency call from the John A. Brown Company asking if I would come down to the store immediately.

Why? I asked—because Mrs. John A. Brown wants to talk to you, the voice on the telephone stated.

Mrs. John A. Brown wants to see me—I do not want to see her—after all that she has done to me, why, my feet are aching now and Mrs. Brown wants to see me—she has nerve—the nerve of her telling me to come down immediately. No, I shall not talk to Mrs. Brown—thank you for calling, but now I'm busy—too busy.

How about tomorrow? I'm all filled up. I'm just too busy taking care of business.

This continued for several weeks.

I could hardly wait to tell my friends and relatives that Mrs. John A. Brown wanted to see me.

I called my mother first and she told me that she thought that Mrs. Brown was a nice lady and that I should go and see her immediately. My mother called my aunt, Mrs. Alberta Felder, and they both talked and fussed at me. I invited them to come on and go down to John A. Brown's with me. They both laughed and told me that I must be the biggest fool in the world. I shouldn't have told them any way.

I called Vera Pigee in Clarksdale, Mississippi and she said Clara, I don't know how you sophisticated Blacks do in Oklahoma, but in Mississippi, when white folks want to talk, we put down everything that we are doing and we go to them and talk. You see, when white folks stop shooting and start talking, we are happy to talk.

The sit-inners also contended that I should talk to Mrs. John A. Brown.

I decided to call Mr. Charlie Bennett, the managing editor of the *Daily Oklahoman,* Oklahoma City's great newspaper. Charlie Bennett was one of the few white men that I really trusted. I would indirectly get his advice on my seeing Mrs. John A. Brown. Charlie and I talked about the mayor's committee and some of the problems that we were facing and I casually mentioned the fact that Mrs. Brown had invited me in to have a conference and I had refused. He had no comment and silence fell over the telephone, and I said, "I don't understand, can't you see my side of it. She refused to see me when I wanted to see her and now that we're boycotting her store, she wants to talk. Frankly, I don't see what we have to talk about."

He said, "I'm surprised at you! Now if you want to keep the lines of communication open, you had better forget about minor problems and stick to the real issue. The lines of communication must be kept open at all times. Anyway, what do you have to lose?"

I didn't want to answer him and I tried to change the conversation but he brought me right back to the question in his own way. He was the undisputable executive and now he was compelling me to answer him. I hesitated. He pressured me and I finally answered.

"No, I don't have anything to lose."

"Pure common sense, or any kind of statistical data would show that you might have something to gain."

I hurriedly made up an excuse and terminated the telephone conversation. Why did I call him anyway? I should have called Dr. Charles Atkins. I called him immediately. He was my doctor and his advice had always been respected and carried out, through the years he had been our family doctor. We had depended on both his medical, recreational, and educational advice. He had never missed an opportunity to support the Sit-ins. Mentally or financially. He checked on our welfare daily. His son, Edmund Atkins, was over to my house practically every day. His advice and encouragement had been appreciated. His wife had been helpful in supplying us with new information and materials. Dr. Atkins said, "You had better see her. This is part of being a winner. Never miss the opportunity to do right."

I wrestled with my conscience and after talking with about ten more people, and since I was convinced that I was not going to get any support for my way of thinking, I decided that I would see Mrs. John A. Brown.

Her secretary called and I told her I was so busy that I could not see Mrs. Brown until the next Tuesday, a week later.

In the meantime, the sit-ins continued at John A. Brown's. Every day I was wondering what our conference would be like. During the years, we had been at John A. Brown's, we had never seen her. However, the week was so full of activities that I did not have time to think.

On the next Tuesday, the telephone rang. Mrs. Brown had asked if I wanted her chauffeur to pick me up for the meeting. "No," I said, "I shall have my chauffeur to drive me down." (I was my own chauffeur.) I got into my car and headed for John A. Brown's Department Store.

It was common information at John A. Brown's that Mrs. Brown and I were going to meet. And I could feel the tension as I walked into the store alone and toward her office. I was graciously welcomed by her attractive secretary. She talked to me briefly and told me to go into Mrs. Brown's office and she would be with me in a few minutes.

That day I was ready for Mrs. John A. Brown. All of the frustrations that had been building within me for the last four years were going to come out "right in her white face."

When the secretary opened the door, I walked into an office. I was overcome with history because that office was Mr. John A. Brown's former office. The furniture, the pictures, the papers and in spite of the improvements and re-furnishings that had happened at John A. Brown's, that office was just as it was when Mr. John A. Brown died years ago. My frustrations began to diminish and when Mrs. Brown opened the door, we both stood speechless before each other and with tears in our eyes, we embraced each other as if we had been friends for years. Oh, I know this couldn't be, but it was, and now we were talking. Two women, one black and one white. One rich and one poor.

Historical circumstances had brought us together. We talked about our families and some of the problems that we had faced as we both tried to compete in a man's business world. We both cried again as I told her how I had tried to make it. How I was working on three jobs trying to educate my children and to provide them with the necessities of life. She told me about her husband and how he had died. We talked about how much we had loved and how much we had lost.

Finally, she said, "I have been told that you hate me, is that true?" I said, "No, Mrs. Brown. I do not hate you. I respect you. You have challenged the male oriented business world; you shall always have my respect."

"I have been told that you hated me," I said.

"Oh, no, Clara, I've heard that, but it is not true. I admire your courage. I have stood here and have wondered day in and day out, what you and your children were saying about me. Clara, tell me, please tell me, what the children think about me? What do they say, Clara?"

As I looked at her, I knew that I had to tell her the truth. Her penetrating eyes stared directly into mine.

"Mrs. Brown, they say that they wish you had died in place of Mr. John A. Brown. They said if he were living they believe that they would be able to eat here," I said.

For a few minutes there was complete silence and then she spoke.

"Clara, day in and day out, I have worried about this thing. I just don't know how to deal with it. You see, Mr. Frank Wade has leased space in my store to operate the luncheonette and under his lease he has the sole right to run it in his own way. You see my hands have been completely tied."

"Yes, Mrs. Brown, but we don't know anything about Frank Wade and care less, but John A. Brown's that's different. This is the store where we have spent our money and we can't see how we can be discriminated against under the roof of a John A. Brown store. Even the name John Brown reminds us of the martyr that died for our cause."

We talked for nearly an hour. Mr. Anderson came in and brought us some lemonade. He offered her the first glass and she said, "Serve Clara first."

Finally she said, "Take this message back to the children. Segregation will end at John A. Brown's."

I was so proud of her. She admitted to me that the first time I was arrested, she called and offered to pay my bond. She never missed calling to see if I were all right, she said.

She asked me to do her a favor. To come and meet with all of the executives of the John A. Brown's store and tell them why we selected John A. Brown's Store.

I followed her to a spacious conference room where I told my story. I liked everybody there immediately except Attorney Lyle. He continued to harass me about insignificant things. I had already been warned about him. I started to raise my voice at him, but I looked at Mrs. Brown and she smiled at me. Then, I knew everything was going to be alright.

When I left John A. Brown's that day, I had respect for Miss Ambrosia, Mr. Hardwick and I knew, I had a life time friend in Mrs. John A. Brown.

An agreement was made that day that John A. Brown's Segregation Walls would fall and in less than a week, Blacks were eating at John A. Brown's.

Mrs. Brown and I continued to talk to each other by telephone. She invited me to go to Europe with her. I turned it down because of other commitments and before she went into the hospital for the last time, she called me and told me that she was going into the hospital under a different name and she probably would never see me again, but she wanted me to know that she appreciated what we had done for this city, a city that she loved so well.

Mrs. John A. Brown acquainted me with loneliness in a way that I had never known it before. When she died, I couldn't control my emotions. I went to her funeral and followed the procession to her final resting place.

A white executive of the store said, ''I'm glad you came.''

She was my friend, I loved her and I had to come.

13

THE CASE OF THE DEERSLAYER

Stan Steiner

"Red Power," it was sometimes called. AIM, the American Indian Movement, was perhaps its most visible element. It was, presumably, an "angry young Indian" movement, the 1960s Native American version of Black Power. Yet it was "radical" in a way most people don't understand that word—that is, getting back to the roots. It is personalized, and given an Oklahoma flavor, in the following chapter from Stan Steiner's 1968 book, The New Indians.

In the quiet of the courthouse square the dark-skinned men sat under the leafless trees of spring, waiting. With brooding and ominous eyes they scrutinized the town. Hundreds of Indians squatted there with old pistols in their belts, or they leaned on the aged trees, eyeing their pickup trucks, where they had hidden their rifles.

A hunter was on trial for killing a deer. The deerslayer was a Cherokee named John Chewie.

Out of the windows of the dim courtroom the handful of small-town officials who had gathered watched the crowd of Indians with growing disquiet. Laughing, someone said it was a scalping party.

"The Case of the Deerslayer," by Stan Steiner, first appeared in *The New Indians* (New York: Harper and Row, 1968). Reprinted with permission, Vera John-Steiner.

The whispered rumor spread: "I hear the Cherokees got guns!" It was not to be believed, for it was safer not to believe it; after all, this was not the set of a shoot-'em-up on television, nor could anyone imagine an Indian uprising of the Old West resurrected on the docile Main Street of Jay in uneventful Oklahoma. This was the United States of America, spring, 1966.

Was the ancient Cherokee war chant to re-echo beneath the Coca-Cola signs on the town square?

> Hayi! Yu! Listen!
> Now, instantly, we have lifted the red war club.
> Quickly his soul shall be without motion.
> There under the earth, where the black war clubs shall be
>   moving like ballsticks in a game,
>   there his soul shall be,
>   never to reappear.
> We cause it to be so.[1]

That morning, and the night before, the young men and the old men of the Cherokee villages had been coming out of the hills. Into the town they came, past the GET RIGHT WITH GOD sign on the roadway, the gas stations, the hot dog stands, and the neon-lit bars that were the outposts of civilization.

In twos and threes they came walking along the roadway, with their rifles in their fists, in pickup trucks hunched down to duck the night winds, in old cars that rattled along like farm wagons.

> I am rising to seek the warpath,
> The earth and the sky beside me;
> I walk in the day and in the night,
> The star of the evening guides me.

Jay, Oklahoma, is a little town, population 1,120. Not much more need be said of it. In eastern Oklahoma, deep in the wooded hills of the Ozarks near the Arkansas line, the town is surrounded by fields where game birds gather and rough stands of woods where the tracks of deer and possum are visible to the myopic eye, and mountain brooks. Hunters say the region is a paradise; perhaps it is. It is as well the county seat of Delaware County, a "depressed area," where the hills are crowded with full-blooded Indians.

Hostile in a way so ingrained that no one needs to say anything about it, the town is not off bounds to the Indians. But they rarely come into town, unless they have to. Except, of course, on Saturday nights. It was unheard of for so many to come. One could feel the tension.

The courthouse in the town square is a fortlike building of no particular architecture. It looks like any other county courthouse in rural Oklahoma.

In the corridors of the courthouse there was a residue of exhausted air. The judicial chambers opened upon rows of gnarled and initialed benches. The benches might have been mistaken for the pews of an ascetic church. The pedestal of the judge who sat in judgment on the boredom that passes for sin in a small town was like a pulpit. The jailhouse, an ugly structure of heavy stones, was visible from the courtroom; a reminder of the swift justice that was a tradition of the Old West. The prisoners, on the Ozark frontier, were mostly Indians. John Chewie had waited in this jailhouse.

And still they came, the silent Indians with their silent weapons. "When Cherokees go armed, they generally carry pistols. They may be of almost any type, from ancient .45 caliber 'hot legs,' to modern compact automatics," said a man in nearby Tahlequah. "Pistols tucked under the waistband of pants, in the deep back pocket of overalls or in a coat pocket. Pistols in the glove compartments of cars, or behind the seat of a pickup. Rifles, too, are 'kept handy' in a nearby car or pickup."

"There were four hundred armed Cherokees in Jay ready to use them if that man was prosecuted," said the principal of a rural Delaware County school, Harold Wade, who was in town that day.

In a town of little more than one thousand, the sudden appearance of four hundred armed Indians was frightening. In any town if that many men, bearing loaded guns, were to appear at city hall to surround the town square, not demonstrating but sitting silently, with rifles and pistols cocked, there would be reason to fear. But in Jay these Indians could have occupied the town in hours.

Were it to happen in New York City's Harlem, whose Negro population is about equal to that of the American Indians, or in Los Angeles' Watts, as it almost did, the alarm would ring out, on the wire services, "Insurrection! Call out the National Guard! And the

Life photographers!" But the armed Indians were met with silence. Not with the National Guard; not even with the television cameras. The newspapers, except for the local press, ignored the threat of the armed uprising in the hills.

Was it incomprehensible to the townspeople that the stoic Indians, the long-suffering and eternally enduring, the apostles of patience, were so violently angry? The Indians were the town joke, as they were the national joke. They were not to be taken too seriously.

"Lo, the Poor Indian," mocked the *Tulsa Tribune* in an editorial of fatherly disapproval. And yet the newspaper at the oil capital was somewhat apprehensive too. The reports of rifle-toting redskins would have been easier to laugh off if it hadn't been for scare words like "Red Power" that some of the young Indians were using. The *Tribune* sensed that the rebellion of the Red Muslims, as the new Indian leaders themselves called it, was not being staged for laughs.

The *Tulsa Tribune* feared that "Then would come a militant separatist movement, such as the French-Canadians have in Quebec, and we're back to the Little Big Horn."

In Tahlequah, back in the hills, Clyde Warrior laughed at these words. The young Indian intellectual was one of the angriest of the angry young men of the hills. Not a Cherokee, he had no part in the uprising. But he was its uninhibited, fiery voice to other tribes.

"We have a Southern social structure in eastern Oklahoma," Warrior said. "The only way you change that structure is to smash it. You turn it over sideways. And stomp on it. It appears to me that's what will happen around here. I think violence will come about. And as far as I am concerned the sooner the better."

> Ho, you young men, warriors!
> Bear your arms to the place of battle!

Indeed, something had to be done. That winter, under the cold clouds of discontent, the envoys from Washington had been holding councils of peace. It was tumultuous enough with the urban Negroes once again threatening to disquiet the summer solstice with cries of "Black Power" without rural Indians threatening to do the same with hunting rifles. Quietly, behind the scenes, the emissaries of the Justice Department, the agents of the F.B.I., the mediators of the

Interior Department, and the lawyers of the Attorney General's office in Oklahoma City had gone into the hills surreptitiously, to confer with the armed Cherokees. "To calm the natives down," said Clyde Warrior.

Was all of this because John Chewie had gone hunting? Chewie, an ex-Marine, known as a hard drinker and a hungry hunter, had indeed gone hunting. He had, by killing a deer, become the symbol of the Red Nationalist rebellion.

The rangers of the Oklahoma Department of Wildlife had arrested him for possession of deer meat in his car out of season, and for hunting without a license. He did not deny the charges. He had shot the deer, he said, in the Kenwood Reserve, a region of woodland held in trust by the U.S. Government for the Cherokee Tribe. He was a full-blooded Cherokee and he would not apologize for hunting on land that rightfully belonged to his people; nor did he have to be licensed like a dog by the state. He had hunted because he was hungry, he told the court; to feed himself and his family. It had been the dead of winter and they had to eat.

In the hunter's behalf, Robert Thomas, a sardonic Cherokee anthropologist, testified at the court hearing that these Indians believed that God had put the wild game on earth for the sustenance of man. Were they, believing that, to obtain hunting licenses from God?

Thomas, who directed the Carnegie Corporation's Cross Cultural Project on the Cherokee culture and language in Tahlequah, told the court that the per capita annual income of the Indians in Delaware County was $500. Hardly enough to starve on, he said. He implied that the religious beliefs of the Indians were neither wholly metaphysical nor legally fatuous, but necessary for survival. The diet was simply inadequate, testified Albert Wahrhaftig, the junior anthropologist with the Carnegie Project. So poor was the economic condition of the Indians, he said, that without wild game to supplement their meager food supplies they would have no meat at all.

"I seen my father suffer. I seen my aunt, my own aunt, die of starvation. I seen old womens suffer. I seen the childrens buried in the county coffins." The mourner was a rural Indian, a backwoods dirt church preacher of the Indian Baptists among the Creeks of

Oklahoma, the Reverend Clifton Hill, who shepherded a rebellious movement of his own people in a neighboring county. "Sometimes I goes to funerals, and see the poor Indians, I mean *poor* Indians, who don't have a thing they own, lying in the county coffin. And you don't know what I feel when I see that.

"Go down to the depths of the Creek Nation. We have shabby houses. It's nothing like compared in the city. It's worse. When I talk about poor, I mean *poor*."

> Here on my breast I have bled!
> See! See! My battle scars!
> You mountains tremble at my yell!
> I strike for life!

"These are very poor people in the midst of a land of plenty," said Finis Smith, one of the religious leaders of the Cherokees and the descendant of Chief Redbird Smith. He believed the "exploitation is accelerating." So was the anger of his people.

"In eastern Oklahoma we have a system of peonage," said Clyde Warrior. "The local politicians and local businessmen find it very profitable to keep these Indians in a state of peonage. They work for people as slave labor; they rent from people off their welfare checks. It has been going on for several years; it is just now coming to a head; the anger, you might say, of the Indian people."

"The life of most Oklahoma Indians is very, very bad," said Warrior, "the sickest, poorest people in the country." Because they were so low economically, and felt so low psychologically, the "Oklahoma Indians had no way of relating to urban America," he said, "just like any other poor people."

The weed roots of poverty in the Indian villages were dug up statistically by Graham Holmes, the former Bureau of Indian Affairs area director for the Five Civilized Tribes of Oklahoma. In a survey prepared for Congressman Wayne Aspinall of the House Interior and Insular Affairs Committee in 1962, Holmes laconically noted:

Of 19,000 adult Indians in eastern Oklahoma, between the ages of 18 and 55, an estimated 10,000, or 52.6 percent, were unemployed;

Of the 10,000 jobless adult Indians well over half received no unemployment insurance, or any other welfare assistance—whatsoever;

Of young Indians, when he was queried "How many Indians 16 or 17 [years old] are now employed? Full time?" the succinct official replied: "Very few, if any."

Yet, having tabulated these statistics of poverty, Holmes's document ended happily. He dryly assured the Congress that all was well:

Question: "How is the morale of the Indian people?"

Reply: "Good."

Question: "Are there any evidences of unusual concern by the Indians?"

Reply: "No."

In rural Oklahoma there is little work for the Indian to do. The economic exodus from the rural towns long since left nothing but a residue of odd jobs and seasonal farm work for those who refused to become city Indians.

John Chewie was a farm laborer. He worked in the strawberry and vegetable crops, when there was work. Most of the time he was unemployed. Hands were more numerous than jobs. Like his neighbors, he hoed a hard row. He was a poor backwoods Indian. A friend in Tahlequah said of him: "He is very Indian looking, with a perpetual scared and timid look on his face. He has no ideological axes to grind. He is a hell of a nice guy, with a great sense of humor, but he is the least likely guy in the world to be in the forefront of an Indians'-rights push that you can imagine. I call him 'The Reluctant Hero.'

"But he is all man," the friend added, "and he doesn't like to be shoved around, bribed, and threatened. So he has gotten real angry about this case. He just wants to hunt."

Hunting to an Indian like John Chewie is not a sport. He does not go hunting and fishing to recapture his lost innocence with mass-produced moose-mating horns. The woodsy disguises of the suburbanite in search of a pseudo-primitive manliness are not for him. Nor is he escaping from the office routine. Like most of the Cherokee hunters, he seeks to escape from the statistics of unemployment. It is not to escape into nothingness, but into Indianness. The woods, the hunt, the wild game, the earth itself represent dignity and pride in the Indian ways. Cherokee tribes hunt to reaffirm their way of life, their oneness with nature, the uniqueness of their Indianness, their treaty rights as an Indian nation. And to eat meat.

Hunting has become a symbol of the new tribalism. Wherever the new Indians gather to reaffirm their rights, the Deerslayer reappears. His rifle echoes and re-echoes throughout Indian country.

Up on the high mountain mesas of the Pueblos or the Hopis the traditional chiefs would not buy hunting licenses for young hunters of the tribe. "We are still a sovereign nation. We have never abandoned our sovereignty to any foreign power or government," they said. Chippewas of Wisconsin's Lake Superior shores demanded their "earth right," as a tribal official phrased it, to fish and to harvest wild rice, without interference, or "okay from outside." The fishermen of the Yakima Indians of Washington State patrolled the banks of the Columbia River with rifles, to safeguard their tribal nets and to enforce their treaty rights. In New York State, the Iroquois, the "native nationalists" that Edmund Wilson wrote of in his book *Apology to the Iroquois*, restated their old religious beliefs by an unfettered and free return of tribal hunting bands to the eastern forests. Deep in the Everglades of Florida the Seminoles were doing the same, while the Red Lake Band of Chippewas in Minnesota fought for and won their "ancestral right" to hunt wild ducks without licenses from the state or the United States.

But why had the movement of tribal nationalism taken on so seemingly archaic a form? Why, of all things, hunting rights?

The wild duck hunters of the Chippewas may offer the clue. For generations the tribe hunted wild ducks on the shores of Red Lake. They ran afoul of game wardens with warrants in their jodhpurs, who arrested the Indians in flocks for not buying migratory bird hunting stamps.

Lo, the poor wild duck became a *cause célèbre*. His unstamped death was fought in the corridors of the Interior Department, until one judicious day the then Acting Commissioner of Indian Affairs, H. Rex Lee, consulted with the wise men of the legal staff and declared: "In an opinion dated June 30, 1936 the Solicitor of this Department pointed out that, while the various treaties between the United States and the Chippewa Indians did not reserve the right to the Indians to hunt and fish within unceded lands of the Red Lake Reservation, it was not necessary to reserve such rights because of the larger rights possessed by the Indians in land occupied and used by them, and such rights remained in the Indians unless granted away.

"In view of the foregoing, it is our view that members of the Red Lake Band of Chippewa Indians are not required to obtain a Migratory Bird Hunting Stamp to hunt wild ducks on the Reservation."

Whether to buy or not to buy a migratory bird hunting stamp? It may not have seemed of historic importance. But it was. The Indians by defying the proclaimed rights of the states were proclaiming their right to govern themselves. And they were protecting their ancient way of tribal life, with rifles ready. The Chippewas and the Yakimas and the Cherokees were issuing declarations of independence.

The Navajo Tribe had spoken of this independence when one Fourth of July in the early sixties their tribal newspaper editorialized: "Perhaps, for the Indian, the celebration is a bit premature. . . . The day will come, and it is rapidly approaching, all the time, when the part of Webster's definition of Independence which reads 'self-maintenance' will become a reality. We call it self-determination in Navajoland, but it means the same thing."

In any event, the defiance of Stamp Acts ought to have had a familiar ring. In the Boston Tea Party of 1773, when the liberty-minded colonials fought the King's Stamp Act, they masqueraded as Indians. Now the Indians were taking off their masks of timidity and defying the latter-day Stamp Acts that denied them their independence.

In the definitive *Handbook of Federal Indian Law* the late Felix S. Cohen had recognized that "tribal rights of hunting and fishing have received judicial recognition and protection against state and private interference, and even against interference by Federal administrative officials." But the words did not persuade the deeds. At the Chicago Conference of American Indians held at the University of Chicago in 1961, a resolution on "Hunting and Fishing Rights" noted the "increasing concern" of the tribes that state governments were "encroaching on the rights of individual [Indians] hunting, fishing, trapping, and harvesting wild rice on Indian reservations." The four hundred Indians from fifty tribes who gathered at that anthropological powwow petitioned the Secretary of [the]

Interior for "a favorable ruling on the rights of Indians to hunt, fish, trap and harvest wild rice, and other vegetation on their own lands."

John Chewie had hunted for more than deer meat. He had hunted for his self-respect and for self-determination in his tribal way of life.

He had not gone into the woods by himself. The men of fifty villages in the hills had come together that winter and talked of their hungers for food and pride. Led by Finis Smith, these men had secretly met in snowbound cabins and in backwoods towns. They founded the Five County Cherokee Movement, a society of full-bloods—the silent men with rifles. And in the dark of winter, yet unheard in the noisy towns, they voiced what was to be their declaration of independence—the Declaration of the Five County Cherokees:

> We meet in a time of darkness to seek the path to the light. We come together, just as our fathers have always done, to do these things. . . .
>
> We, the Five County Cherokees, are one people. We stand united in the sight of God, our creator. We are joined by love and concern for each other and for all men. . . .
>
> We offer ourselves as the voice of the Cherokee people. For many years our people have not spoken and have not been heard. Now we gather as brothers and sisters. . . .
>
> We use our right to freedom of speech. This right is the ancient custom of our people. This right is guaranteed by the Constitution of the United States of America. We insist on equality under the laws of these United States. We act now, peaceably but firmly, to carry out the wish of our people.. . . . .
>
> We do this for the benefit of all Cherokees. We do this as a good example to all men. Already we have gathered to protect our rights to harvest fish and game to feed ourselves and our children. . . .

These men went into the woods together. In bands of hunters as in the old days, they hunted for game as their fathers had. Chewie was one of many. He was caught, but he was not alone. The hundreds who stood by his side with their rifles on the day of his trial were his blood brothers. In their tribal oath they had pledged to one another:

"We will go on until our lands and our homes are safe. Until we live within the full and just protection of the law. Until we live as the American authors of the Constitution and the Declaration of Independence intended each of the nationalities in this country to live. As dignified men. As free men. As men equal to all other men. "From this beginning we will go on until the job is done. . . ."

> O Great Terrestrial Hunter, I come to the edge of your spittle,
>   where you repose.
> Give me the wind.
> Give me the breeze.
> Yu!

Inside the courtroom the hearing itself was dull. Hardly was there need of legal evidence to determine what had happened. Even the cross-examination was mostly repartée:

PROSECUTOR: "How many times have you been arrested?"
DEFENDANT: "I don't know. I haven't counted."
PROSECUTOR: "John, do you drink whiskey?"
DEFENDANT: "Don't you?"

Jokingly the State of Oklahoma's Assistant Attorney General, D. L. Cook, invoked his constitutional right not to answer under the Fifth Amendment. The laughter in the courtroom was, on this cue, more polite than prolonged; it was somewhat nervous.

One of the defense attorneys, Stuart Trapp, who had come from Memphis, Tennessee, to represent the American Civil Liberties Union, then took the stand. He did so, the lawyer said, because he sensed that the tension in the town of Jay was about to flare into bloodshed, unless the Case of the Deerslayer were taken out of the State of Oklahoma's jurisdiction. It ought to be judged by the federal courts. The courthouse square was "an unhappy place of considerable tension," Trapp said. He had listened to the Indians talk of injustices for hours, while fingering their rifles.

In deference to the rifles of the silent, and uninvited, witnesses, the Case of the Deerslayer was held over for the federal courts. And, as quietly as they had come, the Indians withdrew from the town.

Once again the town was peaceable. There had been no violence. No shooting. No riot. Not a window shattered. No shouting. No slogans. The young men with rifles had gathered up their rifles and slipped away. It was as though they had never come. By their silence they indicated their disdain of the whole proceeding.

"The Cherokees and the Creeks are a very legal-minded people. They want to try everything that is right and proper," Clyde Warrior said, "because they believe that if they do everything that is legal and proper then justice will prevail. What they fail to see is that in the American system nothing is done legally, honestly, and truthfully. Now, when they find that out, they are going to be pretty damn mad. If that [the legal way] fails, then violence will take place. The country should take heed."

His wrath voiced the frustrations of not only the young, educated Indians. In the hills the country Indians were more and more vocal. And their pent-up angers, so long frustrated by their feelings of hopelessness, upset the rural calm. "These people are becoming more and more aggressive. I do not use the term 'aggressive' lightly. In many areas it is on the verge of militancy," Warrior said.

These views provoked much headshaking among the local officials, especially since the views were supported by hundreds of rifles. In the cities community leaders were troubled.

When the Council of the Five Civilized Tribes of Oklahoma met to discuss the uprising in the hills, there was much dismay. The Reverend James L. Partridge, a Creek tribal councilman of Sapulpa, advocated that the U.S. Congress and the State Legislature pass laws to "stop all this marching and all this violence." It ought to be a federal offense "to lead an act of violence," Reverend Partridge said.

W. W. Keeler, the principal chief of the Cherokee Nation, was more conciliatory. One of the distinguished Indian citizens of Oklahoma and vice president of Phillips Petroleum, Keeler had been a spokesman of the "task force" on Indian affairs appointed by the late President Kennedy. He thought it wiser to soothe, rather than restrict, the dissident full-bloods. "Now is the time to forget these differences" and past "mistakes," Keeler said; let the Cherokees "join hands and work together."

The principal chief was appointed by the President of the United States; he was not elected by the tribe. In the hills they called him "the President's chief"; he was rudely rebuffed by the full-bloods. He was a "white Indian" to the backwoods, dirt-farm rebels.

Finis Smith, the leader of the Five County Cherokee Movement, was blunt: "We do not need to be called to assemblies to be berated for not cooperating in our own destruction. In a strict sense, there are no alternatives to Indian wants. There is no alternative to having control of our own destiny and having our voices heard and taken seriously. . . . We certainly need to strike bargains with the general society, but we do not need to help whites become big shots in Indian affairs [by being] 'good little Indians.' ''

The old tribal leader talked in a tone different from that of a young ''hot-blood'' like Warrior. But his goals differed little.

''The 'best of all possible worlds' for the Cherokee people would have been for the Cherokee Nation to have continued up to the present,'' Smith said; ''for the Cherokee people to live as an *independent republic of Indians,* closely tied and friendly to the United States, under the treaties—as a *modern Indian state* of small communities of kinfolk, taking part in the present industrialized economy of the world, but with a Cherokee government, and legal system in the Cherokee language, with lands held in common, and educational system in the Cherokee language, and with industrial work as an addition to farming and hunting.

''However, we are willing to compromise and modify our aspirations to accommodate to the presence of our white brothers who now live among us.''

> You have brought me down the white road.
> There in mid-earth you have placed me.
> I shall stand erect upon the earth.

In the words with which Finis Smith described the old Cherokee Nation there was a description of the tribal nationalism of the new Indians. What had been forgotten, or merely suppressed, was no longer spoken of as the past. It was to be enlarged to a ''Greater Indian America.''

Finis Smith, being a traditional chief, had a power in his words that the younger man did not. Wherever one went in the hills of eastern Oklahoma, asking what was happening, people said, ''Have you talked to Finis? You have to talk to Finis.'' The merchants of the hill towns whispered that he was ''the redskinned Malcolm X''; to the local newspapers he was a ''dupe'' who was used ''by outside agitators.'' He was a ''menace to the peace of the community,'' said a police officer. ''He is working the Indians up to no good,'' complained a small-town mayor in Cherokee County. "But if you quote me, don't use my name. I got Indian voters." The Reverend Lindy Waters, himself a cousin of Smith's, talked of "his brilliant mind [that] is being channeled in the wrong direction."

The man was revered and reviled, heard and feared. Yet no one talked of him in the old stereotype of the taciturn, the inscrutable, the enigmatic Indian.

He was an old Indian. But he was an outspoken new Indian. In the personnel files of the local office of the Bureau of Indian Affairs the folder on Finis Smith revealed that he had lost several jobs for "trying to stir up Indian workers to stand up for their rights"—as a government clerk confided. Smith had been fired from the Tinker Air Force Base, in Oklahoma City, for what was said to be organizing activity among the Indians.

"We do *all* the compromising, and our white brothers have drawn the arena and made the rules by which life must be lived, and we have no choice but to go along, whether we like it or not," Smith said. "But a compromise must go both ways. To begin with, whites must recognize our existence as a modern and permanent part of Oklahoma; as a *people*. . . . It follows that whites must be willing to modify many Oklahoma institutions, laws, and procedures so that we can participate in a common society with them."

> You have put me in the white house.
> I shall be in it as it moves about.

"The Cherokees have always led the way in every revolutionary concept [in] Indian affairs. Whatever happens in eastern Oklahoma will have a terrific impact on all Indian tribes," said Clyde Warrior. "I've heard it said that whatever the Cherokees do, that's what everyone else will do. I've head it said, in my travels around the country, that Indians are just waiting for the Cherokees to do something. And then it will be like a snowball rolling down a hill."

The Indian tribes throughout the country were waiting to see what would happen to the Cherokees, Smith thought. It had traditionally been true. History supported this belief, wrote John Collier, the former Commissioner of Indian Affairs, in *Indians of the Americas:* "More than any other tribe, the Cherokee Nation furnished the crystallizing thread of the United States government policy and action in Indian affairs.''

It may have been with this vision of the past and the future in mind that the Declaration of the Five County Cherokees was written. For it beautifully and prophetically and simply said what the new Indians, everywhere, believed:

> Now, we shall not rest until we have regained our rightful place. We shall tell our young people what we know. We shall send them to the corners of the earth to learn more. They shall lead us.
>
> Now, we have much to do. When our task is done, we will be ready to rest.
>
> In these days, intruders, named without our consent, speak for the Cherokees. When the Cherokee government is the Cherokee people, we shall rest.
>
> In these days, we are informed of the decisions other people have made about our destiny. When we control our destiny, we shall rest.
>
> In these days, the high courts of the United States listen to people who have been wronged. When our wrongs have been judged in these courts, and the illegalities of the past have been corrected, we shall rest.
>
> In these days, there are countless ways by which people make their grievances known to all Americans. When we have learned these new ways that bring strength and power, and we have used them, we shall rest.
>
> In these days, we are losing our homes and our children's homes. When our homeland is protected, for ourselves and for the generations to follow, we shall rest.
>
> In the vision of our creator, we declare ourselves ready to stand proudly among the nationalities of these United States of America.

> I stand with my face toward the Sun Land.
> No one is ever lonely with me.
> Wherever I go
> No one is ever lonely with me.

And so in the hills of Oklahoma the Indians hold on to their rifles. They sit in their wooded villages, in their highway shanty-towns, in their forest cabins, with their rifles between their knees, waiting to hear if justice will absolve them from the burden of blood that the white man's inhumanity and greed have cast upon them. They wait to see if the white man's democracy and rich abundance, taken from their lands, will be shared with the Indian.

They sit silently, doubting and waiting. They squat, and they clean their rifles. They have waited patiently for a long time, but they are no longer patient.

Somewhere in the hills Clyde Warrior, the Ponca, spoke: "I say there will be an uprising that will make Kenyatta's Mau Mau movement look like a Sunday-school picnic."

Clyde Warrior grinned. He, too, was waiting.

NOTES

1. These religious chants, or sacred formulas, of the Cherokee are reprinted from *Sacred Formulas of the Cherokees* by James Mooney, 7th Annual Report of the Bureau of American Ethnology, Washington, D.C., 1891. Mooney wrote that he had translated them from writings, in the Cherokee language, by religious men of the tribe who had transcribed them "for their own use."

Cherokees believe it is sacrilegious for a non-Cherokee to publish, print, or use these sacred formulas. In deference to these fine, deeply religious people I therefore wish to explain that I have merely reprinted them from James Mooney, as he reprinted them from the writing of the Cherokees of the nineteenth century.

14

BLACK OKLAHOMANS
AND SENSE OF PLACE

Jimmie L. Franklin

Jimmie L. Franklin, professor of history at Vanderbilt University in Nashville, Tennessee, was one of the first blacks to receive a Ph.D. in history from the University of Oklahoma. He has written several books on Oklahoma history, including Born Sober: Prohibition in Oklahoma, 1907–1959 *and* Journey Toward Hope: A History of Blacks in Oklahoma. *The essay that follows is a revised version of a paper given at the Mid-America Conference at Oklahoma State University, September 15, 1989.*

On one of those rare, perfectly sun-kissed days in the American Northwest, Mildred Webb Hayes settled comfortably into her living room chair to talk of a land she had left behind. As a child, Mildred had grown up in the 1930s and '40s on Oklahoma City's northeast side in a home not distant from Douglass High School. In 1950, she graduated from the public schools, and in October of the following year she made her way to Seattle, Washington. A short time later, she moved to Tacoma, just a few miles away. Leaving home had been no easier for her than for millions of other people who had done it, but the powerful pull of opportunity and the excitement of adventure had beckoned, and she had gone forth to make her way in the world. Like others who had voluntarily uprooted themselves, Mildred fought the terrible pain of

265

homesickness and the occasional fear that sometimes accompanies residence in a new place.[1]

Thirty-eight years away from Oklahoma had blurred some of the sharp details of home in Mildred Hayes's keen mind. However, in the summer of 1989, time had not succeeded in blotting out many impressions of the state that still made her heart beat fast with excitment. Life for Mildred in Oklahoma City had been a happy time, playing with young friends, bragging on the street corner about the exploits of the powerful Douglass football team, or shyly and unpretentiously courting during church meetings. But it was Saturday at the Jewel Theater that brought a special joy to Mildred Webb Hayes and the other black children of the Northeast side. Like other students who had studied at Douglass, including novelist Ralph Ellison, she fondly recalled her experiences with Zelia Breaux, one of the finest teachers of music in the history of the State of Oklahoma.[2]

Young children such as Mildred did not understand the intricacies of social policy in Oklahoma, especially segregation and discrimination. During her childhood, law and order as well as custom had set her black community apart from whites, and while that had proved disturbing to the young girl, it did not push her toward a strong social activism. "I really never missed whites," she said smilingly in her Tacoma interview. Although she found exclusion philosophically unacceptable, the magnetism of a rich black experience and a vibrant black community life had a positive influence on her, and that partly provided a shield in earlier years from the harshness of white bigotry. Significantly, the social policy dictated by law in Oklahoma did not produce a racial chauvinism within Mildred; nor, incidentally, did it prevent social contact between many blacks and whites in the years before *Brown* v. *Board of Education* and the age of integration.[3]

By the time Mildred Webb Hayes completed her interview with the author of this article, one thing seemed clear: here was a black Oklahoman who had a strong sense of attachment to her native land. To be sure, her sense of place had much to do with *memory,* and memory is important, for it helps a person fix himself or herself in time, shape identity, and define associations with institutions and things. Mildred Webb Hayes's experiences greatly resembled those of many other blacks who lived in Oklahoma but later left the state. But even the experiences of those who parted Oklahoma say much about the blacks who stayed at home, who lived out their existence in a Jim Crow society.

There existed within Oklahoma (and other southern states) a racial system that limited black aspirations and that frustrated the creation of a more powerful sense of place. Racial prohibitions, nevertheless, did not lead to the outright rejection of American ideals, as the life of Mildred Webb Hayes readily attests, but to a kind of "twoness" that troubled the souls of black folk. Just four years before Oklahoma entered the Union, social critic and scholar W. E. B. Du Bois had eloquently stated the problem in his *The Souls of Black Folk:* "One ever feels his twoness,—an American, a Negro; two souls, two thoughts, two unreconciled strivings; two warring ideals in one dark body, whose dogged strength alone keeps it from being torn asunder."[4]

Oklahoma had actively begun to establish its racial restrictions that fostered this twoness in 1907, and by the end of the first decade the state had a racial code firmly in place. At the heart of the racial system was the belief in separation of whites and blacks. And along with that separation went economic, political and social discrimination, similar to that of the Deep South. Indeed, most of Oklahoma's founding fathers had agreed with William ("Alfalfa Bill") Murray, president of Oklahoma's constitutional convention, that blacks should remain porters, bootblacks, barbers, and farmers. It was a false notion, Murray had told his colleagues at Guthrie, that "the negro [*sic*] can rise to the equal of a white man in the professions or become an equal citizen to grapple with public questions." Murray and his cohorts at the convention, of course, postponed the development of a complete Jim Crow code at the convention, but at the first Oklahoma legislature in 1907, the Democratically controlled body moved swiftly to pass a statute that put firm flesh on the hard bones of Jim Crow.[5]

The legislation designed to separate the races proved disappointing to black Oklahomans. So did the movement to disfranchise them, and it had a negative effect upon sense of place. Of course, Oklahoma's founding fathers had desired disfranchisement at the time of the Constitutional Convention, but they chose not to test the resolve of President Theodore Roosevelt, who had threatened a veto of Oklahoma statehood if the delegates at Guthrie stripped blacks of the ballot. Unified political action by blacks in behalf of Republican party candidates shortly after statehood, however, gave Democratic politicians the needed pretext for black disfranchisement. Thus, in 1910 the legislature passed the infamous Grandfather Clause, a measure approved by the people in a referendum and designed to cripple the Republicans and to drive black Oklahomans from the ballot box. That clause, of course, required persons to be able to read and to write in order to vote, but it exempted many white people, but hardly any blacks, from the provisions of the act. While the 1915 *Guinn* case knocked the legal props from under the Grandfather Clause (and, incidentally, gave additional life to the youthful Oklahoma branch of the NAACP), it did not ensure the uncontested ballot for black people, for other measures and custom operated to frustrate the exercise of the black franchise. Only the 1965 Voting Rights Act would bring greater opportunity to blacks to vote without fear of intimidation in Oklahoma and other southern states.[6]

The response to Oklahoma's racial code tells something about place and how black people viewed their land, their state. Obviously, Jim Crow represented a heavy burden, and practically all blacks rejected the restrictions that circumscribed their lives, reduced their happiness, and curtailed the exercise of their political liberties. Rejection, then, stood readily in evidence, and migration appeared as a symbol of dissatisfaction. But scholars should cautiously draw conclusions about this important phenomenon in the state's history and about its relationship to blacks and place. Rejection is only one consideration in the black migration phenomenon. A number of other causes account for black movement away from Oklahoma during the Jim Crow era, including some nonracial push factors. Certainly, the deep agricultural distress at the turn of the century, the Dust Bowl of the 1930s, and the lure of better jobs in the North during World War I and World War II were important motivations for leaving home. There is some evidence which indicates that actual racial conflict—except in the case of the infamous Tulsa race riot of 1921—never produced major migration out of the state, although one should not interpret this lack of movement as black satisfaction with existing racial conditions.[7]

Important in the analysis here is that many of the blacks most equipped to leave Oklahoma did not move. A significant reason for the willingness to remain in the state was the attachment to the idea of place. Even when black Oklahomans left home, they took with them not only the memories of their place but visible reminders of their culture. Home gardens replete with all the tasty vegetables for "soul food" dishes reappeared in Wichita, Kansas City, Los Angeles, and Chicago. And black Oklahomans joined with others of the race in re-creating the churches that retained ministers who preached the fire-and-brimstone sermons that moved more than one sinner to come to the Lord, and they joined in choirs similar to the ones described in Joyce Carol Thomas's *Marked by Fire,* a novel set in Ponca City.[8]

Migration did sometimes serve as an escape from the harshness of segregation, but clearly it could not, and did not, completely abolish the cultural effect of place. The settlement of blacks in black towns, like migration, also tells us something of the old Jim Crow system, but again the development has a great deal to say about black attachment to place. Oklahoma has had between twenty-five and thirty all-black towns during its history. By and large the black people who established these towns had clear objectives. They were not necessarily antiwhite, nor did they, nor could they, close themselves off from mainstream society. To be sure, many of the black people who came to the towns had suffered as victims of slavery, southern oppression, and discrimination, and some of them saw an all-black community as a protective shield from the cruelties of a Jim Crow system. Total protection from racial bigotry proved impossible, yet blacks did find an opportunity to share in the control of their lives, and participation in this very process often whetted the democratic appetites of blacks for fuller involvement in the broader society.

Economic problems, good roads, urbanization, and other forces adversely affected the all-black towns, and with the passage of time they either declined or totally disappeared. Two students who have studied some of Oklahoma black communities were correct when they wrote that "the Negro in the all-black community . . . hoped to find . . . a solution to a situation which showed little promise of imminent improvement." The all-Negro community, they said, "was in no sense a retreat from the American standards and values which [blacks] had learned to cherish, nor was it an anachronistic revival of Africanism, but rather it constituted an attempt to develop fully and to exploit completely the American culture."[9]

Disappointment did sometimes lead to a more radical rejection of Oklahoma. Some blacks very early gave up hope of finding a new and equal status in the state. Even before Oklahoma statehood, a few blacks left the territory for Africa. In March 1899 the *Daily Oklahoman* reported that 130 blacks embarked for New York, where they supposedly took a boat to Africa. Called the Cunningham Liberian Colonists, the group consisted of a mixture of both old and young who carried all their belongings with them. Interestingly, the *Daily Oklahoman,* which became a mouthpiece for Jim Crow before and after Oklahoma statehood, did not hide the reasons blacks were leaving the state: they wanted "better homes, living conditions, security, and freedom than is found in the territory."[10]

The most notable back-to-Africa movement in Oklahoma came with the Chief Alfred Sam movement during the early part of the state's history. Like similar movements at other times and at other places, it had to confront the strong ties of home—sense of place— that kept blacks attached to Oklahoma. Rooted principally in eastern Oklahoma, especially the black towns, Sam's proposed venture held out hope of a prosperous return to Africa, the ancestral home of black Americans. Uncertain of their future and disenchanted with continued discrimination, Sam's followers saw Africa as a haven from the trials and tribulations of life in a predominantly white and racist America. Confronted with the reality of an America that had not yet redeemed its promises of fair play and equality, a few black Oklahomans "fell upon Sam as they had upon no other leader in their history." Sam represented an escape which they believed was a solution to their problem in America. But they were not cowardly moving to Africa "as beaten men and women, but were [going] instead to their homeland, full of the ideas that residence in America had taught them, and equipped with the skills which had made the nation famous throughout the world."[11]

The pull of place that had defeated previous movements also defeated Alfred Sam's efforts. Unquestionably, Sam's brief heyday in Oklahoma and his limited success reflected a dissatisfaction "so deep that it amounted to hopelessness among some blacks," but it failed to come to grips with the intense determination of most blacks to fight for equality, to achieve their goals and their own identity within the land for which their fathers and grandfathers had fought and had helped to build.[12]

Less than a decade after Sam's venture into Oklahoma, another back-to-Africa movement surfaced in the United States and later appeared in Oklahoma. But Marcus Garvey's back-to-Africa movement proved as ineffective as that of Chief Sam, and it attracted even fewer supporters. Garvey made an appeal to race pride, and he admonished blacks to overcome the idea of inferiority that whites tried to thrust upon them. Although Garvey probably exaggerated the size of his following in America, he did receive considerable support, and a number of blacks, mostly in the urban East, participated in his business schemes.

Garvey found advocates in Oklahoma, although determining the full shape of the movement in the state is difficult. There existed an Okmulgee division of Garvey's Universal Negro Improvement Association, and for a time before Garvey's eventual indictment and imprisonment for mail fraud in 1925, black Garveyites in that branch met on a regular basis, usually at the Knights of Pythias Hall. Okmulgee Garveyites placed emphasis on a return to Africa, but little evidence exists to show if any blacks from Oklahoma actually ever left the state for Africa during this period. In time, bad business practices, opposition to established black organizations, and Garvey's jail sentence snuffed the life from the movement. Roscoe Dungee of the *Oklahoma City Black Dispatch,* a strong critic of back-to-Africa movements, came close to calling Garvey dishonest or incompetent, and although Dungee had doubts about the trial that ultimately sent Garvey to prison, the Oklahoma City editor stated, "It ought to make some of the rest of us a little more humble as to the big race panaceas up our sleeve."[13]

The black church had often appeared hostile toward Garvey and black nationalist movements in general. In Oklahoma the church played a leading role in fostering a sense of place, while it also cushioned blacks against some of the difficulties of segregation and discrimination. Except for the possible exception of the school within the black community, the church fostered the healthiest notion of a sense of place. Some scholars have viewed the black church before the reformist activities of Martin Luther King as too orthodox and too oriented toward the rewards of heaven, much to the exclusion of worldly considerations. Significantly, however, the faith that historically undergirded black religion encouraged blacks to believe in a human community that embraced love and justice. All life, their faith taught, was interrelated and interdependent, and blacks believed that divine providence linked all people in a common destiny. While such a faith was not peculiar to black people, they used it effectively as a powerful tool against the social evils they faced, and they persisted in the belief that one day they would share all the favorable benefits of place. God would not forever leave His children in the wilderness of discrimination. Put another way, the black church proclaimed the redemptive power of love and the idea that humans fulfilled their moral responsibility by reflecting the love of God in their social relationships. Although this belief sometimes appeared disguised among blacks in Oklahoma and the American South, it contained enormous power, and it served in the days of Jim Crow as a continuing incentive to make real a democratic culture where blacks could enjoy a quality life in broad, mainstream society.[14]

Progressive black ministers in Oklahoma forcefully articulated a religious belief grounded in humanism before the modern era of civil rights. If they seemed sure that God would set things straight, they also appeared equally certain of their sentimental attachment to a state they had helped to build. Oklahoma had imperfections— whites had made it that way with their racial policies—but black people still constituted an intricate part of the state's fabric. Even before the 1960s, black ministerial alliances in cities such as Tulsa, Chickasha, and Muskogee boldly confronted the issue of segregation and attacked the shallowness of a Christian practice in Oklahoma that permitted the denial of human justice. But they placed faith in universal laws that aligned justice on their side, that would correct the imperfections of Oklahoma society. The Reverend E. W. Perry, pastor of Oklahoma City's Tabernacle Baptist Church, served as an example of a clergyman who despite his strong dissent from prevailing racial practices effectively used religion and his spiritual faith to reinforce a sense of place.

Perry served for many years as the leader of black Oklahoma

Baptists, and he was also an important figure in the National Baptist Convention. The minister's religion pushed him toward an appreciation of cultural pluralism. Life in Oklahoma had not made Perry bitterly antiwhite, and although he disavowed the idea of "social equality" (which suggested interracial marriage to many whites), he attacked Oklahoma's white supremacy. When the black minister told a group of white clergymen that the blood of Jesus Christ flowed through the veins of both blacks and whites, he said much about his view of both culture and life in Oklahoma, and he also implied that both races partook of many of the same experiences. Perhaps some clergymen felt more at home with the ideas of the Reverend Charles Jeffrey than with those of Perry. Jeffrey found himself tied to both Oklahoma and the nation but could not exactly explain why. At one point he proclaimed that he would go back to fight for his nation and for Oklahoma if it became necessary, but the Tulsa minister found it difficult to explain his decision. He concluded almost to his regret that perhaps he was a "conditioned black." More accurately, he was an acculturated black who had been entrapped by the strong pull of place despite the hardships of that place.[15]

The work of journalists and writers of Oklahoma has said much about the attachment to place. Their own personal experiences, too, have contributed to an understanding of place. Poet Melvin Tolson came to Oklahoma in 1947 and lived in the Sooner State until his death in 1966. His work at Langston University and his involvement with activities in the state shaped an appreciation for the land despite his Missouri and Texas background. Shortly before his death, he expressed the wish that people regard him not as just another poet, but as an *Oklahoma* poet, and he requested burial near Langston University. Novelist Joyce Carol Thomas left Oklahoma at a young age, but two of her works are set in her own Ponca City, and they often reveal those ingredients that make for strong cords of attachment. One could argue that ten years in a place, the amount of time Thomas actually spent in Oklahoma, is not enough to develop a meaningful attachment. However, little doubt exists that Thomas's return visits to the state, and her continued association with her family, helped to develop notions of place that shaped her literary outlook.[16]

Perhaps no one has symbolized the powerful pull of place and the effect it has had on blacks as much as the noted writer Ralph Ellison. Born in Oklahoma City, Ellison attended Douglass High School, where he tried to fashion himself into what he later called a "renaissance man." He wrote as a mature adult that "the concept of the Renaissance Man has lurked long within the shadow of my past, and I shared it with . . . my Negro friends. How we actually acquired it I have never learned, and since there is no true sociology of the dispersion of ideas within the American democracy, I doubt if I ever shall. Perhaps we breathed it in with the air of the Negro community." Maybe, he said, he picked it up from some transplanted New Englander whose shoes he had shined on one Saturday morning. Most likely, Ellison commented, he got it up from some book or from some black teacher, some dreamer seeking to function responsibly in an environment made difficult by the demands of race and segregated education.[17]

Young Ellison, like Mildred Webb Hayes, set out to extract the best from both the black segregated world and the world beyond. He absorbed the rhythm of black life, especially its music, and he appreciated his community's zest for living even with a society that sought to restrain black individuality. What happened in Ellison's quest to obtain a sweeping view of knowledge, to become a renaissance man, was an inescapable drift toward a healthy cultural pluralism that abetted democratic reform. Ellison, an inductee into the Oklahoma Hall of Fame, has rarely missed the opportunity to speak of his Oklahoma. In his series of essays, *Shadow and Act,* the Oklahoman spent much of his introduction reliving his youthful Oklahoma days. But undoubtedly, some of his most profound comments on the place called Oklahoma appear in *Going to the Territory.* The chapter in that work with the same title as the book and the chapter entitled "Portrait of Inman Page" best represent the subtle (and sometimes not so subtle) influences a state or a region can have on black people.[18]

Ellison's essays often echo the belief that whites and blacks have a history so interwoven that only through great difficulty can people separate out certain features of their social and cultural life. Ellison put it lucidly in "Going to the Territory" when he wrote: "By ignoring such matters as the sharing of bloodlines and cultural traditions by groups of widely differing ethnic origins, and by over-looking the blending and metamorphosis of cultural forms which is so characteristic of our society, we misconceive our cultural iden-tity." In Ellison's judgment, the problem prevailed because "we dread to acknowledge the complex, pluralistic nature of our society, and as a result we find ourselves stumbling upon our true . . . iden-tity under circumstances in which we least expect to do so."[19]

Ellison's careful language goes to the very heart of the argument in this article. Throughout Oklahoma history, there have been within the black community persons who prided the concept of a healthy pluralism, and they consistently shied away from a narrow racial provincialism. Their focus abetted a strong sense of place, aided attachment. Like Ellison, black Oklahoma leaders preached that American cultural life was a composite of many ingredients and that it has developed through contact and communication across race, class, and religion. In 1986, Ellison wrote persuasively that on the level of culture no one group has managed to create the defini-tive American style, and surely his Oklahoma experiences provided some evidence for his contention.[20]

There are those, of course, who contend that Oklahoma's history has mitigated against a strong sense of place. Arrell Morgan Gib-son, the distinguished Oklahoma historian, argued this point shortly before his death in 1987. In an article entitled "Oklahoma, Land of the Drifter: Deterrents to Sense of Place," Gibson contended that exploitative economic frontiers such as mining and cattle "thwarted root establishment." That exploitation, he said, continued after the beginning of the twentieth century as the Great Depression, high farm tenancy, the presence of military operations, and increasing urbanization operated to shatter the notion of place. Some parts of Gibson's analysis possess great strength, but there is evidence that he had begun to rethink parts of his thesis and that he might have revised it to some degree had he lived to complete a longer projected study.[21]

Historians can no longer doubt the visible effects of place among black Oklahomans. Roscoe Dungee's life in Oklahoma makes the strongest case for attachment of blacks to the state. And it is appro-priate to end this study by again turning to this distinguished black journalist and fighter for equality. Dungee came to Oklahoma Territory in 1892 with his family, and he later followed in the footsteps of his father by publishing a paper. In 1915, Roscoe Dungee purchased a printing press in Oklahoma City and founded the *Oklahoma City Black Dispatch,* which for half a century was the most powerful black journal in the state. Dungee laid claim to the conscience of white Oklahomans. He disturbed their notions of the reality of a moral society built on justice, and his democratic axioms consistently confronted them with the truth of racial injustice in a supposedly free land. Understanding Dungee proved difficult for most whites, for he showed signs of real American patriotism, cared little for black nationalism, and bitterly criticized Marxist doctrine and communism.[22]

Oklahoma also laid claim to much of Dungee's allegiance. For over seventy years it seared its history into practically every sinew of his body and soul. It sought to engulf him, and he breathed the intoxicating air of its environment, yet he was discriminating enough to reject those societal forces that sought to co-opt his vision of justice. The noted black editor and "Little Caesar of Civil Rights" cultivated a relationship with his surroundings that enabled him to enjoy *his* state and to *criticize* it for over a half century. Roughly fifty years before Mildred Webb Hayes sat quietly in Tacoma and talked of Oklahoma, and fifty years after the famous Run of 1889, Roscoe Dungee wrote lucidly, although somewhat indirectly, about place—the Oklahoma place. Dungee had experienced much in Soonerland since his arrival as a young boy, and for that reason his readers may have forgiven him for the nostalgia that showed through in his April 22, 1939, editorial in the *Oklahoma City Black Dispatch.*

Dungee's long historical commentary told the story of an early Oklahoma, with its hardships and joys, its challenges, and its people's responses. Assuming the role of historian, he recalled the first wild night of the new pioneers who had come to realize their hopes and dreams in the "Land of the Fair Gods." Other memories also came to the editor's facile mind in 1939. He could remember those days when he went with friends to church suppers in dugouts and ate parched corn. And a smile must have come to his face, and a fast heartbeat to his chest, when he recalled those romantic days of early spring when he and his young male friends walked down the old trails with their girls, optimistically anticipating a future bright with hope. Dungee wrote that "friendships were formed then that have lasted across the fifty years that have fled. Those friendships, many of them, were interracial, for the finest sort of feeling existed between the white and black races during that period."

The black Oklahoman ended his editorial with lines that give away a sentiment that never left this tenacious fighter for civil rights:

Fifty years in the hills and valleys that stretch [across Oklahoma]; fifty years of blood[,] sweat[,] and tears. All our tender recollections of a half century are wrapped up in the land where mother and father are buried and where we first studied readin'[,] 'ritin[,] and 'rithmetic. As we look back down the Sooner Trail toward the black jacks, brush arbors, stubbed toes and the creek where we used to swim, as we think of the Sunday afternoons, when we would come home to delicious meals of clabber, green onions and navy beans, and the ice cold watermelon we would pull out of the well: those were the golden days, imperishable in memory. This is home; we love Oklahoma![23]

NOTES

1. Mildred Webb Hayes, personal interview, Tacoma, Wash. June 29, 1989.

2. Ibid. Ralph Ellison lauds Zelia Breaux in *Going to the Territory* (New York: Random House, 1986), 136–37. For other comments on this fine musician, see Zella J. Black Patterson, *Langston University: A History* (Norman: University of Oklahoma Press, 1979), 238–39, and Kaye M. Teall, *Black History in Oklahoma: A Resource Book* (Oklahoma City: Oklahoma City Public Schools, 1971), 201.

3. Hayes interview.

4. E. B. Du Bois, *The Souls of Black Folk; Essays and Sketches* (Chicago: A. G. McClurg, 1903; repr., Millwood, N.Y.: Kraus Thompson, 1973), 3.

5. The best article on the development of Jim Crow in the new state of Oklahoma is Philip Mellinger, "Discrimination and Statehood in Oklahoma," *Chronicles of Oklahoma* 49 (Autumn 1971): 340–77. The Murray quote is from Jimmie Lewis Franklin, *Journey Toward Hope: A History of Blacks in Oklahoma* (Norman: University of Oklahoma Press, 1982), 40. See also Danney Goble, *Progressive Oklahoma: The Making of a New Kind of State* (Norman: University of Oklahoma Press, 1980), 143–44, 219.

6. Although flawed in places, a creditable study of the grandfather clause is Gerald Hickman's "Disfranchisement in Oklahoma: The Grandfather Clause of

1910–1916'' (thesis, University of Tulsa, 1967). See also Teall, *Black History in Oklahoma*, 217–19, and Franklin's chapter, ''Ballot Security and Party Allegiance'' in his *Journey Toward Hope*, 108–27.

7. Unfortunately, data can not show accurately if persons who left an Oklahoma town where violence appeared actually went to another state or only moved to a nearby location. Internal migration has been a difficult task for census takers to measure.

8. The last two decades witnessed a number of studies on blacks and their life in northern cities. Among the best of the most recent books is James R. Grossman, *Land of Hope: Chicago, Black Southerners, and the Great Migration* (Chicago: University of Chicago Press, 1989), especially 66–160. Joyce Carol Thomas has told an engaging story of a young girl, her family, and the black Ponca City community in *Marked by Fire* (New York: Avon Books, 1982).

9. Norman Crockett has included three of Oklahoma's all-black communities—Boley, Clearview, and Langston—in his *The Black Towns* (Lawrence: University Press of Kansas, 1979). See also ''The Black Oklahoma Towns,'' in Arthur L. Tolson, *The Black Oklahomans: A History, 1541–1972* (New Orleans: Edwards Printing Company, 1974), 90–105. The quotation in the paragraph is from William E. Bittle and Gilbert Geis, *The Longest Way Home: Chief Alfred C. Sam's Back-to-Africa Movement* (Detroit: Wayne State University Press, 1964), 210.

10. *Daily Oklahoman*, Mar. 11, 1899.

11. Bittle and Geis, *Longest Way Home*, 211.

12. Ibid. See also Teall, *Black History in Oklahoma*, 286–88, and Franklin, *Journey Toward Hope*, 56–58, for comment on the Chief Sam movement.

13. Tony Martin has written two books on Marcus Garvey that deserve mention here: *Marcus Garvey, Hero: A First Biography* (Dover, Mass.: Majority Press, 1983), and *Race First: The Ideological and Organizational Struggles of Marcus Garvey and the Universal Negro Improvement Association* (Westport: Greenwood Press, 1976). But see also E. David Cronon, *Black Moses: The Story of Marcus Garvey and the Negro Improvement Association* (Madison: University of Wisconsin Press, 1955); and Amy Jacques-Garvey, ed., *Philosophy and Opinions of Marcus Garvey* (New York: Antheneum, 1969). Sources for the Okmulgee chapter of the Garvey organization and Garveyism in Oklahoma are Robert A. Hill, ed., *The Marcus Garvey and Universal Negro Improvement Association Papers,* (Berkeley: University of California Press, 1983), 3: 466–67, and Martin, *Race First*, 121–366. See the *Oklahoma City Black Dispatch*, July 19, 1923, for Dungee's editorial on Garvey.

14. The view of the church as a conservative force within the black community before the era of civil rights is reflected in E. Franklin Frazier, *The Negro Church in America* (New York: Shocken Books, 1963). Black liberationist theologians of the post-1960s also criticized the black church for its relatively passive posture during the King era of nonviolent resistance. For an illustrative example, see James Cone, *For My People: Black Theology and the Black Church* (Maryknoll, N.Y.: Orbis Books, 1984). The conclusions in the above paragraph are drawn from exten-

sive conversations with religious scholar Lewis Baldwin, who shares an interest in culture and place.

15. A brief treatment of the black ministry and the church in Oklahoma is Franklin, *Journey Toward Hope*, 160–66; see 197–98 for Jeffrey's reaction.

16. On poet Arthur Tolson, see Joy Flasch, *Melvin B. Tolson* (New York: Twayne, 1972), 43 especially. A good biographical sketch of Joyce Carol Thomas is in Trudier Harris and Thadious M. Davis, eds., *Dictionary of Literary Biography*, vol. 33, *Afro-American Writers, 1940–1955* (Detroit: Gale, 1988), 245–50.

17. For an excellent biography of works on the noted black novelist and a quick look at Ellison's career, see *Dictionary of Literary Biography* 76: 37–56, and Franklin, *Journey Toward Hope*, 178–80.

18. Ralph Ellison, *Shadow and Act* (New York: Random House, 1964), xii–xxiii; and Ralph Ellison, *Going to the Territory* (New York: Random House, 1986), 120–44; for the chapter by that same title; on Inman Page, see 113–19.

19. Ellison, *Going to the Territory*, 125.

20. Ibid., 141–43.

21. Arrell Morgan Gibson, "Oklahoma, Land of the Drifter: Deterrents to Sense of Place," *Chronicles of Oklahoma* 64 (Summer 1986): 5–13. For a related article that rejects the notion of black attachment to one particular region of the South, see William Turner, "A Sense of Place among Black Appalachians: A Review of the Question among Blacks in Harlan County," in *Sense of Place in Appalachia*, ed. A. Mont Whitson (Morehead, Ky.: Morehead State University, 1988), 183–89.

22. Roscoe Dungee still awaits his biographer, although he has received considerable notice in notable secondary works. See Teall, *Black History in Oklahoma*, 196–99, 273–75; Gene Aldrich, *Black Heritage in Oklahoma* (Edmond, Oklahoma: Thompson Book and Supply Company, 1973), 82–83; Jimmie Lewis Franklin, *The Blacks in Oklahoma* (Norman: University of Oklahoma Press, 1980), 35–37; and Franklin, *Journey Toward Hope*, 21, 29, 54–57, 102, 103, 115, 118–19, 122, 126–27, 163, 198–99.

23. *Oklahoma City Black Dispatch*, April 22, 1939, and ibid., April 29, 1939, for an article that also reveals Dungee's sentiment toward place. The black editor graphically captures the excitement of the early years of statehood in "When Oklahoma Was Young," ibid., April 26, 1941.

15

THE SOUTHERN INFLUENCE ON OKLAHOMA

Danney Goble

Is Oklahoma part of the West? The Mid-West? The Southwest? The South? Where does it belong? Most state historians give the overwhelming impression that it is part of the West, and the cowboys-and-Indians image is one of the dominant ones, it seems, when folks think of Oklahoma.

Just as Frederick Jackson Turner insisted that the European background did not explain everything about American civilization, and that the frontier perspective provided a much needed corrective, so Danney Goble, in the essay which follows, insists that the frontier perspective does not explain everything about Oklahoma's history, and a southern perspective helps us understand some parts that do not fit the western pattern.

Goble has established himself as a major historian of the State of Oklahoma. Born in the state, he left to get his Ph.D. (at the University of Missouri), but returned, fortunately, to teach at Tulsa Junior College and to make important contributions to the state's history in Progressive Oklahoma: The Making of a New Kind of State, Oklahoma Politics: A History *(with James R. Scales), and* Little Giant: The Life and Times of Speaker Carl Albert *(with Carl Albert), all three published by the University of Oklahoma Press in 1980, 1982, and 1990, respectively. Goble is currently historian in the Carl Albert Congressional Research and Studies Center at the University of Oklahoma.*

There used to be a story told in graduate schools of history about a fellow who invented a tale involving Alexander the Great and published it in a highbrow magazine. According to him, Alexander had put his alchemists to work to invent a method of telling time. The alchemists had come up with a series of chemical solutions. A piece of cloth dipped in the solutions would change color according to the differing angles of the sun's rays as it passed overhead. Delighted, Alexander had ordered his soldiers to wear the strips of treated cloth tied to their wrists. Each strip, the author concluded in a perfectly deadpan tone, was known as "Alexander's Rag Time Band."

But the real point of the story was what lay ahead. It seems that over the next couple of decades, the original author discovered that a series of textbooks began to include a discussion of Alexander's interest in alchemy, some mentioning that it had led to the invention of a primitive wristwatch. Apparently, a scholar singularly lacking in humor had read the original story, missed the pun (and the point), and put it (*sans* punchline) in his textbook. Other writers had borrowed his story and had repeated it in their own. What had begun as a joke thereupon became a "fact" of history.

Another story is more familiar. It is the last scene in *The Dead Poets' Society*—the scene in which the students salute their departing teacher. As Robin Williams's character leaves his classroom for the last time, his students begin, one by one, standing on their desks. To the consternation of the school's administrators, they thereby demonstrate that their teacher has taught them the most valuable lessons of all: you have to look at things in different ways, and what you see depends on how you look at it.

Both of those stories seem appropriate to this collection of essays. Each rejects merely repeating what the last textbook said was so. Each in its own way is an alternative view precisely because each looks at familiar things in unfamiliar ways. This essay does that deliberately and directly.

I

Transcending nearly every "fact" of Oklahoma's history is the overall context in which it is cast. Usually that is a regional context. Since the time of Frederick Jackson Turner, historians have approached the histories of separate states within a regional—or sectional—framework. In many ways the father of professional, "scientific" history in this country, Turner taught that states took on their importance to the nation's history only as they worked within broad currents of sectional interests and affairs. Of course, to Turner one section in particular had powerful national significance. The American West, Turner declared, was the most American of all sections. In his celebrated thesis "The Significance of the Frontier in American History" and elsewhere, Turner claimed a special role for those states that could establish a western identity. The currents that shaped their histories had made America's history as well.[1]

As much as anything, it may have been the professional prestige of Turner and his western emphasis that accounted for the conventional way that historians came to view Oklahoma's history. Personality probably entered into the equation, too. Edward Everett Dale, a onetime cowpuncher from Oklahoma's short-grass country, left home for Harvard not long after statehood to take a Ph.D. in American history. There he studied at the master's feet before returning to teach history at the University of Oklahoma. The history that he taught there for decades was a version of Turner's history, and it made Oklahoma's history a version of western history.[2] The students that he taught themselves took that version into the state's classrooms. Sometimes they repeated it in the textbooks that they produced.

However presented, the story turned out pretty much the same. As a western state, Oklahoma was shaped by the frontier experience. Of course it had its peculiarities—"anomalies," Arrell Morgan Gibson called them—but its basic contours were familiar to every western state and familiar, too, to the readers of Frederick Jackson Turner.[3] The story moved in Turner's famous stages. It began with European adventurers who opened the frontier (and Oklahoma's history) upon primitive Indians. The adventurers were followed by traders and trappers. These, in turn, were followed by the earliest settlers. There was a lot of anomaly here, for these were Indians—"civilized" Indians—who came to the frontier through no desires of their own. Nonetheless, because they were civilized, they pretty much did what all settlers did on the frontier. They built institutions, formed governments, and got messed up by the Civil War. Thereafter, the story returned to its familiar paths. Railroads opened up the land, miners and cattlemen exploited it, and hardy farmers—*white* farmers, this time—finally settled it. The frontier thereupon ended, and if Oklahoma's history did not quite end, at least it got awfully boring. All those governors! Give us Coronado, Chouteau, and Geronimo instead.

The western cast of Oklahoma's history had much going for it. It put Oklahoma's past squarely in the middle of one of the leading schools of academic history, thereby giving it respect. It also imposed a logic upon that past, thereby giving it a narrative structure and an interesting one at that. Besides, it pretty much became the only way that the state's history was ever taught or written.

All of these things may account for the prevailing way to understand Oklahoma. They—not just geography—have led us to see Oklahoma as a western state, its history just another reflection of western history.

Maybe it is time to look at it differently. We do not even have to stand on our desks to do so. Just look at a map. Notice that the state that is west of the Mississippi is also south of something else: the Mason-Dixon Line. Much of the state is further south than Memphis, Tennessee; Dahlonega, Georgia; and Greensboro, North Carolina. Nearly all of Oklahoma is to the south of the entire state of Virginia, and its capital is well south of Richmond, the capital of the Confederacy.

What the map suggests, history must recognize. If Oklahoma is in the western part of the United States, it is also in the southern part. But history's point transcends geography's. History's point is that if a western perspective allows us to see much of Oklahoma's history, a southern perspective would, too. It is just that a southern perspective would allow us to see some things a bit differently. Sometimes it would put us in a place to see things that we might otherwise never see at all.

This essay does not even attempt to do that for all the state's history. Instead, it intends to do it in only two ways, each merely suggestive of what a full-blown southern perspective on Oklahoma might produce. A western perspective shows us much about Sooner explorers, cowboys, and pioneers. A southern perspective can reveal much about race and culture, particularly as they both got mixed together in a stew of southern political gumbo.

II

Not every contemporary southern historian would ascribe fully to U. B. Phillips's dictum that the "central theme" of southern history is the conviction that the South "is and would remain a white man's country."[4] Still, southern historians are especially likely to be unusually sensitive to the role of race—particularly black-white relations—in a state's history. Around the continuing crucible of race, not a vanishing frontier, they build interpretations that attach meaning to whole series of events.

Oklahoma is one place where that can be done. Lost in much of the hoopla surrounding the recent centennial of the original Oklahoma land run was the fact that a good number of the celebrated '89ers were black. That was true, too, of the subsequent openings that created Oklahoma Territory, roughly the entire western half of the present state. Similarly, it generally passes with little notice that the Five Civilized Tribes of the Indian Territory (the eastern half of modern Oklahoma) originally were designated as "civilized" partly because they joined their southern white neighbors in holding black slaves. After slavery's demise, blacks—like whites—began moving onto the Indians' domains until they eventually overran them, forced their dissolution, and established the basis for statehood combined with Oklahoma Territory. When statehood came, 112,000 blacks (about 8 percent of the total population) became citizens of the new state.[5]

What is important is that many of them were in Oklahoma precisely because they wanted to be citizens of a new state—even of a new kind of state. The total black population had jumped by a factor of six in only seventeen years. Those were seventeen years of rapid and steady decline for black Americans, particularly black *southern* Americans. They opened in 1890 with Mississippi's disfranchisement of nearly all of its black population. Other southern states swiftly copied Mississippi's example. By 1907, Oklahoma offered southern blacks what had become a rare chance—the chance to cast a ballot.

It offered more. The South had followed disfranchisement with systematic legal separation of the races. From cradle (in separate hospitals) to grave (in separate cemeteries) and everywhere else in between, elaborate statutes prevented southern blacks and whites from ever meeting as social equals. "Jim Crow" was the system's name, and Oklahoma offered a chance to escape its reach.[6]

For all of these reasons, blacks had poured into both territories. There, they had found much of what they had sought. If life was hard on the South's newest (and final) frontier, it was no more so for black pioneers than for white. Certainly it was more promising than the life they had fled—a life without economic opportunity, without social promise, without political power. In the West, black farmers claimed homestead land, plowed it, and reaped the profits. In the East, freedmen and their mixed-blood descendants of Indian masters shared in the allotment process. They, too, cleared, plowed, planted, and reaped. Blacks did all of those things, and they did them independently of white planters.

In the exploding towns and cities, blacks entered every profession and occupation. In many cases, they controlled entire towns, as several all-black communities sprang up in both territories.

Politically, they were a force demanding white recognition. Although the Indian Territory had no formal territorial government, it did have municipal governments, and in them blacks both voted and held office. In Oklahoma Territory, black hands reached for the lever of political power. The Republican party narrowly but steadily dominated territorial politics. Because roughly one Republican voter in six was a black voter, blacks held the balance of power in territorial affairs. They knew it, and white Republicans did, too.[7]

The sum of all those things was important to Oklahoma's history. It accounted for that sizeable black migration and likely for its special pride and independence. It was no less important to the history of the South. The collapse of Reconstruction in the 1870s had left its promises of black power and hope bare bones. The disfranchisement and segregation campaigns of the 1890s had turned them into dust. After the first, blacks had fled by the thousands into Kansas.[8] After the second, they had fled by the tens of thousands into Oklahoma. In both cases, blacks had left the South, moving not northward but westward. That westward migration continued through the first years of this century as even more southern blacks came to the maturing territories. As those territories merged into a state, however, the story would change. The change would have decided effect upon Oklahoma, the South, and the entire nation.

The approach of statehood for Oklahoma gave its people promise of more than a new star in the flag. Free of federal oversight, they could replace Washington's domination with their own constitution, its "carpetbag" appointees with their own elected officers, its regulation with their own statutes, and corporate power with industrial democracy. The door of opportunity seemed to be thrown open. Through it clamored a small army of reformers, all determined to make the state over in their own image.[9] Among them were those, largely of southern ancestry, who wanted to make it in the image of the South.

As southerners, most of these were Democrats. In the bitterly fought 1906 campaign for seats in the constitutional convention, they pledged their party to the southern position on race with platforms demanding segregated schools, transportation, and accommodations. Precisely because that campaign was so bitterly contested, the Republican opposition met those demands with no opposition at all. Calculating that a strong endorsement of continuing black rights would cost them white voters and that black voters had nowhere else to go but to the party of Lincoln, Republicans either ignored those demands or weakly endorsed them.[10]

The consequence was decisive for Oklahoma. Despite nearly two decades of Republican supremacy in both territories, the Democrats elected 99 of the 112 delegates to the constitutional assembly. The explanation was not at all concealed. Republican voters—particularly black Republican voters—deserted the party that had deserted them. With nowhere to go, they had not gone to the polls. The drop-off in Republican turnout (a loss of twelve thousand voters compared to 1904 in Oklahoma Territory alone) decided the election.[11] It meant that Democrats, by-and-large southern Democrats, would write Oklahoma's constitution.

They did, and they made the most of their opportunity. Article 13, section 2, mandated the legislature to provide "separate schools for white and colored children." For a population of considerable Indian blood, it further defined "colored children" as those of "African descent" and "white children" as "all other children."

Only after President Theodore Roosevelt vowed to withhold approving any document similarly requiring segregated transportation facilities did the convention drop that demand. Without the president's approval, the constitution could not be submitted to a vote for ratification. With it—and with the success of that vote—Oklahomans could do anything they wanted in statutes and subsequent amendments.

The president approved the document and the vote came in September 1907. United behind a strong slate standing four-square on their proposed constitution, the Democrats described their only opponents as "Carpetbaggers, Corporations, and Coons." Actually, the Republican opposition was rent with division. In no small part, that division turned upon race. Only a few Republicans attacked their rivals' embrace of Jim Crow. More tried to stretch their own ambitious arms about it. Most tried to ignore the whole thing.

But it could not be ignored—not by black voters. All they could ignore was the party ignoring them, and again they did. As had happened the year before, black voters stayed home on election day. The consequence was the same. Democrats swept every statewide office on the ballot, took strong majorities in both legislative chambers, and won overwhelming approval for their constitution.[12]

It did not take them long to get down to business. No sooner had the legislature assembled than it whooped through Senate Bill Number One. Swiftly signed by the governor, the state's first statute mandated racially separate coaches, waiting rooms, and compartments in all public transportation. It was the classic and humiliating symbol of southern segregation.

The black response was swift and predictable. Blacks had not come to Oklahoma for this, and they would not take it. At Taft, an all-black community on the Midland Valley line, blacks burned the newly segregated station to the ground. Elsewhere they besieged segregated trains, including one carrying the new lieutenant governor.

Ultimately, however, blacks recognized that their problem was political. White Democrats had written the constitution, and white Democrats had passed the law. If black stay-at-homes had helped make that possible, they would stay at home no longer. In 1908, Oklahomans went to the polls again, for the third time in three years. This time, blacks went, too. When they left, Democratic heads rolled. The party barely got a plurality for its presidential candidate and not even that for three of its five congressional nominees and dozens of its legislators. The black vote was real, and the Republican resurgence was, too.[13]

The Democrats' counterattack was no less real. If black votes cost them the election, they would disfranchise much of that electorate by means of a literacy test, one that exempted nearly all nonblack voters. These would be exempt because the test would not apply to any voter lineally descended from any person eligible to vote on January 1, 1866. The date was convenient but not accidental. That was before Reconstruction had established mass black suffrage. Thereby known as the "Grandfather Clause," the move would require the voters' approval.

Taking no chances, Democratic officialdom ordered that it be given voters in a singular fashion. Printed at the ballot's bottom were the words "For the Amendment." Crossing through those words rendered a negative vote. Submitting an unmarked ballot counted as an affirmative vote, however that ballot found its way into the ballot box. In 1910 the deed was done. Oklahomans amended their constitution to decimate the black electorate. As many as twenty thousand of the votes, however, entered ballot boxes under conditions so suspicious as to amount to ballot box stuffing.[14]

If so, it would not have shocked the southern sensibilities. Southern states had done the same thing for the same reason. Oklahoma merely had taken it into an art form. Now complete, segregation plus disfranchisement gave Oklahoma the "honor" of completing the South's commitment to legalized racism.

It was a southern commitment, made in southern style. For Oklahoma, it would have decisive results. With many of its potential black voters disfranchised, the state's Republican party withered toward nothing. Any subsequent opportunity that the party had for power depended upon just that—*opportunity*. The party thereupon became and long remained a party of negativism and opportunism. They were *against* the Democrats rather than *for* anything. Any chance for success depended not upon what Republicans did for themselves but upon what the Democrats did to themselves.

Through that process the GOP long lost its chance for effective service, and Oklahoma entered the ranks of the one-party "Solid South."

For the nation, the effect would be more subtle but more important. Up until Oklahoma's segregation and disfranchisement campaigns, real black progress had lain along the lines of physical black movement. Until that time, that movement always had been westward. No longer would it be. After 1910, blacks continued to leave the South, searching for rights and power. But they would not go westward. Oklahoma had closed that door. Future black migration would turn northward, toward Detroit, Chicago, Philadelphia, New York, and Boston. After 1910, that migration would change America.

Finally, Oklahoma's embrace of the South's style of race relations would have great—if delayed—effect upon the South itself. Even if most of the nation disagreed (whether from malice or blindness), black leaders asserted that segregation and disfranchisement were not only wrong but also unconstitutional. The Fourteenth Amendment explicitly guaranteed to all persons "equal protection of the laws." The Fifteenth directly forbade states' denial of voting privileges on the basis of "race, color, or previous condition of servitude." Upon those two rocklike constitutional principles the ship of discrimination eventually would break apart.

That would happen, though, only when the nation's courts moved to apply those constitutional principles to southern affairs. That, in turn, awaited impassioned litigators and courageous clients. Men like Charles Houston, James Nabrit, and Thurgood Marshall provided the first. Often it was Oklahoma that provided the second.

It began as early as 1915, and it involved the state's new Grandfather Clause. A group of Creek County blacks who had been denied the right to vote under that provision initiated the legal action that went before the U.S. Supreme Court as *Guinn* v. *United States.* Unable to ignore the transparency of the device, the Court unanimously overturned the Oklahoma amendment. It was the first time that the Fifteenth Amendment had been enforced to strike down any state's discriminatory election machinery, and it was a precedent for future action to give life to its words.[15]

Most of that action lay well in the future. In fact, twenty-four years passed before the Court invalidated another suffrage law, and again it was Oklahoma's. An unrepentant state legislature had met the *Guinn* decision with a statute that required all those ineligible to vote in 1914 (that is, blacks) to register and gave them exactly two weeks to do so or forever lose the right to vote. Not always tightly enforced, the law nonetheless merely replaced one form of discrimination with another. In *Lane* v. *Wilson,* the Supreme Court struck it down as well, Justice Felix Frankfurter declaring that the Constitution "nullifies sophisticated as well as simple-minded modes of discrimination."[16]

That line almost certainly drew a smile from James Nabrit. A black attorney working alongside Houston and Marshall for the National Association for the Advancement of Colored People (NAACP), Nabrit argued that particular Oklahoma case as part of what had become a coordinated attack upon southern discrimination in general. The object was nothing less than the Court-ordered execution of Jim Crow. The noose was to be the Fourteenth Amendment's "equal protection" clause. The trapdoor was to be public education. Kill Jim Crow there—force the Court to declare that segregated education was unconstitutional because it was unequal—and legally enforced segregation would die everywhere.[17]

If a piece of that strategy was visible in *Guinn* and *Lane,* it emerged full-fleshed in two subsequent cases, both arising in Oklahoma. The state constitution's mandate of segregated schooling had been buttressed by an impressive series of statutes designed to keep blacks in their place: out of white schools. These included colleges and universities. State funds paid for black undergraduate education only at Langston. Blacks seeking professional and graduate degrees not offered there were compelled to go to state universities out of Oklahoma. The state pretended to meet its responsibilities by paying their out-of-state tuition fees. Several black Oklahomans refused to let the state off so easily.

One was Ada Lois Sipuel. Raised in Chickasha and a graduate of Langston, she applied for admission to the University of Oklahoma's College of Law, the only publicly supported law school in the state. As Oklahoma's law required, the university denied her admission and did so solely on the grounds of her race. With Thurgood Marshall at her side, she began a struggle that wound through state and federal courts before twice going to the Supreme Court in 1948. The Court chipped away a large brick in segregation's wall by voiding the out-of-state tuition scheme. It ordered Oklahoma to provide Sipuel (and any other blacks) a legal education in the state.[18] The wall, nonetheless, remained, for Oklahoma hastily roped off a section of the state law library and designated it the Langston University College of Law. Its one student refused to attend.

Meanwhile a group of eight black Oklahomans had applied to OU's graduate school. All were denied admittance. A weary Thurgood Marshall returned to Oklahoma and took one of those eight, George W. McLaurin, with him before a three-judge federal court panel.[19] The judges repeated the decision of the *Sipuel* case and ordered Oklahoma to "provide the plaintiff the education that he seeks."

The state's response exceeded even the ingenuity of the *Sipuel* affair. Rather than create an overnight graduate school in some basement, Oklahoma did admit McLaurin to its university at Norman. But under the authority of a new statute, it proceeded to segregate the new student within the university. Scheduling each of his classes in the same room, the school seated McLaurin in a small alcove apart from the white students. It similarly assigned him a separate table in both the library and cafeteria, although it allowed him to use the latter only when whites were not scheduled to eat.

Angry but exhilarated, Marshall returned to Oklahoma and from there returned to the Supreme Court. Oklahoma unwittingly had given him the exact issue that he wanted. However practiced, segregation was always justified legally by the doctrine of "separate but equal"—that is, that the Fourteenth Amendment's requirement of "equal" protection did not preclude "separate" facilities.[20] To Marshall, McLaurin's ordeal struck right at the heart of the constitutional issue. Not even he would deny that Oklahoma afforded McLaurin "equal" education in every material respect. After all, he heard the same lectures, read the same books, and ate the same food as every white student in his classes. Was the fact of his separation alone a denial of his rights? In other words, could segregated education by definition ever be equal education?[21]

In 1950 a unanimous U.S. Supreme Court came right up next to the answer. Declaring that state-imposed barriers unconstitutionally handicapped McLaurin's education, the court ordered them dropped.[22] For the moment the Court would go no further. Four years later in *Brown* v. *Board of Education* it had no choice. A small army of black lawyers commanded by Thurgood Marshall and armed with the *Sipuel* and *McLaurin* precedents won the judicial victory that had been a long time coming. "Separate but equal" had no place in the American Constitution.[23] Jim Crow was hanging in a constitutional breeze.

Subsequent decisions would expand upon the *Brown* decision as well as the *Guinn* and *Lane* precedents. With the help of new federal laws—most notably the Civil Rights Act of 1964 and the Voting Rights Act of 1965—a revolution in black civil rights and political power began to remake the South. Because southern white resistance would be strong, that revolution would take a while. When it was complete, the South would look something like what black pioneers had expected when they sought opportunity, position, and power in a new kind of state. In Oklahoma, they eventually had made it a new kind of South.

III

In the matter of race, Oklahoma's history fits a southern pattern. Shaped by southern will, it had changed southern reality. In politics, too, Oklahoma bears a distinctly southern identity, and it does in several ways intimately related to political culture.

The most obvious is the persistent voting habits that have shaped Sooner politics. Those habits go back to the very beginning, back to Oklahoma's original settlement. The northern and western portions of the future state were especially likely to draw their first settlers from the American Midwest, particularly Kansas but also Nebraska, Iowa, and Illinois. To the flat lands so much like their original homes they brought their familiar crop, wheat. Upon that land's surface they placed Church of Christ and Methodist churches. When they voted, they voted for the party of Lincoln and the Union, the Republican party.

The southern and eastern portions tended to draw population from different sources, the surrounding states of Texas and Arkansas plus Louisiana, Mississippi, and the rest of the Old Confederacy. To the rolling hills and wooded valleys that were so much like their first homes they brought their familiar crop, cotton. When they worshiped it was likely to be in Baptist churches. When they voted, it was usually for the party of Jackson and the Confederacy, the Democratic party.[24]

Old habits die hard, and in Oklahoma these habits have died not at all. A century or so later, the state's political geography mirrors almost exactly the original patterns of settlement. Start at Oklahoma's extreme northeast corner and trace a diagonal straight to its middle. From there proceed due west to the border with the Texas Panhandle. Lacking a map, just use the highways. Follow the Will Rogers and Turner turnpikes to Oklahoma City and head due west on Interstate 40. The land lying north and west of those lines (or highways) remains to this day Republican country. That lying south and east is still described as Little Dixie, the beating heart of Oklahoma's Democratic party. Along those lines are counties in which the original settlement tended to be roughly balanced between midwesterners and southerners, Republicans and Democrats. Those became the "swing counties," sometimes going Republican, sometimes Democratic. As such, they usually determined who won in statewide races.[25]

The resulting political map is remarkably durable. Consider two gubernatorial elections, separated by over seventy years. In the state's very first election, the Democrats nominated Charles N. Haskell of Muskogee, then the metropolis of eastern Oklahoma. The Republican nominee was Frank Frantz, a midwesterner living in Guthrie as territorial governor. In 1978, the Democratic candidate was George Nigh of McAlester, the most populous city in southeastern Oklahoma. The Republicans ran Ron Shotts of Weatherford, a western town lying—like Guthrie—near our imaginary line. In both cases, the Democrats (Haskell and Nigh) won fairly close elections. What made them both close and similar was that seventy of the state's original seventy-five counties voted exactly the same way in 1978 as they had in 1907.[26] The only five to vary their allegiance did so narrowly, and all lay upon the geographic dividing lines of political partisanship.

Oklahoma's continuing sectional basis in politics really has no western counterpart. It is, however, a phenomenon familiar in many southern states. Eastern North Carolina is historically Democratic, western North Carolina traditionally Republican. The same division is found in Virginia. Tennessee, Louisiana, Arkansas, and Alabama similarly have longstanding pockets of Republican or independent strength amid overall Democratic supremacy. In every case, the ultimate basis of those continuing divisions is the same. Those areas most loyal to the Union during the Civil War continue to display that loyalty generations later at the polls. Those caught up with the Confederacy still prefer Democrats, sometimes of the "yellow-dog" variety.[27] Though transplanted in Oklahoma, those Southernlike divisions have taken deep root and bear biennial blossoms.

The Southernlike cast of Oklahoma's voters has its parallels in the state's political leadership. Observers have long noted that southern politicians tend to be unlike western politicians or, for that matter, those of any other section. The difference goes beyond foolish stereotypes about windbag senators wearing string ties and cursing modernity. The real difference is that politics in the southern style tends to be a profession, not a calling. It is no place for amateurs and not much of one for causes. As professionals, its practitioners early learn and master the rules of the game, both the formal and the inside varieties. They rise up definite career ladders until they fill the nooks and crannies of power and influence. Once there, they tend to stay there, for politics is their profession and their life.

One reflection of that difference is in the U.S. Congress. Presidents come and presidents go. National parties regularly exchange the White House. But over this entire century both the House and the Senate have been dominated by southerners. In men like Richard Russell and Carl Vinson, both of Georgia, and Sam Rayburn and Lyndon Johnson, both of Texas, the Congress has found its leaders and its masters.

If that testifies to the natural superiority of southern politicians, Oklahoma's experience adds at least a footnote. The major figures who have dominated the state legislature usually have been southern and eastern Oklahomans, born and bred in professional politics, southern style. Start with the first speaker of the state house of representatives, Bill Murray of Tishomingo, go through Speaker Red Phillips of Okemah and Senate President Pro Tem Raymond Gary of Madill. Add the only two men to lead both the state house and senate (Jim Nance of Purcell and Tom Anglin of Holdenville), and you come up to McAlester's Gene Stipe, uncrowned but reigning king of the Oklahoma legislature.

Look, too, at Oklahoma's governorship, remembering our line dividing the state's voters. A few of Oklahoma's governors have come from the counties straddling that line. This is especially true most recently, when the large metropolitan vote of Oklahoma and Tulsa counties give great advantage to their sons. Nonetheless, the striking long-term fact is that thirteen of Oklahoma's governors have come from south or east of our line. In contrast, only three have come from the north or west of it. Of those three, one (Henry Bellmon) was a Republican, one (Henry Johnson) was impeached, and one (E. W. Marland) never won another election in his life.

The southern flavor of Oklahoma's political leadership finally is reflected in two careers. In fact, it is embodied in the two Oklahomans who have won the greatest national distinction. Both were Democrats. Both were professional politicians. Both were of southern ancestry. Both were born and raised in southeastern Oklahoma. But in the careers of Senator Robert S. Kerr and Speaker Carl Albert one sees two different strains of an overall southern political culture. One is more typical of the modern, urban South. The other is more common to the older, rural South.[28]

In ideology, the differences are, at best, subtle. It is not that one is "liberal" and the other "conservative," as those terms are commonly understood. Rather, it is that the first focuses upon government's role in promoting economic growth, particularly by heavy spending on "worthwhile" public projects, where worthwhile usually means for the politician's constituents. The second tends to lack any ideological focus at all. In it, politics turn on what the man *is,* not the votes that he casts.

The difference is more visible in campaign styles. In the first, political campaigns are like business ventures. Tightly organized, they consume vast quantities of money in slick advertising and calculated media appeals. In the second, campaigns are much less businesses, much more personal: a few "speakings," a billboard here and there, mostly calls upon friends and neighbors of long-time personal acquaintance.

Over time, those repeated campaigns allow a politician of the first style to build something of a political machine. The money and business connections generated on his behalf can be turned to other candidates as well. In contrast, the personal alliances typical of the second can rarely be transferred beyond the candidate himself.

Political success for the first type breeds political success. Power consists of the ability to win federal projects for his supporters. Those most directly benefited thereby, especially contractors and other businessmen, gratefully repay their benefactor with campaign contributions that reassure his election and otherwise add to his power. Both at home and in office, this politician works with business associates.

Political success of the second style, like everything else, remains largely personal. At home, it continues to rest upon old alliances of personal, not economic, origins. In office, it tends to depend upon similar personal alliances with senior men able to boost one's career. In both cases, this politician depends not upon associates but upon friends.

Consider in this framework the careers of Senator Kerr and Speaker Albert.[29] Bob Kerr once declared his ideology in a single sentence: "I'm against any deal I ain't in on." Kerr was successively Democratic national committeeman, Oklahoma's governor, and the "Uncrowned King of the United States Senate," and his "ideology" put him squarely in the middle of deals worth tens of millions of federal dollars for Oklahoma. Carl Albert's Third District was one beneficiary of those funds, but his career in the House had a different purpose. He was an "inside" man who mastered the House's procedures and personalities and built influence upon that mastery. As for ideology, he once shrugged off a vote that was especially unpopular with his constituents (his vote for the 1964 Civil Rights Act) by saying that "my district understood that my career in Congress was more important than any vote I would ever cast."

Kerr's campaigns were legendary extravaganzas. Pulling money out of his own deep pockets and those of his fellow oilmen, Kerr spent millions to put his signs on every fencerow, his face on every billboard, and his voice across every airwave. Carl Albert's first campaign for Congress in 1946 cost but a few thousand dollars, most of that contributed from his wife's wartime savings. Thirty years later, he retired from Congress. At that time he had accumulated a campaign war chest of exactly seven thousand dollars. Over fifteen elections in between, he probably had spent only a fraction of what Kerr had spent on a single primary. For fifteen elections, his friends, classmates, and neighbors were his entire campaign organization.

Senator Kerr's organization came to stretch into every county and corner of the state. It not only assured his own elections but did as well those of his allies. It even survived the senator's death to elect Fred R. Harris to take the Kerr seat in the Senate. In contrast, Carl Albert's personal organization evaporated with his retirement announcement. Charles Ward, Albert's long-time administrative assistant and the aide closest to district affairs, lost the Democratic primary to fill Albert's Third District seat to Wes Watkins, an Ada politician who had steadily built his own personal following for just such an opportunity.

Kerr's power in the Senate was legendary. Invincible at home, he rarely lost there either. The key to his influence—aside from his will and intelligence—was his power on the Senate Finance Committee and his tight control over appropriations through its rivers and harbors subcommittee. No senator got something for his state without Bob Kerr's getting something for Oklahoma. Carl Albert was no less ambitious nor intelligent, but his rise in the House came without a single powerful committee assignment. Rather, he early won Speaker Sam Rayburn's sponsorship and parlayed that into a position that won him friendships independent of party, philosophy, or section. If Bob Kerr's associates made him powerful, Carl Albert's friends made him Democratic whip, majority leader, and House Speaker.

During their days together in Washington—the late 1940s through the early 1960s—Kerr and Albert led a delegation that was regarded as pound-for-pound the strongest state delegation in the U.S. Congress. Men like Russell and Johnson, Rayburn and Vinson regarded them as their equals. They were. They were part of that longstanding Southern domination of Congress. Like the Georgians and the Texans, these Oklahomans were Southern politicians of different but of the highest order.

IV

It is unlikely that this discussion either of race or of political culture in Oklahoma will end the state's reputation as a western state. After all, western states, no less than Southern ones, have had their own problems with race and their own strains of political culture. Oklahoma's do seem to be more typically Southern than western in form, however, and the state's dealings with them have had greater impact upon the South than upon the West.

That, though, is not the point. The point is really Robin Williams's—that we have to look at things in different ways. If we did that consistently, we might not learn a single thing new about Coronado, Chouteau, or Geronimo. There is no guarantee that we will even learn anything interesting about all those governors. But we could begin asking some serious questions about what happened in Oklahoma after Turner's famous frontier closed. We might wonder just why the Southern style of race relations encountered so little opposition among other white Oklahomans. We might question just how the early expectation of something better continued to shape black experiences after Jim Crow's rise. We might ponder, too, just why Oklahoma's inherited political styles have been so durable.

From a Southern perspective, we might consider, too, Oklahoma's economy. Has it been—like much of the South's—largely extractive and imprisoned in a colonial relationship? Culturally, we might wonder how the South's legacy of defeat in the Civil War parallels Oklahoma's shame from the Great Depression and the Dust Bowl migration. Socially, we might wonder why the state has been so like the South in its attitudes on women, the family, religion, and schooling.

Each of these is a big question of, as yet, unknown answer. But history is just that—a set of questions derived from urgency and pointing to understanding. It always requires us to look at familiar things but to do it in unfamiliar ways.

The opposite view—that history is merely familiar facts endlessly repeated—is not history at all. After all, it was a different Alexander who gave us the ragtime band.

NOTES

1. Turner's seminal thesis on the frontier's significance is found in his *The Frontier in American History* (New York: H. Holt, 1920). His work on section is found in *The Significance of Sections in American History* (New York: H. Holt, 1932). A full—and sympathetic—study of Turner's life and influence is Ray Allen Billington, *Frederick Jackson Turner: Historian, Scholar, Teacher* (New York: Oxford University Press, 1973).

2. On Dale's work and influence, see Arrell M. Gibson, ed., *Frontier Historian: The Life and Works of Edward Everett Dale* (Norman: University of Oklahoma Press, 1975).

3. Gibson, *Oklahoma: A History of Five Centuries* (Oklahoma City: Harlow Publishing Company, 1965). Gibson's is easily the best available college-level textbook on Oklahoma's history, and it is written from a western perspective. The same is shared by the only competition: Edwin C. McReynolds, *Oklahoma: A History of the Sooner State* (Norman: University of Oklahoma Press, 1954), and the textbook originally written by Dale, himself, and later revised by Gene Aldrich, *A History of Oklahoma* (Edmond: Thompson Book and Supply, 1972).

4. Phillips, "The Central Theme in Southern History," *American Historical Review* 34 (1928): 30–43.

5. U.S. Department of Commerce, Bureau of the Census, *Population of Oklahoma and Indian Territory, 1907* (Washington: Government Printing Office, 1907).

6. The classic account of the era's disfranchisement and segregation remains C. Vann Woodward, *The Strange Career of Jim Crow,* 3rd rev. ed. (New York: Oxford University Press, 1974).

7. The best available history of black Oklahoma is Jimmie Lewis Franklin, *Journey Toward Hope: A History of Blacks in Oklahoma* (Norman: University of Oklahoma Press, 1982). On this period, see 3–33.

8. Neil I. Painter, *The Exodusters: Black Migration to Kansas after Reconstruction* (New York: Alfred A. Knopf, 1977).

9. Danney Goble, *Progressive Oklahoma: The Making of a New Kind of State* (Norman: University of Oklahoma Press, 1980), 166–94.

10. Ibid., 141–43, 200–201. See also Phillip Mellinger, "Discrimination and Statehood in Oklahoma," *Chronicles of Oklahoma* 49 (1971): 340–78.

11. The difference is that between the Republican vote for Oklahoma Territory's congressional delegate in 1904 and the total received by all Republican convention candidates in 1906. The lack of a comparable earlier election for the Indian Territory makes comparison impossible there.

12. Goble, *Progressive Oklahoma,* 208–25.

13. James R. Scales and Danney Goble, *Oklahoma Politics: A History* (Norman: University of Oklahoma Press, 1982), 36, 44–45.

14. Ibid., 46–47; Mellinger, "Discrimination and Statehood," 373–77; "The Grandfather Clause in Oklahoma," *Outlook,* Aug. 20, 1910, p. 853. The figure

"twenty thousand" comes from the total vote cast on this question (State Question 10) minus the total vote cast in the simultaneous party preferential races, held at the same polls. Under the circumstances, the two should be exactly equal. They are not—not by 20,364 blank ballots.

15. *Guinn* v. *United States* 238 U.S. 347 (1915): 127–28, 177, 274, 658, 899.

16. *Lane* v. *Wilson* 307 U.S. 268 (1939): 274, 658, 681, 749.

17. Richard Kluger, *Simple Justice: The History of Brown v. Board of Education and Black America's Struggle for Equality* (New York: Alfred A. Knopf, 1975), 165–70.

18. *Sipuel* v. *Oklahoma State Board of Regents* 332 U.S. 631 (1948): 323–26, 334, 335, 344, 354, 367, 725, 773, 889.

19. Marshall later explained his choice of McLaurin. Sensitive to racist charges that integrated schooling somehow would lead to interracial marriage, he had chosen George W. McLaurin, who at age sixty-eight was not likely to marry anyone (even if he were not already married). See Kluger, *Simple Justice,* 334.

20. The doctrine, originally asserted to justify segregation on public trains, came from the Supreme Court in the classic *Plessy* v. *Ferguson* 163 U.S. 537 (1896): 90–100.

21. Kluger, *Simple Justice,* 355–56.

22. *McLaurin* v. *Oklahoma State Regents for Higher Education* 339 U.S. 637 (1950): 335–38, 343, 347–48.

23. *Brown* v. *Board of Education of Topeka,* 98 F. Supp. 797 (1951), 347 U.S. 483 (1954), 349 U.S. 294 (1955): 498, 504–34.

24. Solon J. Buck, "The Settlement of Oklahoma," *Transaction of the Wisconsin Academy of Sciences, Arts, and Letters* 15 (1907): 325–80.

25. The indispensable source for most of Oklahoma's election data is Oliver Benson et al., *Oklahoma Votes, 1907–1962.* It can be supplemented with recent biennial editions of the Oklahoma State Election Board's *Directory of Oklahoma.* A thorough analysis of state voting patterns is found in Samuel A. Kirkpatrick, David R. Morgan, and Thomas G. Kiehlhorn, *The Oklahoma Voter: Politics, Elections, and Parties in the Sooner State* (Norman: University of Oklahoma Press, 1977).

26. Two counties, Harmon and Cotton, were added after statehood, Harmon splitting off from Greer and Cotton from Comanche.

27. The classic description of intrastate Southern political factionalism is V. O. Key, Jr., *Southern Politics in State and Nation* (New York: Alfred A. Knopf, 1949). A recent update is William C. Havard, ed., *The Changing Politics of the South* (Baton Rouge: Louisiana State University Press, 1972).

28. The following typologies (like the earlier description of Southern politicians) are very loosely based upon Daniel J. Elazar, *American Federalism: a View from the States,* 3rd ed. (New York: Harper and Row, 1984), 109–73. Skeptics might note that there is nothing uniquely "Southern" about either of these typologies. They are right, for practitioners of both may be found in every region. What is notable, however, is that both are more likely to be found in the South than in any other section, especially in the West. Moreover, a third typology—what Ela-

zar labels a "Moralistic" political culture—barely exists in the South at all (although he finds it virtually dominant in the West). Close students of Oklahoma's politics would not see much that is moralistic about it, at least not in Elazar's sense (pp. 117–18) of a culture rooted in a commonwealth concept of government and civil life.

29. On Kerr, see Anne Hodges Morgan, *Robert S. Kerr: The Senate Years* (Norman: University of Oklahoma Press, 1977). For Albert, see Carl Albert with Danney Goble, *Little Giant: The Life and Times of Speaker Carl Albert* (Norman: University of Oklahoma Press, 1990).

16

CREATING AN OKLAHOMA RELIGIOUS COALITION FOR ABORTION RIGHTS:
A Personal/Historical Essay

Carole Jane Joyce

Carole Jane Joyce is a dance instructor, choreographer, and freelance writer who lives in Ada, Oklahoma. Her essay is historical in the sense of dealing with an important historical issue and showing change over time, but personal in the sense that she was involved as a participant in the events described. Part of the point of "people's history," as practiced by Howard Zinn and others, is that common people can/do/should make— and write—their own history. Also, recent *subjects in Oklahoma history, especially if they are controversial at all, usually don't get the attention the earlier period does. But who would argue that a woman's right to choose abortion is not a worthy subject for historical study, especially today when the Supreme Court seems to have begun a process of backing off from its 1973* (Roe v. Wade) *commitment to protecting that right?*

It was the spring of 1962 in Oklahoma that I discovered I was pregnant for the fourth time in my short twenty-four years. My husband, a traveling salesman whose work was supposed to bring him home to his family on weekends, seldom made it. Early in my pregnancy he made his final appearance in our home, and I knew that I was fully in charge of everything, including the well-being of our three children. Several days later, while a friend was visiting, I confided in her that I was pregnant and could not afford to see a doctor. "I have no money, no job, and no husband." She suggested that I consider an abortion. I gasped, "No, my family would never allow that, I would never allow that, the Baptist church would never allow that!" My friend kept talking in a steady, calm voice: "You are the one who is responsible, not your church or any member of your family, only you."

Inside my head and heart a deep well of anger and conflict brewed. Every day was unbearable. I faced the outside world with an "Isn't life wonderful" attitude, while inside terror reigned. I finally decided to have an abortion. That presented another set of problems now, including where I would get the money for an abortion, where it would take place, and who would take care of my children while I was having it done. With the help of my friend the answers came slowly. We called the doctor, set up the appointment and raised the $150.00. To this day the memory of that trip remains quite clear.

We drove to the small town of Morris, Oklahoma, late in the evening and waited in a parking lot of an empty motel. I was beginning to have the feeling of being a criminal at that point. Soon another car pulled up beside us and the voice inside the car asked our names. He then held out his hand and asked for my money. "Follow me." After a long ride, during which time I felt as though I was watching this crime instead of being the main participant, we stopped on the outskirts of town, behind a small farmhouse that looked as though no one lived there. I remember it was so dark that my friend and I held hands until we reached the back door. The man told my friend to have a seat. She sat down. He called me by name and asked me to come with him. As I left that dimly lit living room, I looked at my friend and she looked at me; the look of fear on her face was one I had never seen. We were in the hands of strangers and had no control over anything, not even where we were. I entered a bright room with a huge dentist-type chair in the middle of it. An elderly woman in a dark dress and cardigan sweater took over. Dressed in the hospital gown given to me, I sat down in the chair, and the woman put me to sleep. As I was coming to, I thought I heard the doctor's voice, but I never saw his face. It was over. As the next few days passed, I realized that I was one of the lucky ones; the doctor had been good, and I was without complications of any kind.

Sixteen years later, in 1978, I became a member of the highly visible All Souls Unitarian Church in Tulsa. I was elected chair of Religion in Action, the social action arm of the church. My first duty was to meet with the minister and discuss the upcoming year and possibly get some input about what he thought the committee should accomplish. Dr. John B. Wolf had one thing on his mind at our meeting, and his words are still ringing in my ears: "Stop the Right-to-Lifers." I heard myself say, "Okay."

The widespread changes in abortion laws, according to Colin Francome in his book *Abortion Freedom: A Worldwide Movement,* have been influenced by a variety of factors, including the role of the women's movement, the views of the courts, and the influence of religion. At the outbreak of World War II there was no country where women were expressly given freedom of choice on abortion. Francome goes on to say that while abortion was not freely available under law, many countries made at least some provisions for it.

During the 1960s religious groups began to challenge the church's right to decide what was right and what was wrong where morality was concerned. Young people had access to the "pill," and birth control clinics for single people were now available. One could engage in premarital intercourse with fewer worries.[1]

Two important events happened in the 1960s that had an effect on public opinion relevant to the need for abortion reform. The first was the case of Sherri Finkbine of Arizona, whose request for an abortion when she realized she might be carrying a thalidomide-deformed fetus was turned down. The second event was the filing of disciplinary charges against two prominent San Francisco physicians, Paul J. Shively and Seymour Smith, by the California State Board of Medical Examiners for performing abortions on women with German measles. The two doctors admitted they had performed therapeutic abortions on women exposed to rubella, abortions that had been approved by their respective hospital abortion committees. Although they had the medical community behind them, the controversy halted all abortions in the city of San Francisco. The accused doctors received suspended sentences; physicians across the United States were now in a more visible position where abortion was concerned whether they chose to be or not.[2]

The drug thalidomide, prescribed for morning sickness, and its horror made public by Sherri Finkbine, and the case of the California physicians prompted many to believe there was a need for abortion reform in this country.

In 1967 the American Medical Association (AMA) House of Delegates at its meeting in Atlantic City considered a policy recommendation on abortion, a proposal that abortion should be allowed for threats to the life or health of the woman, when the infant might be born with incapacitating physical or mental deformity, and when there was evidence of rape or incest.[3]

In 1970 the New York legislature passed a law giving abortion on request in the first twenty-four weeks of pregnancy. Some states passed similar laws. Oklahoma was not one of them. The Oklahoma abortion laws prohibit virtually all abortions, and the state will not provide Medicaid funding for abortion unless the woman's life is in danger. Then in 1973 the landmark Supreme Court case, *Roe* v. *Wade*, legalized abortion.

In May 1978, I attended the National Conference on Social Justice in Washington, D.C., and it was there that I began my education on the pros and cons of abortion. One of the four workshops I attended was entitled "Abortion and the Freedom of Choice." The consensus of the workshop was that the passage of a "right to life" amendment would endanger our religious freedom. The First Amendment states that "Congress shall make no law respecting an establishment of religion, or prohibiting the free exercise thereof." To place into the Constitution the theology of one particular religion concerning the beginning of life compels every citizen to accept that doctrine.

If abortion were banned, those individuals whose religions teach that abortion may sometimes be a moral solution to a problem pregnancy would be unable to practice the tenets of their faith. Religious groups hold diverse and conflicting doctrines with regard to when life begins.

If the American people allow the first clause of the Bill of Rights to be amended, then possibly none of the other clauses would be secure. The first clause protects our religious freedom—the freedom to choose. Without this basic freedom, we would no longer have the right or the responsibility of family planning. The workshop was over and I was inspired.

I began work to establish in Oklahoma a Religious Coalition for Abortion Rights, an organization that had been in existence in some states since 1973. I decided to begin with a meeting with Modern Oklahomans for the Repeal of Abortion Laws (MORAL). Tulsa's chapter was having little effect at this particular time and decided to reorganize. Dorothy Dessauer, the coordinator, and I talked for what seemed forever on the subject of abortion. In the end she and her backers felt that a new voice, a religious voice, was exactly what was needed in the middle of the Bible Belt.

In December 1978 the first meeting of the steering committee was held on the campus of the University of Tulsa. Reverend Thad Holcombe of United Campus Ministry supplied the meeting place for the next year and a half. Without Holcombe and a place to get together for discussion, the project could not have progressed. He was and is a strong supporter of choice. In attendance at those early-morning meetings—early morning because 7:30 A.M. was the only time available to meet—were ministers from five different churches (one rabbi, the chair of the University of Tulsa's religion department, district representatives of two different religious groups, and a chaplain from a local hospital), and two lay people. Some Tuesdays we would be few, but we always met.

At each meeting we progressed toward the requirements to form a state affiliate: a minimum of five denominational memberships; a minimum of ten individual sponsors within the religious community; and a Policy Council, made up of one representative from each member denomination or organization, whose responsibility is to develop state policy and action on abortion rights legislation, citizen education, and constituency development.[4] We also discussed the media and how to handle them and when to handle them. At the early stages of our meetings we desired complete secrecy. The media of Oklahoma were one of the most persuasive forces in the state, we concluded, and we should be formed and ready to work before their knowledge. Because I was somewhat naïve, I never once thought we would not succeed.

Funding for Planned Parenthood was deleted from the Tulsa United Way in 1979.[5] We felt this was another reason we had to be strong and completely educated when the media were introduced to us. The right-to-life organizations were gaining strength and were highly visible. Because of our meetings several churches began education on abortion in a new and enlightened way. A workshop on the subject was held for all ministers at All Souls Church in February 1979.

As we progressed, our goals became more apparent: The religious community needed guidance on the issue. We would explain medical procedures and spend many, many hours debating the law and morality. We talked about the word *abortion* and how many people could not deal with the emotional word, but we decided it was imperative that we use it. And last and most important, we all agreed that each religious viewpoint of how or when personhood begins would be respected. Meanwhile, I was in close touch with the national headquarters of RCAR in Washington, D.C., not only by mail but also in person. I met several times with Patricia A. Gavett, national director, and Robert Z. Alpern, chairperson, while in Washington. Freddye Hodges, the field director and my contact during the forming of Oklahoma RCAR, and I spent many hours of constructive time. I not only traveled to our nation's capitol but also to Texas, Louisiana, Arkansas, and Kansas. I visited with social action groups in each of the states and received helpful input. Texas was the only state at that time that did not have some form of organizing taking place.

Religious Coalition for Abolition Rights put out a newsletter that included information on Oklahoma and how we were progressing:

Organizing efforts are being carried out in the Tulsa area by a Unitarian social action director and the MORAL coordinator. A state-wide coalition of pro-choice organizations has recently been formed, and the need for participation of the pro-choice religious community is critical. . . . State is predominantly Protestant.

State legislation: Medicaid funding is based on federal guidelines. The constitutional convention resolution was withdrawn under pressure in 1978, but memorials were passed in 1973 and 1977. A comprehensive anti-abortion bill was passed this year which combines all the worst provisions relating to facility requirements, informed consent, reporting, counseling, and advertising regulations. Another bill permits hospitals and medical personnel to refuse to perform abortions.

Congressional delegation: Oklahoma senators are pro-choice. Representatives are split, with three generally voting pro-choice and three voting anti-choice. Delegation is heavily Protestant.[6]

The Christian Church (Disciples of Christ) of Oklahoma's Northeast District was the first to present its board with a proposal to form an RCAR chapter. The following is an excerpt from their board minutes dated June 18, 1979: "Nancy Wirth, of Harvard Avenue, who represents the District on a steering committee to form a Religious Coalition for Abortion Rights (RCAR), presented the board the proposal approved by the Cabinet that we be one of the five denominational judicatory bodies needed to form this coalition. After much discussion pro and con, Bill Imhoff made the motion that we do endorse and agree to be a part of the Religious Coalition for Abortion Rights in Oklahoma. It was seconded and carried."[7]

Nancy Wirth was constant in her concern and leadership where the steering committee was concerned. She had presented her board a clear picture of what RCAR had to offer our community. In her remarks to the district meeting she included the creed of RCAR: "To encourage and coordinate support for safeguarding the legal option of abortion, for ensuring the right of individuals to make decisions in accordance with their consciences; and for opposing efforts to deny this right of conscience through constitutional amendment of federal and state legislation."[8]

Wirth's life had been touched in 1962 by the case of Sherri Finkbine of Arizona.[9] Like Sherri, she was pregnant during that year, but unlike Sherri, she was carrying a healthy fetus and was secure in her pregnancy. She followed the news about Finkbine faithfully and remembers the feelings she felt when the court of Arizona refused Finkbine an abortion even though she had taken the drug thalidomide and it had done its dirty work inside her womb. "I realized the importance of choice for every woman during that trial," Wirth reported to me recently in a telephone conversation. She also had felt that her naïveté kept her from ever feeling that her board would not agree to RCAR's terms.

The Union of American Hebrew Congregations was the next support for an Oklahoma RCAR. Rabbi Charles P. Sherman of Temple Israel in Tulsa received the following statement from the board on August 10, 1979:

Dear Rabbi Sherman:

The response from our board was entirely favorable. Please feel free to use the name of the Southwest Council in support of the Oklahoma Chapter of the Religious Coalition for Abortion Rights.

Respectfully,
William M. Lucas, Jr.
President, Southwest Council
Union of American Hebrew Congregations[10]

Rabbi Sherman had spent seven years, beginning in 1969, counseling women with problem pregnancies in the state of Connecticut, where abortions were illegal and counseling about abortion was prohibited. He told me by phone:

What I learned during that period of my life was that most of the women I counseled wanted an abortion. They simply did not have the money to drive the three hours to another state for the operation. They had no choice. I would counsel not only about abortion but also marriage as an option or possibly adoption, but the majority wanted an abortion. When I realized the plight of these women and began to feel in 1978 that out of religious faith people were wanting to turn the clock back, I wanted to put some of my knowledge, that I had gained from my experience in Connecticut, to use.

He added: "The nosy minority angered me."

Although the rabbi disliked our early-hour meetings, he was a rock in the community and with us every step of the way.

The Southwest District of the Unitarian Universalist Association followed with their approval, and needless to say, Dr. Wolf was pleased. Wolf would spark our discussions with historical facts. One fact stands out among all others. The Catholic church itself had seesawed back and forth in its dogma regarding abortion. Dr. Wolf explained:

In 314 A.D. the church prescribed ten years' penance for abortion. Thereafter theologians debated the point at which the fetus is "animated" with a rational soul and therefore "murderable." Thomas Aquinas proposed that the fetus acquires its soul in stages, acquiring a fully human soul at about two months. Based largely on St. Thomas' ideas the Catholic church in the 13th century established that abortions were to be permitted when performed within 40 days of conception for a male fetus, and 80 days for a female. For a brief period of five years Pope Sixtus V (1585–90) made abortion an excommunicatory sin when performed at any stage of the fetus' development. But, the next pope, Gregory IV, reversed that decision and decreed excommunication only if the abortion were performed after the fetus was 40 days old. This view prevailed for almost two centuries until in 1869 when Pius IX reverted the church's position to that of Sixtus and held that the soul begins at the moment of conception.[11]

Wolf believed that the issue of abortion was just one more way the fundamentalists had of keeping woman in her proper place. "A religion should free people," he said. It angered him that the Bible was being used by some as a sort of "recipe book," reducing the Bible to the word of God instead of the words of God, and believing every one to be true.[12]

The quote from Wolf that remains with me is: "To inspire means to breathe, to expire means to die; therefore, life begins when we breathe. Life does not begin with the creation of a human being, life goes on all the time."[13]

The Presbytery of Eastern Oklahoma rounded out four of the five suggested for membership in RCAR. The field director of RCAR felt that our membership would grow and decided that we were a well-planned group and should form Oklahoma Religious Coalition for Abortion Rights. Four judicatories to start a state affiliate was sufficient.

What began two years earlier was about to finish. New faces came into the picture and took the reins. Officers were elected and goals set for the future of this new coalition. In December of 1980 a press conference was held at Southminster Presbyterian Church in Tulsa to announce RCAR's newest member and the state officers. By March of that year there were thirty-one national judicatory members in the national organization.

Today the Oklahoma state affiliate of RCAR has an annual budget of twelve thousand dollars and a part-time state coordinator. It has a nonprofit tax-exempt bulk mailing permit for the newsletter, a listing of over eighty clergy sponsors, a mailing list of over twelve hundred, a network of forty-four legislative alert callers, many volunteers throughout the state, active lobbyists and educators, counselors, public speakers, and cooperative arrangements with organizations in the community who work for choice.[14]

In 1989 the abortion issue was headline news most of the year. President George Bush made his appointments to the Supreme Court, and the country began to speculate on whether an attempt would be made to reverse the *Roe* v. *Wade* decision made in 1973. The National Organization for Women noted that "Life for women under a Bush presidency could become far more unfair." Their newsletter also feared a movement against the right to birth control by this administration.[15] The Supreme Court handed down a decision in *Webster* v. *Reproductive Health Services* (of Missouri) that pushed back the clock where women and abortions were concerned. The attorney general filed a brief urging the Supreme Court to use the Missouri case as an opportunity to reconsider *Roe* v. *Wade*. In the state of Missouri no public funds to "counsel or encourage" a woman to have an abortion are available. Several other abortion-related cases also found their way before the Supreme Court in 1989. Backed by the financial resources of the Reverend Jerry Falwell, Operation Rescue picketed and terrorized Planned Parenthood clinics.[16]

In the summer of 1990 a group calling itself the Oklahoma Coalition to Restrict Abortion (OCRA), with the backing of Fred Sellers, circulated antichoice petitions in churches and turned in more than one hundred thousand signatures by the end of the year to the Supreme Court of Oklahoma in hopes of putting the issue of abortion to a vote of the people. The initiative petition, known as State Question 642, makes it a crime for doctors to perform abortions except in certain situations. It also makes anyone criminally liable who aids or refers someone to an abortion. Conviction of either charge would mean prison terms of not less than four years and criminal fines of ten thousand to one hundred thousand dollars. Choice Legal Defense Fund of Oklahoma organized volunteers to challenge the estimated 104,189 "valid" signatures on the petition; in May 1991 the fund turned over to the Supreme Court of Oklahoma 23,059 signature challenges. These were signatures "not found," or signatures not located by the election boards of their counties. It is assumed that proponents of any petition will be able to reinstate one-third of the names challenged by the opponents, but the Oklahoma Supreme Court referee indicated in February 1992 that the proponents did indeed have enough legal signatures and that the Choice Legal Defense Fund of Oklahoma was 691 challenges short of proving that State Question 642 was not signed by enough registered voters. For a while it seemed likely that SQ 642 would be on one of the 1992 election dates: the primary election on August 25, the runoff on September 15, or the general election on November 3. However, early in August the Oklahoma Supreme Court ruled that State Question 642 was unconstitutional and that the people of Oklahoma would not see this particular issue on the ballot.

On May 23, 1991, the Supreme Court ruled in *Rust* v. *Sullivan* that it is constitutional for the government to restrict Title X funded clinics from counseling women on abortion, even if continued pregnancy threatens a woman's life or health. This regulation censoring the speech of health providers was a decision that devastated pro-choice advocates. RCAR and other religious leaders converged on Washington, D.C., on July 18, 1991, to urge Congress to overturn this "gag rule" on family planning. Over 280 national organizations, including professionals from the medical, legal, public health, civil liberties, and arts communities, joined the campaign to overturn the rule. Federally funded Title X family planning clinics are the primary source of health care for 4.1 million American women.

On the twentieth anniversary of *Roe* v. *Wade,* and after only three days as president of the United States, Bill Clinton ended the Reagan-Bush "gag rule." For the first time in twelve years, choice advocates have a sympathetic president in the White House.

One bill currently working its way through Congress is the Freedom of Choice Act (HR25/SB25). This bill reverses the ability of states to interfere in the reproductive lives of women and would eliminate conflicting state laws regulating abortion. One provision in the act codifies the principles of the 1973 Supreme Court decision in *Roe* v. *Wade*. As currently drafted, however, the bill would *allow* states to require parental consent or notification for minors' abortions and permits states to cut off Medicaid and other public funding of abortion for poor women.

In the current session of the Oklahoma legislature, as in the past twenty sessions, bills will be introduced to limit the right of a woman to a safe abortion. The Oklahoma Religious Coalition for Abortion Rights will continue to play an important role in the effort to pressure Oklahoma legislators to keep the women of our state protected and not to return to those dark days before *Roe* v. *Wade*. No woman should have to hear the words, ''You must have that baby.''

NOTES

1. Coling Francome, *Abortion Freedom: A Worldwide Movement* (London: George Allen and Unwin, 1984), 77, 222.

2. Marian Faux, *Roe v. Wade: The Untold Story of the Landmark Supreme Court Decision That Made Abortion Legal* (New York: Macmillan Publishing Company, 1988), 42–51, 60–62.

3. Francome, *Abortion Freedom,* 104.

4. Patricia A. Gavett, National Director, Religious Coalition for Abortion Rights, to the author, no date, probably 1978.

5. ''A Brief History of ORCAR,'' Mar. 1989, unpublished paper supplied to the author by the Rev. Mary McAnally, p. 3.

6. Gavett to the author.

7. Board Minutes, Northeast District of the Christian Church in Oklahoma, June 18, 1979.

8. *Oklahoma Religious Coalition for Abortion Rights* (pamphlet, n.p., n.d., probably 1979).

9. Linda K. Kerber and Jane De Hart–Matthews, eds., *Women's America: Refocusing the Past,* 2d ed. (New York: Oxford University Press, 1987), 492.

10. Letter from William M. Lucas, Jr., to Charles P. Sherman, Aug. 10, 1979.

11. John B. Wolf, handwritten note to the author, Mar. 3, 1989.

12. John B. Wolf, interview with author, Mar. 3, 1989.

13. Ibid.

14. "A Brief History of ORCAR," Mar. 1989, p. 3.

15. "New Initiatives Action Ballot," National Organization for Women, no date given, probably 1989.

16. Eve W. Paul, Vice President for Legal Affairs, Planned Parenthood Federation of America, memorandum to Concerned Citizens, no date given, probably 1989.

17

VIOLENCE AGAINST WOMEN IN RURAL OKLAHOMA

Elizabeth D. Barlow

Domestic violence is a poignant example of our tendency to avoid serious problems—in history as in life. The following essay is another "personal/ historical" essay, and a prime example of self-empowerment by common people. Elizabeth D. Barlow was the founder and executive director of the organization she describes, Southeastern Oklahoma Services for Abused Women. She has currently returned to school at the University of Oklahoma.

A woman is beaten every fifteen seconds in the United States, according to FBI statistics. An estimated 340,000 women are assaulted by their partners each year in Oklahoma.

I ran from my mobile home in the cold dead of night. I left my children who were crying in their beds. My husband was after me. There were no neighbors within hearing distance. My jaw was broken. He had a gun. Somehow, I had managed to pick myself up after he had kicked me off our 5 foot high porch. My neck was sprained and it was difficult for me to hold my head up, but I ran anyway. After what seemed like a long time I stopped and slept somewhat under the trees, but I was fearing for my life.

The next day I got a ride into town. I went to the hospital, my face was black and blue, my jaw was broken, my neck was sprained. I went to the Sheriff's office, and asked to speak directly to him. He told me that there was nothing he could do. I went to the District Attorney, he told me to "let us know if it happens again. . . ."

—Rosie, a battered woman of eight years

Rural Oklahoma is a supportive environment for violence toward women. Sheriffs must, at a minimum, fill out a report, and the district attorney has a responsibility to inform a victim of her right to file charges upon hearing of an alleged crime. But this woman did not know either of these things. In this case, both the sheriff and the D.A. knew and had socialized with the abuser. Rosie's story is a typical story of abuse, and an especially typical story of abuse in a rural area.

This "everybody knows everybody" attitude keeps many rural abused women from asking for help. Geographic isolation and lack of resources often cut her off from even knowing help is available. Therefore, how the community responds to this problem is and has been different in rural Oklahoma as opposed to urban Oklahoma. This particular chapter of Oklahoma history is about the community of southeastern Oklahoma and how it responded to this problem through the grassroots development in the 1980s of an agency known as Southeastern Oklahoma Services for Abused Women (SOS).

This kind of story is important in part because it is the history of women, and traditionally, history has been about men. During more recent years, there has been a sincere effort to include *famous* women. Although famous women are important to our history, it is erroneous to skip back through the history books and fill in the details with solely the more famous women.

Calling this "contribution history," historian Gerda Lerner says in her chapter in *Liberating Women's History* that it "mostly describes what men in the past told women to do and what men in the past thought women should be. Essentially, they have applied questions from traditional history to women, and tried to fit women's past into the empty spaces."[1]

I believe that we also need the collective call of the *commonplace* woman for a more "universal" history. Lerner goes on to point out that women in history have been deprived of economic and political power, but she says that "they found a way to make their power felt through organizations, through pressure tactics, through petitioning, and through various other means." Finally, Lerner writes, "historians must painstakingly restore the actual record of women's contributions at any given period in history."[2] That is what this is. It is an actual record given from a personal/historical perspective of a group of women making themselves more powerful through grassroots efforts.

The oppression of women is universal. In India new brides are set on fire by husbands so they may be free to marry again for dowry; in Africa female children are circumcised without anesthesia; and in southeastern Oklahoma a pregnant woman is brutally beaten in the genitals with a baseball bat, causing her to abort the baby. Women are not treated differently in Oklahoma than they are anywhere else in the United States or the world.

However, it could be argued that the *excuses* for battering may differ from region to region. For example, I have often heard from the battered woman that the abuser told her she was "getting out of line," or "talking back." This could be construed as a conservative fundamentalist interpretation of family roles of the area. Also worth mentioning is the fact that the *rationalizations* for indifference given by social services and the criminal justice system could differ from region to region. Having heard from law enforcement that "Joe is a good ol' boy and would never beat his wife," one could argue that the Southern traditions of "family and honor at all costs" could be at play in the comment. But pay attention to these details, and you realize it is only semantics. The occurrence of woman abuse is more similar everywhere than it is dissimilar. Abused women everywhere say they were beaten most often for some reason such as arriving home five minutes late from the grocery store; it doesn't matter where they live or what economic class they are in.

As R. Emerson Dobash and Russell Dobash wrote in *Violence Against Wives,* "Through the seventeenth, eighteenth, and nineteenth centuries, there has been little objection within the community to a man's using force against his wife as long as he did not exceed certain tacit limits."[3] Historically, women have been

beaten and are still beaten today because a patriarchal society promotes violence towards women. Nowhere is this more clear than in
the criminal justice system's record. In 1824, the Supreme Court of
Mississippi ruled that a husband should be able to ''chastise'' his
wife without having to fear prosecution, as it would only bring
shame to the parties. Another court ruling in 1864 determined that
the criminal justice system should not interfere in domestic violence
cases. This North Carolina ruling established that the parties should
be left to themselves to make up except in cases of permanent injury
or an excess of violence.[4]

In Oklahoma it has only been in the last decade that battered
women have had any specific legal recourse. During the 1980s, both
the Protection from Domestic Abuse Act and changes in the rape
statutes have provided relief. Only recently, however, on April 13,
1993, did it become illegal to rape your wife. Prior to that date, a
wife could only bring rape charges against her husband if she had
filed for divorce or legal separation, filed a protective order, or was
living apart from her husband. Unless one of these conditions was
present, a husband could still rape his wife in Oklahoma. From this
point on, this paper will focus on issues that make communities in
southeastern Oklahoma particularly unsympathetic to women who
are victims of battery and rape.[5]

Known as the ''last of the outlaw country,'' southeastern Oklahoma had no services for abused women, rape victims, or their
children in the summer of 1981, when SOS was founded. I did not
really know where to start. I only knew that I was tired of seeing
beaten women scooped up off barroom floors, or standing in the
grocery stores with black eyes, with nothing I could say or offer. So
I talked to a few of the women leaders of the community about the
problem.

Unexpectedly, battered women began calling me in the middle of
the night. Obviously, this proved that there were battered women in
southeastern Oklahoma who were just waiting for a way out. I found
myself gathering battered women and their children up in my old car
and taking them to someplace safe in the wee hours of the morning.
I would learn from each encounter what I needed to know about how
to help the next caller. I watched in awe at each woman's strength,

inspired by her ability to survive torture for days on end and still find a way to get self and children to safety. But I needed help.

So I did a little reading and put together a ten-minute speech and went to a church. This seemed to be the best way to get to the community in this Bible Belt area. I took my speech to the Women's Bible Class of the United Church of Christ, and the response was overwhelming. I was never again to get such encouraging energy from people who wanted to jump in and help. I now had volunteers, which made us a "task force."

In March 1982 this task force began providing services. We began to answer calls in our homes, and some of us kept the battered women and their families in our homes. Many of us were survivors of abuse ourselves. The mission of the task force was "to educate the people of Southeastern Oklahoma to the issues of domestic violence and to provide crisis services and a safe place for women and their children who come from abusive homes."[6] In September 1982, the board of directors was formed and held its first meeting. We called ourselves Pushmataha County Services for Battered Women back then because we thought we would only be serving our county. But, somehow, the Valliant Police Department in McCurtain County nearly sixty miles away got our number, and we were soon running all over southeastern Oklahoma.[7] Eventually we would consistently serve eight counties.[8]

There were many factors that made organizing in this area difficult. This was the most impoverished section of Oklahoma, leading in unemployment. Set in the Kiamichi and Ouachita mountains, the area is extremely rural. With the exception of lumbering, there is little major industrial development. Single women with children find it increasingly difficult to find employment in such an economically depressed area.

Although sparsely populated, the geographic area is very large, spread out, and mountainous, with public transportation virtually nonexistent. No buses or taxis run through most of the area. Many survivors have to travel great distances to safety, and most clients do not have a car. For example, in Pushmataha County it is 90 miles round trip to the courthouse from one town. From that same town it is 115 miles to the shelter. Transportation to safety or to the shelter and away from the abuser is difficult and costly. Consequently, SOS, like so many rural organizations, had the responsibility to provide transportation, a most expensive and time-consuming endeavor.

In the beginning, we had to transport to the Tulsa shelter, which was three hours away. Many times going to the shelter in a big city would be more frightening than the abuse. Rural women did not know how to get around in the city. Having grown up in a small community, these women did not want to leave the area. As one battered woman said, "Our families—mothers, aunts, and uncles—live around us and we are not as mobile as people in the big city. It is more difficult for us to leave and go to a place of safety, because many times safety is very far away. Far away from my family, my farm." We were soon to learn that we would need our own shelter.

Telephone calls only a few miles from the county seat are often long-distance calls, making calls for help difficult and sometimes dangerous for the battered women, as the help-line number will appear on their phone bill, alerting the abuser that she is trying to escape. Therefore, SOS accepts all collect phone calls in order to make services available to all clients within the area.

The crisis phone line is the lifeline of an abuse program. It is the only connection or hope for connection that the crisis worker has to the battered woman. It requires twenty-four hour supervision. Often the caller calls in the middle of the night, is hurt, and needs safety immediately or she might be killed.

Traditionally, crisis lines in urban areas use call forwarding or answering services, and whoever is on call answers the phone. This was a major stumbling block to us because these services were not available in southeastern Oklahoma, and without funding, we had no twenty-four-hour office as of 1982. We printed a list of six or seven phone numbers of volunteers and handed it to the police and sheriff's departments, and they would go down the list until they found someone at home. Essentially, the battered woman was on hold until one of us was reached, but that was the best we could do at that time. This practice ended abruptly one day when it was discovered that a local law enforcement office posted this list on their wall in plain view of any abuser. Fortunately, around this time the state legislature enacted legislation for a statewide toll-free number through the state Department of Mental Health. We then published this number, so the battered woman would call Oklahoma City, and the department was kind enough to act as our answering service, diverting the calls to the volunteer on call.

In the beginning our position was such that we did not see the need to work within the system. We were running an underground railroad, working out of our homes, keeping women in our houses, and we kept to ourselves. Law enforcement thought we were crazy; it never occurred to us to ask them for help. Slowly, as we became empowered as an organization, we began to *demand* help from the legal system, marching into the courtroom with these women. We learned about laws and legislation so we could help them demand their rights.[9] We were then in a position to give information about what was going to happen, and we could advocate in the courtroom.

Although local law enforcement states that 33 percent of all calls are domestic disturbance calls, the battered woman was not recognized as a victim of crime. A most important component of social change is to get woman abuse recognized as a crime, although it is already against the law to assault anyone. When an officer of the law arrives at the scene of a domestic disturbance, an arrest is rarely made. When the officer leaves, the victim may be beaten even more severely for calling the police.

Both the battered woman and the rape victim were hesitant to use the criminal justice system before SOS. The judicial system reported that few abused women and rape victims filed against the perpetrator. The abuse victim's hesitancy was based on the system's inability to provide the emotional support she needed and on her lack of faith in the system to protect her. One of the most important jobs of our battered women's organization was to work on the criminal justice system, and initially we were not accepted by most.

Failure to investigate made prosecution impossible. In one case, a thirteen-year-old female had been raped by a forty-year-old male in a park where they were both at a party. The family came to SOS because they could not get anyone to investigate the crime. The sheriff's office said the victim "had a reputation," so they had not bothered to investigate. After talking to the district attorney, the sheriff's department finally relented, but the deputies refused to interview the perpetrator. "He isn't in town," a deputy told me. I told him that everybody in town knew where the offender was and I would be happy to drive the deputy there immediately. The law officer at first refused, but later he did go. On his "investigative report" he wrote "NO ONE was raped by ANYONE!"—forgetting, I suppose, that his job was to investigate and not to judge. This is a common story for battered women. Prejudice against the victim within the system is perhaps the most frustrating problem for me. I believe our justice system has the capacity to deter the cycle of victimization of women but all too often participates in revictimizing the abused.

Because of this bias, SOS initially worked abrasively with the system. We would harass the sheriff until he would serve the papers on the abuser, for the orders were not in effect until they were served. Finally, a few people stepped forward to assist us, enabling us to work more effectively within the system. We began to bypass those who would not work with us and to go directly to those who would. If the sheriff in one county refused to serve papers on a perpetrator, then we went to the judge or to the district attorney, and she or he would make the process happen. Or we went to a police officer who was known to help SOS serve papers. At times a department would want to assist a battered woman but was deterred by lack of funds, a common problem in rural law enforcement agencies. The sheriff's office must transport all prisoners and those legally committed, many times to out-of-town institutions. For some offices this meant traveling as far as 250 miles away, taking one of the three officers away from the community all day. Sheriffs often run out of mileage funds only a few months into the fiscal year. In rural Oklahoma, there is a significant lack of education of law enforcement agencies. Often SOS advocates had a better understanding of the law affecting abused women and children. SOS took on the responsibility for training and education about domestic abuse, homicide rates, protective orders, and new legislation affecting assault. We gained credibility and furthered cooperation.

Associate District Judge Lowell Burgess speaks about the first few years of SOS:

In a community like this one, and I have lived here all my life, ostracism has a lot to do with keeping women down. These women were continually ostracized by the legal system, both executive and judicial. They were banished. The abuse victim didn't know she had rights, so there was no remedy needed. As a result, it didn't come to our attention much back then. Law enforcement was hesitant to file—hitting your wife was seen as a marital privilege. Religion is used as a foundation for society and the community. This is a rural, agrarian, "Little Dixie" with macho attitudes.

SOS brought abuse out of the closet. People were forced to take it more seriously—to admit that it was a crime. It was no longer a defense that "she needed it." It made my job easier. I began to see healthy victims in the courtroom. SOS facilitated the courtroom process by making it a friendlier place. You come in and sit them down so they can look around, the courtroom is no longer a mystery. These women weren't dismissing the charges.

There were many snide comments around the Courthouse about SOS. It was viewed as a left wing, radical organization that nobody wanted around. It complicated things. It awoke their clients to their rights, even though there were already laws on the books that dictated this crime. There was no real change in the law, instead SOS came in and changed the environment in spite of this mentality. The lawyers thought you were just playing—that you would go away.[10]

The battered woman and her children have few options in a community where a family is "not to be interfered with." The legal system is only one example of a system with biases against abused women. Traditional social service systems have not been helpful for battered women. Local battered women report that the Department of Human Services, churches, and other helping services urge the abused woman to forgive and forget, go home, and be a better wife. Victim blaming is the reason that all battered women's programs must advocate for the abused woman in many different ways, but especially in rural programs where the battered woman usually *knows* the people she must ask for help.

The development of the SOS shelter mimics the history of the first shelters everywhere in that we struggled with facilities that were less than optimal. In November 1983, a concerned family in Idabel donated a dilapidated old farmhouse for our first shelter. In June

1986, we were forced to move because the house would not meet state standards. In response to a desperate plea, the local chapter of Epsilon Sigma Alpha sorority raised thousands of dollars from the community to pay for 50 percent of a new shelter, and the remaining mortgage is being paid using the rental income from another donated home. Currently, the Idabel shelter holds eighteen beds, and it is often full.

In Antlers, the Crisis Service Center is located in a home donated by the city. Open during business hours, the office provides transportation to shelter, counseling, advocacy, and community education. The center answers a crisis phone line twenty-four hours per day. Additionally, Hugo also has the same model of Crisis Service Center which recently moved from a city-owned complex to a house.

SOS served 800 people in 1991. This number has grown considerably over the years. In 1984 SOS served 130 people, in 1986 it served 310, and in 1987 the number grew to 535. The majority of these women were living at or below the poverty level. Although domestic violence is no more frequent in poorer families, SOS is more likely to serve these families which have fewer avenues of escape. The majority of families served are white, followed by American Indian. African Americans are underrepresented, reflecting the racial isolation in this community.

During their stay, the mothers are provided with advocacy in the areas of housing, employment, educational opportunities, and financial assistance and are assisted through courtroom proceedings. Approximately 68 percent of those in shelter are children. While at the shelter, children are free from violence. Living in a shelter which is designed for safety enables the child to understand there are alternatives to abuse. This supportive environment promotes further community among the women, many of whom choose to share houses and child care upon leaving. Many clients continue to receive counseling and advocacy after they leave the shelter, and even more become volunteers for the program. All services are voluntary.

SOS is designed to meet the very special rural needs of the abused woman. By establishing a *network* of programs to cover the area, SOS was better able to provide comprehensive crisis services to rural women and their children. Only by using volunteers was this possible. SOS was founded by volunteers and operated for many years on solely volunteer labor. These volunteers come from all walks of life; factory workers, business owners, mothers, welfare recipients, ministers, church groups, housewives, carpenters, and teachers are the people who have made this program.

Critical to the stamina of the program was the link with other shelters in the state. In 1982, I contacted the Oklahoma Coalition on Domestic Violence and Sexual Assault (OCDVSA), a network of crisis programs begun in 1978 by just a few women. In 1979 that group approached the legislature, which soon afterwards approved the first state funding for abused women. Today OCDVSA consists of twenty-five programs, and over the years it has been responsible for advocating, lobbying, and usually writing new legislation related to domestic violence and sexual assault. The power of the coalition is that *all* state funding is worked out at coalition meetings, as opposed to each program individually procuring funds from its legislator. Meeting others who were doing this same work gave me strength.

Ann Lowrance, director of domestic violence services for the Oklahoma Department of Mental Health and Substance Abuse Services, has this to say about the success of SOS:

> SOS services were organized to provide rapid response in emergency situations. The program was unique in that it developed, in a few short years, a series of programs spread across the area. SOS took the services to the abused woman, making safety geographically accessible to women who did not have access to car or money to escape.
>
> In 1982 the Southeastern Oklahoma community was readily identified as resistant to the State or an outside agency moving in and putting a social program in their area. SOS was successful because it was established and continues to be staffed by local people—the client trusts the staff because of this.[11]

According to local legend, we were the first feminist grassroots organization to successfully organize southeastern Oklahoma. Our organizational base was a conservative, fundamentalist community, and a radical approach would not work. Instead of saying "Bring down the Patriarch!" we said that "to not help the battered woman is to weaken the fabric of the family," and it worked. Still we had a divorce-promoting, family-bashing, man-hating image to counter. There were those who did their level best to shut us up and shut us down. In the beginning, we functioned in the face of great hostility.

There were many sacrifices made by all of those who built SOS up to where it is today. We worked with no wages and not much sleep.[12] There were times I would get incredibly frustrated, and I would wonder if it was worth it. Maybe "they" were right, and all of this was "unnecessary." But then I would get another call and hear a frightened battered woman telling me that her arm was broken and that her husband was gone but would be back in thirty minutes, all with the children screaming in the background. Suddenly it would be distinctly clear that there was a fundamental responsibility not only to continue, but also to hurry.

People would consistently ask whether I got burned out. My answer was always: I get burned out by the systems and people who believe that the battered woman deserves or somehow asks for the abuse she suffers. I have never once heard a story, however tragic, that burned me out or made me tired. The stories fueled me. Because what this woman was telling me is not that she was tortured, cut, kicked, whipped, or shot at, but that she survived. I was just so proud and happy to see her alive, standing there talking to me.

Fortunately, the response of the systems has changed. There are many supporters. Community education, coupled with the national attention domestic violence has received, has paid off; SOS is a household word.

For all the barriers to battered women, I believe that SOS is a success *because* it is rural. In rural Oklahoma we say that we take care of our own. This was the model we used to develop services for battered women, and the community could respond to this idea. We worked with what we had and we did not yield to troubled times, and by doing so we retained the essence of what living in rural Oklahoma means.

NOTES

1. Gerda Lerner, "Placing Women in History: A 1975 Perspective," in *Liberating Women's History,* ed. Berenice A. Carroll (Champaign: University of Illinois Press, 1976), 360.

2. Ibid., 353–54.

3. Quoted in Susan Schechter, *Women and Male Violence: The Visions and Struggles of the Battered Women's Movement* (Boston: South End Press, 1982), 217.

4. Ibid.

5. Violence toward women includes any assault, beating, or rape. Rape occurs in the United States at one of the highest rates in the world and is believed to be on the increase in rural areas.

6. Excerpted from task force minutes, Aug. 19, 1982.

7. The Valliant Police Department was the first to use SOS for the battered women they encountered. They called consistently and offered many women assistance in leaving their abusive partner.

8. SOS provided services until other programs developed in these counties.

9. In 1982 the Protection from Domestic Abuse Act was passed by the Oklahoma legislature. This was a milestone in justice for battered women. With this act, the battered woman could obtain relief such as ordering the abuser not to abuse, communicate, contact, or otherwise harass her. She could also ask that the abuser leave the home, although some judges were hesitant to order that. No lawyer is needed to claim relief, and it does not cost anything. Before this law the woman was required to file for divorce to get similar relief.

10. Excerpted from an interview, Aug. 19, 1989.

11. Excerpted from an interview, Jan. 25, 1990.

12. The first financial support was given by the Antlers Mental Health Thrift Store and amounted to twenty-five dollars a month. The first major funding was not received until April 1983, when we received three thousand dollars from the Eastern Oklahoma Union Presbytery Self Development of People Fund.

18

OKLAHOMA'S GAY LIBERATION MOVEMENT

Thomas E. Guild, Joan Luxenburg,
and Keith Smith

Homophobia runs deep and wide, including in Oklahoma. In recent years, an additional pressure on the gay/lesbian community has come from AIDS, and the automatic tendency of many to assume that it is purely a homosexual malady. Recently I heard it suggested that AIDS is purely a behavioral problem, that people who get it are trying to get it. And more than one right-wing extremist Christian evangelist has suggested that AIDS is God's revenge on the homosexual community for their sinful behavior. Clearly, there is much ignorance, misinformation, and bigotry abroad in relation to homosexuality. Historical work on the gay rights movement, such as the following essay, should help. Guild taught political science and now teaches business law at the University of Central Oklahoma in Edmond; Luxenburg teaches sociology at the same institution; Smith serves on the Oklahoma and national boards of the American Civil Liberties Union and is the executive director of New Mexico AIDS Services, Inc.

New York City gave birth to the Gay Liberation movement, through the Stonewall uprising in late June 1969.[1] By the early 1970s most communities in America were experiencing some form of cultural and/or political expression of personhood by gays.[2] How each gay community proceeded was dependent upon its resources, its indigenous leadership, and its sense of the prevailing climate for social change in the larger, surrounding community. This paper will present Oklahoma's "coming out"—the development of gay consciousness and the few, but significant, legal battles for gay rights that occurred in the post-Stonewall years from 1969 through 1989.

The background of Oklahoma's gay liberation movement is couched in the nation's gay liberation movement. The larger movement began with the Stonewall revolt.[3] On Friday evening, June 27, 1969, close to midnight, New York City police began a routine raid on a Greenwich Village gay bar, the Stonewall Inn. However, as the bar employees and patrons began to show some resistance, social contagion spread through the gathering crowd of homosexuals outside the bar. Rocks were thrown at police, the bar was set on fire, and rioting broke out. The rioting continued on the next two evenings. Some four hundred police clashed with some two thousand gay protesters. A speech by poet Allen Ginsberg at the Stonewall that Sunday evening called for recognition of the new approach that gays would be taking—the fight for gay liberation.

The Stonewall riots prompted gay leaders across the nation to call for widespread organizing for change. Within a few weeks after the Stonewall triggering event, gay liberation groups throughout the country began forming and making their presence known. While existing homophile organizations had previously sought assimilation (principally through concealing one's identity), the gay liberation movement represented a different strategy.[4] The new stance stepped away from accommodation and toward rebellion—away from tolerance seeking and toward expressing gay pride and accompanying demands for freedom.[5] Rose Weitz has characterized this move as one from secondary to tertiary deviance, in which individuals not only adapt and adjust to the deviant identity but also assert their right to be different.[6] The timing for such a movement was ripe, as the 1960s black civil rights movement, women's liberation movement, and anti–Vietnam War movement served as models for widening horizons. Demonstrations of pride and legal challenges against discrimination would characterize this movement.

Oklahoma would experience its share of gay activism in the 1970s and 1980s. It would witness the growth of a gay community—one that would "come out." Gay Oklahomans would organize to provide political leadership, to combat discrimination, to push for reform, and to fight for their existence. While space does not permit us to mention all of the gay and lesbian organizations, publications, and events of the past two decades, some of the more outstanding contributions are presented here.

ORGANIZATIONS

One of the more influential gay community political groups to form in the post-Stonewall era in Oklahoma was the Oklahomans for Human Rights (OHR), organized in 1979 in Oklahoma City principally by attorney Bill Rogers. That same year, Tulsans began organizing a chapter of OHR. By 1980 the Tulsa chapter was holding meetings with as many as fifty attendees. They also held social events and fund-raisers. According to Paul Thompson, a past president of Oklahoma City's OHR, the organization catered to professionals, many of whom could not be associated with an organization that would have "gay" in its title.[7] OHR began publishing a newsletter known as *Our Time*. One of the individuals associated with the publication later helped start the *Gayly Oklahoman,* a monthly statewide newspaper which premiered in October 1983 and which by 1989 had an estimated readership of thirty thousand to forty thousand.[8]

OHR was instrumental in spearheading the drive to get a gay community center established in Oklahoma City. The owners of Angles (a gay disco in Oklahoma City) donated a nearby building for the center. Members of the gay community contributed materials, labor, money, and so on, to help establish the Oasis Gay Community Center in October 1983.[9] (In 1989, the name was changed to the Oasis Resource Center.[10]) The formal opening of Oasis was celebrated during national Gay Pride Week of 1984 (the week commemorating the Stonewall incident).[11] During the opening of Oasis, the first annual Gay Pride (39th Street) Block Party was held. On North West 39th Street (off of Pennsylvania Avenue) there are several gay bars. This area is generally known by gays as "the strip." Today it includes a gay diner, the Herland women's bookstore, and, of course, Oasis. While there are several gay bars within a few minutes from the strip, the 39th Street area seems to contain most of the gay community's spirit. The annual Gay Pride Parade (first held in June 1988) culminates at this location. Local homophobes derogatorily refer to the strip as "Gay Town" or "Homo Heights," and it has experienced some incidents of antigay harassment and violence.

A few months after Oasis opened, the center's board voted to eliminate OHR from further participation. To keep the center financially supported, Angles began hosting an annual Christmas Carnival fund-raiser. Various gay organizations and local entertainers participate. An estimated three thousand dollars is often raised at this event.[12] Oasis provides an information and referral phone line, meeting space for several groups (including the AIDS Coalition), a food bank, and a clothes closet.

Eventually OHR in Oklahoma City dissipated. The Tulsa branch (known as TOHR), however, remained very active. TOHR's official publication, the *TOHR Reporter,* is distributed monthly and has a mailing list of over 750. The group's mission is to help bring an end to discrimination against persons based upon sexual or affectional preference. Attendance at monthly meetings varies from 30 to 150. Their efforts include an information phone line, an HIV and AIDS testing free clinic, and seed money for Tulsa's AIDS Support Program. A major TOHR event is an annual Benefit Auction and Dinner.

Perhaps the most promising new political group to form was the Oklahoma Gay Political Caucus (OGPC), which held its first annual convention in Tulsa in 1985.[13] OGPC voted in April 1989 to change its name to the Oklahoma Gay and Lesbian Political Caucus (OGLPC). Recent activities of the Oklahoma City–based group include a gay voter registration drive as well as encouraging nongays to support the gay political agenda.[14] Each year the OGLPC presents its Bill Rogers Award of Merit. Alternatively, it presents its Phobie Award or Awards to individuals who have done the most harm to the gay community and its goals. In 1989, Oklahoma City Councilman Mark Schwartz received the Bill Rogers Award for having introduced an ordinance (which subsequently passed) increasing penalties for acts of violence motivated by racist, anti-Semitic, and homophobic hatred.[15]

Some of the more specialized groups promoting gay culture within Oklahoma include the Herland women's collective and the

Oklahoma Gay Rodeo Association (OGRA). Herland Sister Resources began as a small women's bookstore in Oklahoma City in 1980. Barbara Cleveland is considered the main early-day force and is known as "Mother Herland." In 1982 the group began publishing a newsletter, *The Herland Voice,* which has a current circulation of seven hundred. Herland holds annual retreats, sponsors concerts, holds support groups, and maintains a feminist library and bookstore.

The OGRA, formed in 1984,[16] is affiliated with the International Gay Rodeo Association (IGRA). In August 1986, Oklahoma experienced what has been reported to be "one of the most ambitious gay endeavors in Oklahoma history" by hosting the Great Plains Regional Rodeo at the Oklahoma State Fair Grounds.[17] Oklahoma City hosted the event again in 1989.

LEGAL BATTLES

Several important lawsuits were filed in the 1970s and 1980s on behalf of gay rights in Oklahoma. The first of these occurred in 1972 in the city of Norman at the University of Oklahoma (OU). A student group, originally called the Norman Gay Alliance for Sexual Freedom and later referred to as the Gay Community Alliance for Sexual Freedom,[18] sought the same privileges enjoyed by other student organizations at OU. More than 120 people had begun organizing this group as early as October 1, 1971.[19] The group first announced its formation on January 25, 1972, at a breakfast with OU President Paul Sharp.[20] Although the group had complied with university regulations for registering itself and was recognized by the Student Congress on February 15, 1972, the university denied the organization permission to open an account with the bursar, thereby denying the group a host of services (including meeting space). Upon President Sharp's recommendation, the regents for OU voted in April 1972 not to recognize the group. With the American Civil Liberties Union (ACLU) representing the group, on April 13, 1972, Cleveland County District Court Judge Elvin J. Brown issued a writ of mandamus ordering the regents to recognize the group or to show cause in court.

On August 21, 1972, Judge Brown ruled in favor of the organization and stated: "No one has offered a single authority to the effect that a homosexual citizen has any more or less constitutional rights than the heterosexual citizen and for good reason. Not only is there not any such authority, but responsible people involved in this case would denounce such if it existed. Both the homosexual and heterosexual citizen have equal and correlative constitutional rights to equal, fair, and impartial application of reasonable laws, and to be treated equally and fairly by the state, of which the University of Oklahoma is a part.''[21] Judge Brown also said: "Until such time as it is permissible to discriminate against women who have had hysterectomies, men who have had vasectomies, or children who suffer the misfortune of being born asexual or bisexual, it will also be unconstitutionally discriminatory to deny equal rights and privileges to homosexuals.''[22]

Five years later, the ACLU returned to court on behalf of OU's Gay Activist Alliance (GAA). On October 26, 1976, the GAA was denied recognition by the University of Oklahoma Student Association Congress, allegedly ''for the students' own good.''[23] There was some apparent apprehension within the congress that the state legislature would not continue to grant funding for the OU recreation center if the group were recognized.[24]

On February 15, 1977, after exhausting all administrative remedies, the GAA filed suit in the Cleveland County District Court. On August 10, 1978, that court ruled against the GAA.[25] On September 11, 1978, the GAA appealed to the Oklahoma Supreme Court. On December 22, 1981, the supreme court ruled in favor of the GAA (although the court affirmed the district court's refusal of damages). In its majority opinion, the court stated: ''As the record is lacking in evidence showing disruptive or illegal activities, mere undifferentiated fear or apprehension on the part of the University Regents or disagreement with philosophy no matter how repugnant to these officials is not enough to overcome First Amendment freedoms.''[26]

The GAA's next major struggle with the university occurred when the student congress denied funding to them in 1983. A group of students calling themselves the Heterosexual Activist Alliance (HAA) formed in 1983, and its president succeeded in getting the student congress to reject funding for both groups. After a year-long struggle, the GAA finally received funding.[27] The group's funding for 1989–90 was fourteen hundred dollars.[28]

In 1983 the GAA was instrumental in attempting to add sexual/
affectional preference to the list of protected classes in Norman's
antidiscrimination ordinance. The measure, however, was rejected
by the City Council, with only two council members voting in favor
of it.[29]

In 1984 the GAA renamed itself the Gay/Lesbian Alliance
(G/LA). Their current controversy with the university involves the
group's petition to amend the Student Code to include an antidiscrimination clause for gay students.[30] When the university's regents
rejected such an amendment in May 1989, the G/LA staged a protest
demonstration at the U.S. Olympic Festival's opening ceremonies at
the campus in July 1989.[31] As the G/LA pursued that issue, one of
its former officers attempted to establish a Lesbian/Gay Alumni
(L/GA) group within the university's alumni association. A Black
Alumni Society already exists. As of December 1989, President
Richard Van Horn had not approved the L/GA. The group contemplated legal recourse.[32]

The gay student organization at Oklahoma State University
(OSU) in Stillwater also experienced some difficulty in its formation. The group was originally rejected by the Student Government
Association (SGA). When the group solicited the support of the
American Civil Liberties Union and threatened a lawsuit, the OSU
administration recognized the group on March 30, 1984, but in
exchange for such recognition "forced" the name Students for
Homosexual Awareness (SFHA) on the group.[33] A group of OSU
students calling themselves Heterosexuals for Moral Living tried to
form, but were denied recognition on April 20, 1984.[34]

The university arena was not the only setting for gay rights lawsuits. Perhaps the most significant litigation with regard to gay
rights in Oklahoma was that of the *National Gay Task Force* v.
Board of Education of the City of Oklahoma City.[35] Although no
actual firing was involved, the National Gay Task Force (NGTF),
some of whose members are Oklahoma teachers, brought suit in
1980 challenging the constitutionality of a state law enacted in
1978.[36] The case received national attention and caused apprehension on all sides involved, both vicariously and directly for several
years. On March 26, 1985, the case resulted in a U.S. Supreme
Court per curiam opinion in which the lower court's judgment was

affirmed by an equally divided Court.[37] This summary affirmance by the Court left intact the decision of the Tenth Circuit Court of Appeals, which had found parts of the Oklahoma statute unconstitutional. The Oklahoma law in question called for the dismissal or suspension of Oklahoma teachers for engaging in "crimes against nature" with a person of the same sex that was indiscreet and not practiced in private. The court went on to add that the school may constitutionally fire a teacher for engaging in indiscreet public acts of oral and anal intercourse. The "public" element of these activities takes this portion out of the "privacy" model as it is understood by most people.

The Circuit Court analyzed other sections of the Oklahoma statute on grounds of First Amendment free speech and freedom of association and held parts of the law unconstitutional. The court declared that "the First Amendment does not permit someone to be punished for advocating illegal conduct at some indefinite future time."[38] The state statute provided for suspension or dismissal of teachers for "advocating, encouraging or promoting public or private homosexual activity."[39] The Circuit Court found this portion of the law unconstitutionally broad in hindering free-speech rights of teachers. The Tenth Circuit, dealing with the statute, went on to hold that "a state has interests in regulating the speech of teachers that differ from its interests in regulating the speech of the general citizenry. But a state's interests outweigh the teacher's interests only when the expression results in material or substantial interference or disruption in normal activities of the school."[40]

The Tenth Circuit further opined that the unconstitutionally overbroad portion of the statute was severable from the constitutional portion of the law, which merely proscribed public homosexual activity (that is, sexual conduct) by Oklahoma teachers. The appellate court pointed out that a teacher arguing for repeal of the Oklahoma antisodomy statute would be advocating homosexual sodomy "and creating a substantial risk that his speech would come to the attention of school children or employees if he said, 'I think it is psychologically damaging for people with homosexual desires to suppress those desires. They should act on those desires and be legally free to do so.' Such statements, which are aimed at legal and social change, are at the core of First Amendment protections."[41]

The Circuit Court, in essence, said that free speech extends to all issues of public debate, including whether or not to decriminalize certain sexual behavior. Because the U.S. Supreme Court's vote was an evenly divided one, the ruling is binding only upon Oklahoma and the other states in the Tenth Circuit (Colorado, Kansas, New Mexico, Utah, and Wyoming). Oklahoma, however, held the distinction of being the only state in the nation to have such a law.[42] Despite its confinement to only the states in the Tenth Circuit, the decision was lauded to be "a benchmark of the progress of the gay rights movement."[43]

Two federal district court cases out of Oklahoma City in 1983 are also indicative of the federal court system's vindication of the civil rights of homosexuals. In one case, Oklahoma City was ordered by a federal judge to rent agreed-upon space in its Myriad Convention Center to a firm promoting a national pageant for female impersonators. In that case, Federal District Court Judge David Russell ruled that the Miss Gay America Pageant must proceed as scheduled. Judge Russell concluded, "The First Amendment values free and open expression, even if distasteful to the majority, including personally distasteful to this court."[44]

The other case of interest brings us full circle to the Stonewall incident. The case was filed in federal district court by the owners of Angles (the gay disco) against Oklahoma City and certain members of its police department. The police were accused of conducting a campaign of terror, abuse, intimidation, and harassment against customers and employees at Angles. Specifically, it was alleged that during the first six days that Angles had been in operation (in September of 1982), several police officers entered the bar on a daily basis intimidating customers, calling them "queers" and "faggots," shining flashlights in their faces, and so on. Additionally, the police were alleged to have issued the bar citations for offenses that either did not take place or were not in existence. These activities continued into the months of October, November, and December 1982 and January 1983 and included alleged physical assaults on customers.

In February 1983, the bar's owners filed their suit. The case came to an end on October 17, 1983, when a permanent injunction was issued by Federal District Court Judge Luther Eubanks enjoining the city and its police from violating the plaintiff's constitutional rights. Angles was awarded $1.00 in damages (plus over $23,000 in attorney's fees and more than $4,000 as expenses). The consent decree was agreed to by the Oklahoma City Council and the plaintiffs.[45]

CONCLUSION

If one were to compare the gay rights movement in Oklahoma to that of the gay liberation movement in the United States as a whole, it is useful to divide the movement into its different segments: (1) community and political organizing and (2) litigation of claims of discrimination. Since the gay rights movement began nationally with community and political organizing in 1969 (the Stonewall incident) and not until 1979 in Oklahoma (the founding of OHR), it is clear that the climate was not ripe for such action in Oklahoma until approximately ten years after such organizing began in New York City and elsewhere. It would be reasonable to postulate that today, in terms of visible political action and success in developing an internally cohesive community, Oklahoma is in a similar approximate ten-year cyclical lag.

As far as litigation of discrimination claims, the Oklahoma gay community seems to be very much on a contemporary par with the rest of the nation. While it required court action in the 1970s and 1980s for a gay student group to gain recognition at OU, OSU's student organization was recognized later in the 1980s without the need to go to court. Noteworthy is the fact that by 1991 the University of Central Oklahoma (UCO) did not require litigation for its group, Gay Lesbian Alliance for Student Support (GLASS), to gain official status. It can reasonably be assumed that the success of the OSU and UCO groups without resorting to the courts is directly related to the victories which the OU student group enjoyed in its court challenges of the homophobic power structure.

The successful litigation in 1980 challenging the right of Oklahoma City public school teachers to enjoy First Amendment rights also points to the favorable climate of Oklahoma's courts, as well as to that of the Tenth Circuit Court of Appeals. When it came to court battles for Oklahoma gay rights activists in either federal or state courts or on the federal appellate level, the stereotype of Oklahoma as a very religious, homophobic state (the "buckle of the Bible

Belt'') seemed to weaken. The conservative attitudes present among Oklahomans may have inhibited only the initial gay organizing during the post-Stonewall years. When gay activists had their day in court, Oklahoma proved to be quite hospitable to those promoting equality for this minority group.

Clearly there were shades of the Stonewall reappearing in the Angles incident. It was 1982—not 1969—and a couple of thousand miles from New York City that a small community representing gay Oklahoma citizens stood up to police harassment. There was no outbreak of rioting, merely an exercise of rights through the court system. The events of the 1970s and 1980s occurring within the gay community in Oklahoma did not occur in a vacuum. They were part of the collective (though seemingly fragmented) activities that began nationwide following on the heels of the Stonewall incident. Other states dealt with the issues of gay teachers, gay college student organizations, and so on. Each victory for gay rights gave impetus for the next. Each defeat led to a resolve among gays to work harder against the forces that impeded their progress.

It was not a lack of enthusiasm that almost kept Oklahoma's first Gay Pride March from happening. Gay leaders had spoken about a march for several years before its first occurrence in 1988. However, there were fears that antigay violence would mar the event. These fears were not totally without foundation. The prevailing social climate of the surrounding community was not welcoming. The mentality of some Oklahoma homophobes was articulated by a popular Oklahoma City radio disc jockey, who won a 1989 OGLPC Phobie award for having suggested to his listeners that they get in their cars and ''mow down some queers on 39th Street'' during the event.[47] In keeping with the theme for the first year (''Rightfully Proud in '88''), march organizers chose representatives from the local AIDS support program to serve as honorary grand marshals to lead off the parade. Despite rumors that the Ku Klux Klan would protest, there was only one minor counterdemonstration (from a local Baptist church) during the event, which was attended by an estimated four hundred people.[48]

The second annual Gay Pride March in 1989 was even larger. The T-shirt sold by Oasis for the 1989 Gay Pride Week contained a definition of Stonewall on the front. On the back of the shirt was the national Gay Pride Week's slogan for that year, "A Generation of Pride." The shirt's designer (an Oasis board member) remarked to one of the authors that an entire generation has grown up around the country enjoying a sense of gay personhood. Oklahomans are clearly part of that experience.

NOTES

1. For a discussion of the Stonewall incident, see John D'Emilio, *Sexual Politics, Sexual Communities: The Making of A Homosexual Minority in the United States, 1940–1970* (Chicago: University of Chicago Press, 1983), 231–32.

2. See Barry D. Adam, "A Social History of Gay Politics," in *Gay Men: The Sociology of Male Homosexuality* ed. Martin P. Levine (New York: Harper and Row, 1979), 285–300, specifically 291–94. The writers have chosen to interchange the words *homosexual* and *gay* to stand for both males and females who are same-sex–oriented, as well as to use the word *lesbian* at other times to specifically mean a female who is same-sex–oriented or woman-identified.

3. For a comprehensive discussion of the first twenty years of the post-Stonewall gay rights movement in the United States, see Joan Luxenburg and Thomas E. Guild, "20 Years after the Stonewall: Legal and Political Movement in Gay Rights," paper read at the annual meeting of the Society for the Study of Social Problems, Berkeley, Calif., Aug. 1989.

4. Adam, "Social History," 290–94.

5. See Rose Weitz, "From Accommodation to Rebellion: The Politicization of Lesbianism," in *Women-Identified Women,* ed. Trudy Darty and Sandee Potter (Palo Alto: Mayfield Publishing Company), 233–48.

6. Ibid., 245–46.

7. Paul Thompson to the author, Dec. 20, 1989. See also *Gayly Oklahoman,* Oct. 1988, p. 21.

8. Brochure, Gayly Advertising Dept., n.d., n.p.

9. *Gayly Oklahoman,* Oct. 1988, p. 21.

10. Ibid., Dec. 1989, p. 5.

11. Ibid., July 1984, p. 7.

12. Ibid., Oct. 1988, p. 21.

13. Ibid., Sept. 1985, p. 6.

14. Ibid., May 1989, p. 10.

15. Ibid., Apr. 1989, p. 9. See also, *Herland Sister Resources Newsletter,* Apr. 1989, p. 1, for a discussion of Article IV, Sections 25-53 and 25-54, of the Oklahoma City Municipal Code. The ordinance includes sexual orientation as a protected class with regard to intimidation or harassment.

16. *Program, 1989 Great Plains Rodeo,* n.d., n.p., 17.

17. *Gayly Oklahoman,* June 1986, p. 8.

18. Early media reports (such as in the OU student newspaper, *Oklahoma Daily,* Jan. 27, 1972, p. 1) refer to the former name, while later media reports (*Oklahoma Daily,* Sept. 1, 1972), p. 1) refer to the latter name.

19. *Oklahoma Daily,* Jan. 27, 1972, p. 1.

20. Ibid., p. 2.

21. Ibid., p. 1.

22. Speech notes, Shirley Barry (Executive Director, American Civil Liberties Union of Oklahoma), ''You Are Not Alone,'' speech given to Oklahomans for Human Rights, Oklahoma City, Aug. 14, 1983, p. 5.

23. *Oklahoma Daily,* Oct. 28, 1976, p. 1.

24. Ibid.

25. *Gay Activists Alliance v. Board of Regents of the University of Oklahoma,* 638 P. 2d 1116, 1119 (Okla. 1981).

26. Ibid., 1120.

27. *Gayly Oklahoman,* Dec. 1984, p. 5.

28. *OU Update: The Monthly Newsletter of the Gay/Lesbian Alliance* 1, no. 3 (Winter 1989–90): 1.

29. *Gayly Oklahoman,* Dec. 1988, p. 6. See also *Dallas Voice,* Oct. 12, 1984, and *Oklahoma City Times,* Nov. 2, 1983, pp. 1–2.

30. *OU Update* 1, no. 3 (Winter 1989–90): 1.

31. *Saturday Oklahoman and Times,* July 15, 1989, p. 16, and July 22, 1989, p. 15.

32. *OU Update* 1, no. 3 (Winter 1989–90): 5.

33. *Gayly Oklahoman,* May 1984, p. 7, and May 1989, p. 25.

34. *Gayly Oklahoman,* May 1984, p. 7.

35. 729 F. 2d 1270 (10th Cir. 1984), aff'd by an equally divided court, 470 U.S. 903 (1985).

36. 729 F. 2d 1272. See also *Daily Oklahoman and Times,* Mar. 15, 1984, p. 9.

37. *National Gay Task Force,* 470 U.S. 903 (1985).

38. *National Gay Task Force,* 729 F. 2d 1270, 1274 (10th Cir. 1984).

39. Oklahoma Statutes, Title 70, Sect. 5-103.15 (West Supp. 1984).

40. *National Gay Task Force,* 729 F. 2d 1270, 1274.

41. Ibid.

42. Ralph Slovenko, foreword, ''The Homosexual and Society: A Historical Perspective,'' *University of Dayton Law Review* 10, no. 3 (Spring 1985): 453. Slovenko credits former Miss Oklahoma, Anita Bryant, with helping get the law passed when she spoke out against gay teachers before the Oklahoma legislature in 1978.

43. *New York Times,* Mar. 27, 1985, Section 1, p. 9.

44. *Saturday Oklahoman and Times,* Sept. 9, 1983, p. 27.

45. *Cotton-Eyed Joes, Inc., v. The City of Oklahoma City,* No. CIV-83-314-E (W. D. Okla. Oct. 17, 1983). For specific allegations, see ibid., complaint filed Feb. 11, 1983.

46. Some of the more noteworthy cases involving gay teachers in the 1970s and 1980s are discussed in Rhonda Rivera, ''Queer Law: Sexual Orientation Law in the Mid-Eighties: Part I,'' *University of Dayton Law Review* 10, no. 3 (Spring 1984): 514–35, and Rhonda Rivera, ''Our Straight-Laced Judges: The Legal Position of

Homosexual Persons in the United States.'' *Hastings Law Journal* 30 (Mar. 1979): 862–74. For a dicsussion of relevant 1970s through mid-1980s cases involving gay student organizations, see Kenneth Lasson, ''Civil Liberties for Homosexuals: The Law in Limbo,'' *University of Dayton Law Review* 10, no. 3 (Spring 1985): 661–63.

47. *Gayly Oklahoman*, Apr. 1989, p. 9.

48. Ibid.; see also, *Daily Oklahoman*, June 20, 1988, p. 5.

19

EVEN AMONG THE SOONERS, THERE ARE MORE IMPORTANT THINGS THAN FOOTBALL

Alan Ehrenhalt

The following essay by Alan Ehrenhalt, from the November 1989 issue of Governing, probes a very sensitive issue in Oklahoma: education, and the commitment (or lack thereof) to excellence in education. A noticeable and ugly strand of anti-intellectualism has been evident in Oklahoma's history. Richard Hofstadter's Anti-Intellectualism in American Life included a thoughtful definitional section entitled "On the Unpopularity of Intellect," in which he wrote: "Again and again . . . it has been noticed that intellect in America is resented as a kind of excellence, as a claim to distinction, as a challenge to egalitarianism, as a quality which almost certainly deprives a man or woman of the common touch."[1] Just so in Oklahoma, where a governor ("Alfalfa Bill" Murray) can refer to professors as "high-toned bums" and where we, to quote Rennard Strickland, "pay teachers a pittance and then complain that students cannot read and do not know the state's heritage."[2] The $230 million education and tax reform bill passed by the state legislature in April 1990—under pressure from a massive teacher walkout—perhaps offers a note of hope.

Five days before Thanksgiving, the Oklahoma Sooners will take the field against Nebraska for what has become the decisive event of Big Eight college football—the game that virtually always determines the conference championship and sometimes the national championship besides.

The Sooners will be everything Oklahoma football teams have been since the end of World War II: proud, competitive and convinced that, win or lose, no one in the country does their job any better.

They will be everything their university is not.

It has been more than 30 years since the president of the University of Oklahoma, George Lynn Cross, startled a committee of state legislators and attracted national attention by remarking that he wanted to create a school his football team could be proud of. Since then, the Oklahoma higher education system has done a lot of commendable things. It has maintained campuses in every corner of the state and offered college training to thousands of kids, tenant farmers' kids and oil workers' kids, who never expected to get that far. And it has done it at bargain basement prices—it has been difficult to find cheaper tuition anywhere in the country.

What Oklahoma has never had is a great university. By most conventional measurements, it has never even had a good one. The University of Oklahoma in Norman accepts 95 percent of all applicants. Its faculty salaries have been below the average even for Southern and Southwestern schools. When it comes to federal research contracts, OU does not rank in the top 100. It has never been admitted to the Association of American Universities, the organization of 50 high-quality public and private schools that has long included such neighbors and rivals as Texas, Kansas, Iowa and Iowa State.

Oklahoma political leaders have always known that their school was not the equal of Ann Arbor, Berkeley or Chapel Hill, but for most of the postwar years, they did not much care: Oil-financed prosperity allowed them to put aside questions of educational quality. And George Cross may not have built a school the football team could be proud of, but he had created a football team the whole state could worship.

''The commitment to academic life is basically not part of our culture," concedes Paul Sharp, who was president of OU for seven years. "You didn't have to have an education in Oklahoma to stick a hole in the ground and make a fortune. Prosperity was never associated with education."

Oklahoma's attitude began to change on July 5, 1982, the day that Penn Square Bank of Oklahoma City, one of the state's largest financial institutions, collapsed under the weight of hundreds of millions of dollars in uncollectible loans, most of them to small independent oil producers. That was the beginning of the oil price depression in Oklahoma, a calamity with which the state is still struggling. In the climate of economic stagnation, Oklahomans have reached a consensus that their economy has to be built on more than oil.

In the past five years, Oklahoma has begun wooing businesses worldwide, and has found them less interested in the university's football team than in the quality of its physics department. In 1985, after the state launched a million-dollar lobbying effort to attract the federal Super Collider project, only to be told that its state universities were not up to handling the related research, some prominent Oklahomans began admitting that maybe their priorities had been a little askew.

"We prioritized where we finished in football," says Representative Carolyn Thompson, a Democrat, "and we never cared where we finished in libraries. That's changed because of the oil bust."

"It's glibly stated by our athletic fans that we are a great university," adds J. R. Morris, another former OU president. "What it takes to be a great university is beyond their perspective."

But the perspective of the state's leadership, if not of all its football fans, is changing. In July of 1985, the legislature appointed a task force, chaired by Oklahoma City banker James Tolbert, to conduct a massive study of the state's higher education system. Early last year, the task force gave the legislature the unflattering report it was expecting to receive. "Oklahoma's Secret Crisis," the task force called the situation.

"Even prior to recent years of declining resources," the task force stated, "education was not funded in a manner that could produce excellence. . . . No one has defined clearly the elements necessary to shape the future of quality higher education."

It is easy to look at Oklahoma—football-mad, anti-intellectual Oklahoma—and see an eccentric state that owes its higher education troubles to its unique history and outlook. But Oklahoma is different only in degree.

Every state education system has its elitists and its populists. Oklahoma simply has had more than its share of populists—people more concerned about providing some education for the many than a superior education for the few. In the 1960s, as it chose to maintain its sprawling network of colleges and universities, Oklahoma was simply practicing what President Lyndon B. Johnson was preaching in Washington.

"It is the obligation of your nation," Johnson announced in 1965, as he signed the Higher Education Act, "to provide and permit and assist every child born in these borders to receive all the education he can take." As LBJ saw it, going to college—almost any college—was the route out of poverty and into the middle class for people of all races.

Johnson wasn't against excellence; he simply saw no reason why states couldn't maintain great universities while offering college degrees to a mass market. And some states could: wealthy ones, like California, or those with long traditions of academic achievement, like Michigan. But many other states couldn't afford both access and excellence. They chose access.

What the task force told Oklahoma in 1987 was that it needed to re-examine its choice. "It is now time to declare victory in the battle for access," the task force reported, "and make the enormous commitment required for a fundamental increase in the quality of the system."

In this context, one begins to understand the presence of Hans Brisch, Oklahoma's new chancellor of higher education. He is the fourth chancellor the system has had, and the first one who has not been a local product. Brisch was not even born in the United States. He came to this country from Germany in the 1950s and still speaks with a distinct accent. He is a political science Ph.D. and classroom teacher. The Oklahoma state regents hired him away from the governor of Nebraska, for whom he was working as chief of staff.

Brisch arrived in Oklahoma in April proclaiming that the time had come to launch a new era in Oklahoma education, to create a great research university at OU and another at Oklahoma State. He was not hesitant to say things that some of Oklahoma's past educational leaders were reluctant to say—that there are more important things in life than football. "I don't want people just to see the football team as the symbol of Oklahoma," he insisted. "Fooball doesn't capture the essence of what we need to be about. . . . My emphasis is on academics."

But it is not the things Brisch has said that have made him controversial. It is the things that have happened since he showed up. In midsummer, with very little warning, the state regents under Brisch's leadership announced that they were changing the means by which funds for the state's colleges and universities are distributed. No longer would any school receive a fixed amount of money based simply on its enrollment. From now on, Brisch and the regents would fund the schools according to a "peer system." Each school would be compared with similar institutions elsewhere in the country and funded in a way that allowed it to be competitive with those institutions. No official list of peers was published. Anyone was free to conclude that Brisch and the regents were making the idea up to justify their own priorities.

But the effect of the change was clear. Brisch needed money to make the University of Oklahoma and Oklahoma State into the outstanding research centers he envisioned, and the money was going to come out of the budgets of the junior colleges and the four-year regional universities in the system.

The legislature had appropriated nearly $30 million in extra funding for the new academic year, but it was not going to be evenly divided. Under the new system, more than 60 percent of that money would go to the University of Oklahoma or to Oklahoma State; most of the smaller schools would get very little. And the legislature was limited by law to providing a single lump sum for education, which Brisch and the regents could distribute as they saw fit.

Brisch suddenly became a very unpopular man in the legislature. "It's just an insult," said the chairman of the Senate Appropriations Committee, Democrat Stratton Taylor, whose hometown school, Rogers State, was one of the many losers. The House majority leader, Democrat Guy Davis of Durant, said the legislature might well respond by cutting the entire budget for higher education. The new chancellor had not just taken on an educational bureaucracy— he had challenged a crucial element of the state's political system.

Oklahoma is a conservative state. It is also a populist state. It is very reluctant to spend taxpayers' money, but what it does spend it likes to spread among as many regions and interests as it can.

That helps to explain why Oklahoma has what might charitably be described as one of the more unwieldy higher education systems in the country: 27 state colleges and universities for about three million people. Twelve of the 27 are full four-year institutions granting bachelors' degrees. By contrast, Iowa, with almost the same population, has just three four-year public colleges. Florida, with roughly 12 million people, has only nine. "We have too many colleges to support," says Sandy Garrett, who recently became higher education secretary in Governor Henry Bellmon's Republican administration. "We've fallen on hard times. It's hard to support all these institutions."

Oklahoma has always had more public colleges than it needed, but no one has ever succeeded in effectively cutting the system back. To maintain 27 public colleges is to advertise that college training in Oklahoma is for everyone. It is said often, and not in jest, that no person in the state lives more than a half-hour from higher education.

When it comes to football, people all over the state are content to bask in the reflected glory of the Sooners. The people at Panhandle State in Goodwell or the other regional colleges scattered throughout Oklahoma have never begrudged OU its football program—but when it comes to education, the feeling is different. None of the lesser schools want OU to be that much greater than they are. "Football is a statewide pride," says Larry Nutter, the president of Rose State College. "In education, the pride is local."

"There's no national championship of math or history," adds Lawrence McKibbin, former dean of the OU business school. "Who the hells knows who's best? So the least of the institutions can rationalize to its students that they are just as good as those guys in Norman.

"As the state evolved," McKibbin goes on to explain, "the name of the game was how to get a piece of the pie for your town, your region. Each town militantly pursues more than its share of the economic action. In some of these communities, the college is the whole life. It's an enterprise that doesn't go bankrupt.''

Oklahoma's higher education system embodies not only the populist ethos of the state but the values of E. T. Dunlap, the man who presided over it as chancellor from 1961 to 1981. One of 13 children of a rancher in the southeast Oklahoma hills, Dunlap grew up 10 miles from the nearest high school. By the time he had worked his way through college, into the legislature and on to a doctorate and a small-college presidency, he had acquired an unshakeable determination to make higher education available to every last farm boy like himself.

It is in large part because of that conviction that Oklahoma, through the mid-1980s, ranked 47th in the country in the tuition its colleges charged. The state still guarantees every junior college graduate automatic admission to the University of Oklahoma for the following school year—regardless of previous coursework or grades.

Dunlap, still vocal in retirement, says that he is all for what Brisch is doing—that he never wanted to hold down the university in Norman so he could focus on the rest of the system. His critics say, though, that whether it was intentional or not, Dunlap's approach amounted to institutionalized mediocrity. ''We provided access,'' says Paul Sharp, the former OU president, ''at the cost of blocking a strong research university from emerging. It was a high price to pay. But it paid off in the political system of the state.''

Oklahoma's legislature has always reflected the populist approach to education. In 1917, Democratic Governor Robert Williams thought he could make the system more rational by reducing its size, and he closed 10 colleges by vetoing their appropriations. Two years later, the legislature reopened all but two of them, and even created a new one.

Up until World War II, there was no budget for higher education. The presidents of the colleges lobbied the legislature individually for money. ''The presidents would be up at the legislature like a bunch of pigs at a hog trough,'' Dunlap remembers. ''The biggest pig would get all the money.'' In reaction to those excesses, the state in 1941 enacted the law providing for a lump sum appropriation to all schools in the higher education system.

The 1941 reform ended the "hog trough" funding method that so disgusted Dunlap and many others. But it didn't take higher education out of politics. Because the presence of a college is crucial to so many small towns in this still largely rural state, a legislator who represents one of those towns must try and deliver what he can for the local school while he is in Oklahoma City.

Even though the legislature does not appropriate money school by school, it maintains a considerable amount of leverage over the fortunes of all the colleges. The legislature can set up endowed professorships at favored schools. It can pass "intent resolutions" telling the regents how it wants to see money spent. It even has the power to close a school if it wants to. When a college is ignored repeatedly in the distribution of legislative favors, the member who represents it is likely to be questioned by constituents about his or her effectiveness.

But the members are not the only ones who feel vulnerable in this system. The presidents of the 27 colleges, aware that the funding and perhaps the very existence of their institutions is precarious, spend an enormous amount of time and effort keeping their legislators happy.

Perhaps the most vulnerable institution in the entire state network is the University of Science and Arts of Oklahoma in Chickasha. Once the state women's college, it has struggled for a role to play since it became coeducational in the 1960s. In the past decade, it has built a creative curriculum based on interdisciplinary team teaching and has managed to keep alive. But its enrollment is barely 1,000 students, and it is always first on anyone's list of schools that might be closed to save money.

In 1985, when the legislature was forced to raise taxes to deal with the state's growing financial problems, the two legislators from Chickasha tried to vote no. In response, colleagues began circulating a petition on the House floor calling for the school's closing. "In areas where senators and representatives are both not willing to go along," Speaker Jim Barker warned, "those institutions might be jeopardized."

By 1987, the Chickasha delegation was lined up with the speaker in favor of a new tax bill. And Roy Troutt, the president of USAO, was contributing to Barker's campaign and writing to other college presidents in the state to tell them about a fund-raising reception in Barker's behalf.

It was, in part, this sort of educational politics that caused the downfall of Joe Leone, the chancellor whose forced resignation in 1987 led to the arrival of Hans Brisch from Nebraska a year later.

A southeast Oklahoma product like Dunlap, Leone had replaced him as chancellor in 1981. Leone was loyal to the junior colleges and the other lesser institutions—and he solicited campaign money from presidents of the smaller colleges for delivery to state legislators. If a president could not attend a fund-raising event held in honor of a legislator, he normally gave the money to Leone, who delivered it to the legislator personally.

In 1987, a grand jury in Oklahoma City began investigating payments made to supplement Leone's $93,000 chancellor's salary by a private foundation that received some of its budget from the state legislature. No charges were ever filed against Leone, and he might have survived the controversy had Bellmon not been elected governor the previous fall on a platform that included demands for reform in higher education. The alleged irregularities in the chancellor's office provided a crucial opportunity for those who wanted a new approach to the entire subject.

Hans Brisch stepped into this web of loyalties and alliances determined to build a great research university, even if that meant challenging E. T. Dunlap's ''access for everyone'' policy. ''You become known nationally and internationally,'' he says, ''for what your faculty is doing in the creation of new knowledge. What are MIT and Harvard known for? Have you heard much about their teaching lately?''

Brisch has some important allies. Governor Bellmon, as a Republican, has few ties to the politics-and-education network centered in the Democratic legislature. Equally important, Bellmon and Brisch have a working majority on the nine-member state regents board. Only three of the nine are Bellmon appointees, but two others are solid supporters of revamping the system.

There still is no hard evidence that the average Oklahoman places an elite research university high on his list of priorities. But there are other forces for change: the national and international corporations that maintain facilities in Oklahoma.

For most of the state's history, the only business community that counted was the oil industry—and what the oil industry wanted out of OU was a good program in petroleum engineering. But one by-product of the 1980s oil depression has been a reduced presence by the oil industry in the councils of Oklahoma business. Filling the gap have been companies with a more cosmopolitan outlook, especially Goodyear, Weyerhaeuser and Western Electric, major Oklahoma employers. All three have been strong supporters of the education task force: Of Bellmon's first appointments to the state regents, one was a Goodyear executive and another a member of the Weyerhaeuser family. All three firms are concerned about how they will attract the talent their Oklahoma operations need. And all of them worry that it will be difficult without a better research university.

In the coming months, the people are going to be asked to accept more changes than they may be aware of now. Having revamped the funding process for the state schools, Brisch and the regents plan to make the University of Oklahoma a more selective school. "We can't have open admissions," the chancellor says, "and talk about raising our standards." But earlier this year, when the regents decided to test the waters by raising the entrance requirements at Northeastern Oklahoma State in Tahlequah, they were besieged by charges of elitism from the school and its political adherents. Gene Stipe, one of the most influential Democrats in the state Senate, accused the regents of trying to create "an elitist society" in Oklahoma. Open admissions at OU may not be impregnable, but they are a key component of Oklahoma's populist education system and will not be easy to change.

Making the university more selective at least has the virtue of being relatively cheap. Other things Brisch wants to do will be expensive. He thinks there is a current $400 million funding gap between OU and the schools he would like to compete with in the Southwest and Midwest. The task force reported that the University of Texas was paying its faculty members an average salary of more than $38,000; OU needed to go up more than $5,000 per teacher to match that.

The need to raise so much money inevitably means the end of low tuition. Right now, an Oklahoma University student pays for 26 percent of the total costs of his education. The regents want to bring that figure up to 30 percent by the early 1990s.

And if it is all accomplished, will the state be on the road to solving its economic problems? Brisch thinks so. The task force certainly thought so. It reported back to the legislature last year that "quality higher education is the catalyst necessary for emergence from the current depression."

Necessary? Perhaps. Sufficient? No. The University of Texas is in many ways the school that the University of Oklahoma would like to be—renowned for its ability to draw top-flight faculty, skillful at attracting federal research dollars—and yet its quality did not prevent Texas from suffering almost as much oil depression misery as Oklahoma.

Nearly everyone involved in the debate agrees, however, that even if educational reform proves disappointing as an economic panacea, something in the state's collective psyche has changed in a way that will never change back. "What really is different," says OU political science Professor Don Kash, "is that now, whether you are liberal or conservative, the conventional wisdom is that the future of the state is tied up with brains and intellect."

And that development will please many of the University of Oklahoma's most dedicated supporters, even some of its most loyal football fans. After George Lynn Cross retired as OU president in 1968, he wrote a personal history of the school's football program. He called it *Presidents Can't Punt*. He wrote nostalgically of the glory years under Coach Bud Wilkinson, the national championships, the tradition of excellence that remains intact a quarter-century after Wilkinson's departure.

But on the final pages, as he summed it all up, his confidence seemed momentarily to desert him. "Oklahoma football," Cross wrote, "has been extremely effective in bringing the state to the attention of the nation. But . . . has football been a good thing for the University of Oklahoma?"

"Frankly," he said, "I do not know."

NOTES

1. Richard Hofstadter, *Anti-intellectualism in American Life* (New York: Alfred A. Knopf, 1970), 51.

2. Rennard Strickland, "Oklahoma's Story: Recording the History of the Forty-sixth State," in *Oklahoma: New Views of the Forty-sixth State,* ed. Ann Hodges Morgan and H. Wayne Morgan (Norman: University of Oklahoma Press, 1982), 263.

INDEX

The following abbreviations are used: OU (University of Oklahoma); O.C. (Oklahoma City); and COs (conscientious objectors).